"ARE YOU CALLING ME A RACIST?"

"ARE YOU CALLING ME A RACIST?"

WHY WE NEED TO STOP
TALKING ABOUT RACE
AND START MAKING
REAL ANTIRACIST CHANGE

SARITA SRIVASTAVA

NEW YORK UNIVERSITY PRESS
New York

NEW YORK UNIVERSITY PRESS
New York
www.nyupress.org

Library of Congress Cataloging-in-Publication
Data Names: Srivastava, Sarita, author.
Title: "Are you calling me a racist?" : why we need to stop talking
about race and start making real antiracist change / Sarita Srivastava.
Description: New York, New York : New York University Press, [2024] |
Includes bibliographical references and index.
Identifiers: LCCN 2023030084 (print) | LCCN 2023030085 (ebook) |
ISBN 9781479815258 (hardback ; alk. paper) | ISBN 9781479815265
(paperback ; alk. paper) | ISBN 9781479815272 (ebook) |
ISBN 9781479815296 (ebook other)
Subjects: LCSH: Antiracism. | Racism. | Equality. | Social change.
Classification: LCC HT1563 .S75 2024 (print) | LCC HT1563 (ebook) |
DDC 305.8--dc23/eng/20230713
LC record available at https://lccn.loc.gov/2023030084
LC ebook record available at https://lccn.loc.gov/2023030085

This book is printed on acid-free paper, and its binding materials are
chosen for strength and durability. We strive to use environmentally
responsible suppliers and materials to the greatest extent possible in
publishing our books.

Manufactured in the United States of America

10 9 8 7 6 5 4 3 2 1

Also available as an ebook

CONTENTS

INTRODUCTION

THE STORY OF MEGHAN AND HARRY, OR WHY
READING ABOUT WHITE FRAGILITY IS NOT ENOUGH

As Meghan Markle prepared to marry Prince Harry in May of 2018, some observers suggested that she should search the internet for "racism, British royal family."[1] One may presume that she did not take that advice.

If she had done so, she might have been less surprised by the behavior of the British media and the royal family, an experience that reportedly led the couple to abandon both Britain and their royal duties. In an incriminating interview with Oprah, Meghan and Harry revealed that members of the British royal family had expressed concern about the skin color of their baby, asking, "What will the kids look like?" The disturbing implication, said Meghan, was "if you were to be brown that would be a problem." She then rhetorically asked Oprah, "Which is really hard to understand, right?"[2]

Hard to understand, perhaps, if one neglects a history of colonialism and slavery, and isolates a few striking comments of individuals. Whether or not she studied up on "racism and the royal family," Meghan Markle was most likely aware that she was marrying the same Prince Harry who, while serving in Afghanistan, once found it amusing to film himself mocking fellow soldiers with racial epithets such as "Paki" and "raghead."[3] She would also likely have heard the oft-quoted comments of his great-grandmother, the Queen Mother, who reportedly opined, "Africans just don't know how to govern themselves . . . what a pity we're not still looking after them."[4] Yet each of these instances, just like the royal family's alleged concern about the color of Meghan and Harry's child, can be dismissed as the ignorant misstep of a genuinely good person. After all, almost everyone agrees with the abstract principle that racism is wrong. If someone's actions appear not to align with this agreed-upon principle, the problem is most easily explained by focusing on errant individuals and well-meaning ignorance. No wonder that the Queen's response to Meghan and Harry's revelations of racism was to say that the issues "will be addressed by the family privately."[5] Megan and Harry's concerns were immediately traced to the interiority of family dynamics and individual actions—actions whose meaning is measured by a vague tenet that racism is both unforgivable and rare within the realm of respectable society.

It is this relegation of conversations about racism to either individual culpability or abstract principle that explains Meghan Markle's quizzical tone. If she thought it was "hard to understand" why British royalty might be concerned about having brown family members, it is perhaps because she saw these comments as divorced from Britain's history of racial purity, racism, slavery, and colonialism. Yet Meghan and Harry's interview aired only a few months after Black Lives Matter protestors in the UK toppled a statue of prominent slave trader and town leader Edward Colston,[6] heightening public awareness that established institutions rest on a bedrock of racism and colonialism. (As a rebuke to this history of slavery, for example, some prominent Black Britons have turned down their appointments to the Order of the Empire.[7])

While the arrival of Meghan Markle's African heritage into the royal family was heralded by some as a turning point in this history, others such as British journalist Yasmin Alibhai-Brown more skeptically asked, "Can the royal wedding change centuries of racism and classism in Britain?"[8] Meghan herself provided an answer of sorts when she walked down the aisle wearing a veil embroidered with flowers from each of fifty-four nations colonized by the British Empire.[9]

Meghan and Harry, like many, do not appear to make any meaningful connections between these seemingly disparate moments. Rather than connect the intimate comments of individuals to an ongoing backdrop of racism and colonialism, we tend to approach the everyday challenges of equity and diversity in individual, moral, emotional, or abstract terms. The ensuing debates and conflict are, not surprisingly, focused on both individuals and grand rhetoric. This approach might, as in Meghan and Harry's case, evoke a theatrical emotional spectacle of public outrage and controversy, including a talk show host storming off the set and resigning in defense of the monarchy.[10] Or it might end in the familiar tension, discomfort, and undertones of fear, shame, anger, and tears that we so often see when we broach questions of race and diversity.

You might reasonably ask what the royal family's racial conflict has to do with, well, anyone else's. Admittedly, it is hard to resist the drama of racial conflict in the royal family or the buzz when Meghan wears an off-the-rack dress. But I began with this provocative example precisely because, while far removed from our community and work lives, it shines an unavoidably bright spotlight on how emotion, morality, and individual scrutiny are tenacious undercurrents that underlie all our conversations about race. I draw on this story to remind us that we feel these same undercurrents everywhere—whether people are defending royalty or engaging in introspection about their own racism.

This story also highlights the disjuncture between the individual and the systemic, the distance between abstract principles and concrete practices, that underlies many efforts at equity and diversity. Rather than embracing both historic roots and future practices, conversations become overwhelmingly preoccupied with isolated moments and questions of the innocence, ignorance, worthiness, and morality of individuals. Institutional solutions focus on training and talking. Diversity workshops often devote energy to defending, recuperating, educating, and inwardly reflecting. It is a therapeutic approach that I first observed when I began researching community organizations two decades ago. But rather than fading away, the therapeutic or reflective approach has become even more familiar in corporate and educational spaces. The popularity of books like *White Fragility: Why It's So Hard for White People to Talk about Racism*, and related workshops, is the most well-known marker of this therapeutic style.[11]

Yet research shows that diversity efforts and anti-bias training often have limited results and can even make things worse.[12] Is there a problem with the techniques, the goals, the motivations? Yes, yes, and yes.

To be clear, I am not opposed to workshops and education. As someone who has spent years teaching university students, I am deeply committed to education and pedagogical practice.

Nor am I opposed to emotions or to therapy. When I give a public talk, people sometimes ask, "Don't you think emotions are important to our work?" Yes, passionate engagement is key to social movements. Yes, emotional awareness and care is important in all relationships.

But sporadic workshops that focus on ignorance, bias, interiority, emotions, and self-transformation have not been successful routes to organizational change.

The origins and core of this book lie far from the royal family and celebrity culture. I began thinking about race and equity over two decades ago when I was working as an activist, supporting environmental, feminist, labor, and Indigenous sovereignty movements, as well as community radio. In the environmental organization where I worked, I was the first person of color hired in a leadership position.

What I saw surprised me. Inside progressive spaces filled with progressive people committed to fighting sexism and racism, we were nevertheless confronted with familiar conflicts over racism, sexism, and diversity. I saw racial justice and social justice as integral to environmental activism, but not everyone in the movement shared this view. I, like many, had assumed that social movements were supposed to be the places to *challenge* sexism and racism, not to create new conflicts. While the content of these conflicts about racism or sexism was not unfamiliar, their tone and scale were new to me: these conflicts were not only highly intense and emotional, they would also embroil an entire organization and even spill over into the public eye and news media. Feminist organizations were a frequent site of these conflicts.

The tendency for many organizations to respond to these challenges with therapeutic, conflict-resolution approaches was frustrating. "How do you feel about what she said?" a facilitator might ask. The focus was on the individuals, rather than on changing organizational practices. (This continues to be a go-to model for talking about race.)

It was the desire to better understand these events that brought me to academic life. I left my work as an environmental activist to do a PhD in sociology and began an empirical study of antiracism in social movement organizations. For several decades, I have been preoccupied with trying to understand why efforts at equity and diversity so often yield unsatisfactory results. In a sense, I have been thinking about these contradictions for my entire life, reconciling the discourse of color-blindness with the racism I experienced as a child.

When I first began this project, I was very interested in the historical and local specificity of antiracism efforts. How, I wondered, are community organizations distinct from public school or corporate contexts? My original project explored how the ideals of social movements and activists uniquely shape their responses to racism and antiracism.

I was surprised to learn, however, that many people found my research relevant across a range of organizations, communities, and countries, wherever questions of diversity, equity, and antiracism arise. So I have widened my analytical lens: I now think about how "feel-good" racial politics shape not only community organizations, but also popular culture, social media, universities, and workplaces. I hope to convince you that, despite the distinctions among these sites—which remain nevertheless interesting for scholars to study—there is a vast emotional and moral landscape that impedes all of us from making progress on racial justice.

This book reflects my wide-ranging project to understand what is standing in our way. It draws on my empirical research in Canadian feminist and community organizations, on cultural and philosophical analysis, and on my own experiences as an activist, professor, and now academic leader. I focus on understanding the common historical threads that sustain conventional approaches to diversity and equity. I use this research to explain why conventional diversity approaches have had limited impact and why the inwardly reflective approaches we see in *White Fragility* workshops do not usually lead us to the positive, collective transformation we might hope to see. The broader ambition of this book is to highlight the emotional and moral landscape we are navigating as we attempt to journey toward racial justice.

We can read the story of Meghan and Harry as a marker of this landscape. If, like Meghan and Harry, we elide the historical and systemic and stick to the path of individual guilt and ignorance, then our journey toward racial justice will also be limited. Their story also reflects the proliferation of what I call the "Let's Talk" approach—the tendency to talk about racism in terms of individual biases, feelings, and experiences.

But talking is not enough. Even if it is to one's queen.

1

The Feel-Good Politics of Race

WHY EQUITY AND DIVERSITY ARE SO ELUSIVE

The indignant response, anger, the rage that turns into tears,
the foot-stomping, temper tantrums, which are very typical
responses. Every single organization that I have been in, every
single one.
—"Rayna"

We believe that feelings are immutable, but every sentiment,
particularly the noblest and most disinterested, has a history.
—Michel Foucault, "Nietzsche, Genealogy, History"

"*You're calling me a racist?*" This is the incredulous
sentiment that lies at the heart of failed attempts to
speak sagely and act wisely on race and diversity. Whether it is an angry
outburst, an indignant rejoinder, or a mortified retreat, "You're calling
me a racist?" is a familiar emotional response to conversations about
antiracism; it is also guaranteed to derail any meaningful progress.

In the spring of 2020, in the wake of massive protests against George
Floyd's murder by police in Minneapolis, most organizations made
public declarations against racism. Within days, the number of people
expressing support for Black Lives Matter rose exponentially.[1] In place
of the familiar moves to downplay racism, many folks and organizations became newly anxious to acknowledge racism. The discovery of
the unmarked graves of Indigenous children who were taken from their
families and who never returned from Canadian residential schools also
marked an emotional reckoning with racism and genocide.[2] Many were

moved to declare, in one way or another, "I feel so terrible about racism," racial violence, and colonialism. Yet whether people are expressing shock, hurt, indignance, denial, or even apathy, these are all emotional responses, emotions that often arise from the desire to distance oneself from the ugliness of racism. The moment people focus on their own emotions, guilt, goodness, or ignorance, however, attempts to transform institutional practices cease.

The title of this book, *Are You Calling Me a Racist?*, is meant as a provocative signal for these complex emotional and moral undercurrents that shape all racial encounters—whether in politics, workplaces, or intimate attachments. Rage, denial, fear, hurt, shame, pride, guilt, self-righteousness—powerful feelings are evoked by even the most understated of conversations about race or diversity. Debates about race in classrooms or boardrooms are as likely to end in a stalemate of hurt, confused, and angry feelings as in any movement toward change.

But these open expressions of emotion are only part of the picture. Emotional and moral undercurrents shape all manner of racial encounters even when we are not aware of feeling anything at all. Imagine the following typical scenarios: A politician is called out for a racist remark. An organization hires their first non-white manager. An organization makes all their employees take antiracism training. College students demand that their English literature curriculum be made more diverse and more global. A nonprofit group is writing a diversity policy. Well-meaning whites ask their friends, "What should I read about racism?" In each of these scenarios, emotional, psychic, and moral preoccupations often trip up meaningful antiracism actions, despite training and good intentions. The politician or well-meaning whites might be swayed by deep-seated fears about being called racist, by a focus on their moral culpability rather than their responsibility, or by fears of becoming vulnerable by taking leadership on antiracism; the English professors and the nonprofit group might be motivated by deep nostalgia for the way things were, or by a sense of idealistic purity about how they should be.

It is a perplexing conundrum: Why does antiracism flounder where it seems it should be most likely to succeed—in organizations already dedicated to equity and social justice? This is the key question I pose— not the larger question of why racism persists, but why meaningful change and thoughtful analysis is elusive even when there is good intention, resources, and commitment. For decades, community organizations, educational institutions, labor unions, social movements, social service agencies, and corporate spaces have been working to increase racial, ethnic, and gender diversity and equity. Outcomes are often superficial. The resulting debates can be fractious. Diversity efforts often arise from a seed of desperation and falter on a field of recriminations. Despite concerted plans toward equity and diversity, most fall short of profound change.[3,4]

On the surface, we are nevertheless making progress. In his book *Diversity Regimes: Why Talk Is Not Enough to Fix Racial Inequality at Universities*, sociologist James Thomas points out that the project to increase racial diversity in universities is, by some measures, succeeding.[5] In the 1970s, about 80 percent of US undergraduate students identified as white; that figure had decreased to just under 50 percent by 2019.[6]

Racial conflict on campuses has increased, however. Thomas highlights blatant expressions of racism and racist violence among students and experiences of isolation and everyday racism for non-white students. The problem, he argues, is that while university diversity policies have proliferated, their day-to-day diversity efforts are inadequate at coordinating meaningful change—indeed, he finds that commitments to diversity often sustain racial inequality, as they limit "material transformations in how power, resources, opportunities, and decision-making are distributed."[7] These are the central contradictions I explore: the contradictions between good intentions and weak outcomes, as well as the contradictions between increasing diversity and ongoing cultural and structural inequities.

Conversations begin, good intentions are voiced, perhaps a policy is written, a workshop is held, but organizations often fail to make ongoing changes in the way they do things. The detailed and difficult work we need to do to see genuine change is often neglected, whether that requires allocating resources; creating accessible services; changing the way we make decisions; hiring new people; mentoring; designing new products, spaces, and diverse content; and so on. Broader changes that focus on decolonization, reconciliation, and transformations in culture, goals, values, and governance are even more elusive. Instead, an anti-bias session or a diversity policy has become the go-to organizational approach. Too often the focus remains on individual training.

Consider the case of two men who sit waiting for a business meeting in a Starbucks café in Philadelphia. An employee approaches and says they must order something or leave, and then calls the police. By the time their business acquaintance arrives for the meeting, they are in handcuffs.[8] This 2018 incident garnered international scrutiny because it was filmed and posted on social media by another patron. Despite this evidence, many people were disbelieving. The patron who filmed the incident wrote on Twitter, "Ever since I posted this, I've had white strangers AND friends say 'there must be something more to this story.'"[9] Yet there is no other explanation, except that the men arrested for sitting in a café are Black.

Not surprisingly, anti-bias training was the most visible organizational response to the Philadelphia arrests. The following month, Starbucks shut down eight thousand cafés for an afternoon of antiracism training, spending tens of millions of dollars on this one session, much of it delivered to employees gathered around iPads.[10] Similarly, after the singer SZA posted on social media that a Sephora employee had called security on her, the cosmetics chain closed all its US stores and offices for an hour of diversity training.[11]

Anti-bias training, in other words, has become a typical response to concerns and conflicts about racism, in both corporate and community settings. Civil rights and employment equity legislation has also made anti-bias training a routine and often mandatory requirement in almost all large corporations, government agencies, and about half of all midsize companies in the US.[12] With a renewed interest in racial justice, this training is on the rise. Police departments, universities, communities, and corporations continue to spend millions of dollars on antiracism and diversity training. In 2017, the New York Police Department signed a $4.5 million contract for anti-bias training.[13]

The notion of "anti-bias" training stems from important research that highlights how "implicit" biases shape everyday decisions and practices, even without explicit intent to discriminate. Social psychologist Jennifer Eberhardt, author of *Biased: Uncovering the Hidden Prejudice That Shapes What We See, Think, and Do*, understands bias as a "social agenda" in which racial stereotypes influence interpersonal interactions such as a police officer's treatment of Black males or a landlord's refusal to rent to racialized tenants.[14] A study of the Oakland police department, for example, revealed that police officers spoke in more friendly and respectful ways to white members of the public.[15] Eberhardt's proposed solutions are myriad and focused on everyday and structural practices such as data collection, not simply general and short-term training.[16]

Yet short-term, generalized anti-bias and diversity training has become the norm, the go-to and readily accepted approach to addressing inequity in organizations. Diversity consultants are now part of a growing multimillion-dollar industry, and much of their work is dedicated to workshops.[17] A Google search for best-selling books on EDI or DEI easily reveals at least fifteen titles published between 2019 and 2022 (including *DEI for Dummies*). (While these efforts vary in their nomenclature, origins, and approaches—they may be termed diversity, equity, EDI, DEI, or antiracism—they are growing. I place them all under the same analytical lens.)

Does diversity training make things better? There is little evidence that conventional diversity policies or training create employment equity, reduce racial prejudice, or increase cross-cultural sensitivity.[18] In their article "Why Doesn't Diversity Training Work?," sociologists Frank Dobbin and Alexandra Kalev reviewed dozens of studies showing that anti-bias training "does not reduce bias, alter behavior or change the workplace."[19]

The emotional minefield of these workshops makes them particularly ineffective approaches to organizational change. Diversity trainers often sidestep talking about race directly, using mundane examples that are "less charged than the racial biases," says anti-bias trainer Noble Wray, a former police chief, even though "the 800-pound gorilla in the room is racial bias."[20] Evidence also shows that conventional diversity training produces problems of its own.[21] As my own research demonstrates, the typical mandatory diversity training and policies can exacerbate organizational tensions without supporting organizational change.

The ineffectiveness of conventional training is hardly surprising since its focus is often on individuals, their knowledge, their biases, and their inner reflections, rather than on changing organizational practices. Yet, with the recent rise in anti-bias training, we are in danger of repeating these same mistakes. If we instead scrutinize how these affective and moral preoccupations limit our efforts, we could develop more effective ways of making equitable organizations that contribute to racial justice, decolonization, and reconciliation. Vociferous and painful debates on racial violence,[22] migration, mass incarceration,[23] genocide, residential schools,[24] reparations, anti-Semitism, and Palestine[25] have done much in the last few years to expose the explosive racial undercurrents of social and political life. Yet, even after the 2020 uprising for racial justice, we seldom acknowledge the emotional tenor of these contemporary racial politics. Instead, the popular narrative of multicultural progress places emotional racial conflict in a distant place or time. Meanwhile, even well-meaning workplace debates about race and diversity erupt or dissipate into a range of emotional and moral narratives that are tinged with apathy, denial, and indignance and infused with notions of white liberal innocence.

I have seen well-meaning organizations flounder over accusations of racism while people leave, withdraw, rage, cry, insult, or rant. I have attended painful antiracism workshops and listened to well-intentioned folks downplay racism; I have tried to change my own organizations with antiracism policies, meetings, research, and equity training. As a scholar, I draw on all these experiences as the starting points for my research on the troubled antiracism efforts in community, feminist, educational, and activist sites.

The aim of this book is to uncover the ways that emotional and moral preoccupations prevent progress on diversity and racial justice. It is not a diversity manual or antiracism toolbox. But it does advocate a clearer path to concrete, locally specific practices and systemic changes. In the last chapter, I outline practical steps to begin this process.

Antiracism educator and author Robin DiAngelo uses the term "white fragility" to capture these typical "defensive responses" and "anger, fear and guilt" that she has often confronted as an antiracism trainer.[26] Like the term "micro-aggression," "white fragility" has rapidly come into common parlance, providing a ready phrase to capture the nuances of everyday racial encounters. But keeping our attention on psychological phrases like "white fragility" and "micro-aggression" falls short as a solution. Like so many efforts at equity and diversity, these approaches highlight the missteps of individuals. They encourage personal reflection, rather than actively remaking systemic practices in the places where we live and work. Social media intensifies this tendency at a higher emotional pitch, cultivating a culture that cancels and calls out those who misstep.

What is perhaps more surprising is the failure of diversity and equity efforts in places that are already committed to equity as a central part of their values and goals—progressive community organizations and institutions, social movements, schools, and universities. Why have efforts at equity failed in precisely the places where one would most expect them to succeed—the spaces where people are gathered to make egalitarian communities? Even when all involved agree that diversity is good, efforts to achieve it are fraught with rancor.

This is the irony of failed attempts at diversity. Even within spaces whose very existence is oriented toward the pursuit of social justice and egalitarian community, profound shifts toward antiracism and diversity prove elusive.

Witnessing this unsettling contradiction in my own work as an activist compelled me to write this book. When I was an environmental activist in Toronto, I became immersed in antiracism and equity efforts. At first, I was taken aback by the sexism and racism within social movements. Then I tried to challenge it. I wrote antiracism policy, organized an equity workshop, attended facilitations and training. Most of the time I felt that I was failing to make a difference. The experience was emotionally intense and profoundly disheartening; that seemed to be its primary impact.

I became a sociologist to understand why these efforts fail. In my first job as a sociology professor, however, I experienced many of these same, familiar dynamics. Once again, I assumed that, because I was in a relatively progressive space, people would welcome antiracism efforts. Working with a supportive colleague, I proposed an equity committee, and was surprised by the disinterest and suspicion from some colleagues. While our equity committee made some progress over the years, we also saw apathy and sluggish change. Today junior faculty of color and graduate students continue to work toward equity and racial justice at the university; however, they tell of feeling marginalized and discouraged. I am reminded of a colleague's angry response to our equity work, ending with the phrase, "But if I say anything I'll get called racist." I have reflected many times on how I might have responded. This book is my response.

These kinds of individual preoccupations with who is and who is not "racist" give us a sense of the ground on which these efforts fail. We need to more closely examine these moments in which antiracism efforts falter. Most studies of race and antiracism have not studied the everyday practices within organizations and communities that make change both stormy and elusive. Before proposing more empty diversity campaigns or creating more antiracism workshops, we must understand where these conversations go awry. For this reason, much of my research is centered in social movements and community organizations; the book begins with a look at the early days of antiracism battles in community and feminist organizations in the 1980s and 1990s.

To understand why antiracism efforts so often fail or lead to conflict, I interviewed staff, management, and activists[27] working in a variety of community, social service, and advocacy organizations that had been through difficult conflicts over race and equity.[28] I also analyzed coverage of these battles in mainstream and feminist print media, and observed and participated in antiracism workshops, meetings, and events.[29] Looking closely at some of the earliest, most explosive, and most emotional debates on racism in community organizations during the tumultuous period of antiracism struggle between the 1980s and early 2000s, I explore the emotional crises and moral distractions that keep us from more profound antiracism practice. I complement these interviews with analyses of contemporary events, histories ,and theories of race, emotion, moral regulation, and social movements, and recent studies of diversity in organizations, broadening my analysis to times and places beyond my initial study.

The people I interviewed worked in community organizations and feminist groups in Toronto, a large, diverse metropolitan area of about six million people, over 50 percent of whom identify as "visible minorities." All had been involved in diversity or antiracism efforts in their organizations, and all expressed either an abstract or active commitment to antiracism. They identified themselves in a variety of ways in their interview transcripts—"white," "mixed-race," "woman of color," "racialized," and so on. Out of respect and convenience, my descriptions echo the terms of identity used by the interviewees. These terms of racial identity reflect historical categories and social movements, and are not definitive statements about the individuals themselves; throughout the book I use a variety of terms, depending on what is used in the literature or by community members. The organizations and individuals remain anonymous and are identified by pseudonyms; identifying details have been altered.

My research shows that racial encounters among well-meaning people are ironically hindered by the emotional investments they have in being good people. The failures of antiracism efforts can be traced to emotional, psychic, and moral concerns: the desire to both *feel* good and *be* good. I use the phrase "*Feel-Good politics of race*" as a shorthand to describe the affective and moral terrain of racial politics, a terrain in which racial encounters are drenched in histories of moral regulation. Feel-Good racial politics reflect the desire not only to believe that we *are* good—moral, upstanding, and innocent—but also to *feel* good—positive, warm, hopeful.

Feel-Good racial politics train our focus on the redemptive and the therapeutic, limiting our abilities to develop difficult conversations and concrete practices that could move us toward equity. These Feel-Good racial politics shape not only professional interactions, but also the political realm. They touch even our personal, intimate, and community lives.

The anger, tears, and fears that arise when we confront race and antiracism are not just momentarily obstructive. These emotional responses also teach us about the historical, moral, and ethical landscape of racial encounters today. Profound investments in racial histories, moral identities, ethical paths, and ideals of nation and community evoke deep emotions. This book explores the powerful emotions and moral concerns that not only burden everyday conversations about race, but also hamper efforts to profoundly challenge histories of racialization.

Global antiracism protests in the spring of 2020 represent a turning point in public engagement with antiracism. Polls in June 2020 show a sharp and rapid increase in the number of Americans who support Black Lives Matter from 40 percent to over 50 percent in the two weeks after George Floyd was killed by Minneapolis police officers.[30] The number who think that "racial discrimination is a big problem" increased from 51 percent in 2015 to 78 percent over just a two-week period in June 2020.[31]

But does a dramatic shift in public opinion lead to genuine transformation in racial inequality? Will this new antiracism wave be more effective than previous waves—the civil rights movement of the 1960s and 1970s or the antiracism activism of the late 1980s and early 1990s?

Ordinary people and public institutions are asking in unprecedented numbers: "How can we make sure we are on the right side in the fight against racism?" Yet many of the sentiments that motivate these questions also lie behind the familiar failures of diversity efforts. Individuals and organizations are too often motivated to feel good and appear good—to appear non-racist, antiracist, or diverse. As a result, their actions are largely ineffective—symbolic practices such as training, workshops, conflict resolution, or policy writing that can make things worse.[32]

Organizations typically take one of two approaches to dealing with the emotional content of conversations about race and diversity: either they counter "irrational" emotions with rational education and policy or they defuse emotions with conflict resolution and therapeutic talk. All these approaches neglect the necessary work of dissecting and transforming mundane institutional practices. In either approach, workshops and conflict resolution inevitably focus on individuals, their emotions, and their knowledge. Individuals' emotional reactions to racism deflect attention away from the process of achieving antiracism goals. When discussion goes deeper, it often turns inward to self-reflection or therapeutic conversations, rather than to organizational change.

This book shows that the very moral imperatives that inspire the fight for racial justice can also be its undoing. Whether the terrain is calm or tumultuous, emotional and moral considerations are central to understanding contemporary racial politics. The most ordinary of tools, such as the antiracism workshop, and the most ordinary of feelings, such as nostalgia and guilt, can derail the best of intentions.

So efforts at diversity *multiply* the challenges of diversity: we see a multiplicity of forms of resistance, dysfunctional adaptation, and even creative engagements. Institutional attempts at diversity shift the landscape of racial encounters in unforeseen and surprising ways—they can produce not just recalcitrance, but also earnest attempts at embracing change. What, for example, is produced out of the desire to be a good antiracist person?

In this introductory chapter, I first highlight the limitations of conventional approaches to "diversity" and antiracism in organizations—how has the diversity project been defined and why has it been unsatisfactory?

The rest of the chapter looks more closely at the key arguments of this book. I argue that we can trace the shortcomings of diversity efforts to the following discourses, practices, and histories:

- Feel-Good racial politics, in which conversations about race are shaped by concerns with psychic comfort and morality
- Key myths about emotion and race and the profound links among relations of race and affective relations
- Deep intersections among notions of morality, emotion, and race, including the characterization of racism as a personal trait and moral flaw
- A focus on dialogue, therapy, and self-examination as a route to equity and antiracism
- An individualistic emphasis on education and knowledge as an antidote to racism
- The unique context of progressive spaces and social movements that express commitments to equity and justice

WHY IS IT SO HARD TO ACHIEVE DIVERSITY?

We have been working on "the problem of diversity" for decades. Public institutions, community groups, and private corporations, prompted by social movements and employment equity legislation, have expended great effort on training, retreats, policies. Many of these efforts are grounded in profound values of egalitarianism. Others are based in corporate responsibility, profitability, avoidance of corporate liability, or the cultivation of sound human resources.[33]

Almost all large companies and universities have diversity policies and diversity training. It is estimated that over half of large US companies have a chief diversity officer. And the spotlight on racial justice in 2020 led to a sharp increase in the number of diversity officers appointed that year.[34]

By some measures, these efforts have worked. University campuses, for example, look very different than they did a few decades ago. In 1976, white students earned almost 90 percent of all bachelor's degrees in the US; by 2018 that figure had fallen to 63 percent.[35] After concerted efforts at diversity, the percentage of racialized students rose significantly in the last few decades. Indiana University, for example, saw a fourfold increase in Hispanic students between 2002 and 2021. The number of Black undergraduate students in the US increased by 178 percent between 1976 and 2013.[36] In 1976, Black students made up about 10 percent of undergraduate students; by 2011, they made up 15 percent.

But by other measures, diversity efforts are falling short. Corporate leadership, for example, has seen limited changes in racial diversity: Black executives represent less than 2 percent of chief executive officers in the S&P 500 index—there were only four Black CEOs in the top five hundred US companies in 2020, six in 2022.[37] Although a study led by Seung-Hwan Jeong found that the market responds more positively to the appointment of a Black CEO than to the appointment of a white CEO, changes in corporate leadership have been slow for many years. Jeong et al. also confirmed that the bar for Black executives is much higher, so that those progressing to the level of CEO have more years of education and are more likely to have an advanced degree.[38] To paraphrase an executive acquaintance, "We've been working on these issues for decades, but eighteen out of twenty people on the board still look like me."

Even the gains for Black students have been waning in recent years.[39] While all college enrollments in the US fell by about 8 percent during the pandemic years of 2020 to 2022, the enrollment decline of Black students was even more severe, almost 17 percent.[40] And this is not just a pandemic phenomenon. The underrepresentation of Black students has been worsening over the past two decades. A survey of the top public universities in the US shows that since 2000 the percentage of Black undergraduates has dropped at six out of ten of those institutions.[41] At the University of Michigan, Black students declined from around 8 percent of all undergraduates in 2002 to 4 percent in 2021. According to former university president Michael Nietzel, "the majority of universities in the Big Ten Conference have a smaller percentage of Black undergraduates enrolled at their institutions than they did 20 years ago."[42] There are notable exceptions, as many university campuses have seen increases in diversity—while about 60 percent of top universities decreased their percentage of Black students over this time period, about 40 percent increased it, and over the last decade the overall diversity of students at many campuses has increased to reflect the diversity of the communities around them.[43]

But do the professors or deans on those campuses reflect the diversity of their students? In most universities across the US and Canada, the racial diversity of faculty members and leaders has not kept pace with the racial diversity among students. While less than half of all undergraduate students in the US identify as white, about 75 percent of full-time university instructors in the US identify as white; about 6 percent are Black, and less than 1 percent are Indigenous. If we look at senior professors and leaders, the numbers are even more striking—in a 2019 study of Canadian universities, about 8 percent of deans identified as racialized as other than white, a figure that dropped off sharply at the highest level of leadership. The percentage of non-white university presidents, vice presidents, or provosts was too low to report.[44]

It is no wonder that diversity officers have a high rate of turnover. The job has high expectations and a narrow scope for change; it has been observed that "the very nature of the role lends itself to emotional fatigue."[45]

The irony in these striking statistics is that too often equity and antiracism are assessed only by the measure of numerical, demographic diversity. But this yardstick too falls short. It's important to acknowledge that any figures tell only part of the story.

If we assess curriculum, campus culture,[46] and everyday experience in universities, or if we apply a more substantive, qualitative analysis to any organization, we often get a different picture. Even when diversity programs bring in new students and faculty, their campus experience can be very challenging. James Thomas suggests that "racially diverse campuses may produce long-term psychological and social gains for their students, but research suggest these gains are greatest for white students and weakest for racial and ethnic minorities."[47]

Racial diversity is a feature of campus life, but so is, as Thomas high-lights, everyday racism, racial conflict, and violence.[48] In the US, college campuses are the third most likely location for a hate crime;[49] 8.5 percent of hate-crimes targeting race or ethnicity happened on college campuses in 2018.[50] Seventy percent of hate crimes on US campuses were moti-vated by race, ethnicity, or religion, accounting for a total of 563 incidents in 2018.[51] In Canada, 16 percent of nonviolent hate crimes targeting race or ethnicity occurred at an educational institution.[52] And Black students report that surveillance by campus security and students regularly singles them out as threats, rather than part of the campus community.[53]

Too often the response to incidents of racism focuses on anti-bias and diversity training. Yet reviews of hundreds of studies find that anti-bias and diversity training creates either short-term changes in attitudes or none at all.[54] Nor should attitudes and "bias" be the measure.[55] Changes in attitudes and reduction and bias do not necessarily have any cor-relation with increases in diversity, changes to organizational culture, decision-making, recruitment, or hiring practices. Diversity policies and workshops, like other commonly proposed solutions—conflict resolu-tion, consultants, examining one's own racist thoughts, developing empa-thy,[56] being color-blind—have often failed to change day-to-day practices.

This is perhaps not surprising. Changing concrete practice is rarely the stated goal of workshops and policies. Conversations begin, good intentions are voiced, policies are written, but profound changes in or-ganizational practices, culture, and hierarchies remain elusive. Changes in hiring or programming are slow or uneven. Formal efforts at diversity have failed to make deeper shifts in organizational culture and practice.[57] Even the most successful diversity efforts can be superficial, aiming to "include" marginalized groups, rather than to transform an organization to work in more equitable ways.

Despite being anemic in their impact, diversity policies are never-theless met with resistance and recalcitrance. Many of the community organizations I observed were wracked by battles over race and diversity. Universities have also been perennial hotspots for these debates about diversity and difference.[58] As Sara Ahmed writes, doing diversity work in a university requires "the physical and emotional labor of 'banging your head against a brick wall,'"[59] echoing what is the first-hand experience of many students and academics.

Many diversity efforts are, as my research shows, steeped in emotional fallout. Too often, raising concerns about racism or equity leads to greater tensions or even explosive, drawn-out battles.[60] Ann Russo describes how even a routine committee meeting at her university lead to "an emotional outburst" when race and diversity were raised; one committee member began to cry, offering to step down from the committee to make room for a person of color.[61] Turning their attention to reassure the weeping woman, the other committee members quickly abandoned the discussion of diversity. This is the same story told to me by the women I interviewed. One woman shared the exhausting experience of seeing the same typical emotional responses to discussions of racism in all the community organizations where she has worked:

> The indignant response, anger, the rage that turns into tears, the foot-stomping, temper tantrums, which are very typical responses. Every single organization that I have been in, every single one.

It is a dynamic of emotionality and guilt common to the organizational discussions of racism described in this book.

Tears, anger, recriminations, fear, and shame—all these can easily become the currency of board meetings or antiracism workshops. Failed diversity efforts, in other words, cultivate not just a lack of diversity, but also personal conflicts, political divisions, emotional trauma, and organizational discord.

In other words, not only do these efforts often fail to make lasting change, but they can also make things worse. Diversity practices, for example, may simply reinforce the fact that an organization is historically not diverse. Jane Ward's study of a queer community organization in Los Angeles with a national reputation for multiculturalism highlights this irony. The organization's non-white staff are less than impressed with this national reputation for diversity; in their eyes, it continues to function as a white-centered organization.[62] The organization's so-called Diversity Days only emphasize the need to perform and justify diversity—in other words, they underscore the normative whiteness of the organization.[63] Cameron Greensmith's analysis offers a similar critique, highlighting the complex ways that queer and trans service providers use diversity as a tactic that can instead create further exclusion.[64]

Researchers speculate that not only is diversity training ineffective in preventing police violence against racial others, but also that it may contribute to tense and dangerous dynamics between police officers and marginalized communities.[65] Researchers inferred that because diversity training can heighten the fear that white participants have of being seen as racist, it can in turn increases tensions and fear between whites and non-whites.[66] To demonstrate this effect in an experiment, Phil Goff and colleagues showed that white participants who were concerned about being seen as racist actually set their chairs farther away from Black participants before an upcoming discussion. Moving a chair "may not be a dire racial injury," but the researchers ask us to imagine how this kind of racial distancing and tension—averted eyes, lack of warmth, mistrust—can affect relationships between police and community members.[67] Even trying to avoid talking about race causes white participants to have more negative affect and reduce nonverbal friendly gestures.[68] These experiments show that the effort it takes to appear non-racist means that whites make fewer friendly nonverbal gestures; in other words, their body language is less friendly. They also fail to give Black participants important information because they fear being seen as racist.

In more progressive environments, the same fear of being seen as racist can lead to more expository and exhibitory strategies: confessing one's racism or declaring one's commitment to antiracism, for example, becomes a typical strategy to avoid accusations of racism. However, studies show that these kinds of egalitarian statements are effective at deflecting criticism or sanction for discriminatory actions. In group situations, the more people feel they are among enlightened egalitarian colleagues, the more likely they are to take a discriminatory action in, for example, a hiring decision. As I show in this book, these emotional, therapeutic, and moral self-absorptions also direct attention away from creating equitable practices.

It is perhaps not surprising that corporate workshops and online training appear to have little effect, particularly when many employees resent or resist this mandatory training.[69] Diversity efforts even inspire outright rebellion; a faction of lawyers in the Law Society of Ontario successfully organized in 2018 to overturn a new rule requiring lawyers to establish their own policies on diversity and equity.[70]

The problem is not just that conversations about race get emotional. The typical pattern of emotional responses to antiracism challenges—anger, fear, and tears—are produced by implied challenges to what counts as a good person, a good activist, and a good citizen. Rather than simply document emotional responses, we must acknowledge how these are rooted in deeper and broader psychic investments in racial hierarchies and representations and how these are linked to our political ideals, notions of community, national imaginings, imperial history, and moral identity. The standard approaches to challenging inequity and increasing diversity—workshops, policies, public education, dialogue, and facilitation—do not work, because they are anchored in and hampered by the deeper emotional and moral undercurrents of histories of racism.

For those who think of themselves as egalitarian, the fear of appearing racist can be so deeply troubling that it doubles back and perpetuates racial tension. Yet as people work to distance themselves from the taint of racism, their emotional discomfort also distances them from the work of creating antiracism practices. Even positions that have been seen as the most benign—being color-blind, for example—can shape conduct in harmful ways by denying and perpetuating everyday racism.

FEEL-GOOD RACIAL POLITICS

The idea that racism is an evil perpetrated by bad people makes it hard to imagine that anyone, least of all oneself, might be implicated in racism. The simplicity of this framing of racism as good versus evil makes it impossible for us to embrace the genuine complexity of individuals and therefore the challenging complexity of the solutions. Yet this simplicity continues because it is deeply comforting. *To Kill a Mockingbird*, a cherished literary novel with an antiracist hero, illustrates this contradiction perfectly.

Atticus Finch may be a fictional character, but this has not prevented him from becoming a cherished hero in the fight against racism and injustice, a model of justice and integrity whom many hope to emulate.[71] The hero of *To Kill a Mockingbird*, Atticus Finch, and his unsuccessful fight to defend a falsely accused Black man have moved many to name their children after him[72] and encouraged generations of readers to become lawyers.[73] Inspired by Atticus Finch to fight for justice, UK lawyer Shami Chakrabarti writes, "None of us will ever be as unimpeachable as Atticus, but it can only be a good thing to try."[74]

Days after Chakrabarti wrote those words, the first draft of Harper Lee's *To Kill a Mockingbird* was published, over fifty years after it was written. Marketed as a sequel, *Go Set a Watchman* was the author's first attempt at *To Kill a Mockingbird*, rejected by publishers in 1957. In this first version of the novel, however, Atticus Finch is depicted as an openly racist advocate for segregation, espousing ideas that his daughter, Scout, despises.[75] Like the first Atticus Finch, this Atticus has also evoked passionate and emotional responses from readers—shock, denial, sadness. Unwilling to reconcile the two versions of Atticus, many refused to read the "sequel." One man asserted, "I will keep the Atticus we know from *To Kill a Mockingbird* as my Atticus." As one book club member worried in a Facebook post, readers felt they would be "heartbroken" on reading about a racist Atticus.[76]

The character of Atticus Finch is based on Harper Lee's father; her original characterization of Atticus reflected his complexity. Yet there is little room in people's minds and hearts to embrace Atticus as a man who simultaneously defends a Black man and holds racist beliefs. Our relationship to this revered character illustrates the false and polar boundaries that we uphold between polite and blatant racism, between enlightened citizens and ugly racists. The striking separation of good from evil, making it so clear exactly who the hateful racists are, is why readers receive such "psychic nourishment"[77] from stories and movies like *To Kill a Mockingbird*. As a lawyer, Atticus Finch represents a system where the only choices are innocent and guilty. (As a friend remarked to me, "I long for racial politics to be that simple.")

Racism and goodness, in other words, are seen as mutually exclusive. And not only with regard to our literary preferences. Whether in cultural representations or in everyday language, our ways of thinking about what racism is (and who "a racist" is) suffer from this core incompatibility of meaning. Culpability for racism is conveniently sloughed off onto bad people; conversely, racist words, gestures, and entire histories are excused with references to good intentions or ignorance. Racism is a broad set of practices—it includes the everyday, cultural, institutional, and historical ways that racial and ethnic difference, discrimination, and violence are cultivated. Well-meaning people and benevolent institutions participate in and benefit from these practices. But most people reserve the word "racism" for distant historical events and for hateful people that we do not know. It is this good-versus-evil framing of racism that prompted US presidential candidate Hilary Clinton to cast the controversial aspersion that Donald Trump supporters are a "basket of deplorables" who are irredeemable,[78] and, in conversation with Black Lives Matter activists, to refer to slavery to as an "original sin."[79] The pursuit of goodness and diversity are then also linked; as Hilary Clinton said in a presidential campaign debate: "America is great because America is good," for it "celebrates diversity."[80]

This good/evil dichotomy does not fully explain the highly emotional responses, not only to Atticus, but also to all debates on race. Both the passionate reverence for Atticus and the heartfelt distress at his racism are emotional responses that echo the *Feel-Good politics of race* which limit all attempts to challenge racism. The Feel-Good impulse in debates about race does not render happy participants, however; instead, Feel-Good racial encounters are laden with continual concerns about one's innocence, redemption, and psychic comfort. We mire ourselves in guilt about distant injustices because it makes us feel like good people. It also helps us to avoid taking actions.

As David Goldberg points out in his analysis of *racismo cordiale*, 90 percent of Brazilians think racism is a problem in Brazil. Only 10 percent of them think they themselves are part of the problem, even though most agree with a variety of racist statements.[81] This contrapuntal relationship between racial innocence and guilt is not only central to any conversation about race, it is also its historical anchor and its ongoing scaffold. This desire to represent ourselves as innocent underlies and undermines all our discussions about race, whether these are organizational or national. Sherene Razack, for example, shows us that these notions of innocence and benevolence work to produce an image of Canada as a tolerant nation besieged by immigrants.[82]

In our desire to be good and feel good, we either deny the existence of everyday practices that cultivate racial inequality or turn our lenses on questions of our individual moral fitness or knowledge. These Feel-Good racial politics suffuse not only angry battles about race and difference, but also the best intentions to address racial injustice, equity, and diversity.

There are three ways in which Feel-Good racial politics lead our conversations and organizations astray:

First, the profound fear of appearing racist means that energies go toward propping up one's moral standing rather than toward making institutional change.

Second, the fear of appearing racist can conversely increase tensions; studies show that the trepidation and lack of trust that accompany this fear can increase racial tensions.[83]

Third, Feel-Good racial politics animates the notion that racism is linked to ignorance and "not knowing better." This claim leads to ineffective educational strategies that focus on correcting ignorance rather than on changing practices.

Feel-Good racial politics are the reason we neglect the more uncomfortable conversations that neither prop up our innocence nor parade our culpability. We also neglect the far more crucial work of rolling up our sleeves and changing the way we have always done things. The Feel-Good impulse is so pervasive that it becomes a protective cloak that is difficult to penetrate. Unless we can loosen that cloak, even the decrees to examine our own racism or to support antiracism become simply another route to goodness.

One outcome is that, whether debating police violence or promoting diversity, all conversations about race have become overlaid with emotional attachments to innocence. Instead of focusing on how to change institutional practices so that they are more equitable, diverse, and antiracist, we become mired in misdirected anxieties about who is and who is not racist. Atticus Finch and the intense emotions he provokes are an integral part of a cultural and political memory, a memory which sustains the Feel-Good story of racial justice and racial innocence that hampers so many efforts to challenge racism. We can trace the failure of personal, organizational, and political attempts at diversity to this affective and moral terrain.

EMOTION AND AFFECTIVE RELATIONS

I did not ask antiracist activists how they feel about their experiences of racism. Yet I was struck by their vivid descriptions of the strong emotionality arising from discussions of identity and antiracism in organizations. Many antiracism activists begin with the perhaps naive assumption that if we simply pointed out the existence of a problem, our colleagues would respond readily and agreeably. Often, however, as my interviews show, diversity efforts are often met with emotional resistance and denial, anger, or indignance. Co-workers speak in an emotional manner about their solidarity and express guilt, self-doubt, anger, and pain that they have been accused of their complicity with racism. I too have heard subtle variations on these emotional responses when equity and diversity is discussed. The emotional landscape of conversations about race is broad, from the angry emotions of conflict to the feelings of shame felt by well-meaning folks to the pride people express about diversity.

When I began studying social movements and race, there were few sociologists writing about emotion, let alone emotion and race. One of the reasons sociology has historically sidestepped the study of emotions is the mistaken tendency to see them as belonging to the psychological realm, rather than to the social. But emotions are not simply personal expressions of how an individual feels. Certainly, that is one way to think about emotions—as the complex set of feelings that express our own personal states and lives. But we cannot fully understand social problems unless we acknowledge that emotions are not merely individual, physiological, and ahistorical impulses. Emotions are also integral to social and cultural relations.[84] Scholars such as Arlie Hochschild pioneered a new "sociology of emotion," arguing that emotions are centrally relevant to explaining social problems.[85] As Sara Ahmed asserts, attending to emotion "allows us to address the question of how subjects become *invested* in particular structures."[86]

Indeed, emotions have meaning because of social relations, because of the concerted activities of people working to create meaning and to organize their relationships and institutions. Emotions help to shape these social relations; the converse is also true. Emotions, their expressions, and the meanings we give them reflect and profoundly shape social and historical relations of power, including life and death. Expressions of remorse by people accused of a crime, for example, are central to how their innocence and guilt is assessed. In cases of wrongful conviction, because the accused show a lack of remorse, they receive longer sentences and are denied parole and compassionate leave.[87]

These linkages between emotions and the social world may be thought of as *affective relations* or as an *affective sphere*, a concept which refers not to emotional relationships between individuals, but to the broader relations that join the emotional, psychic, social, and political.[88] Although the term "emotions" is a straightforward way to signal the feelings that shape conversations about race, the term "affective relations" is both more precise and more encompassing. Following Sara Ahmed's concept of "affective economies,"[89] in her book *The Cultural Politics of Emotion*, I am using the term "affective relations" not just as a synonym for emotions, but also as a way of highlighting the continual undercurrent of emotions in social life.

The term "affective relations" is useful because it is not tied to any evident expression of emotions. Indeed, we do not have to actually feel a particular emotion in a particular moment, or be aware of feeling anything at all, to be shaped by the affective relations of the political and social debates around us. We may feel emotionally neutral or oppositional to the emotions that most others are feeling (pride or benevolence toward racialized migrants, for example), and yet we are still acting within the social circulation of these emotions and the cultural history of these affective relations.

This approach suggests an analytical focus on the discourses and techniques of emotional expression and their link to social relations. In other words, by asking which emotions are considered acceptable, when and how they are expressed, what they communicate, and how they influence the meaning of social and political events, we emphasize the intermeshing among emotion and practices of power and knowledge.[90]

How, then, do knowledge and power relations of race circulate through the emotional, psychic, and affective realm?

Imagine that a person of color enters a store in a mostly white, well-to-do neighborhood. The manager notes that the customer is racially and ethnically different from her usual clients; she decides that the customer must be a recent immigrant or refugee. What are the affective relations that shape this interaction? Reflect for a moment on the emotional histories that permeate these kinds of community relationships. The manager, if asked, might say that she feels benevolence and pride about welcoming new immigrants. The manager might also attempt to hide or overcome feelings of condescension or irritation, to keep her feelings neutral or to represent them as positive. Perhaps she feels that she is an exception to the average white person and feels self-assured. Perhaps she has a longing to be more antiracist or even to be other than white. Yet the manager may not be aware of feeling anything at all.

But imagine that the customer does not return the manager's cheerful repartee, stepping outside the manager's expectations of deference or gratitude. The customer then browses for a long time but doesn't buy anything. How then do the manager's feelings of benevolence change? Perhaps the manager is more likely to feel affronted, hurt, angry, or vindictive. Perhaps she now begins to watch the customer; perhaps she calls security. The emotional undercurrents of a very ordinary moment can lead toward damaging actions and away from transformative change. Imagine that, after this unfortunate incident, the manager and the customer are asked to repair community relationships by attending a conflict-resolution meeting and an antiracism workshop. They reflect on their biases, express their feelings, discuss experiences of racism and migration with empathy, tears, and anger. Not long after, the manager moves to another job. Since the conflict resolution focused on the relationship between the customer and the manager, and since the antiracism workshop focused on individuals sharing stories, it is unlikely that these efforts will have much impact on how the store operates, hires people, treats customers, deals with security, and builds community relations.

While this example draws on the story of two individuals, it does so only to illustrate a pattern of historical and social relations. We cannot effectively address racial justice and equity without understanding these affective relations of race.[91] The emotional currents in debates about race are not just matters of individual psychology. In other words, they are shaped by histories of racialization; emotional expressions are in turn also interpreted through a racial lens. Anger is interpreted differently depending on who is expressing it and whether their anger is seen as justified.

Some scholars have suggested that emotions be made more central not only to the study of social life, but also to the very work of organizations.[92] Putnam and Mumby, for example, argue that "an emphasis on work feelings" in organizations would counter bureaucratic rationality and that "sensitivity to other people's feelings is essential for understanding diversity in the workplace and may form the foundation for organizational change."[93] However, a look at social movement organizations—many of which have already embraced this approach for several decades—shows that there are serious pitfalls. While we must add emotion to social analysis, the use of emotional disclosure as organizational practice is entirely another matter.

My project is quite the opposite: I highlight how emotions about race are derailing organizations.

I am not, however, advocating that we override emotions and turn to composed rationality as an alternative. Nor am I saying that "we just need to calm down." Instead, I argue that the unexamined emotionality of racial encounters is a crucial impediment to meaningful change.

In this project I draw inspiration from the work of scholars who have highlighted both the psychic *investments* in long histories of racial hierarchies as well as the psychic *effects* of racial oppression.[94] The roots of these psychic, emotional, and moral investments in racial hierarchies are anchored firmly in histories of conquest and colonialism. As Joanne Nagel's historical analysis shows, for example, the conquest of Indigenous nations was shaped and justified by the fifteenth-century desires and fantasies of Europeans.[95] Moral investments in racial hierarchies continued to be evident in the day-to-day arrangements of colonial life and education in Asia and Africa, as Ann Stoler outlines.[96] And today, these moral and emotional investments are echoed in global relations and development work, as Barbara Heron and Gada Mahrouse show.[97]

MYTHS ABOUT EMOTION AND RACE

Popular notions about racism and emotion reflect two key myths that have misguided our intellectual and political progress toward racial justice.

The first myth is that the emotional or angry racial politics is in the distant past, or in distant places with distant people.

Too often, the emotionality of racism is represented as a drama that happens far away from us in time or place—angry racists in historic civil rights battles, ardent white nationalists, or isolated hate crimes. The recurrent use of 1960s images of angry racists help to underpin this hopeful chronicle. These are the documentary and TV images I saw growing up: the angry racists picketing school children going to desegregated schools, the KKK burning crosses; these all made racism seem far away and defeated—even as I lived it in the schoolyard. The 2016 film *Hidden Figures*, documenting the history of Black female mathematicians at NASA, repeats this narrative. In one scene, actor Kevin Costner uses a huge mallet to march across the compound and dramatically destroy the "colored" washroom sign. As the sign comes crashing down, it is meant to signal the demise of blatant racism and racial segregation. The implication is that as technology advances to put a man on the moon, so society advances toward a gentler time of racial desegregation and multiculturalism. These narratives suggest that we have left emotional racism, anger, and hate behind us.

Many people believe this narrative of redemptive progress toward antiracism or make a pretense of believing it. Never mind the everyday racial epithets, stereotypes, and taunts hurled at us as in streets and school hallways that we never spoke about when we were growing up. Even as anti-immigration and neo-Nazi groups became active in the 1980s, they were often seen as marginal rather than as part of a continuum of racial thinking and politics. The rise of white nationalist groups today elicits a similar response—they are bracketed as on the outside fringe rather than as threads in a fabric. When we do talk about racism, in university seminars perhaps, our analysis often turns to "polite racism," the everyday, well-meaning, and bloodless interactions without the blatant expressions of racial superiority that ironically help to perpetuate racism by diminishing its impact.[98] The term "racism without racists," coined by Eduardo Bonilla-Silva, so aptly describes the paradox.[99]

The second myth is that blatant and angry racism is not only in a distant place or time, but is also inevitably more harmful than polite, dispassionate, color-blind racism.

We are often prepared to imagine (or perhaps to hope) that blatant racism may be relegated either to the dustbins of history or to the margins of society. "Polite" and "blatant" are not easily distinguished as separate categories of racism, however. They are inextricably linked. Racism does not confine itself to discrete categories such as polite or blatant, but is a broad and historical set of practices both subtle and brutal, both polite *and* blatant. Individuals may act in polite or dispassionate ways toward racial others, for example, yet be enacting explicitly discriminatory practices on a large scale;[100] several studies have measured this effect in the screening of job candidates.[101] Employers reviewing job applications may consider themselves to be unbiased and non-racist, yet studies across several countries show a strong bias toward white job candidates and against Black and ethnic-minority candidates.

Polite and blatant racial politics not only coexist today, they also help to produce and sustain each another. The current resurgence of blatant racism, for example, can act as a prop for polite, well-meaning racial politics: expressing outrage at blatant racism reassures folks that that they are good people. It displaces their fear of being racist and makes them less likely to examine the multitude of everyday ways that racial injustice is perpetuated.

This book challenges the tidy dichotomy of emotion versus dispassion, one in which messy emotions about race are seen as either attached to the stormy past or to blatant and angry acts of racism. For one, debates about race and social justice are as emotional and turbulent as they have ever been. Race, diversity, and equity are among the most volatile flashpoints of contemporary politics, whether we are talking about policing, schooling, immigration, community organizations, or universities. The speed and anonymity of social media has even further heightened the emotionality of debates about race and diversity.[102] This emotional milieu in turn supports the targeting of racialized people. One example is the simmering resentment and anger that has fueled anti-immigrant campaigns around the globe. Paula Ioanide highlights this emotional framing when she argues that "feelings trump facts" in US political debates about racism, immigration, and crime.[103] Emotionality is not just a way of framing 1960s civil rights battles or the sentiments of fringe white nationalists. Emotions shapes racial politics in the here and now, in contemporary politics, in our everyday conversations and community spaces.

HOW DID WE GET HERE? HISTORIES OF RACE AND MORAL REGULATION

So how did we get here? To transform the ongoing practices that sustain ideas about race and difference, we must also tease out their roots. These practices include institutional ways of doing things, the ways that we use language and the symbolic, the techniques we use to express connection or aversion, produce knowledge, manage people, make decisions, and articulate who and what we value. As local or individual acts they may seem insignificant, but these "micropractices" are noteworthy because of how they are anchored to broader and long-standing relations of power.[104] Together these practices produce a distinct social formation or assemblage such as racism, one that varies across place and time and yet is anchored in common histories.

The affective field on which relations of race are played has well-anchored historical foundations. While philosopher Michel Foucault was largely silent about emotion,[105] his work on the historiography of modern power relations is useful in highlighting not only the historicity of feelings,[106] but also their importance as "the main field of morality."[107] Feelings about race and racism, in other words, do not arise naturally; they have a history shaped by colonialism and moral regulation. If we want to understand why Feel-Good racial politics are so tenacious and so resistant to change, we must unearth these underpinnings. This is not merely an intellectual inquiry, for when we recognize that these practices are neither fixed nor inevitable, we also assert that they are open to continuous transformation.

The making of the racialized subject has a historical trajectory that is intertwined with representations of culture, nation, and empire. Studies of imperial history show that morality, purity, and race were linked in a myriad of explicit ways, not only through legal and political systems but also in the organizations of households and communities.[108] Moral superiority and moral regulation, in other words, were both key to racism under colonial rule.

These imperial representations of whiteness[109] as both benevolent and morally superior have a long-standing and ongoing resonance. A century ago, sociologist W. E. B. Du Bois wrote of the "moral satisfaction" that "white souls" experience by giving to "humble black folk."[110] David Goldberg has argued that moral reason itself has been racialized by "constituting racial others outside the scope of morality."[111] In tracing modernity's emphasis on rational capacity as a basis of moral reason, Goldberg draws on the late medieval category of the "savage" or "wild man"[112] who was excluded on a putative absence of morality.[113] These medieval categories of exclusion, while not explicitly racial, prefaced the racial categories of modernity and postmodernity.

In the prevailing moral discourse of modern liberalism, rationality and moral capacity came to be used to cement racial categories. The color white has been historically associated in Western culture with purity, virtue, and honesty. A close study of visual representations of white people in Western culture shows that this moral symbolism of the color white is in turn reflected in the repetitive association of white skin with virtue.[114]

While we may find the white-hatted good guy and black-hatted villain to be a laughable cliché of early Hollywood westerns, it has remained a common binary representation,[115] one which shows us that this trajectory continues within the moral politics of contemporary racial debates and popular culture. Tracing visual and literary representations from Renaissance painting to Hollywood film, Richard Dyer argues in his book *White* that the equation of whiteness with goodness underlies all representations of white and non-white people. Concludes Dyer, "To be white is to be at once of the white race and 'honorable' and 'square-dealing.'"[116] Even when whites are portrayed as bad characters, for example, they are often seen to possess physical characteristics of non-whites.

The image of the good, caring woman has also been anchored by imperialism.[117] In imperial contexts, white women have been represented as the "custodians of morality,"[118] as scholars such as Ann Stoler have shown. English women in colonial settings, for example, styled themselves as the "overseers of black souls" and "guardian of white morals."[119] These gendered and racialized representations of virtue in turn justified oppressive colonial laws, such as the White Women's Protection Ordinance of Papua, to protect white women from men of color.[120]

Representations of morality, honesty, and benevolence have not only been a historical foundation of whiteness, bourgeois respectability, and femininity,[121] but they also continue to be echoed in contemporary work[122] in psychotherapy,[123] international development,[124] and teaching,[125] as well as in ongoing feminist debates.[126] In a study of white women doing development work in Africa, for example, Barbara Heron shows that they were motivated by their desire to "make myself better by doing something for someone somewhere."[127] Similarly, in her research on white women psychotherapists, Kerstin Roger calls this the "good fairy" image, one that still operates in powerful ways. In analyzing the gendered and racialized nature of the "good fairy," Roger suggests that white women in helping professions produce their innocence about racism through the guilt of the white men in their family. By declaring how horrified they are about their father's or uncle's racism, they aim to demonstrate their own antiracist feminist positions.[128]

Several writers have challenged this moral positioning, and instead forward the moral dilemmas of "white complicity"[129] with racism, suggesting that whites must develop new ethical and spiritual paths.[130]

Sociologist Michael Young's historical analysis shows that this kind of productive shift has indeed been possible in the past: the movement to abolish slavery was invigorated by new conceptions of sin and paths to salvation.[131]

The problem is that there is no inevitable nor causal relationship between acquiring a new moral identity and dismantling racism. On the contrary, one may have undertaken a renovation of one's soul and still benefit from racism. Maryam Kouchaki's experiments suggest that identifying with an egalitarian moral position offers some absolution and therefore can make discriminatory actions more likely. Participants who were told that their group was "more moral" than others or who read about a group member's nonprejudiced actions were *more* likely to discriminate against Black and Hispanic job candidates in a hiring scenario. The heightened sense of collective morality had the effect of providing a kind of "moral license."[132]

The prevalent self-image many people have of themselves as tolerant, just, and non-racist clearly shapes talk and action on ethical questions such as racism. For example, academics have focused on the implicitly non-racist constructions of Western nations such as Canada, the Netherlands, and New Zealand, and more broadly on liberal values of color-blindness,[133] notions that are contradicted by state policy on race, immigration, and Indigenous rights.[134] In her study of Canadian student teachers' reflections on racism, Carol Schick found that claims to innocence drew on a national image of tolerance. Canada was described a "lovable," "not evil" place where everyone receives equitable treatment.[135] In the Netherlands, writes Philomena Essed, the national self-image of tolerance and nondiscrimination underlies the reluctance to admit racism.[136] New Zealanders, observe Wetherell and Potter, use typical discursive strategies of denial to avoid being seen as prejudiced.[137] Denial of racism and assertion of innocence is clearly a pattern that crosses organizational and national sites.

These Feel-Good racial politics are in part rooted in the color-blind ethic that was cultivated following the civil rights movement of the late

1960s and early 1970s. One counterpoint to legal inequality and racial violence was to diminish the significance of racial categories entirely; the most common ethical positions on race have involved claims not to see racial difference at all.[138]

The anger, tears, fears that arise when race and antiracism are the topic are not just momentarily obstructive; they also teach us about the historical, moral, and ethical landscape of racial encounters today. Deep investments in racial histories, moral identities, ethical paths, and ideals of nation and community evoke deep emotions. This book is concerned with the practices that continue to cultivate these psychic conditions and that prevent us from cultivating different ways of doing things. Conversations about race and diversity too often move toward personal ethical and educational journeys instead of toward organizational change.

EDUCATION AS AN ANTIDOTE TO "IGNORANCE"

Learning more about racism appeared to be a brand-new pursuit after the spring of 2020, inspiring a spate of popular books, public discussions, corporate training, YouTube channels, and blogs. But even before employment equity legislation spawned workplace training in the 1970s and 1980s, education has long been the default approach. Why has education become the key strategy for addressing concerns about racism, diversity, and equity?

The belief that well-meaning ignorance is the cause of racism is a widespread and comforting one. When ignorance is posited as the root of racism, then education and knowledge are inevitably offered as the antidote to racism. This is an unshakeable foundation of most diversity workshops.

The conviction that ignorance is the root of racism is closely related to the notion that racism is a matter of individual guilt or innocence; in this framing, one is either guilty of racism or innocent of racism, either racist or antiracist. Ignorance conveniently helps to establish one's innocence. It is common, for example, to describe a well-meaning person as ignorant, as someone who "doesn't know better," as a way of minimizing their culpability. Whether we are assessing ignorance or innocence, however, the focus remains on the individual as the source of the problem and the focus of the remedy. Not surprisingly, education serves as a convenient but ineffective antidote.

In the novel *To Kill a Mockingbird*, for example, the characters most guilty of racism are those who are also represented as most ignorant— those who are uneducated and working-class. As sociologist Jennifer Pierce shows in her book *Racing for Innocence*, racist villains in Hollywood films are usually working-class, poor, and marginal. The "anti-racist white hero," on the other hand, is always elite—a lawyer, a teacher.[139]

In *Good White People*, philosopher Shannon Sullivan refers to this as the "sharp bright line" drawn between good middle-class antiracist white people and bad working-class white racists.[140] Good middle-class people maintain this line by knowing that they should "refrain from making derogatory remarks about race, support multicultural celebrations in their communities, and so on."[141] Sullivan and Pierce suggest that both scholarly and popular representations emphasize working-class racist attitudes,[142] reinforcing the notion that it is the "uneducated" who are more racist.

Most antiracism and equity training approaches assume that lack of knowledge is the core problem. Yet what does it mean to be ignorant of race and racism, and how is this ignorance produced and sustained? Ignorance, as Charles Mills, Sharon Sullivan, and Nancy Tuana show,[143] is not accidental or passively received, but rather produced through relations of power.

There are two approaches commonly proposed for addressing this supposed ignorance: "contact" and "literacy." The first is the familiar notion, represented in the psychology and sociology literature as the *contact hypothesis*, that to reduce prejudice people need to have more contact with each other. The second, which we might call the *literacy hypothesis*, refers to the acquisition of knowledge and skills to navigate cross-racial interactions. There is a wide range of approaches to "racial literacy"[144] and some are more broadly focused on learning about the structural aspects of racism.[145] In most cases, however, in many cases racial literacy refers to either learning facts or learning "the capacity to decipher racial grammar."[146] Harrelson, for example, describes racial literacy as "the ability to recognize, describe, and respond to the racial nuances of complex social settings."[147]

As originally proposed by psychologist Gordon Allport, the contact hypothesis only works to reduce prejudice between groups under several quite particular conditions, including that the groups have equal status and are working toward a common goal.[148] The contact hypothesis is so alluring and enduring, however, that it has become the basis for so many initiatives and efforts at diversity and antiracism—and yet, under less than ideal conditions, even extended contact has no effect or actually increases prejudice.[149] Even in a city with a high degree of contact and marriage between Indigenous residents and white settlers, for example, sociologist Jeffrey Denis found that whites continued to maintain a sense of collective superiority.[150]

Of course, I am not opposed to social contact and education in cultivating change: thoughtful connections and intellectual engagement are important in building movements and communities. But I am concerned that these enduring notions have made dialogue, conflict resolution, and education the conventional, unquestioned, go-to approaches for challenging racism, without sufficient analytical attention to how these approaches are best conceived and whether they are making a difference. Most dialogical and pedagogical approaches that draw on the contact or literacy approach neither address nor equip people to challenge structural and historical inequalities. As I argue in chapter 3, dialogue, conflict resolution, and more education should not be the primary strategies for challenging systemic racism in organizational, institutional, and public spaces—though they often are. As an alternative, my final chapter proposes the ACT approach, a process for collaborative analysis and action.

INSIDE SOCIAL MOVEMENTS: "THIS IS WHAT DEMOCRACY LOOKS LIKE?"

I have seen racial tensions arise in every movement or organization in which I have been involved, whether the environmental movement, the feminist movement, community radio, or labor organizing. And yet there is an expectation that social movements and progressive institutions are enlightened spaces, where racial conflict and inequity are the exception. But this idealism merely makes it more difficult to confront histories of racism, colonialism, and sexism or to integrate a broader social justice framework.

In the 1990s I worked as an environmental activist; in my organization, I was the first person of color in a leadership position, and the movement had few non-white activists. I witnessed the inspiring rise of the environmental justice movement, and met the new generation of Black and Indigenous activists working to highlight the links between racism and environmental damage.[151] I worked with long-time labor advocate Stan Gray to integrate environmental and labor issues and to support a Green Work Alliance.[152] But when trying to integrate concerns about labor, aboriginal self-government, poverty, and racism, I was often told that the environment was not a social justice issue. I observed that "the environment" was constituted as nonsocial, while strategies to save it were the largely led by white, middle-class professional activists.[153]

Decades later these gaps remain, as Sharmeen Khan demonstrated in her well-circulated article "The Whiteness of Green," about the whiteness of the environmental movement. As she reflects, "I wonder if sometimes they stop and look around and ask, 'Why are we so white?'"[154]

I learned several things from my experiences as an activist. For one, I saw clearly the idealistic assumptions of social-movement purity that proscribe discussions of racism, sexism, and harassment. Secondly, I discovered that interpersonal approaches were the primary response to conflict; when organizations had to deal with charges of racism, sexism, and harassment, they often referred to personality differences and inter-personal conflict resolution. Finally, I learned that these kinds of battles are emotionally draining and depressing, with long-lasting effects.

The community organizations I studied were very similar. I observed an emotional defense of the boundaries of feminism often expressed through nostalgia and ideals of purity. This emotional defense coex-ists with heartfelt desires for broader antiracism visions. The tensions among these diverse impulses are mediated by focusing on the personal, the emotional, and the experiential. My research also shows that there are certain features of social movements that can shape or stall discus-sions of equity: a profound investment in a particular, universal vision of equity; an assumption that social movements are uniquely egalitarian spaces; a strong sense of familial, emotional, and political community; and, quite often, a closet full of informal and formal tools to produce political knowledge and to express emotions and experiences.

It is precisely in those places where we are most preoccupied with working toward justice that efforts at talking about racism can become especially mired in emotional attachments to innocence and goodness. These responses point not only to deep psychic investments in racial hierarchies and representations, but also to how these are linked to no-tions of community, national imaginings, colonial history, and moral identity. Ethical practices, or the ways that we monitor and make ethical selves, are particularly crucial in social movement spaces, spaces whose whole existence may be trained toward producing a better world.[155]

In this book I show how the history of progressive social movements adds another layer of moral imperative to historical constructions of racial innocence, a non-racist position seen as central to being a good feminist, a good radical, or a good liberal. The ideals of social justice, solidarity, and egalitarianism common to progressive social movements have ironically initiated *and* limited discussions of antiracism. These egalitarian ideals are so central to the moral identity of progressive folks that when antiracist activists point out a movement's limitations on ques-tions of justice and race, they are often resisted in deeply emotional ways.

Of course, intense internal battles over the central values of social movement organizations are not new. As long ago as 1911, sociologist Robert Michels concluded that all political organizations, no matter how democratic or socialist their principles, would get more hierarchical and more conservative with time and increased size.[156] While not all politically progressive organizations fall subject to this pattern, one that Michels called the "iron law of oligarchy," his research highlights the contradiction that often exists between egalitarian intention and everyday practice. Organizations whose very purpose is to support social justice may nevertheless cultivate hierarchies and practices that in turn perpetuate the very inequities they are working to undo.

But these exclusions and omissions are not simply incidental oversights; they have come to structure the very nature of social movements.[157] Race was constitutive of the US labor movement in the nineteenth century, in which only the white man was seen as a worker.[158] David Roediger's historical analysis shows us that the development of a working class and whiteness went hand in hand.[159] Similarly, the history of racism in the British trade union movement was central to its role in securing jobs and wages for white workers.[160] Historians of first-wave feminism have also highlighted how constructions of benevolent and pure white femininity were inseparable from the goals of feminists in the nineteenth and early twentieth centuries.[161] For example, in the US and Canada, the women's suffrage movement argued that women should gain votes so that they could uplift the race and purify the nation. "Until women have electoral value, their reforms . . . their dreams of an uplifted race, a purified country . . . will lack fulfillment," argued an article published in an 1892 issue of *Women's Journal*.[162]

The contemporary politics of diversity and race have offered particularly glaring examples of this contradiction between egalitarian visions and social movement practices.[163] The racial tensions in queer and trans communities, for example, confirm this conundrum.[164] "Should the rainbow have black and brown stripes?" asks Sylvia Grills in her research investigating this "central fracture" within queer organizing, one that expresses a commitment to antiracism but makes it secondary, invisible, or subsumes it with slogans such as "gay is the new black."[165]

Scholars such as Cindy Patton and Abigail Halcli have shown that AIDS organizing, while both innovative and successful, was defined not by the full spectrum of people living with AIDS but primarily by white, middle-class activists.[166] Histories of racial exclusion have also kept activists of color away from anti-globalization protests, prompting some activists to add an ironic question mark to the familiar chant, "This is what democracy looks like." Local activist Jinee Kim asks, "Is this really what democracy looks like? Nobody here looks like me."[167] The minimal presence of people of color in the protests against the World Trade Organization meetings in Seattle had activists asking, "Where is the color in Seattle?"[168]

Most Western social movements, with the exception of the civil rights and abolitionist movements, have historically failed to integrate an anti-racism analysis. George Dei notes that "in movements for social change, race concerns have always been pushed to the background or denied."[169] So our work should be oriented not toward discovering racism and sexism in social movements—its existence has been well-documented— but toward understanding how the discourses and practices adopted in social movements shape inequality.

It is the feminist movement, however, that has been the battleground for some of the most conspicuous and discordant conflicts over race. Beginning in the late 1980s, these organizational conflicts over racism increased not only in frequency but also in their level of controversy.[170] Battles in local organizations even became national disputes, and then the subject of books and textbooks.[171]

In the 1990s, I attended a gathering to welcome the first non-white president of Canada's national women's association, NAC.[172] We felt that we were living in an exciting moment of change: concerns about race and diversity in social movements had become front and center, and the presence of women of color was visible, both in the feminist movement and in the media, in a way it had never been.[173] We saw organizations falter and leaders ousted in the face of these challenges. Decades later, we hear striking echoes of decades-old battles, not just in the feminist movement, but in almost all social movements and community organizations. The 2017 Women's March on Washington to protest the inauguration of Donald Trump was marked by division over race; Pride Day organizing has battled over race and policing; queer community organizations have been grappling with their lack of racial diversity.[174]

These controversies demonstrate that while emotional aspects of solidarity have always been vital to building social movement communities, at the same time these are the unsteady foundations upon which antiracism change falters. They also demonstrate how engaged, over many decades, the feminist movement has been with questions of social difference and antiracism. Bell hooks's 1981 book *Ain't I a Woman: Black Women and Feminism* is one of the earliest catalysts that fueled antiracist feminism. In Britain, Hazel Carby's 1982 essay "White Women Listen! Black Feminism and the Boundaries of Sisterhood" was a turning point that inspired further activism and writing.[175] This period of antiracism feminist scholarship has been one of the most vibrant areas of engagement with questions of racial justice and talking across difference.[176] What this scholarship lacks, however, is a close analysis of the day-to-day antiracism battles going on inside organizations and movements.[177]

In the chapters that follow, I expand these antiracist feminist critiques to look at specific organizational practices and histories, detailing a pattern of knowledge production about race and antiracism. I show that organizational discussions of antiracism often focus on the desires of some white participants for "better" knowledge of people of color, for greater self-knowledge, and for an innocent non-racist self or a more ethical antiracist self. I demonstrate that techniques such as consciousness-raising, popular education, and feminist therapy, drawn from the central belief that the personal is political, have been interpreted in individualized ways that shape how knowledge about race, racism, and antiracism can be produced. These techniques have often been used to turn the spotlight alternately on people of color as knowledge resources and on the emotions and moral deliberations of some white participants rather than to develop measures for organizational change. (While I offer several critiques of antiracism workshops, I am also disturbed by misguided interventions by state and federal governments to ban antiracism workshops and education about systemic racism. Ninety percent of states in the USA have proposed legislation to limit teaching about system racism, and about seventeen states have succeeded in these bans.)[178]

At one level, this book documents the tremendous impacts that antiracism has made on the social movement landscape. It contributes a detailed analysis of key organizational debates that have accompanied antiracism challenges. At another level, this book is an exploration of how typical practices of discussion and problem-solving have limited the ability of these organizations to work toward equity and racial justice.

In uncovering this story, I knit together interviews and media accounts into a partial historiography of antiracism. It is an approach inspired by a methodological approach known as "history of the present," which examines how our present knowledges and practices are historically constituted.[179] Put most simply, it begins with an analysis of the present rather than of history and asks "how did we get here?"[180] In contrast to conventional historiography, its aim, writes Wendy Brown, is the "disruption of conventional accounts of ourselves—our sentiments, bodies, origins, futures."[181] This historiographic project has the potential to lead us to some contemporary trajectories: to disrupt the conventional accounts of ourselves within the racial project, and to disrupt the conventional diversity project.

Despite its title, this book is not an incitement to scrutinize who is and who is not racist. Public debate about racism often focuses on individual culpability. It is precisely this trend that I challenge—not because I wish to absolve or ignore racist actions, but because this trend only leads us away from organizational, social, and political change. The focus on individual culpability also leads us toward polarization. Concepts like "white fragility" and "micro-aggressions" have become conveniently catchy phrases, but they also keep us in the realm of the individual, focusing on traits, habits, and feelings rather than on challenging the systemic practices that produce these moments.

A few years ago, a media scandal erupted when Donald Sterling, former owner of the LA Clippers' basketball team, was recorded making racist comments during a personal phone call. As a result, Sterling was banned from attending NBA basketball games and required to sell his team. Many observers downplayed the eighty-year-old's racist remarks with comments such as "He's not racist, he's senile." Like so many debates about race, this sets up mutual exclusions between intelligence and racism, niceness and racism, even mental well-being and racism. I urge us to shift our energies from branding particular individuals as racist, or "fragile," or good, and instead turn to analyzing all of our ongoing daily engagements with practices and histories of racialization.

The Black Lives Matter movement in May of 2020 sparked many antiracist statements and legislative discussions. But, as scholar Keeanga-Yamahtta Taylor suggests in her book *From #BlackLivesMatter to Black Liberation*, we will need more concerted organizing and coordination if we are to move beyond protest to a genuine movement for racial justice.[182] This new wave of antiracism will not bring the profound change we need unless we move beyond conventional therapeutic and educational approaches, and begin the thoughtful, detailed work of analyzing and transforming everyday practices in the spaces we inhabit.

2

"Nostalgia for a World We Never Knew"

AMBIVALENT ENCOUNTERS BETWEEN FEMINISM AND ANTIRACISM

> But suddenly racism and "women of color" appear as phrases
> or topics thrown into books as chapters, producing tight
> little breathless paragraphs or footnotes. If certain themes
> and peoples are so important, we wonder about their sudden,
> urgent, yet parenthetical appearance.
> —Himani Bannerji (1993)

IN 1982 Hazel Carby wrote "White Women Listen!"—a blunt admonishment to "white feminists" about the "boundaries of sisterhood." "What exactly," she asked crisply, "do you mean when you say 'we'?"[1]

With this simple query, Carby challenged what was once a defining principle of the feminist movement—that all women share a universal condition and a global solidarity.

Hazel Carby's urgent tone and sharp critique of the limitations of "sisterhood" signaled a dramatic shift in the social movement landscape. One of the most significant and turbulent struggles over racism inside a social movement had begun. Carby was part of a new wave of antiracist feminists who, in speaking forcefully about the histories of racism, slavery, and colonialism, unsettled the notion of a common experience among all women.

It was a painful reckoning. The battles were intense and bitter, whether inside organizations, universities, or scholarly texts. Starting in the 1980s, sharp critiques by antiracist feminists such as Hazel Carby, bell hooks, and Gloria Anzaldúa pointed out that feminism's goals, leadership, and membership had been shaped by the experiences of white women and had been led by white women.[2] Activists in the US, Canada, and Europe tried to bring the insights of antiracist feminist writers into their organizations, sometimes with rocky outcomes.

It is a reckoning worth revisiting. Why, you may be wondering, are decades-old debates about race inside feminist organizations still relevant to equity and racial justice today? The first reason is that these battles represent a uniquely focused effort to confront racism. It was arguably the first time a social movement had such an intense, widespread, and sustained confrontation with the politics of race *within* their own sphere of action, practices, and goals. The civil rights movement of the 1960s and 1970s focused primarily on challenging racism in institutions and public life. New social movements and the counterculture of the 1960s and 1970s also looked inward, exploring new ways of being, living, organizing, and relating to each other. In the 1980s and 1990s, antiracist feminist activists and scholars brought these two threads together, devoting time and emotional energy to challenging the core ideals of their own movement. These efforts, as Winifred Brienes suggests, have been a "microcosm of the racial project of American society,"[3] efforts that have also been active across the globe.

All social movements and institutions are riven with internal battles—not just power struggles, but genuine debates about their core values. The feminist movement's engagement with question of race and difference is unique however, because it has been sustained and theorized over decades. The deep and long-term engagement of feminist scholars and activists looking inward, debating, and continually remaking their own organizations, theories, and tenets in the context of racial justice provides a rich body of material for analysis.

The second reason is that this history presents a salient case study and echo of the battles that continue to this day in so many institutions and movements. Not only do these feminist struggles continue to the present day but, as I show in this book, their history also remains influential in other sites. The Women's March on Washington in 2017 was a large, public example of these continuing battles, resonant with long-time debates over racism and diversity in the feminist movement: Does a "Women's March" mean that being "women" supersedes other issues and identities? As Karen Grigsby Bates reports in a story about the Women's March for National Public Radio, "All that diversity came with a cost: racial tension—not just around the march itself, but around the feminist movement, who leads it and why." Grigsby continues, "Some bemoaned the discord as a distraction from the march, saying on this occasion, 'we should all be women first.'" There are countless examples within local feminist groups, online fora, journals, events, and social media that reveal these difficult tensions every day.

These tensions also reveal the deep roots of our uneven progress toward racial justice. A close look at this tumultuous history exposes familiar stumbling blocks that we see in contemporary equity efforts. We observe not only a trajectory of antiracism strategies and successes, but also typical avenues of opposition and failure. The harsh battles within feminist and community organizations in the 1980s and 1990s offer a rich study of this divergent and seemingly contradictory relationship that so many organizations have had with antiracism change.

The story of the feminist movement's encounters with antiracism reveals an ongoing pattern of ambivalence, one that continues to be apparent in efforts at diversity and antiracism today. Progressive organizations often celebrate or promote diversity while at the same time failing to challenge racism in practical ways. Damien Riggs notes the contradiction between public celebrations of diversity such as Sydney's "Kaleidoscope"-themed 2014 Gay and Lesbian Mardi Gras, and the fact that there is "little evidence of modern gay advocacy organizations confronting race or racism either within or without" in any systemic ways.[4]

The battles over diversity in the 1980s and 1990s are not merely historical artifacts, in other words. They should interest us because they continue to echo inside nonprofit organizations today. While the US becomes increasingly racially diverse, the percentage of people of color as board members and executive director/CEO roles of nonprofit organizations is largely unchanged for the last twenty-five years, remaining under 20 percent. A 2017 study found that 90 percent of chief executives and 84 percent of board members of US nonprofit organizations were white. Over a quarter of nonprofit boards were 100 percent white.[5] This composition has remained steady over decades. As one study respondent said, "One of the big problems in the nonprofit sector is that the leadership of nonprofit organizations doesn't represent the racial/ethnic diversity of the country." Similarly, there has been a lack of people of color in positions of leadership in queer community organizations.[6] Sylvia Grills's research explores this "central fracture in queer social movements," noting that "queer and antiracism social organizing does not necessarily coalesce."[7] Yet, as Kelly LeRoux shows, racialized leaders and staff of nonprofits are more likely to engage in advocacy, mobilization, and education on behalf of the racialized communities they represent.[8]

Finally, as I explore in subsequent chapters, the history of antiracist feminism has been generative in ways that continue to shape equity efforts today: consciousness-raising, emotional disclosure, therapeutic, and pedagogical approaches have all been profoundly influential and also obstructive.

In this chapter, I explore the ambivalent and uneven relationship between feminism and antiracism by tracing key conflicts in events, organizations, and news media.[9] I show that feminist politics has seen a complex dance between progression and regression on the question of race. As the phrase "antiracism" became increasingly central to feminist politics in the 1980s and 1990s, so too did a pathology of resistant response.

I use battles in Toronto as a case study and exemplar of these global and transnational conflicts over race in social movements. A metropolis of almost six million, the greater Toronto area is one of the most multiethnic cities in the world, with about 50 percent of the population identifying as an ethnicity other than "white" and about 50 percent born outside Canada.[10]

There is no doubt that the last thirty-five years have seen some important shifts in how organizations think about and engage with antiracism. Still, activists have argued that antiracism activism of the 1980s and 1990s was not able to make profound changes. One study found that even after a decade of antiracist activism, the majority of national women's organizations had made little progress toward greater diversity.[11] More recently, Callander, Holt, and Newman note "there has been little change or challenge to the whiteness of gay institutions" since the 1980s.[12] Looking more closely at antiracism efforts within the feminist organizations helps us understand why progress toward equity has been hampered there and elsewhere.

Any organizational gains have been *contested* gains. Eager embrace of diversity coexists with trepidatious, sometimes angry resistance to organizational change. Contradiction and ambivalence characterize debates on race and equity in most organizations and public spaces. While almost everyone agrees on the desirability of diversity and the undesirability of racism, responses to antiracism efforts can easily careen from enthusiastic support to ambivalence, indifference, and anger. Even nominal efforts at antiracism elicit emotional debates.

This ambivalence is in part rooted in *nostalgia*—nostalgic imaginings of community and nation that limit broader antiracist, anti-imperial visions. A look at the debates within feminist organizations shows that, while activists have been ethically compelled to consider how their visions of justice do not address the full dimensions of social inequality, there is a corresponding impulse to protect a fragile, imagined unity that may be harmed by divisions within the movement. In particular, this resistant response often demonstrates a nostalgia for certain harmony of common goals—a harmony has been disturbed by supposedly peripheral concerns of race. Todd Gitlin similarly uses the phrase *The Twilight of Common Dreams* to mourn the loss of a common vision that accompanied what he calls the "fetish of difference"[13] of feminist and

antiracism politics.[14] The desire for the "universalism" and "commonality"[15] of past activist struggles evokes novelist Bharati Mukherjee's
phrase, "nostalgia for a world we never knew"—in the sense that it is a
world of commonality only known by some. It is a nostalgia for a "party
of commonality"[16] that has had limited membership. This nostalgia that
she and other white feminists feel, writes Winifred Breines, is born of a
longing for the vision of racial harmony activists worked for in the civil
rights movement.

An eruption of writing, scholarship, and activism beginning in the
1980s called white feminists to account for leaving women of color and
racism at the margins of the struggle. Appearing on an almost silent
stage, "women of color" became a collectively identified force in feminist politics. In the US, the hugely influential 1981 anthology *This Bridge
Called My Back* is considered the first major collection to bring together
feminist women of color across a variety of communities.[17] Its essays
and poetry spoke poignantly about the authors' experiences of racism
and marginalization in the movement, and it became an inspiration for
new visions of antiracist feminism. The first publication in Canada to
be edited by a collective of women of color, the 1983 special "Women
of Colour" issue of the feminist journal *Fireweed*, was also notable and
inspiring.[18] During the 1980s and 1990s, activism by a diverse group of
women of color and immigrant women appeared to move from silent
stage to center stage: there was an exponential explosion of debate about
antiracism, diversity, and inclusion. As journalist Michelle Landsberg
wrote, "A new revolution is brewing. . . . Every major feminist organization . . . has been or is about to be met with tough articulate demands
from women who want to share the power."[19]

For some, it seemed that the attention was excessive. The conventional wisdom was that "identity politics" led to the decline of feminism: "If feminists had only focused on what united women, they say,
instead of what divided them, the women's movement would have remained strong."[20] Despite supposedly excessive attention to "diversity,"
ten years after the groundbreaking "Woman of Color" issue of *Fireweed*,

antiracist feminist scholar Himani Bannerji still wrote about the "silencing" of women of color in feminist intellectual texts.[21] Feminists may have listened to Hazel Carby, Angela Davis, bell hooks, and the other Black feminist writers who challenged "white feminism," but negotiating meaningful changes in the practices, landscape, and vision of feminist organizations would be both painfully slow and explosive. The rising tensions meant that even a poetry reading could become a brawl. In 1991, a fierce debate broke out when a Black woman reading a provocative poem about "white feminism" was heckled at a large Canadian feminist conference; the resulting fight was so emotional and raucous that it became a headline on the front page of a national newspaper: "Feminist conference disrupted by fracas: poetry reading ends in shouting match."[22]

Herein lies the central contradiction that has defined—and continues to define—political and organizational responses to antiracism. On one hand, there are urgent desires to embrace "diversity" and appear "inclusive." Black women, for example, are invited to read poetry at national conferences. On the other hand, there is also subtle resistance and even open censure that, at its most disapproving, frames the attention to antiracism as excessive and dangerous. On the one hand, there were eager nods to antiracism policy and practice; the phrase "women of color" was included in feminist texts and events, sometimes with great fanfare. At the same time, these superficial inclusions of women of color in feminist texts and organizations were often forced and marginal—a presence, Bannerji argues, that speaks only to the true absence of critical discussions of race. Rather than simply "rendering their visibility"[23] by adding Black women to feminist theory, as Carby argued, feminist theory must begin to move toward more complex understandings of the relationship between race, class, and gender.

It is a tug of war that has been unsatisfying for those attempting to make meaningful antiracism changes, as Bannerji observes.[24] This ongoing *ambivalence* continues and has come to define contemporary debates on "diversity."

The political and scholarly efforts by feminists to work across difference have received only passing attention in historical accounts of the
women's movement.[25] Incisive critiques of feminist theory have been
quite prolific, focusing on how the dominance of a white, middle-class,
heterosexual analysis has led to a lopsided understanding of, for example, reproductive issues or the family.[26] However, the tenor of these debates within organizations are rarely detailed in a comprehensive way.[27]
Mary-Jo Nadeau's careful analysis of "one of the most transformative
organizational struggles over racism" in the national women's group in
Canada (NAC) is a notable exception,[28] as is the careful accounting of
the International Women's Day/March 8th Coalition's[29] slow and bitter
progression toward diversity.[30] Yet we need more analyses of how movements deal with these critiques: How do they resist, progress, and evolve
under this kind of critical scrutiny?

My aim is not to document the "true" story of antiracism and feminism,
but to understand what challenges to "white feminism" have meant—how
have feminism and feminists been constituted through antiracism, and
how has antiracism been constituted through struggles in feminist organizations? As historian Joan Scott reflects, a poststructuralist approach to
gender history means that we are interested not only in the "things that
have happened to women and men," but also in how the very categories
of gender identity have been shaped and transformed.[31] The chronologi-
cal narrative in this chapter should not be interpreted as a definitive story
of what "really happened" in feminist politics in the 1980s. For the most
part, it is only the recorded public events and interviews that appear here.
Even if they are partial, however, the stories that we tell each other about
political events help us make sense of our communities. I take inspiration from Ana María Alonso's approach to historical sociology; she shows
how a "multiplicity of personal, local and regional" accounts are woven
together as a representation of "what really happened," accounts that in
turn conspire to constitute national and community solidarities.[32] My
own patchwork methodology similarly brings together anecdotes, local
events, national media stories, feminist texts, and personal memories into

one imagined story of the antiracism struggle of women in the feminist movement. As a "history of the present,"[33] this account looks to the past to explain the roots of contemporary debates about diversity.

RACE AND THE FIRST WAVE

Race has been not only an ongoing theme of conflict in the feminist movement for over a hundred years, it has also been constitutive of its strategies and goals.[34] The "first wave" of the feminist movement, which succeeded in its fight for the right to vote, had roots in the movement to abolish slavery. However, Vron Ware shows that, after abolition, the women's movement did not integrate an antiracism message but rather exploited the moral imperative and language of equality and liberation of antislavery discourse to bolster its aims for women's emancipation, "without needing any longer to refer to the slaves whose bondage had once outraged and inspired them"[35] Indeed, appeals to racism were central to the strategies of the "first wave" women's movement as it fought for the right to vote at the turn of the century.[36] The National American Women's Suffrage Association (NAWSA) argued that giving white women the vote would help preserve the superiority of the race—it was the most expedient strategy for getting the vote in Southern states where whites were concerned about newly freed Blacks attaining voting rights.[37] Feminists in Canada followed a similar strategy. Cartoons in the newsletters of the Women's Christian Temperance Union (WCTU) strategically depicted the outrageous racial injustice of "'ethnic,' Chinese, and aboriginal men going into polling booths while respectable Protestant ladies were forced to remain on the sidelines."[38]

Mariana Valverde's careful analysis of these strategies shows how discourses of whiteness, light, and purity in the Canadian feminist movement produced an image of vote-deserving women as the cultural, moral, and biological "mothers of the race," a position clearly inhabitable only by some white women.[39] Similarly, the temperance and "white slavery" campaign strategies of prominent North American first-wave

feminists such as Canada's Emily Murphy also helped to perpetuate racist stereotypes of non-white and immigrant men as either dangerous or
lacking in self-control and "childlike."[40]

Challenges to racism in feminism are not new either. As Paula Giddings's historical analysis shows, Black leaders fighting for the vote
found that "white women, including suffragists who should have been
their natural allies, often became their most formidable adversaries."[41]
Throughout the first-wave, Black feminists continually fought against
their exclusion from the women's movement.[42] Black feminist Ida B.
Wells, for example, was publicly attacked by Frances Willard and other
prominent leaders of the WCTU, who tried to muffle her anti-lynching
campaign.[43] In 1913, Ida B. Wells was ordered by NAWSA to walk at the
back of the suffragist march on Washington, an order that she cleverly
defied.[44] Most resonant of contemporary debates is an 1899 exchange in
which a Black delegate tried and failed to get NAWSA to take a stand
against segregated seating for Black women on the trains. Prominent
feminist activist Susan B. Anthony lead the refusal to support the resolution. As Giddings recounts, "It was at that convention that Anthony
helped put NAWSA on record as saying that woman suffrage and the
Black question were completely separate causes"[45]

SISTERHOOD AND KEEPING THE SISTERS IN LINE: 1980S–1990S

Susan B. Anthony's assertion about the "the Black question" has unfortunate echoes in ongoing debates about racism. The notion that concerns
about racism are distinct, definable, and separable from other concerns
has continued to shape political debates. Almost a hundred years later,
Frances Beal, leader of the Third World Women's Alliance, was walking
in the 1971 Women's Liberation Day march when she got into a debate
that has parallels to the NAWSA debate of 1899. Beal was carrying a
"Free Angela Davis" sign to support the release of the Black feminist
activist and scholar from prison.[46] A white woman from the National

Organization of Women (NOW) chastised Beal angrily: "Angela Davis has nothing to do with women's liberation." Beal retorted, "It has nothing to do with the kind of liberation you're talking about, but it has everything to do with the kind of liberation we're talking about."[47]

Over a period of a hundred years, the crux of feminist debates around racism remained unchanged—what is feminism and who is its keeper? Historically, white women had been positioned as both the makers and the keepers of feminism's idealist purity. Yet there are important differences between the first- and second-wave women's movements. The foundational backdrop of the civil rights movement[48] means that a liberalist non-racism is an implicit tenet of the second-wave women's movement and many other social movements that grew out of the 1960s. These movements added new ideals of social justice while retaining the old trustees. The result is a curious contradiction between egalitarian collectivism and imperious custodianship—a sense of custodianship that underlies the feelings of ambivalence, defensiveness, and nostalgia that often accompany debates about antiracism.

Early attempts to tackle "the race question" in mainstream feminist publications demonstrate this balancing act between sisterhood and keeping the sisters in line. Social movement periodicals were, especially until the late 1990s, a vital way for activists to connect nationally and internationally. They also communicate and contest the core ideals of the movement and can highlight some of the tensions. As Agatha Beins suggests in her study of US feminist movement periodicals, they "illuminate patterns in the representation of feminism" that can help us understand its development over time. Like the periodicals presented here, the US feminist periodicals of the 1970s studied by Beins were "written and edited primarily by white women."[49]

Broadside was one of two national feminist periodicals in Canada, published monthly during the 1980s.[50] In its pages we can trace the nature of the ambivalent and tumultuous debates over racism in the movement.[51] In 1983, Broadside ran an article by Sheila Wilder that directly addressed racism in feminism. In "Racism Unresolved," Wilder wrote,

"Perhaps some criticism may well be 'sour grapes'; nevertheless when it comes from women it must be taken seriously."[52] Clearly a fledgling attempt at tackling race and feminist theory, the author began with an ambivalent stance that managed to recognize concerns about racism while undermining and individualizing them. Wilder's article shows how broadening feminism and making it more "inclusive" was still seen as a double-edged sword, something to be done, Wilder worried, "without compromising the central concerns of women." On the one hand, it is the concept of gendered collectivity, or universal sisterhood, that rational-izes Wilder's interest in racism—a belief that anything that comes from women has merit. On the other hand, Wilder uses the same concept to undermine antiracism critique. In her piece, "women" refers only to the abstract, collective sisterhood. This abstraction allows feminism to be imagined as a protectorate—the sisterhood is not only a collectivity, but also a protectorate of women who defend its "central" ideals against "sour grapes." The phrase "sour grapes" is trivializing, but also has a precise meaning: the unfair disparagement of someone else's position because you cannot attain it yourself. It works well here to frame antiracism cri-tiques as outside insurgencies by jealous and frivolous dissenters. Wild-er's article foreshadows a move that some white feminists continued to make in response to antiracism: her foray into antiracism recenters and celebrates an implicit whiteness as constitutive of the ideal feminism.

A survey of the *Canadian Feminist Periodicals Index* shows that, in the thirteen years between 1972 and 1985, feminist periodicals in Canada carried a total of only nine articles referring to "racism." In the same thirteen-year period, feminist periodicals carried only eleven references to "women of color," most in book reviews. Despite prolific activism and writing by feminists of color,[53] the mainstream feminist movement, or the organizations and periodicals that were predominantly directed by white feminists, were quiet on the subject in the 1970s and early 1980s. For example, a 1983 *Broadside* special feature on issues in feminist pub-lishing did not mention race at all, ironic given the raging controversies over race and representation in women's presses that would surface by the end of the decade. (At the same time, antiracist feminist activism on the ground was active in the 1970s and 1980s, focusing on police violence and immigration policy.)[54]

But as challenges by women of color gradually increased during the early 1980s, the large movement organizations did not remain indifferent. Toronto's International Women's Day (IWD) events, drawing as many as ten thousand people at their peak, provide a gauge for these shifts. As early as 1981, IWD event organizers had been challenged by groups such as Women Working with Immigrant Women (WWIW) who spoke out against the "single-issue approach" to concerns of immigrant women and women of color. According to an account by International Women's Day organizers, these interventions by WWIW had significant impact; for the first time IWD pamphlets were printed in languages other than English.

As antiracism challenges increased exponentially in the decade between 1983 and 1993, the debates also become more contentious. The year 1983 stands out as a turbulent turning point. In the spring of that year, a group of seven women of color edited a special issue of the feminist journal *Fireweed*. The first of its kind in Canada, the "Women of Colour" issue was a national rallying cry for antiracist feminism. In a personal account of her own route to antiracism as a white feminist, Lorna Weir recalls, "In the local Toronto circles to which I belonged, the *Fireweed* 'Women of Color' issue . . . marked a watershed."[55] The "Women of Colour" issue was a clear accomplishment and turning point both for antiracist feminism and for the women who organized it. Yet even in their tremendous accomplishment, the guest editors of *Fireweed*, Nila Gupta and Makeda Silvera, revealed their own serious concerns. Why, they wondered, did the *Fireweed* collective suddenly become interested in doing a "Women of Colour" issue? Only a year and a half earlier, "after a number of frustrating and fruitless meetings," the *Fireweed* collective had rebuffed their idea of a special issue edited by women of color.[56]

Skeptical of *Fireweed*'s sudden openness to a "Woman of Color" issue, Gupta and Silvera were aware that it echoed the rapid appearance of interest in diversity. There was an apparent urgency, a "hurried anxiety" with which women of color were newly acknowledged.[57] Yet it also seemed to be a contradictory and ambivalent urgency—the appearance of women of color was at once "sudden, urgent and parenthetical."[58] Underlying both impulses—the rush to embrace as well as the reluctance, anxiety, and even anger—is the protection of the integrity and unity of the movement.

Events at the 1983 International Women's Day in Toronto demonstrate that this ambivalence is rooted in nostalgic emotions about ideals of universal feminism. One of the themes that year was anti-imperialism. Organizers hosted a panel titled "Women's Liberation, Disarmament and Anti-Imperialism," inviting speakers to speak on liberation movements in Eritrea, Palestine, Nicaragua, el Salvador, and the Philippines, including a woman from the League of Arab Democrats. Preceding the march, women spoke on struggles in South America, and one speaker led the crowd in a series of rallying cries in Spanish: "Women of Latin America, now and forever! Women of Africa, now and forever! Immigrant Women, now and forever!"[59]

The response from a number of white feminists was disappointment and indignance, perhaps not surprising given previous feminist debate on the Middle East.[60] Yet these women objected not only to the Palestinian view on the Middle East, but more broadly to any discussion of anti-imperialism. In April 1983, the national feminist paper *Broadside* carried Lois Lowenberger's article "IWD: Lip Service to Feminism." Criticizing the organizers of International Women's Day, Lowenberger expressed her dismay and anger at the inclusion of anti-imperialism as a theme, arguing that it was, at best, only "peripherally relevant" to feminism. Seeing "a celebration of *women* together" as the framework for International Women's Day, Lowenberger implicitly refers only to women whose roots are in the northern hemisphere, claiming that "many working-class women are not very interested in South America." Lowenberger's implicit argument is that thinking about issues elsewhere in the world is an elitist position, one that neglects working-class women at home.

In the same issue, feminist academics Mary O'Brien and Freida Forman of the University of Toronto[61] took a similar tone in their cutting
letter to the editors of *Broadside*, citing the "erosion of feminist content"
in IWD events. They wrote,

> We were particularly disheartened by the rally preceding the march: not
> once in the entire round of slogans and speeches was the word "feminism"
> mentioned nor indeed did a feminist perspective prevail. . . . We were
> told that we were working women, immigrant women, lesbians, even
> vegetarians; were there no feminists there at an IWD rally? . . . More
> alarming still was the introduction of a highly divisive and deeply con-
> troversial issue: the Middle East (reduced at the rally to a Palestinian
> struggle only). . . . And . . . to be told, like robots, to show our solidarity
> by chanting in Spanish? (Is that the universal language of struggle now?)
> Is an IWD rally, a day when presumably we show our sisterhood with all
> women, the time and the place to shout simplistic Spanish slogans which
> are certain to divide us?[62]

Their objections were so strong that they threatened to retract the
endorsement of IWD by the University of Toronto's Women's Research
and Resource Center. According to their letter of objection, on a day
when we "presumably show our sisterhood with all women," celebration of diversity is undesirable. "Immigrant women," "lesbians"—these
are mutually exclusive or subordinate to some overriding and universal "feminist" identity. The letter's incredulous and sarcastic references
to "Spanish" ("Is that the universal language of struggle now?"), and
the dismissive reference to the "robots" who might chant these "simplistic" slogans, blithely dismiss other languages and ethnicities as
trivial. Just as Susan B. Anthony confidently dismissed feminism and
"the Black Question" as "completely separate," these writers are able
to argue for a feminist purity that excludes a consideration of imperial and regional histories. They are unable to reconfigure feminism as

fully transnational—for them the heart and center of feminism remains explicitly North American and homogeneous.

There were other sentries anxious to defend the borders of "universal" sisterhood. In the next issue of *Broadside* (May 1983), another letter of protest suggested that the more "acceptable" IWD position would be to focus on those issues more directly relevant to all women (such as day-care and maternity leave), and to disregard the more "peripheral" issues:

> probably the wisest [is] to concentrate on International Women's Day on those issues directly connected with women on which there is general agreement within the women's movement. There are certainly enough problems of immediate relevance to women, e.g. better daycare, better maternity leave, protection against sexual assault, that there is no need to raise on IWD issues with only a peripheral connection with the women's movement.[63]

This Toronto debate on anti-imperialism closely echoes Vron Ware's account of a socialist feminist conference in London in 1979. A woman in one workshop, recounts Ware, "expressed anger that we were discussing imperialism at all, asking what it had to do with women anyway."[64]

These concerns about diluting the pure and true cause of a movement are neither new nor have they ended with the battles of the 1980s and 1990s women's movement. Activists and scholars have highlighted this same tension in queer communities, where, as Lenore and Dryden point out, racism and colonialism are seen as eclipsing the "real" and central issue of sexual diversity: "Discussions of racialization, diaspora, settler colonialism, and empire] are often framed as extraneous to the authentic, 'real' question of the insider-outsider status of 'sexual minorities.'"[65]

All of these perspectives recall author Bharati Mukherjee's phrase "nostalgia for a world we never knew,"[66] in this case the longing for an imagined movement that existed before antiracism challenges messed things up. The concept of "imagined community" is Benedict Anderson's;[67] he uses it to explain the concept of the nation as an imagined political community, one in which members do not know each other, but share "the image of their communion." To parallel Anderson's phrase, sisterhood is an imagined community of women who do not know each other but "share the image of their communion." Much of feminist or queer politics has depended on a belief in the universally shared commonality of experiences. Robin Morgan, editor of *Sisterhood Is Global*, speaks of the "common condition which, despite variations in degree, is experienced by all human beings who are born female."[68] While Morgan's particular concept of sisterhood has been challenged, an imagined community or family of women has historically been a core precept of feminist thought and practice. However, as Judy Rebick points out in her history of feminist organizing, "Women have never been united in their views. . . . If uniting across race proved more difficult, the fault lies not with those demanding that their voices be heard but with those who walked away."[69]

Resistance to antiracism has often been couched in a nostalgia for this imagined solidarity that antiracism has supposedly damaged; white feminists who resist "diversity" often position themselves as the keepers of this mythical unity and purity.[70] When the universal values of progressive social movements are challenged the result may be, as Wendy Brown observes, a reactionary response to safeguard them,

> clinging without logical ground to the last comforting frame in the unraveling narrative—pluralism, the working class, universal values, the Movement, standpoint epistemology, a melting pot America, woman's essential nature—whatever it was that secured the status of the true, the status of the good.[71]

In writing about her own activism in the feminist movement, sociologist Winifred Breines suggests that it was "white nostalgia" that made it difficult for her to let go of her utopian ideals:

The promise of the early 1960s shaped me and others of my generation. I have not easily let go of a humanistic, universal, racially integrated sisterhood and brotherhood ideal where, hand in hand, we would work to create a just world.[72]

She recognizes, however, that "I was able to be nostalgic for integration and the insignificance of race because of my whiteness."[73]

For a certain community of white feminists, the experience of having outsiders unsettle their defense of the sisterhood and decenter them as leaders of the women's movement was clearly traumatic. As Kai Erikson's studies of communities in trauma show, the realization that "we" no longer exist is traumatic for communities.[74] For those who felt they were the leaders, founders, or carriers of the imagined universal sisterhood, the portents of its dilution were painful. Yet, as Erikson discusses, at the same time as people feel a loss of community integrity and unity, their experience of trauma can also create community. Clearly, just as some feminists felt a loss of feminist community, they also felt compelled to continually re-create and reassert this imagined solidarity.

These resistant responses to the theme of anti-imperialism at International Women's Day in 1983 did not represent the entire feminist community. On the contrary, the *Broadside* letters sparked an open dispute, illustrating the divide between those white feminists who resisted these antiracism efforts with those who were able to integrate them into a socialist feminist or antiracist feminist perspective. Almost the entire "Letters" section of the May 1983 issue of *Broadside* was devoted to the debate. There was a boycott by *Broadside* readers and an angry protest by graduate students at the University of Toronto,[75] where the letter originated. One former student involved in the protest told me about meetings held by Third World students furious about the O'Brien-Forman letter: "It was very emotional. We were out for blood," she recalls.

Feminist activists and academics spar around the central question: What is feminism, anyway?

To the women active in the debate at the time, this fight was a symbol of age-old rifts between socialist and other feminists; to socialist feminists, the fight against imperialism was an acknowledged part of their socialist politics.[76] No wonder that, in both articles of protest, the IWD approach is slammed as characteristic of "the male left"—the O'Brien-Forman letter opined that anti-imperialist language was "the worn out and destructive language of patriarchy," while Lowenberger's article argued that IWD was "increasingly becoming dominated by male-oriented leftist issues." Their disdain of the "male left" certainly speaks of historical divisions among socialist, radical, and liberal feminists.[77]

But this emotional exchange also shows that the historical defense of the "true" woman-centered feminism was clearly racialized. In the 1983 debate, anti-imperialism and antiracism were treated as an external demand: white feminism was, as always, described as the center to be defended from dilution by outsiders, immigrants, and so on. In the Canadian feminist movement, the metaphor of outside insurgency is particularly relevant as many prominent challenges were made by immigrant women's groups. This response—seeing antiracism as an external demand destroying the true spirit and heart of feminism—was to become a recurring theme.

At the same time, however, a multiracial, transnational, antiracist feminist analysis was also arising. Responding to the controversial 1983 letter by O'Brien and Forman, Mariana Valverde used a very different concept of unity; she turned the protestors' understanding of unity on its head. Comparing the recent struggle over race and class to earlier struggles about heterosexism, she wrote,

As lesbians, we have had to be blatant about our sexuality in order to redress a historic imbalance, a historic silence. In being blatant, we may have indeed appeared to be acting in a "divisive" way, but the eventual result has been (in some places) to unify all women around an understanding of how heterosexism oppresses us all. If the women's movement is to deal with the issues of class, imperialism, and race in a non-tokenistic way,

it will have to go through a struggle similar to that around lesbianism. . . .
I am confident that we can integrate issues such as anti-imperialism and
class exploitation in a way that will strengthen, not dilute, what we have
already built.[78]

The International Women's Day Committee's official response took up
almost a whole page of May 1983 issue of *Broadside*, and argued precisely
for the links between feminism and anti-imperialism:

One: surely one key root of the racial and ethnic discrimination that we
see every day in Canada is a heritage from colonialism and imperialism?
And can we talk about immigration policy without referring to the impe-
rialist underdevelopment of many nations—which forces people to come
to Canada? Two: surely we cannot talk about decent jobs for all without
talking about the role of imperialism in securing a high standard of living
for some and a living hell for the rest of the world?[79]

As an early and very public criticism of feminist anti-imperialist efforts, O'Brien and Forman's letter was so far-reaching in its effects that
it prompted commentary from the editorial collective even in the final
Broadside editorial six years later.[80] The debate sparked by their letter
highlighted the core issues that polarized feminist debates on race. On
one side are those arguing that International Women's Day should be
focused "on issues particular to women" rather than those "peripherally
relevant to women."[81] This argument centers around the existence of
supposedly universal feminist issues common to all women: day care,
maternity leave, and assault. On the other side are those arguing that
imperialism is central to the oppression of women; this approach seeks
not only to broaden the range of "feminist issues," but also to question
even the concept of "common" women's issues.

Debates about anti-imperialism, representation, and racism became a
defining feature of feminist politics in the 1980s. The 1986 International

Women's Day celebrations in Toronto and Vancouver explicitly named racism as a theme. Working together, groups such as Women Working with Immigrant Women, the Latin American Women's Collective, and the Coalition of Visible Minority Women produced a joint recommendation that the feminist movement "recognize in a very public way that the struggle against racism is our struggle.[82] The slogan of the IWD events that year was clear, strong, and simple: "Women say NO! to Racism/From Toronto to South Africa." Clearly the climate of debate had shifted; IWD organizers were enjoining women to make transnational links between racism in South Africa and racism at home.

The antiracism theme drew many women of color into International Women's Day organizing, many of whom "directly challenged existing methods of organizing and political attitudes."[83] Yet it was an analysis of racism still tied to a modest activist message—"just say no."

The following year saw "dramatic changes" and intense conflict; by 1987 about one-third of the coalition were women of color, Black women, Indigenous women, or immigrant women.[84] These challenges led to deep conflicts: the Black Women's Collective withdrew in protest from IWD organizing in 1987. Once again, debates about diversity and racism were characterized by both rapid progression and acrimonious conflict.

In a striking departure from previous editorials, the *Broadside* editorial collective also took up the challenge in its 1986 editorial "No to Racism."[85] The editors advocated the need to build "diversity" and noted for the first time the links between antiracism and feminism and "the growing profile of women of color within our political and cultural movements." The editorial went further to acknowledge that their writers had "received harsh criticism for racist comments" and ended by declaring, "We have to begin by fighting racism in our own community."

Both the International Women's Day organizing committee and the *Broadside* editorial collective had proclaimed the dawn of a new era. The 1987 keynote speech on International Women's Day gives a sense of the tremendous shifts and fissures of the time:

Last year on International Women's Day we said we were going to build a new women's movement in Toronto. In this year's coalition, we, women of color, Black women, and Native women, are providing leadership in an atmosphere which demands dialogue and accountability.[86]

The *Broadside* collective writes in 1986 that "the challenging process of building a movement of all women has begun."

Quickly and exponentially, racism and antiracism came to the forefront of conversations within feminist and community organizations. By 1991, the annual number of articles concerning racism in Canadian feminist periodicals had increased almost twenty times, when compared to any year of the previous decade.[87] An analysis of the *Canadian Feminist Periodicals Index* shows that in the six months between May and September 1991 alone, for example, there were eight articles on racism—as many as appeared in the thirteen years between 1972 and 1985. As the frequency of talk about feminism and racism increased, the language also gradually shifted. In September of 1991 the *Canadian Feminist Periodical Index* created a new category called "racism and feminism," and by 1994 the index was tracking articles under yet another new category, "antiracism." This parallels the rise of articles in mainstream Canadian print media. A review of the *Canadian Periodicals Index* shows that the number of articles on racism was ten times greater in the decade from 1989 to 1998 than in the eight-year period between 1981 and 1988.

By the early 1990s, critiques that had begun with feminist writing were also returning to influence women's studies programs in universities. Sociologist Lorna Weir, for example, tells us that it was the debates within the International Women's Day Committee that in turn gave her greater awareness of "white dominance within feminist [university] courses."[88] That awareness led her to make significant changes in her own teaching in the women's studies program at the University of Toronto. In particular, she says that between 1985 and 1987 she expanded her feminist teaching to include "Third World women's movements and the new international division of labor." Her essay topics now included

one on "the development of antiracist feminism: the impact of antiracism critiques on the concept of sisterhood."[89]

By the end of the decade, these events and these new theoretical perspectives had left their mark on the feminist movement. In 1989, in their
final issue, the *Broadside* collective looked back at the past decade of
feminism and highlighted the central significance of antiracism: "The
most crucial aspect of feminism in the past few years has been the efforts to incorporate antiracism perspectives into feminist analysis."[90]

In just a few years, the nostalgic, white-centered threads within
feminist organizing had begun to unravel. Only a few years earlier, the
focus of the feminist periodical *Broadside* had been on fighting racism "out there" or on integrating the concerns of immigrant women.
In 1989, *Broadside* was instead talking about "incorporating antiracist
perspectives."

When *Broadside* published its last issue, the collective members
pointed to their own dissolution as a sign of this major antiracism shift.
In its final editorial, the *Broadside* collective noted that it had been an
all-white one and "was formed in an environment of White feminist
perspectives." The editorial claimed that *Broadside* was folding in part
because "White women have been forced to deal with the issues raised,
forced to face the fact that it may no longer be the role of White women
to frame the debate and direct the struggle."[91] It is not clear why the
editors chose to make this statement about "being forced to deal with"
questions about race. Perhaps it reflects tension within the editorial collective, or perhaps it represents the deep ambivalence about race that
we have seen in so many other debates. The editors appear to simultaneously place blame on antiracist activists while also expressing commitment to antiracism critique. If white custodianship of *Broadside* was
responsible for its demise, it raises the question of why its editors chose
to shut down rather than to make wholesale changes.

The national women's association, NAC, was also forced to deal with
these issues and in 1988 undertook an organizational review. The review
reported that "some women feel excluded from and lack ownership of

NAC. It is viewed as elitist, racist, classist and not addressing the needs of many women."[92] The proposed solutions, however, offered "an equal opportunity model in a context in which an affirmative action program would have been more effective."[93] In other words, although feminist organizations had begun grappling with difference and power among women, the practice of challenging it head-on was still nascent.

As antiracist feminism became a recognized force in feminist politics, the focus had shifted to changing everyday practices within community organizations. Not surprisingly, new battles ensued. The challenge to "the way things had always been done," began to be heard in many places. Two challenges to feminist organizations in Toronto made particularly lasting marks on the landscape. The first was at the Women's Press, a feminist publishing collective, the second at Nellie's Hostel.

Between the fall of 1987 and 1989, the Women's Press was the public stage for conflict about racism and cultural appropriation. An early snapshot of the racial conflict simmering in feminist publishing is the 1986 anthology *Dykeversions*. In a boldly titled preface, "Notes about Racism in the Process," the editors wrote:

> There were times when we were on the brink of leaving and withdrawing stories we had solicited or written, and letting the anthology be what it would have been without our energy—a white women's anthology that included racist content.[94]

These conflicts soon to come to an angry and rapid boil, culminating in a national news story about a heated internal controversy at the Women's Press: short stories that had already been accepted for publication were later challenged by a Women's Press policy group as racist.[95] After several bitter meetings, a group of women formed the "Front of the Bus" caucus within Women's Press to promote a new antiracism mandate. The new *Anti-racist Guidelines for Submissions* sparked vigorous conflict about racism and cultural appropriation not only within the women's movement, but also among writers' groups and cultural agencies more broadly.[96] A power struggle ensued: a staff member was fired and a new splinter press was created.[97]

Several things are notable about the Women's Press conflict: it was public, tumultuous, and centered on specific organizational practices.[98] It was also the subject of national mainstream media coverage; this kind of attention raised the stakes for all organizations attempting to deal with race.

CONFLICT AT NELLIE'S HOSTEL

As public as the Women's Press controversy was, however, it was far surpassed by the furor at Nellie's Hostel for women in Toronto. Nellie's Hostel was started by June Callwood, a well-known and widely respected social activist and journalist who founded a number of similar shelters. By 1991, many community organizations like Nellie's Hostel had become aware of the critiques of antiracist feminism and were experiencing the challenges of putting them into practice. Like other organizations, Nellie's Hostel responded to these critiques by increasing "diversity"— adding two women of color to their twenty-one-member board and hiring women of color for the staff. Not surprisingly, adding women of color to Nellie's without a corresponding look at organizational practices and vision led to considerable conflict. In response, women of color on the board and staff formed the five-member Women of Color Caucus and began to talk about racism in programming and decision-making at Nellie's.[99]

At a highly emotional board meeting in December 1991, the Women of Color Caucus presented a document that cited systemic racism at Nellie's and called for employment equity, antiracism, and grievance policies, as well as staff evaluation and training. June Callwood retaliated against the accusations of racism. The staff member who read the document had herself stayed at the shelter long ago; Callwood asked her pointedly, "Are you the same woman we helped for over a year?"[100] The staff member replied, "You want me on my knees forever."[101]

A rancorous battle ensued and lasted for months with eventual demands for Callwood's resignation. By the time June Callwood finally resigned from the board in May of 1992, five staff and board members in the Women of Color Caucus had filed complaints with the Ontario Human Rights Commission. By the fall of 1992, the two new women of color on the board of Nellie's had resigned. In fact, all but three of the twenty-one members of the board had resigned.

The explosive events at Nellie's Hostel demonstrate some themes familiar to other debates about antiracism. One is the nostalgic references to the ideal of a movement in which all women share universal solidarity and common goals. Before her resignation, June Callwood mused, "In the past there was a general assumption on the part of women of no color that we were all fine, because we seemed to be one happy family."[102] During his interview with Callwood, CBC radio host Peter Gzowski suggested that women's groups stick to common goals such as breast cancer as "an issue that presumably would embrace all women in the way that perhaps the issue of racism would not."[103]

As in earlier debates, there is a focus here on a mythological commonality of "all" women—and a concomitant dismissal of race as something that does not affect "all" women. The Nellie's conflict showed that debate about racism in feminist organizations would continue to be defined by the same polarity: Antiracism or feminism? On one side were activists who saw antiracism as central to the purpose of feminist organizations. On the other side were members who framed the antiracism challenges at Nellie's as diverting energy from the "true" work of the hostel. Callwood referred to antiracism challenges as divisive "garbage."[104]

This dismissive denial of antiracism challenges meant that meaningful change was all but impossible. As former chair of Nellie's board Marilou McPhedran commented, "The board failed to act. The alarm bell was ringing around race and around meaningful inclusion. It rang for a long time, and it wasn't answered. The issues raised by the women of color were valid. People are in massive denial."

The battle at Nellie's underscores the emotional intensity of debates about race. It began with the emotional and tearful reading of a letter to the board; by the end of that board meeting, Callwood was also sobbing.[105] The emotional fallout lasted long after the board meeting, leaving those who were personally involved demoralized and depressed.[106]

But the battle over racism at Nellie's was also emotional for people across the country. It demonstrates how an antiracism challenge inside a small community organization can become a highly emotional, explosive, national debate. Nellie's was not the first antiracist feminist organizational conflict to receive national media coverage; however, the involvement of June Callwood, a prominent and celebrated philanthropist, dramatized, shifted, and intensified the debate around racism in feminist organizations. A heightened antipathy toward so-called "political correctness" in the early 1990s was also key in bringing attention to incidents at Nellie's, the Women's Press, and elsewhere. (The term "political correctness" became a popular way to disparage social justice efforts.)[107] Antiracist feminism caught the eye of the news media and the public in a way it had never before. Columnists across Canada offered their commentary on internal struggle at a local feminist hostel. With titles like "Wrongful Dismissal"[108] and "White Woman's Burden,"[109] many of these articles were variations on a theme: if Callwood was racist, the world was upside down.[110] "If Callwood is 'racist,'" one columnist opined, "then the word has been trivialized and with that, the experiences of all those who have really experienced the evils of racism." The most controversial and disparaging piece was the feature article "Wrongful Dismissal" in *Toronto Life* magazine, whose cover picture of June Callwood was accompanied by the headline, "Battered woman: Why angry women of color drove June Callwood from the shelter she created."[111]

Even a national editorial, "A question of the pot calling the kettle white," was dedicated to the defense of Callwood.[112] The corresponding concern and alarm of Canadians everywhere was evident in numerous letters to the editors of national and local newspapers and magazines.[113]

All of these letters, both supportive and critical, came from people outside Nellie's, indicating a unique level of public involvement and interest in the internal battle of a women's organization. As one example, these kinds of letters took up two pages of *Toronto Life* in May of 1993. The majority were supportive of the Women of Color Caucus at Nellie's; several others, however, praised the magazine for its courage "at this time of political correctness and very fragile sensitivities."[114] The mainstream media's interest in what one journalist called feminism's "dirty laundry"[115] had become a continual presence hanging over organizational debates.[116]

Nationalistic defenses of June Callwood were common. Many Canadians felt that criticism of June Callwood was like "being shot in one's Canadian heart—and something for us all to be concerned about."[117] Well-known Canadian author Pierre Berton was one of the first columnists to rush to Callwood's defense in a piece with the incredulous headline, "If Callwood is a racist then so are we all."[118] This image of two iconic Canadian personalities simultaneously denying and demonstrating the nature of racism in Canada uniquely highlighted the Nellie's debate. Through June Callwood, recipient of the Order of Canada, Nellie's had become the symbolic focus for expositions on Canadians' non-racism. At the same time, lack of Canadian citizenship was used as a basis of attacks against Sunera Thobani when she was elected as the first non-white president of the national women's organization.[119] Being an icon of national pride defends one against charges of racism, while being seen as a national interloper makes one a target of racism. National pride so often becomes a *defense* against charges of racism. Conversely, notions of national purity make the supposed interloper a *target* for racism.

One magazine headline, "White Woman's Burden," echoes Rudyard Kipling's 1903 poem on imperialism, "The White Man's Burden."[120] Kipling's poem highlights the supposed burden of colonialism on white men: despite their contributions to the colonies, they will be scorned. Like Callwood's rebuke to the Black woman at Nellie's, many hastened to express their indignance that her benevolence may have been rebuffed.

This media focus on June Callwood also highlighted the individualistic nature of so many debates about race and diversity in organizations. The lens shifts immediately to one individual's culpability or innocence rather than to the histories and systemic practices of inequality. In that sense, this incident was a precursor to the phenomenon of "calling out" and "cancel culture" we would come to see in social media debates.

The conflict at Nellie's provoked more fear and vilification of antiracism and of women of color. The media coverage of Nellie's characterized antiracist women of color as raging, power-hungry extremists.[121] In her "exposé" article, "Wrongful Dismissal," journalist Elaine Dewar wrote that women of color at Nellie's were "obsessed with gut-wrenching antiracism," "antifeminist," "hardliners," and "angry."[122] Dewar claimed that women of color "aren't interested in sharing power, nor do they value the feminist ideals at the heart of Nellie's":[123]

> If [Callwood] could be pushed to resign it would be a hands-off signal to others. . . . Anyone planning a run at Nellie's could surmise that if Callwood was pushed on the subject of racism, she might leave—the way certain female birds divert predators from their nests by offering themselves as broken-winged victims.[124]

Shortly afterward, an article in *Quota*, a lesbian monthly, provides an echo of this image of women of color:

> [Callwood] is astonished by women who grab power. "I didn't think women did that, I believed we shared." Evidently, one underlying notion in antiracist activism is that of the superior leadership skills of women of color.[125]

Nevertheless, the Nellie's incident was also a dramatic turning point in antiracism organizational change, and created greater pressure for antiracism. One *Toronto Sun* column, titled "Politically Correct 'n' Ridiculous," asked, "Is the world upside down?"[126] In a sense, the world had been turned upside down. Antiracism activity in women's organizations had been energized by the women of color recently included in boards and collectives all across the country. The Nellie's incident showed, however, that adding young activists of color to the boards of these organizations would not leave the movement unchanged. In other words, early attempts at "inclusion" led—unexpectedly for some—to more profound antiracism efforts. Later June Callwood said, ruefully, "I wish I'd had a better sense of how things have changed!"[127]

The words "Nellie's" and "June Callwood" came to carry broad symbolic and psychic weight—both as clear signifiers of the supposed dangers of antiracism, and as representations of systemic racism in community organizations. Kim, one of the women I interviewed, describes a debate with her co-worker over these multiple meanings and memories of Nellie's. "In fact, this white woman said to me, 'It must have been a really horrible, terrible thing that happened at Nellie's.' I said to her, 'Well, it could happen here too.' And she said, 'No, I don't think so, it's such a small organization.' Then I said, 'Well, things happen on different scales,' because I had already in my mind pegged the organization as having systemic racist issues, but decided not to name it. So I would say things like that to her. . . . And then I left it at that, so I was in a way saying something, but not saying, 'I think you have racist behavior.'"

The co-worker's "No, I don't think so" implies that conflict over race could only be imaginable elsewhere: in other kinds of organizations, in larger organizations, in organizations with big problems. The name "Nellie's" simultaneously signaled the hope for antiracism transformation, the consequences of resistance to antiracism change, and the fear of antiracism challenges. The co-worker's response typifies the denial and minimization that can occur as a reaction to trauma ("It will never happen to me").[128] Caruth argues that while psychic trauma "involves the recognition of realities most of us have not begun to face," the greatest confrontation to reality may also occur as a numbing to it.[129] Kim's co-worker's reference to the unimaginability of Nellie's hints at the emotions of denial and resistance that would surface (and did later surface in her own organization) if she were to face an antiracism challenge.

In social movements and nonprofit organizations, the Nellie's incident hung over all those fearful of antiracism as a moral lesson and a lingering nightmare. The individuals who knew or admired June Callwood were perturbed—in denial or in shock. One woman of color I interviewed remembers the support she had to give her traumatized white fellow board members at a women's shelter. The Nellie's incident took a toll on those directly involved; many quit the board, others withdrew from activism. Several years later, a woman I interviewed observed that many of the Nellie's women of color had been so affected emotionally that they were still "in hiding."

The Nellie's incident also generated another level of antiracist feminist activism. One progeny was a new group, the Coalition of Women of Color in Women's and Community Services, who organized a protest against the *Toronto Life* article about Nellie's.

Both progress and conflict continued into the early 1990s. Efforts began to shift from more general concerns about diversity and racism to more precise language about colonialism, Indigenous self-determination, and US imperialism. A button from International Women's Day 1991 reads "From Oka to the Gulf—Make the Links," urging us to make the links between Oka, the site of a protracted uprising by the Mohawk community of Kahnesetake, and the invasion of Iraq by the US. It was an explicit message acknowledging racist and colonialist violence as feminist issues. Despite this slogan's emphasis on Kahnesetake, the integration of Indigenous issues and decolonization into IWD organizing was still rocky. In 1992, IWD commemorated the five hundredth anniversary of European colonization of North America, and Indigenous issues came to the forefront. Yet in 1992 and 1993, the Native Women's Resource Center clashed with organizers over the serving of alcohol at the IWD dance, leading them to withdraw from IWD in 1993.[130]

We also begin to hear notes of optimism and momentum. In 1991, five members of the International Women's Day Coalition in Toronto wrote optimistically: "Within the last few years, the grassroots women's move-ment has experienced significant changes . . . through the active partici-pation of previously marginalized sectors of the women's movement."[131] In May 1992 feminist columnist Michele Landsberg wrote prophetically of the revolution these women had brought:

> A new revolution is brewing: a revolution of rising expectations among women who have always been relegated to the margins. It's the target of the revolution that's so fascinating. Every major feminist organization in Canada has been or is about to be met with tough, articulate demands from women who want to share the power. . . . The challenge itself: femi-nist groups must become more genuinely inclusive.[132]

Landsberg's language presages the 1993 election of Sunera Thobani, the first woman of color to be president of the national women's organi-zation (NAC), a change that helped shift how feminist issues in Canada were defined; immigration policy was formally taken up as a feminist issue.[133] Yet critics erroneously claimed that Thobani was an illegal im-migrant, creating a frenzy of media attention that shows how contested is the task of diversifying leadership.

The public spotlight on race and the feminist movement continued. In the subsequent 1996 election for NAC president, front-page stories focused heavily on the racial elements of the election: one of the candi-dates was white, the other Black. A national front-page story carried the headline, "NAC to vote for more than a president/NAC has fallen into 'skin trap,' critic says." Racial conflicts had made routine elections within a national women's organization highly newsworthy.

THE LIMITATIONS OF DIVERSITY

These public controversies, such as the uproar at Women's Press and Nellie's, were merely a visible tip of the proverbial iceberg. Bound for certain collision, some organizations headed for lifeboats—eighteen of twenty-one members of the Nellie's board resigned. But organizations also began to think about redesigning the ship. Increasing the representation and leadership of women of color, establishing antiracism policy and education—these became part of accepted discourse of women's organizations.

However, antiracism activists would also become aware of the limitations of these organizational strategies for change. Approaches such as writing diversity policies and having antiracism and consciousness-raising workshops can be not only ineffective, but also conflictual, obstructive, and painful, as subsequent chapters will show.

One of the barriers to access and equity in community and nonprofit organizations has been the historical absence of people of color at every level, including boards of directors.[134] Not surprisingly, efforts aimed at greater and "better" representation of non-whites in staff, clients, services, images, and decision-making positions have been at the heart of much antiracism organizational change.[135]

Jane Ward's research in queer community organizations confirms that increasing racial diversity among staff has been a priority. Funding agencies have encouraged organizations to become more "representative" of the communities that they serve.[136] For many activists I interviewed, more women of color in key staff positions was the central key to change; as one woman insisted, "But what I think is really critical is representation. Because with representation you have a chance."

In practice, however, the tasks required to actually ensure greater representation—careful attention to practices of recruitment, selection, interview, and retention—are often not followed through, or must be undertaken by the one or few antiracism staff and board members. Despite reporting high levels of dissatisfaction with current board demographics—particularly racial and ethnic diversity—boards are not prioritizing demographics in their recruitment practices. Nearly a fifth of all chief executives report they are not prioritizing demographics in their board recruitment strategy, despite being dissatisfied with their board's racial and ethnic diversity[137] Callander, Holt, and Newman write that, since the 1980s, "there has been little change or challenge to the whiteness of gay institutions."[138] A number of recent studies indicate that there is a stark lack of diversity in nonprofit leadership and discuss the difficulties organizations have in achieving inclusivity among board members.[139]

Questions about who should be "included," who they are representing, and what they should be doing in those positions complicate this vision. Recruitment is often haphazard, with most organizations focusing on some marginalized groups, while ignoring others.[140] "Diversity" can become translated in ways that are simply dovetailed to the existing culture and vision of the organization. The promise of diversity often shows itself to be unsatisfactory and unfulfilled.

The isolation and oppression that minority "representatives" experience has been one reason for failures of this strategy. A study of twelve national women's organizations reported that when they tried to increase diversity by recruiting a woman from a marginalized group to be on their staff or board, most were unsuccessful because of the lack of support she received:

> the marginalized woman was expected to be solely responsible for advancing all issues of inclusion and diversity within the organization, entirely on her own.[141]

Ironically, the recruitment of one marginalized person can also halt further change:

> It seems that once the marginalized woman was recruited, the pressure was lifted from other members of the organization, and progress towards real inclusion and diversity was halted.[142]

Some women I interviewed had come to the conclusion that, in and of itself, winning this kind of representation can be not only a hollow victory but also a painful experience. Over and over, women told me of their refusal to become the sacrificial representative of people of color. Ayesha talks of her disillusionment with "representation" as a strategy:

> When I first started, I thought it was really important for me to be represented at these organizations, or boards—if I wasn't there, then my community wouldn't be represented. I don't believe that any more. I'm not willing to work in those organizations anymore. Even if I just limited myself to working-class Black lesbian trade unionists—a seemingly small group—there would be plenty to do. *(interview transcript)*

Overall, efforts at equitable representation of people of color have had limited success. At the end of the 1990s, activist Pramilla Aggarwal observed:

> in community-based organizations the representation in the agencies and on boards is still very white. In the power structure, where I would have hoped revolutionary change could have happened in the last 15 or 20 years, change has not really occurred. In the front-line staff, we have some Black women, but mostly all decision-making power in all the mainstream institutions, as well as in the non-mainstream institutions, has not changed. It is still white, and that is disheartening. There are no Native people there, there are no Black people. What the heck is going on? Where is the movement in terms of change? . . . I find that throughout my work, both in the community and in the college where I teach, equity has only been given lip service. . . . After a lot of struggle in small pockets, we have not made a big dent. I'm hoping I'm wrong.[143]

THE LIMITATIONS OF DIVERSITY POLICIES

Many organizations in my study had no formal grievance policy or hiring policy, let alone a policy on antiracism. In the 1990s, there began to be a focus on developing these kinds of policies, and funding agencies began to require organizations to have a diversity or multicultural plan.[144]

However, a 1995 study found that the majority of national women's organizations in Canada had no formal policy to implement "inclusiveness and
diversity."[145] The study found that developing policy was not only difficult, but also often ineffective; "all respondents mentioned a considerable
amount of tension and conflict surrounding the issues because of different
ideological standpoints, understanding and/or lack of knowledge."[146]

Yasmin describes how the burden of the policy not only fell entirely
on her shoulders, but that, once it was done, its presence was barely
noticed:

> And again, it was something that I had to initiate—apply for funding to
> have somebody come to work with women, do the training, work with
> staff, work with board. And then, finally, when it was done, and we de-
> veloped it, it was myself who wrote it out, typed it out, printed it out.
> There was not any initiative coming from other people to take that on.
> (interview transcript)

Policies such as these are considered proof of good intention and
meaningful action. Yet, as Yasmin observed, organizations rarely support such policies with any concrete organizational measures. The 1995
study concurs:

> Some of the organizations referred to what they considered to be inclu-
> sive language. . . . None . . . had a specific policy or concrete implementa-
> tion plans to promote meaningful representation.[147]

Almost thirty years later, many more organizations have diversity policies, but "concrete implementation plans" are still lacking.

CONCLUSION

What do we learn from this account of antiracist feminism? For one, the
progression of debate on race becomes clear in historical perspective.

Antiracism began in the 1980s to become a central part of feminist conferences, scholarship, and activism; an antiracism or multicultural policy became de rigueur for social services and nonprofit organizations, and even required by funding agencies. Many of the feminist antiracist, anti-imperialist, and decolonial critiques that came to the fore in the early 1980s continue to be integrated into scholarship and organizational practice.

Yet, as feminism in North America shifted from a universal to an antiracism frame, we can trace increasing resistance against it—nostalgia for a familial and political harmony, and even indignant backlash and hostility. Sad, angry, and hostile emotions become openly and explosively expressed in feminist fora, in print media, and in face-to-face fights in the boardrooms of feminist organizations. Furthermore, the "anti–politically correct" radar of the 1990s focused media attention on any racial conflict in organizations, so that these emotional battles inside organizations not only came under public scrutiny, but also became the topic of national and nationalistic debates. On the one hand, increasing organizational, institutional, state, and organizational support for antiracism in the 1980s and 1990s put political pressure on organizations to have antiracism policies, antiracism workshops, and people of color on their boards. On the other hand, the inevitable failures of these strategies became public debacles that sometimes fed greater conflict and private hardships.

These fights are not as black-and-white as they are sometimes portrayed, however. Rather, there has been an ambivalent and evolving relationship of white women to antiracism and to women of color. The passion inherent in any social movement enterprise often translates into an implicit quest for purity; as we have seen here, this passion underlies both an openness to change, as well as a protective stance against outsiders. In other words, that passion for justice has fueled both progression and regression on the question of race. So just as the boundaries of the imagined community of women have been shaken, so have they continued to be defended. A close look at the history of feminist debates about race tells neither a story of linear progression and evolution nor one of monolithic resistance by white feminists. History shows a seemingly contradictory dance between retreat and approach, a dance between resistance and rapprochement, that characterizes the relationship of social movements to questions of race.

This history sets the stage for ongoing contradictions, obstacles, and emotional preoccupations in equity efforts in other movements and spaces. As Pastrana's study found, "lesbian and gay organizing efforts make strategic use of identity politics, sometimes suppressing notions of identity while at other time celebrating them"[148]

Finally, while their influence in antiracism work grew in 1980s feminist groups, the techniques of consciousness-raising, antiracism workshops, emotional disclosure, and personal reflection have continued to thrive, proliferate, and shape most organizational efforts at diversity and equity today.

TABLE 2.1. CHRONOLOGY OF ANTIRACISM IN TORONTO WOMEN'S ORGANIZATIONS, NOTABLE EVENTS 1981–1993

1981 International Women's Day organizers are challenged by groups like Women Working with Immigrant Women. For the first time, IWD pamphlets are printed in languages other than English.

Feminist monthly newspaper *Kinesis* publishes "The Politics of Visibility: Addressing Third World concerns," by Maylynn Woo and Prabha Khosla.

1983 *Broadside* publishes "Racism Unresolved," by Sheila Wilder.

Feminist journal *Fireweed* publishes the first "Women of Color" issue in Canada.

Letters protest IWD's focus on anti-imperialism and immigrant women. Angry debate follows.

1985 Sister Vision Press, "a black women and women of colour press," is founded. *Tiger Lily* begins publication.

1986 For the first time, the International Women's Day theme is antiracism; the slogan is "Women Say NO! to Racism/From Toronto to South Africa."

1987 One-third of the IWD coalition is women of color, Black, Indigenous, or immigrant women.

Himani Bannerji's *Introducing Racism: Notes Towards an Antiracist Feminist* appears.

Black Women's Collective withdraws from the IWD coalition.

1987–89 Staff at Women's Press have a bitter battle over racism and appropriation; "Front of the Bus" caucus formed.

1989 Feminist newspaper *Broadside* publishes its last issue, noting that it has been an "all-White collective."

1991 "Racism and feminist" first appears as a category in the Canadian Feminist Periodical Index. Staff and board members at Nellie's Hostel form the Women of Color Caucus and challenge programming and decision-making.

IWD slogan is "From Oka to the Gulf—Make the Links."

1992 June Callwood resigns from Nellie's board. Five staff members file complaints with the Human Rights Commission. Coalition of Women of Color is formed.

IWD commemorates five hundred years of colonization with the theme of aboriginal rights.

1993 Coalition of Women of Color stages a demonstration at the office of *Toronto Life* magazine. Sistering, a women's drop-in, receives a grant to do antiracism organizational change.

Sunera Thobani is elected as the first non-white president of NAC.

Native Women's Resource Center withdraws from IWD organizing coalition.

1994 "Antiracism" appears as a category in Canadian Feminist Periodical Index.

1996 Joan Grant-Cummings elected first Black president of NAC.

3

"Let's Talk, Cry a Little, and Learn About Each Other"

THE FAILURES OF DIALOGUE, THERAPY, AND EDUCATION AS THE ANTIDOTE TO RACISM

We talked about how we experience racism in the organization. . . . But Denise never said anything except, "I feel bad." All Denise would say was, "Thank you for sharing."
—Ginny *(interview transcript)*

But how are we supposed to learn? We *have* to have a dialogue.
—White university students challenging a classmate of color

IN the years following the racial justice uprisings of 2020, organizations have turned to antiracism workshops with new interest and intensity. Many of the techniques they are using, however, are not new. When Aruna, a schoolteacher, recently mentioned to me how irked she was about a mandatory workshop on racism, her story seemed familiar. All teachers in her school were required to read a popular book on racism and briefly discuss it in small groups. Aruna was particularly annoyed at the discussion question—"How did the book make you *feel*?"—which asked them to share their "physical and emotional feelings." As Aruna describes it, they met in awkward sessions and listened to some white colleagues confess past racist thoughts or actions.

Dialogue is our perennial strategy for approaching almost any dispute. There are few approaches to conflict resolution that are as widely accepted as talking through our differences, whether in a boardroom or a therapist's office. So it is understandable that leaders at Aruna's school might assume talking to each other about diversity or racism will make things better. The enduring belief that talking about our emotions and sharing our stories will lead to profound change is a powerful pedagogical thread in diversity debates.

The aim of dialogue is to learn more about others, or even for participants to learn more about themselves and their own emotions. This faith in dialogue is underscored by the belief that more knowledge is always the answer. When ignorance is implicitly framed as the root of racism, knowledge is seen as a ready remedy. Learning more, particularly learning more about "others" is then seen as a key path to mutual appreciation and harmony. This interest in facts and knowledge peaked in 2020, when millions became newly keen to learn more about racism through reading. Articles such as *Forbes*' "20 Books for 2020: A Reading List on Race in America," which declared "it is incumbent upon us to do the work to get educated,"[1] appeared frequently. No wonder, then, that the discussion about antiracism at Aruna's school began with an educational project—a directive for all teachers to read a book about racism. Mandatory workplace training on diversity also takes a knowledge-based approach—it may include general knowledge about bias, equity policies, and what discrimination looks like. The notion that knowledge is the antidote to racism is a tenacious one.

These are alluring ideas. Dialogue, therapy, and education are standard strategies for diversity and equity work in most organizations. The workshop at Aruna's school, for example, reflected all these familiar strategies. I refer to these strategies, and the ideas that underlie them, as the "Let's Talk" approach.

The problem is that dialogue, therapy, and education garner such deep faith that they foreclose conversations about how to make concrete changes to everyday practices in our own organizations. The attempt to raise consciousness is not only a familiar first step toward equity and diversity; too often it is also the last. As Aruna said about the workshop for teachers:

I guess they feel that introspection is the first step. But I don't think that there is going to be a step 2 or step 3. *(interview transcript)*

I too have initiated, participated in, and facilitated a number of these workshops, even while writing about their limitations. As an environmental activist, I organized an antiracism workshop for all campaign and administrative staff in my organization. We talked to each other, did some role-play, and shared our experiences. There were some tears. At the time, it was one of my proudest accomplishments. Until then, "conflict resolution" between two individuals had been the answer to any grievances about harassment or racism—so a collective antiracism workshop seemed to me to be a huge leap forward.

It was also the thing to do. For several decades, such workshops had been a standard tool in the equity and diversity toolkit. With origins in the civil rights and other social movements, and honed by affirmative action and human resource departments in the 1970s and 1980s, equity training was becoming standard in many organizations by the 1990s. The growth of antiracism in the 1990s brought the antiracism and equity workshop to the forefront as a solution that could be easily embraced in corporate, organizational, and educational spaces. School boards drafted new equity policies and developed workshops for teachers and students; funding agencies began requiring community organizations to have equity policies; the Anti-Racism Secretariat[2] in Ontario provided a flush of funding for community workshops. It would be tempting to dismiss these events as having minor historical significance; the community and corporate workshops of the 1990s, however, did not fade away, nor were they superseded by a new model of antiracism.

Instead, these diversity and antiracism workshops have grown exponentially. The pedagogical approaches to diversity that became widespread in earlier decades are ubiquitous today. In progressive organizations and nonprofit and corporate settings alike, the diversity workshop is standard and increasing in scale and frequency. In their 2016 US survey, Dobbin and Kalev found that most large corporations have diversity training, that two-thirds of universities have diversity training for faculty members, and that one-third require it. Since 2016, the demand for diversity workshops, and particularly for workshops that focus

on race and whiteness, has only intensified. Respected antiracism trainers have seen their business increase dramatically in the last few years;
Glenn Singleton, author of *Courageous Conversations*, reportedly saw
business increase by over 100 percent between 2016 and 2020; after the
Black Lives Matter protests of May 2020, demand for antiracism trainers
like Singleton and DiAngelo again increased exponentially.[3]

Yet what kinds of successes can we claim for any of these interventions?
Despite the continual use of diversity workshops for decades, the progress
of antiracism in organizations has often been disheartening for activists
and educators. While some approaches to workshops may be more successful than others, many participants have expressed a deep dissatisfaction with the perennial equity and diversity workshops and discussions on
racism. The evidence shows that the formal, facilitated discussions, workshops, and trainings that are common to many organizations have largely
failed to effect the desired changes in beliefs, consciousness, practices, or
employment equity.[4] Reviews of dozens of studies shows that these workshops either do not reduce bias or produce only short-term reductions of
bias and that, more importantly, they do not change behavior or the workplace in ways that lead to equity.[5] Educational efforts attempt to correct
ignorance, rather than to support collaborative problem-solving.

One of the remarkable emblems of these failures is the emotional
fallout produced by dialogues on racism. Volatile discussions percolate
with a range of complex and even explosive emotions. Writing about the
antiracism workshops of the 1990s, Susan Friedman noted that "discussions about race and racism often collapse in frustration, anger, hurt,
yelling, silence, withdrawal and a profound belief that different 'sides'
are unable to listen and learn from the other."[6] These practices have also
been criticized as being especially painful for many non-white participants and unnecessary for making antiracism change.[7] These observations are still apt. Debates about racism may have shifted in the last few
years, but their emotional weight has certainly not attenuated.

If these emotional dialogues produced genuine change, then we
would be willing to brave them. Instead, these kinds of dialogues can

contribute to open conflict and lingering tensions. The damaging effects on workplace communities and on mental health can be long-lasting. They can be particularly discouraging, draining, and painful encounters for people of color, many of whom drop out and refuse to participate in antiracism workshops.

Not surprisingly, then, workshops can themselves become a focus of debate and conflict. While organizations continue to have Diversity Days and diversity training, many participants resist them in direct or indirect ways. Not only participants, but reactive state and federal governments have resisted antiracism initiatives by challenging and banning education about systemic racism. In September 2020, US president Trump banned antiracism training in federal agencies, and between January 2021 and February 2022, forty-one states in the US introduced legislation to restrict or ban teaching about racism.[8] Antiracism workshops are not only the *site* of conflict, but also the very *subject* of conflict.

Should we entirely dismiss attempts at dialogue and pedagogy, and resign our past efforts to some historical dustbin of good intentions and necessary compromises? How might we reconcile the enduring belief that talking and learning makes things better, with the recurring observation that antiracism workshops produce either stasis or conflict? I too am caught by this tension: As an academic I continue to believe in deep and sustained scholarly conversations about racism and equity as part of any educational trajectory. I continue to act in ways that reveal optimism for teaching and talking about racism. Yet I am troubled by the pitfalls of the educational and therapeutic approaches we see in so many organizations.

If there any hope for creating approaches that better support antiracism, diversity, and equity—and I believe that there is—a key step is to understand the roots and effects of past failures.

In this chapter, I explain why conversations about race and equity fall short, and why we keep doing the same things. I trace the techniques, origins, and adverse effects of these dialogical and pedagogical strategies—which I refer to as the "Let's Talk" approach—to explain why they are both enduring and damaging.

I begin by outlining some typical workshop techniques that characterize the Let's Talk approach, such as the sharing of experiences, stories, feelings, and knowledge about racism.

What makes this Let's Talk approach so enduring? We can better understand its influence by tracing myriad historical threads that anchor it, the intertwining discourses and practices that produce and justify this approach. Deep-rooted theories of knowledge, liberalism, feminism, consciousness-raising, and the "personal is political" come together with pedagogical techniques, sometimes in contradictory ways, to anchor the Let's Talk approach. This chapter traces each of these threads to help explain how the Let's Talk approach operates within antiracism workshops, and how it remains enduring.

Finally, I draw on my interviews and my observations of workshops[9] to demonstrate the damaging effects of the Let's Talk approach and strategies. As I show, these techniques of diversity workshops not only defuse and deflect efforts at change, they also unintentionally reiterate stereotypes of racial identity and emotion. Diversity efforts are so ubiquitous that the impact of these approaches on how we think about race, diversity, and organizational change is profound. In a 2020 investigation of antiracism workshops, Daniel Bergner notes, "As their teaching becomes more and more widespread, antiracism educators are shaping the language that gets spoken—and the lessons being learned—about race in America."[10]

The emotional costs of these conversations also weigh on participants; in a workplace, the material risks of disclosure can be great. In the following chapter, I look more closely at these emotional risks and the therapeutic tenor of these workshops.

WHAT DOES A DIVERSITY WORKSHOP LOOK LIKE? LET'S TALK

Disclosure of personal feelings, stories, and experiences has become formalized as a form of political education, analysis, and conflict resolution in many organizational settings.[11] I call this the "Let's Talk" approach. This widespread tenacity of this Let's Talk approach explains why discussions of antiracism have also become dominated by a range of techniques for producing knowledge and resolving conflict through expressions of experience and emotion. Let's Talk techniques were evident, for example, in the sociologist Jane Ward's study of diversity culture in LGBT community organizations; Ward describes a long list of typical workshops, with titles such as "Can We Talk?," that accompanied a Diversity Day at the LA Gay and Lesbian Center.[12]

I use the phrase "Let's Talk approach" to gesture toward a collection of longstanding and well-respected principles and strategies of discussion, problem-solving, and education common to many organizations.

There are a number of key elements within the Let's Talk approach:

- Knowledge: more knowledge of each other and more knowledge of racism are seen as the key to progress.
- "The personal is political": personal experiences, stories, feelings, and consciousness are seen as the route to change.
- Therapy: self-reflection and emotional expression are the goal; self-knowledge and self-transformation are cultivated as a form of organizational change.
- Conflict resolution: talking through differences, feelings, and motivations and resolving individual conflicts.

All these elements are commonly found together in organizational efforts at diversity and antiracism, often even integrated in one discussion. Together they form a Let's Talk approach for discussion about race and racism, one that uses techniques of pedagogy, therapy, and conflict resolution to shape who talks and what they say. These techniques are enduring, partly because they are anchored and supported by political ideals and practices that originated in collectivist social movements such as feminism.

In practice, this Let's Talk approach, common to social movements and collective organizations, is a variable mix of diverse theories and approaches, various streams with a common bedrock: knowledge and emotion. Some approaches to diversity will emphasize an educational approach, others a therapeutic approach. Often these approaches have a common derivation and parallel effects. Let's Talk includes a number of recurring ideas or approaches: attention often remains on the individual's emotions and experiences. Sharing emotion and experience is encouraged. Whether the focus is therapy or training, workshops are pedagogical projects in which the production of some kind of knowledge is an important goal. And in most cases, this knowledge or self-knowledge is produced in a supposedly egalitarian and participatory environment. Finally, there is the notion that equity and diversity require more authentic knowledge; the sharing and disclosure of personal feelings and experiences is framed as desirable, principled, and important for conflict resolution and reform.

One result is that the Let's Talk approach often elicits experience, stories, and knowledge about racism from racialized people; these may be the participants, but also the presenters or sources of outside knowledge—histories, statistics, laws. While white participants may display their feelings and self-knowledge, those racialized as other than white are generally expected to share their experiences of racism. Discussion is often aided by a professional or informal facilitator who uses techniques of experience sharing to elicit, discuss, and analyze personal experiences, as well as to solicit feelings about those experiences and even about co-workers.

The Let's Talk approach may look very different in a large university compared to a small, feminist collective, and it may be interpreted differently over time. Let's Talk isn't a fixed or defined set of practices or values. Instead, the phrase Let's Talk is a way of pointing to a configuration of historical and contemporary practices and discourses that focus on shifting individual knowledge and emotions, rather than shifting systemic practices and values.

A TOOLBOX OF TECHNIQUES

An identifiable toolbox of techniques drawn from consciousness-raising, therapeutic, conflict-resolution, and popular education approaches shapes these Let's Talk discussions. These are techniques explicitly aimed at shaping group dynamics and physical space, techniques designed to encourage a participatory and egalitarian environment in which experience can be shared. In one workshop model, non-white participants may disclose stories of racism, while white participants may share their feelings of feeling empathetic, dismayed, racist, non-racist, and so on. While less concerned with interpersonal relations and therapeutic reflections, the popular education approach may also include the solicitation of emotion and personal experiences. The following techniques represent some typical pedagogical approaches to elicit shared experiences and feelings:

- Telling and analyzing personal stories, sharing emotions, and disclosing difficult experiences of racism or of being racist
- The "go-around": each member of the whole group is compelled to speak in turn about their thoughts and feelings, or experiences
- The use of a flip chart, digital, or physical whiteboard to record the sharing of stories about racism through visual techniques, including drawing and diagrams
- Role-play, or acting out of stories or imagined scenarios of racism or antiracism
- Body sculpture, a form of role-play or theater
- Physical or spatial arrangements of bodies, such as individuals standing up to indicate their relationship to oppression or privilege

The most common of these techniques is the discussion, presentation, and analysis of personal experiences of racism. The analysis may be structured and formal, or an informal part of the process. Various methods such as small or large group discussions or presentations or "go-arounds" (everyone speaks one by one) are used to elicit personal experiences of racism or of being racist. The facilitator or small-group leader may record them on a digital or physical whiteboard, display them, or do an oral presentation. I attended one antiracism workshop for a mixed group of community members, activists, and professional antiracism workers that demonstrates this model: we were asked to speak about our experiences in small groups, present our discussion to the larger group, and then had our comments displayed on the wall. A board of education manual for youth antiracism workshops prescribes very similar techniques.[13] Asking students to "share personal experiences of racism" is a frequently suggested activity. Facilitators are told to then use the participants' personal experiences of racism as "raw material" for social analysis. They are asked to prompt the young person for details and "get them to describe their experiences and feelings in the most vivid way possible."[14] They then record and organize the experiences under general categories.

How should we interpret the practice of eliciting people's "most vivid" descriptions of their experiences of racism?[15] Presumably, vivid and emotional stories are seen as more effective for countering supposed ignorance of racism and for persuading others of the significance of racism. These kinds of emotionally painful incidents are, in other words, seen as educational. One antiracism educator I spoke with called these "opportunities for learning." Another told me, "But it's good because some white students have never heard that before"; when he says "it's good," he means that hearing the story has educational value because it addresses a supposed gap in knowledge—a story "never heard before." More likely is the kind of story to which they had never before paid attention, rather than one they have "never heard." Either way, it is difficult to avoid the conclusion that both the intent and the effect of these tactics is to use one student's trauma to teach another student.

Tracing the origins of these workshops approaches in long-standing theories about knowledge and experience helps to understand why they are so tenacious. A genealogy, a methodology Foucault also called "history of the present," can help to explain contemporary practices by tracing their roots in the past. However, using the term "genealogy" to describe this historical investigation of the Let's Talk approach might imply that it has a straightforward lineage. The lineage of current workshop practices is neither linear nor logical, however. Here a better term for the genealogical historical method might be the term "bricolage," or the practice of putting something together from the available materials and tools;[16] the methodological approach that I use similarly sifts through a mix of historical ideas and practices about knowledge, consciousness, therapy, and social change, and connects them to present-day discourses about race and equity. Bricolage is also an apt term to refer to diversity strategies, which are remade over time and place, taking on both familiar and recombinant forms.

The Let's Talk approach is inspired by an inconsistent mix of seemingly incompatible discourses and practices, including contemporary interpretations of liberal theories of social reform through knowledge, interpretations of the enduring notion that "the personal is political," and the articulation of these theories to therapeutic and pedagogical practices. As we trace each of these threads, we can see how they help to sustain the workshop as a regulated space in which participants' knowledge and feelings about racism and racial categories become the target of change, rather than organizational systems and practices.

WAYS OF NOT KNOWING: THE EPISTEMOLOGIES OF IGNORANCE

Acquisition of knowledge is the starting point for most organizational approaches to diversity and equity—so workshops and training are often the focus of efforts. Why do efforts at diversity in organizations assume that more knowledge is the primary problem? What kinds of ignorance is this knowledge addressing?

Organizational workshops cultivate several areas of knowledge, including:

- General knowledge about historical and current inequities
- Equity policies and laws
- Self-knowledge of one's privilege and emotions

- Experiences and stories of racism
- Reflections on our own biases
- History and contemporary examples or statistics
- Knowledge of racial others, their communities, and their culture
- Cross-cultural knowledge of cultural differences and practices

For example, an antiracism lecture and workshop by popular educator Robin DiAngelo was described by a participating journalist as "an onslaught of statistics" about racism and whiteness:

Soon she projected facts and photographs onto the screen behind her. No lone image offered anything surprising, yet the series caused a cumulative jolt: the percentage of state governors who are white, of the 10 richest people in the country who are white, of the people who directed the 100 top-grossing films of all time, worldwide . . . and so on.[17]

We also often see an assumption that the knowledge required is best available and most authentic by hearing the stories of people close at hand—rather than by acknowledging the array of readily available knowledge about racism.

This production of knowledge about racism is meant to remedy a supposed lack of knowledge about racism, to combat a putative "ignorance" of racism. Coexisting with the well-documented analysis that racism is rooted in systemic, historic practices and institutions is the popular sentiment that racism is produced by the ignorance or faulty knowledge of some individuals. It is a sentiment echoed in an antiracism slogan once used in Toronto: "Racism: 100% ignorance." The corollary is that knowledge is seen as the antidote to racism.

The idea that ignorance of racism can explain racism belies the knowledge of race and racism that is already readily available to everyone and in daily use. Philosophers Tuana and Sullivan urge us to use to examine the power relations and "political values at work in our knowledge practices," particularly when it comes to race.[18] We might apply this epistemological lens to the question of how whites come to know racist knowledge, as well as how and why they might avoid knowledge of racism and colonialism when the facts are close at hand.[19]

Charles Mills has argued that whites have an interest in ignoring these facts.[20] The term "white ignorance," says Mills, refers not to an accidental lack of knowledge but to the "vested group interests of . . . white citizens of the white settler states in not wanting to face the truth about the origins and development of their societies in processes of colonialism, conquest, and racial exploitation."[21] The disjuncture between apparent ignorance and a plethora of everyday and historical knowledge about racism is not accidental, nor is this lack of knowledge accurately described as a lack.[22] Ignorance of racism should not be thought of as a blank space or passive absence but rather an active practice.[23] Philosopher Linda Alcoff refers to so-called ignorance about race as a "substantive epistemic practice."[24]

Ignorance about race is not, as is often conceived, a regretful lack of access to education, but is actively produced, even if it is through a history of benign neglect and with a backdrop of good intentions. Although "ignorance" is often the result of systemic omission or repeated neglect that can appear passive or incidental, there are also psychic and material reasons for communities and individuals to be invested in ignorance of racism.

Yet mistaken assumptions about ignorance or "ways of not knowing" about racism persist. These assumptions underlie many diversity workshops and equity training efforts, leading us to ineffective strategies.

Educational approaches often make the following mistaken assumptions:

- Ignorance is an originary cause of racism; i.e., the very root or origin of racist practices is ignorance itself.
- This ignorance can be corrected by presenting people with knowledge about bias and inequity; people will have the interest and motivation to retain this knowledge and use it, and bias will be reduced.
- Reducing individual bias or prejudice will lead to more equitable practices, less discrimination, less racism, and so on.

These practices are buttressed by pervasive principles of liberalism that underscore the importance of knowledge and education as a route to social progress. Common principles of liberalism include reason, the rational individual, and the supposition that "all social arrangements may be ameliorated by rational reform."[25] The assumption, in other words, is that greater knowledge will bring liberating truths: "if the truth is inherently opposed to power, then its uncovering would surely lead us on the path to liberation."[26] A further guiding principle of liberal modernity is the assumption that morality flows naturally from rational thought. As David Goldberg argues, the inevitable analytical outcome is that racism is judged as immoral because (and only when) it is considered irrational. This returns us to educational strategy: the policy commonly drawn from this liberal analysis is that "racism can be eradicated for the most part by education."[27] In other words, the assumption is that, if one acts in a more rational manner, one will be less racist; to act in a more rational manner, one needs information and education. In discussing the contact hypothesis, for example, Geoffrey Short assesses it in terms of its effect on the *reasoning* ability of participants: "the holding of any attitude without good reason is irrational . . . the criterion for judging the value of inter-racial contact [should be] whether it permits [participants] to think more rationally about 'race' and ethnicity."[28]

These ideas are pervasive as ways of thinking about tolerance and diversity. As Cynthia Wright wryly observes, the critical response to a terrorist attack by Christian fundamentalists would hardly be to screen *The Ten Commandments*—and yet a screening of the *History of Islam* was the response of campus activists seeking critical discussion following September 11.[29] In the end this representational strategy merely highlights that violent actions by whites are not causally linked to ethnicity and religion. Why not examine instead how knowledge of Muslim fundamentalism is represented by North American mass media? Instead of supporting the belief that racism—in this case against Muslims—is irrational and can be countered by greater knowledge, this strategy can instead show that dominant representations of Islam in Western media provide rational support for Western foreign policy. As Goldberg demonstrates, contrary to this popular discourse of racism as irrational, not only is racism supported by rationality, but liberal rationality is also founded in some measure on racism, in part by the ranking of who is and who is not seen as rational.[30] Not only are men represented as more rational than women, but whites are also represented as more rational than non-whites, Christians more rational than Muslims, and so on.

In the *Good White People*, Shannon Sullivan points out that this analysis is used to cast racism as worst among uneducated, working-class whites.[31] Racist individuals are often represented in popular culture and everyday discourse as uncouth and uneducated. This distinction is highlighted, Sullivan says, because of the practical skills that many middle-class whites have of how to demonstrate appreciation for diversity.

These assumptions about knowledge and rationality, and the belief that we must begin by addressing ignorance, lead us to ineffective educational proposals. The two most prevalent proposals are the "contact hypothesis" and the "literacy hypothesis"; here I question both.

THE CONTACT HYPOTHESIS AND THE LITERACY HYPOTHESIS

What kind of knowledge is used to try to erase the knowledge of racism?

This notion that we need more knowledge to challenge racism is evident in two key hypotheses: the well-known "contact hypothesis" and what I am calling the "literacy hypothesis."

- The contact hypothesis proposes that more contact with others, more knowledge of others, will diminish prejudice.
- The literacy hypothesis proposes that more general knowledge about racism, racial others, and white privilege will diminish racism.

Proposed by psychologist Gordon Allport, the contact hypothesis suggests that direct contact between groups reduces animosity and prejudice.[32] The more cross-cultural contact that groups have with each other, and the more they know about the other, the less prejudice they will have. Allport developed these ideas in the 1950s, at a time when racial segregation was being challenged, and his hypothesis was offered as evidence in favor of desegregation.

The contact hypothesis, as proposed by Allport, is quite narrow in its framing, but it is often interpreted quite broadly to imply far-reaching benefits of any kind of contact, even when the contact is virtual or incidental. The most well-known interpretations of the contact hypothesis are the diversity efforts that celebrate multiculturalism and ethnic difference, taking what I call a 3-D approach—one that celebrates dance, dress, and dining—but fails to take into account the multiple dimensions of racial and social inequality. Because it has been so widely influential and misinterpreted in ideas about multiculturalism, diversity, and antiracism, the contact hypothesis deserves some close analysis.

The contact hypothesis specifies that four quite precise conditions should be in place for contact between groups to reduce prejudice: equal status between the groups; common goals; cooperation; and support from authorities. The problem is that real-life, cross-racial interactions are exceedingly complex since the confluence of all these conditions is uncommon or inconsistent. Many of the conditions set by Allport, such as the presence of both collaboration and equal relationships, are not common.

While research to test the contact hypothesis has been extensive, the results have been neither universal nor definitive. Certainly, there is experimental evidence that contact can reduce prejudice under the ideal conditions specified by Allport. However, some studies contradict the contact hypothesis, showing that under certain conditions contact can actually increase prejudice. If the contact includes negative experiences, for example, contact between groups has been shown to increase prejudice, rather than decrease prejudice.[33] In general, in observations of real-life conditions of sustained contact, the contact hypothesis often does not hold. There are many examples of racially integrated communities with significant intergroup contact that are still rife with racial prejudice. In a study of high schools in Belgium, diverse classrooms did not decrease ethnocentrism; however, ethnic tensions within a school actually strengthened prejudice when measured two years later.[34]

A study by sociologist Jeffrey Denis showed that even with a high degree of contact, friendship, and intermarriage between Indigenous and white residents in a Canadian city, whites continued to maintain their sense of superiority and their racist beliefs about Indigenous communities.[35] In this study, contact between Indigenous and white communities did seem to reduce "old-fashioned prejudice." However, "it does not diminish whites' superior sense of group position, at least, in part, because the historically rooted racial structure remains intact."

Interactions between groups can be exceedingly complex—they may be negative, brief, or neutral. In addition, any benefits of contact often fail to extend beyond individuals one meets or beyond the immediate situation. Reductions in individual prejudice toward the people one meets during cultural exchanges often do not generalize to all members of the group.[36] In one study, white employers evaluated their Black domestic employees more favorably than whites as a group, but continued to demean Blacks in general.[37]

Dixon and his colleagues note that, on a collective level, contact between communities can even have the effect of cultivating more racism and new forms of segregation.

> [Contact] may heighten perceptions of threat among the wider membership of the communities involved. This may result not only in an increase in aggregate levels of racism but also in the emergence of new systems of segregation, designed precisely to regulate the possibility of contact.[38]

Finally, prejudice reduction is not necessarily always a valid or useful goal. As Dixon and his colleagues ask in their assessment of the contact hypothesis, if the goal is fighting systemic racial injustice, is getting everyone to like each other even helpful?[39]

The "literacy" hypothesis proposes that the antidote is more knowledge about racism, about one's own biases, one's own defensive emotions, and so on. Some antiracism educators advocate a particular kind "racial literacy" or "white racial literacy"[40] that focuses on ability to navigate relations of race. Harrelson, who teaches racial literacy to his white university students, defines racial literacy as "the ability to recognize, describe, and respond to the racial nuances of complex social settings"[41]—in other words, white racial literacy is the individual recognition and navigation of the social relations of race. The desire for this kind of racial literacy and general knowledge has increased, and the increase in educational resources and books about racism shows that people see this literacy as linked to racial justice and action.[42]

Gordon Allport proposed the contact hypothesis, on which so many educational efforts are based, in part because this literacy approach was so limited. As Allport pointed out, "Prejudice has too profound a functional significance to such individuals to be changed by exhortation, by knowledge or by argument."[43]

Since much of the general knowledge presented in workshops has been easily available for decades, would making it more available make any difference? Or can we assume a kind of chosen ignorance, blissful ignorance, or willful ignorance? Harrelson distinguishes between "willful ignorance" and the "ignorance" of his well-meaning white students, as if one is caused by intentional action and the other is the result of passive neglect. But, whether intentional or passive on the part of the individual, ignorance of race and racism nevertheless represents a set of active practices and histories that produce certain kinds of knowledge about race. As Deborah Britzman asserts, "ignorance is not the lack of knowledge but rather constituted by knowledge itself."[44] David Goldberg similarly posits that "racial knowledge is not just information about the racial Other, but its very creation, its fabrication."[45]

The 2015 report of the Truth and Reconciliation Commission is a careful documentation of residential schools and the genocide of Indigenous communities in Canada.[46] It recommends mandatory education on residential schools to address the "ignorance" of Canadians about the genocide of Indigenous communities in which generations of children were taken away from their families; thousands never returned. Yet even after the publication of this report, many non-Indigenous Canadians remain "ignorant" of this history and were shocked by the discovery in 2021 of the graves of hundreds of children. After the discovery, a poll reported that despite the fact that 72 percent of Canadians said they were saddened by the news of the mass graves of Indigenous children, only 10 percent of Canadians were familiar with the history of the residential school system.[47] And yet a decade earlier, the Canadian government issued a formal apology to Indigenous communities for residential schools.[48] In this context, what does it mean to continue to say, "I never knew"? It may mean, "I never thought to read past the headline; it didn't interest me; it was in the past," and so on.

A few years ago, sociologist Melissa Forcione, then one of my graduate students, began her research from the starting point of her own ignorance about colonialism. How, she wanted to understand, could she and her fellow white community members have grown up so ignorant of Indigenous and colonial history? As Forcione documents in her dissertation, "(Un)settling Education," despite the presence of a former residential school a mere fifteen-minute walk from her own school, she had never heard that Indigenous children were taken from their families. The very first time she learned about residential schools was through a conversation with a customer when she was bartending. Yet the knowledge and even the material evidence was more than readily available her whole life. This kind of ignorance, shared by so many, is not accidental; it requires an active, systemic, epistemic practice that continually produces local and formal knowledge that absents colonialism and Indigenous communities. Why, as Forcione asks, were these histories missing from her schooling and everyday conversation? The fact that her town's existence depends on resources extracted from unceded Indigenous territory suggests that that there is an implicit interest in maintaining that ignorance.

What strategies would be able to undo this active practice of igno-rance? Do we simply need to counter with more rational facts? Paula Ioanide suggests that the emotional content of racism prevents people from seeing the facts; she is concerned that in public conversations about race, "feelings trump facts."[49] While I agree that these conversa-tions about race are deeply emotional, I argue that we should not coun-terpose factuality as a sort of antidote to emotion. On the contrary, the idea that we require more knowledge, facts, and education to achieve racial equity can itself be part of the problem. If we were to need more education, what kind of education would be most effective in advancing racial justice? Who needs to be educated, when, about what?

These questions are rarely closely examined in our organizational efforts. If we remain convinced that the problem is produced by well-meaning folks who simply don't know better, our default solution will always be education and dialogue. Yet these tools rarely lead us to mean-ingful change. Either they are seen as an end in themselves, or they lead to nominal changes, or they end in indifference, disillusionment, tears, and even conflict.

It is this epistemology of ignorance, or what I call the "ways of not knowing," that is most relevant to understanding the shortcomings of the diversity workshop. Exploring this relationship between knowledge, ignorance, and education helps us to query the notion of the antiracism workshop as an antidote to racism. The knowledge that is circulated in diversity and antiracism workshops is not an antidote, but rather can sustain fixed representations of marginalized others.

The racial literacy approach advocates reflecting on one's own emo-tions, learning new emotional responses, and acquiring facts. DiAngelo, for example, directs white readers to "Breathe. Listen. Reflect," to cul-tivate new kinds of feelings, and to seek out new sources of knowledge to educate themselves.[50] Learning about racism or about one's feelings about race does not, however, lead to racial justice. In most cases, these strategies and workshops direct energy toward the interior psychic and moral reflection of white participants, rather than toward remaking specific practices of our organizations and institutions. As important as it is to challenge the obstructive patterns that are so common in discussions of racism, we must move beyond self-reflection. More education, more contact, more self-reflection, more awareness of one's whiteness, and even more empathy do not, however, lead ineluctably to better equity practices. There is no necessary equation between greater knowledge and awareness of what other folks feel and experience and practices that support equity and cultivate greater diversity.

An instructive example comes from Jasbir Puar's analysis of violent attacks on Sikh men who were assumed to be Muslim. Instead of challenging the racist portrayal of all brown men as dangerous, Sikh civil rights groups tried to educate people about the Sikh religion and turbans, treating it a problem of mistaken identity that required people to be better educated about religious and ethnic distinctions.[51]

It becomes inevitable, then, that stories may be used in an instrumental way—to "better" teach white participants about racism. The contact hypothesis—the mistaken notion that more contact diminishes prejudice—continues to have influence in institutional efforts at antiracism. As educators, activists, and academics, we implicitly hold close the notion that there is an automatic association between knowledge and conduct.[52]

"THE PERSONAL IS POLITICAL"

The Let's Talk approach is not particular to social movement or nonprofit organizations. Popular psychology, therapy, the talk show, even popular film and TV drama—all reflect the prevalence of personal disclosure as a form of knowledge and problem solving.

However, the assertion that "the personal is political," a phrase most recently associated with the feminist movement, adds a layer of political imperative and passion to the popular, therapeutic threads of the Let's Talk approach. Rooted in social movements such as feminism, socialism, and anarchism, "the personal is political" has in turn become a foundation for the Let's Talk approach in a wide diversity of spaces, including public institutions, community organizations, universities, and corporate spaces that aspire to reflect collectivist values of social justice. Drawing on personal experience as a basis for initiating analysis or organizational change is a familiar practice in sites inspired by these social movement ideals.[53] To put it another way, the "personal is political" framework uses personal experience as the basis for generating the knowledge and analyses needed for progressive social change. We see these practices of group process and discussion reflected in many organizations, suggesting that "the personal is political" has a strong and continuing influence.

It is a deeply rooted influence. For over a hundred years, "the personal is political" has been a foundational principle for many social movements, connecting consciousness to social structures. This historical foundation helps explain why, in movements that share any historical links to socialism, collectivist anarchism, or feminism, talking about experience, consciousness, and emotion is not seen simply as a vehicle for therapeutic self-disclosure. It is instead seen as integral to the production of knowledge that leads to social and organizational change.

It is inevitable then, that the discourse of "the personal is political" has also formed an historical framework for the production of knowledge about race; the considerable historical breadth and depth of "the personal is political" has given weight to this framework in a variety of public and corporate sites. However, a review of this history shows that, while "the personal is political" has been both tenacious and widespread, it has also gradually evolved away from the political and toward the personal, so that its original intention has been diluted or subverted.

"The personal is political" is familiar to many as one of the most significant and distinctive expressions to come out of second-wave feminism. Yet the concept of "the personal is political" not only predates but also spreads well beyond second-wave feminism. Its most obvious roots are in Marxism; the relationship between social structure and individual thought or action apparent in feminism's "the personal is political" has its origins here. In Marx's theories, human "consciousness," as well as "dominant ideas," are directly determined by relations of material production. Marx argues that "the phantoms of the human brain are . . . necessary sublimates of men's material life-process."[54] Our ideas and consciousness are, according to Marx, shaped by what we do.

Despite Marx's links among social life, human thought, and social, economic, and political structure, Marxist theory does not encourage individual exploration of this relationship. In fact, the Marxist-Leninist model of political organizing has been criticized by feminists for being dismissive of feelings. As Jaggar says, "some Marxists, indeed, tend to dismiss concern with feeling and emotion as a self-indulgent luxury of the privileged classes."[55]

We begin to see a stronger emphasis on the personal, however, in the egalitarian philosophies of early communitarian or social anarchist experiments. For these nineteenth-century communities, the personal and everyday issues of parenting and sexuality were confronted as central to their political enterprise.[56] Early anarchist writing emphasized the link between human relationships and political goals. Scientist and anarchist writer Peter Kropotkin,[57] for example, proposed that the principle of "mutual aid," or communal feeling rather than competition, forms the basis of progressive social evolution. Those periods when mutual aid was most evident in institutions, Kropotkin argued, "were also the periods of the greatest progress in arts, industry and science."[58] This link in Kropotkin's writing between human relationships, social progression, and the feelings and actions of individuals formed the groundwork for the more explicit expression that "the personal is political."[59]

Not surprisingly, then, the link between the personal and political was important even in the first-wave women's movement of the late nineteenth and early twentieth centuries. An analysis by Myra Ferree and Beth Hess suggests that "moral reform" feminists, who, among other things, fought against prostitution and alcohol, had "a vision of human relationships that affirms the dignity and value of each person, and a commitment to social and economic arrangements that would make such interpersonal relationships possible."[60] We can hear echoes of the contemporary "personal is political" in the demand by first-wave moral reform feminism "for consistency in personal and political life [and] the belief that women are 'natural' pacifists or the bearers of a distinctive ethic of care."[61]

These early roots of "the personal is political" reappeared in the "counterculture" and new social movements that flourished in the 1960s and early 1970s. Radical feminism, for example, had strong parallels with early social anarchist theories; it emphasized the making of alternative communities and collectives in which women's relationships, ways of living, and making decisions were central political issues. Marxist thought was also influential on early second-wave feminism; many young feminists learned Marxist and other critical social theory through their participation in the civil rights and New Left movements.[62] Marxist thought was a direct theoretical inspiration for these early expressions of "the personal is political." One of the first appearances of "the personal is political" in feminism was the 1969 "Redstockings Manifesto," which asserts, "We regard our personal experience, and our feelings about that experience, as the basis for an analysis of our common situation."[63] A central point of the manifesto was that personal and intimate "conflicts between individual men and women are *political* conflicts that can only be solved collectively."

Ferree and Hess argue that in asserting that "the personal is political" feminists of the 1970s created a new interpretation of Marxist principles, as they

> stood conventional New Left practice on its head; rather than starting with theory, as in Freudian or Marxist analysis, and then trying to fit contemporary patterns into the theoretical model, New Left women began with life experience and then developed an explanatory framework.[64]

This feminist interpretation gave "the personal is political" a unique and central significance, one that has in turn been widely influential in other sites. In their study of feminist organizing, Adamson argues that, together with "sisterhood is powerful," "the personal is political" stands out as the most important idea to come out of the feminist movement.[65]

Not only have these political ideas been among the most enduring to emerge out of feminist thought, but they may have had the widest influence. "The personal is political" formed a powerful political core for grassroots feminist movements, playing a key role in shaping their analyses, direction, forms of organization, and impact.[66] In the broadest sense, "the personal is political" made concerns about women's supposedly "personal" or private lives into legitimate political issues, including women's feelings, sexuality, personal relationships, and the home. Adamson argues that originally the central intentions of "the personal is political" were to challenge the deep-seated emphasis on the individual over the social, and to counter the separation of the private and public. Most significant, however, was "the way 'the personal is political' situated women's personal experiences in a larger political context, and oriented women towards a collective struggle for social change."[67] We might say that "the personal is political" is an originating political principle of the feminist movement. Laura Brown goes so far as to call this principle a "holy truth of the feminist vision."[68]

This centrally significant principle has had profound effects in two related areas: organizational structure and interpersonal modes of expression. The influence on organizational structure or form is clear in the collectivist feminist organization, which has its roots here. Briskin calls these collectivist organizations an "outgrowth" of "the personal is political."[69] The basic elements of the collectivist or grassroots feminist group include collective organization, sharing of all tasks, consensus decision-making, and "emphasis on personal experience."[70] In reaction to the rationalist, hierarchical organization, "collectivist"-style organizations have instead emphasized personal relationships. Rather than bureaucratic efficiency, it is consensus, solidarity, and egalitarianism that are favored.[71] For example, Lustiger-Thaler distinguishes the Green Party in Montreal from other environmental groups because of its focus on "process." For the Green Party, he says, "the notion of process was itself a large part of the task of being political."[72]

The other enduring outcome of "the personal is political" is its profound effect on interpersonal modes of expression in community spaces. The emphasis on personal and emotional experience that has become a common way of approaching collective problems has its roots here. Feminist interpretations then cemented the link between "the personal is political" and theories that emphasize the importance of valuing women's emotions. One of the underlying intentions behind "the personal is political" was to challenge the hierarchical dualism of reason over emotion and to value the emotional experiences of women. As Linda Briskin puts it, "the personal is political . . . challenges the . . . overvaluation of the rational and concomitant devaluation of the affective."[73] In a sense, "the personal is political" is the practical expression of feminism's gendered analysis of the reason/emotion hierarchy. This historical weight helps explains why, in organizations that share a common history or principles with collectivist, feminist organizations, the sharing and disclosure of personal feelings and experiences is framed as desirable, principled, and important for conflict resolution and organizational change.

The belief that conflict over racism is resolvable by personal sharing is supported not only by enduring interpretations of "the personal is political," but also by predominant liberal conceptions of racism as traceable to individual prejudice. Assumptions about how racism may be countered by better knowledge then support personalized conflict-resolution, therapy, and consciousness-raising techniques. as well as popular education.

CONSCIOUSNESS-RAISING AND POPULAR EDUCATION

As a central social movement premise, "the personal is political" has both a solid historical foundation and a strong contemporary emphasis on the personal and emotional as a route to analysis and knowledge. What has this meant for the practice and techniques of social movement organizations? What are the implications of "the personal is political" for organizations attempting to address racism? To answer this question, we need to understand the organizational techniques that have arisen out of the premise that "the personal is political."

Consciousness-raising groups and feminist therapy are the two most notable practices to stem directly from "the personal is political." Popular education, education for and of the people, also shares the same foundational philosophy. These three social movement practices—consciousness-raising, therapy, and popular education—are joined by organizational practices such as conflict-resolution and human-resource training to form the configuration of organizational attempts to address racism and equity. The following chapter examines the therapy mode more closely; in this chapter, I explore the techniques of consciousness-raising, popular education, and conflict resolution.

The consciousness-raising group, once referred to as the CR group, has likely been the most influential feminist technique to be linked to "the personal is political" philosophy. Josephine Donovan argues that "the practice of small group consciousness-raising, with its stress on examining and understanding experience and on connecting personal experience to the structures that define our lives, is the clearest expression of the method basic to feminism."[74] Particularly common during the early years of second-wave feminism, these were small groups of women who met regularly and spoke informally, usually without a structure, on any and all issues relevant to women's lives. Like "the personal is political" itself, the consciousness-raising technique was inspired by Marxist theorists of the twentieth century who emphasized the importance of "consciousness" in explaining historical change. Drawing heavily on this foundation, socialist feminism "claims that an effective revolutionary strategy must include techniques . . . for demystifying . . . prevailing ideology . . . and for developing alternative forms of consciousness."[75] Just as Marxist theory emphasized the creation of a political unity and common interest among oppressed peoples,[76] consciousness-raising groups were also considered key to realizing a common identity and to overcoming isolation.

There have been parallel developments of the consciousness-raising model in other social movements. The use of personal experiences has, for example, been an important starting point for popular education and other alternative educational efforts. Popular education, literally education for or of the people, was conceived as a radical alternative to conventional or "banking" education;[77] Paolo Freire is well-known for his development of this approach, also referred to as "education for critical consciousness."[78] In most popular education models, as in the consciousness-raising model, an important aspect of gaining this "critical consciousness" is the analysis of experience. Popular education techniques advocate using the lived experiences of participants as a starting point for a collective analysis of the relations that structure those experiences[79] with the goal of changing those social relations.[80] These techniques have been widely used in many organizational and community settings, such as unions, social service agencies, First Nations, and community groups.[81] As Sherene Razack argues, this "storytelling has been at the heart of our pedagogy" for social change.[82] In discussing her human rights course, for example, Razack writes that her goal was "to forge a politics of alliances based on this sharing of daily experiences."[83] It is inevitable, then, that antiracism education[84] reveals a common history with the consciousness-raising group. Practitioners of antiracism education emphasize the diversity of "personal experience and lived realities as a source of knowledge."[85] The use of experience and local knowledge from multicultural perspectives is advocated as a way to challenge the universalism and racism of curricula and texts.[86]

However, while both consciousness-raising groups and popular education are based on Marxist definitions of consciousness as the system of ideas that both supports and is determined by the system of production, in practice many interpretations of "consciousness" have often been far more personal. In her detailed study of consciousness-raising groups, for example, Cassell defines consciousness as "an individual, subjective experience."[87] The purpose of consciousness-raising was "to understand our personal lives and experiences, not to build a mass movement."[88]

This emphasis on personal experience has had immense appeal and tremendous success, both within and outside women's groups. As Adamson notes,

> the CR group emerged very quickly as a powerful tool for grassroots organizing. By focusing on the reality of each woman's life, it was able to reach, and, ultimately, activate women in a way that more abstract calls to organize around an issue would not have done.[89]

Consciousness-raising groups have even been described as the key to feminism's success. Patricia Carey has argued that feminism's "survival and consistent progress can be attributed to one of its most frequently trivialized symbols and political vehicles: the consciousness raising session."[90]

Precisely because of the very broad appeal of these techniques, the consciousness-raising model evolved into one that privileges personal experience and stories over political analysis. In other words, the phrase "the personal is political" has also come to imply an equivalence between the personal and the political. In this interpretation, everything personal comes to have political significance. This interpretation has become part of the culture and history of the feminist movement[91] and is evident far beyond the peak of the consciousness-raising group in the 1960s and 1970s. For example, Carey noted that the consciousness-raising group has continued in a far more informal form.[92]

The format of the consciousness-raising group has been continually used by feminist groups to explore racism.[93] Gail Pheterson, for example, describes an elaborate five-month series of feminist consciousness-raising sessions on racism, anti-Semitism, and heterosexism.[94] Consciousness-raising sessions were also the strategy used by a feminist publishing collective in my study; when Maya raised concerns about racism at the collective, her white co-workers responded by holding "consciousness-raising" sessions for all the staff and collective members.

Similarly, in her study of diversity in queer community organizations, Jane Ward suggests that the ideal multipronged approach to diversity should operate not only on the political and organizational levels but also the "social-psychological," by developing a new "consciousness."[95] Ward and others advocate that people develop this consciousness by using "their own experiences, culture, and emotions as a means of connecting to forms of oppression that they do not directly experience."[96] It is a form of transformation that begins with the self.

THE DEMAND FOR STORIES

As Aruna pointed out in her assessment of the antiracism workshop at her school, raising consciousness may have been intended as the "first step," but it also became the last step.

The demand for speech as a form of knowledge has a particular history: philosopher Michel Foucault argued that the incitement to speech as a way of gaining more information about individuals is a characteristic of modern techniques of governance. The key to understanding the relationship of pedagogy to the modern subject, Foucault shows, is that the modern subject "must talk."[97] He refers to this ritual of discourse as confession, and argues that it has become a main ritual for the production of truth.[98] While the confession was first associated with thirteenth-century Christianity, eighteenth-century pedagogy and nineteenth-century science developed it into a widespread practice.[99] We have, Foucault argues, become "a confessing animal."

The intimate disclosures and emotional outpourings of talk shows and social media are only the most visible symbol of an increasingly confessional culture.[100] In areas such as education, psychoanalysis, and criminal justice there is a continuum of techniques of knowledge production that make the individual into an object of knowledge, into a modern subject who must talk and whose words must be interpreted by experts to produce knowledge about individuals and to govern individuals.[101] Recall this confessional mode in the teachers' workshop Aruna was required to attend; she sat in a small groups and awkwardly listened to her white colleagues talk about the times they had been racist. Aruna reports, "They want white people to talk about how do you feel about being a white person; it's a ritual, to check a box" *(interview transcript)*.

Antiracism workshops are not simply mirrors of the confessional talk show, however. Rather, as I have shown, in these sites several approaches conjoin to produce a muddle of pedagogical practices complicated by relations of race. In confessional modes of antiracism discussion, requests for personal reflections do not necessarily elicit the expected intimate self-disclosures of the support group, therapeutic relationship, or talk show. Instead, participants are more obviously objects of knowledge. Their utterances are meant to contribute to the self/knowledge project of the listeners—a project to create a certain knowledge about racism and one's own character, one's own feelings.

In one interview account, Carmen relates how the demand for her personal experience became suddenly urgent, required by her coworkers only in the context of a diversity workshop:

> I remember the facilitator just said to me, "So Carmen, why don't you tell us what it's like to be a lesbian in a straight office?" I thought, "What do you mean, what is it like, why do I have to tell you what it's like? Why can't you figure it out? Why can't *you* talk about it?" And I remember I just said stupid things like, "Well, you can't walk down the street holding hands with your partner"—because it was just too painful to talk about in terms of the office, to say *you've never once before asked me about my life. (interview transcript)*

The knowledge of Carmen's life is newly demanded and read within the context of antiracist organizational change and conflict resolution. As Carmen's commentary highlights, what it's "really like to be a lesbian in a straight office," what it's "really" like to be a woman of color in a white organization, will not be revealed. That knowledge may not even be sought. Carmen, as her commentary shows, struggles to present a story that will meet the needs of the workshop yet do so without revealing her true feelings and experiences.

Her stories are not confessions of inner self, but are produced to fit the needs of the listener. Speaking about these kinds of pedagogical moments, Sherene Razack asks, "What tale will I choose to tell, and in what voice?"[102] Elizabeth Ellsworth suggests that the answer will depend on our assessment of the power relations in the room.[103] Those who are marginalized—made other by virtue of race or sexuality—enter the self-knowledge project as a dangerous place. For in the context of the antiracism or diversity workshop, any confessions of self are also grist for the self-knowledge project of others.

This request for knowledge about life experiences of oppression can become persistent. This dynamic reminds me of the suggestion by some classmates in my graduate courses to hold an antiracism workshop. When the request was refused by a student of color, her refusal was challenged by the white students making the proposal, who confronted her after class, saying: "But how are we supposed to learn? We *have* to have a dialogue." Their demand for dialogue was founded on their desire to educate themselves. In analyzing the problematic use of "storytelling" in her own human rights course, Razack recalls how a South African woman finally left in tears after she was twice "confronted" by fellow students "with a firm 'Why don't you tell us about your experiences?'"[104] Gloria Anzaldúa describes a similar scene in her university classroom, underscoring the emotional urgency of these demands for knowledge:

> Several whitewomen stood up in class and either asked politely, pleaded or passionately demanded (one had tears streaming down her face) that women-of-color teach them; when whitewomen wanted to engage women-of-color in time-consuming dialogues, *las mujeres-de-color* expressed their hundred years weariness of trying to teach whites about Racism.[105]

Linda Carty writes that these expectations of knowledge from experience also shaped her experience as a Black woman teaching university students: "What was clearly expected of me, the Black woman instructor, was to bring to class *my personal experience* of the issues being discussed (I was actually told this more than once by some participants outside of class)."[106]

It becomes clear that organizational and pedagogical efforts to deal with race bring together a variety of threads. Practices of knowledge production and emotional disclosure that are common to new social movements intersect with liberal ideas of rational social reform and modern interpretations of the confession. In this complex, sometimes contradictory mélange, the techniques of "the personal is political" are at times recast through liberal conceptions of the individual, racism, knowledge, and social progress. While this liberalism may appear to sit uneasily alongside "the personal is political" and its ideals of systemic analysis and radical change, it is well anchored by social movements and organizational settings that, to one degree or another, also echo humanist visions of social change. The feminist movement is an example of this uneasy alliance. While poststructuralist feminist scholarship has profoundly challenged liberal conceptions of the individual, in everyday practice many feminist approaches reflect an ambivalent yet persistent embracing of individual experience as the ground of knowledge. Foucault's analysis informs poststructuralist feminist critiques of experience; however, his description of the confessional relationship also characterizes some modes of discussion in feminist and community organizations. These contradictions sit alongside each other in the same spaces. As Mariana Valverde remarks of feminist scholars,

> Even those of us who can deconstruct a humanist subject at twenty paces often feel nostalgia for "experience," for the humanist subject and for her ethics of personal authenticity. . . . There is thus a contradiction between the emotional and interpersonal dimension of becoming and remaining a feminist, on the one hand, and on the other hand the theoretical tools that deconstruct binary opposites and interrogate the cultural assumptions of narrative forms used to tell one's tale.[107]

The belief that emotion and personal experience provide truth is, in other words, a compelling one. The allure of personal experience as a route to truth is particularly compelling for those who are familiar with the culture and practices of feminist and community organizations.

According to many interpretations of "the personal is political," since personal experience provides an alternative way of understanding social relations, and since "true" emotion supposedly reveals "true" experience, disclosure of one's experiences and emotions becomes an important form for resolving conflict and producing knowledge about racism.

WHAT KINDS OF KNOWLEDGE ARE PRODUCED?

What are the implications of using personal experience as the basis of knowledge and action in antiracism discussion? What are the effects of this conception of knowledge in antiracism workshops and in organizations?

It has been observed that racism rests not on the lack of knowledge, but on the production of knowledge about racialized peoples.[108] Equity and diversity workshops contribute to this production of knowledge— they are not simply transferring knowledge, but workshop practices are also inadvertently producing new knowledge about racism, antiracism, and racialized categories. Workshops can, for example, produce and re-produce simplistic representations of identity—the stereotypical "angry woman of color" or "weeping white woman."

To be clear, these workshop practices are not intended to be exploit-ative or extractive of Black and Indigenous people and people of color; on the contrary, they have often been designed to honor their expe-riences. Gurnah, for example, describes Racism Awareness Training (RAT) workshops in Britain as "rightly concerned with people's personal experience of racism."[109] McCaskell similarly notes that antiracism edu-cation "requires a particular type of *pedagogy* . . . based on learners' real social experience."[110]

When used as originally intended, a popular education approach provides a way for a community to create an analysis of inequity that reflects the social relations and history particular to its own location. As a starting point for inquiry, reflections on direct experience can potentially allow us to examine the local and historical conditions that produced that experience. If this knowledge project is undertaken as a community or group, it can help to build a collective analysis and a collective strategy for change. Egalitarian dialogue and exchange of this knowledge is at the heart of pedagogical and political tactics founded on "the personal is political" and popular education.[111]

This is not the approach or the goal of most diversity and equity workshops, however. In most workshops or organizational discussions, the "equal" sharing of experiences and feelings is not explicitly directed toward collective analysis or collective change. On the contrary, the sharing of experience is overshadowed by the inequitable relations of telling. In most of the cases I studied, the tellers—people of color who share their experiences—are seen as primary resources. As we have seen, the required knowledge is drawn from its most "authentic" knowers— participants racialized as other than white. Techniques are created for participants to discuss and present, role-play, and analyze their personal experiences of racism. The goal becomes knowledge about race that is produced by and about people of color, knowledge for scrutiny, rejection, or gratitude by white participants. This kind of "dialogue," while represented as a collective educational project, can ironically be shaped by coercive demands.

For this reason, the invitation to a collective space of sharing is often declined—it is well-intentioned, but specious. Silence or withdrawal is not an unusual outcome of attempts at discussions of racism. In one workshop I attended, the chairs were arranged in circles, a common technique to encourage a more participatory learning experience. Yet the inner circle became occupied by white participants, the outer circle by non-white participants, and the egalitarian and participatory intent of this technique was refused and inverted. The circle becomes a hierarchical space because of the vulnerability of sitting in the center, the danger and undesirability of being the center of attention. Similarly, Razack's student left the classroom rather than give in to demands from others to speak their experience.[112] Sleeter's research describes how some teachers are puzzled or frustrated when Black children resist and refuse to discuss their cultural background at school.[113] Yet the teachers' desire for Black children to share their cultural heritage stands in sharp contrast with the devaluation of Black histories and cultures in school curriculum and society.

Ironically, then, these educational techniques may reproduce the same relations they seek to uncover. In other words, the relations of race that we are trying to investigate are not absent from antiracism workshops and can be only momentarily forgotten. Dorothy Smith proposes that we address both the "conditions as well as the perceived forms and organization" of direct experiences by looking beyond their circumscriptions.[114] In this case, the meaning of these stories can only be understood by examining the social relations that shape not only the "original" experience, but also the telling and retelling of these experiences. Because the Let's Talk technique often individualizes racism as a personal experience, these collective discussions often glide over a concerted examination of social relations. The result is that these techniques help to produce a certain analysis and knowledge of racism—ones in which racism, sexism, and heterosexism are easily opposed by changing individual feelings and attitudes.

The technique of role-play, used to draw out and reenact the stories of racism, further accentuates the writing of this script. Role play is sometimes used as a workshop activity, an impetus for discussion as well as an object for transformation. For example, in a popular theater workshop on antiracism that I attended, people were asked to replace one of the actors in a role-play (usually the target of racism) and replay the scene differently. White people volunteered to replace the person of color; men replaced the women. As they took the stage to replace the "victim," they effortlessly and powerfully confronted the abuser with phrases such as "Don't do that again," or with rational explanations of the behavior's unacceptability. In imagining that the workplace power relations did not exist, the role-play created an image of racism and sexism as easily eliminated by the individual. "If only she would just say 'fuck off,'" to her harasser, one participant repeated over and over uncomprehendingly, if only she were not so passive. In one incident, reported in the *New York Times*, a teacher demonstrated the extreme example of this technique when she organized a classroom role-play of slavery in which the Black children were treated as slaves.[115] These incidents emphasize that the retold experiences are not mirrors of people's lives, but are stories that align with the requirements of the workshop. As performances of our understandings of racism, these role-plays are part of the knowledge relations through which conceptions of racism and antiracism are created. Not only are people's experiences displayed, but they are also used to produce and reinforce a collective knowledge that often denies how the relations of power have produced those experiences.

Similar to role-play, another technique asks participants create a theatrical vignette or pose to analyze power relations and transform them. In a community workshop I attended, an Indigenous man created a scenario to show how a racist teacher had discouraged his interest in music. Everyone attending the workshop participated to collectively analyze and transform his vignette of racism; gradually all of the workshop participants who had been discouraged in their musical pursuits now placed themselves within this man's vignette. Now "empowered" and smiling, they all played their imaginary instruments. The facilitator never returned to or perhaps never recognized this man's initial observations about the racism he had experienced, despite the explicit intention of the exercise to analyze power relations. The focus on everyone's individual stories, and also on the power of the individuals to easily change the story in a celebratory way, obscured the discussion of racism.

The "equal" sharing of experience is also subverted by the more direct denial, dismissal, and competition of stories, a phenomenon described in interviews and observed in workshops. The denial is at times paradoxical, when some participants first desire and then reject stories. In response to stories of racism, for example, one man in an antiracism workshop proclaimed that it couldn't really be this racist in Canada. Many variations on this statement surface in and outside antiracism workshops.[116] For this reason, a Board of Education manual on youth antiracism workshops alerts facilitators that guilt and defensiveness can be a problem for the "process."[117] A common event, the manual notes, is participants' comparing racist abuse to name-calling sometimes experienced by white students. In one youth workshop, after a student shared a story of racism, a white American teacher compared it to his own experience immigrating to Canada. The diversity workshop can provide a space and format for these forms of comparison and implicit dismissals of racism.

It becomes clear, as previously touched upon, that the typical techniques of diversity workshops can produce and reproduce simplistic representations of race, emotion, and racial identity. Workshop practices of self-expression, pedagogy, and conflict resolution not only shape how we speak about racism, but also shape representations of participants and their emotions. The casting of racialized participants as educators on racism, the stereotypes of the angry woman of color, and the "fragile" or resistant white participant or "weeping white woman"—these are key examples of the ways that equity work shapes the language of race and emotion.

While it is inevitable that discussions about race and diversity may make participants emotional and cause emotional trauma, it is the tendency of diversity workshop approaches to focus on individuals, their emotions, their actions, and their moral positions that produces representations of race and emotion such as the "angry woman of color." In turn, these representations undermine individuals, limit organizational analysis, and help to sustain inequitable relations of race. While people may become emotional when discussing race, an individualistic focus on their anger, "fragility," culpability, or personal histories can also derail detailed analyses of organizational practices. These dynamics are not exclusive to formal workshops, and some of these ways of approaching conversations about race will be familiar in other group or workplace contexts.

Emotion is facilitated, valued, elicited, encouraged. Why? Because, in both the popular education and the therapy manifestations of the Let's Talk approach, experience and emotion are seen as more authentic knowledge. When a co-worker and I facilitated an antiracism workshop, she struggled to keep tears back during her introductory remarks. We spoke cynically and angrily afterward about how persuasive and effective her tears seemed—appreciative people went out of their way to tell her how much she had moved them. This echoes Sherene Razack's classroom experience, in which she describes her students' "feeding off the tears" of other students' testimonials.[118] Why do tears provide nourishment when listening to stories of about racism? Do tears signal a more "authentic" or a deeper knowledge, or is it the emotional connection, trust, safety, and potential for redemption that these tears signal?

Ginny's experience in a small women's drop-in center provides another illustration of this familiar Let's Talk approach, in which participants share their experiences, feelings, and reflections on racism. Ginny and another co-worker raised concerns about racism in the distribution of tasks and in programming for women coming to the center. Ginny hoped that an antiracism facilitator would help to focus discussion on organizational changes. Instead, the discussion took a personalized turn. At times the discussion focused on resolving the conflict between co-workers, and at other times it was a theater in which Ginny and co-workers told their stories for an emotional audience:

> We talked about how we experience racism in the organization and in women's organizations. But Denise never said anything except, "I feel bad." . . . All Denise would say was, "Thank you for sharing." *(interview transcript)*

While Ginny and a co-worker spoke about their experiences of racism, their white co-worker Denise only responded by alternating between gratitude and sorrow for their "sharing." This exercise creates a racialized dynamic between teller and listener, between spectacle and gratitude. Participants of antiracism workshops report that their stories may elicit not only gratitude and sorrow, but also anger and denial.

Overall, the effect of these pedagogical approaches is to produce a knowledge of racism and racial identities that supports individualized and emotional strategies for antiracism rather than organizational ones.

THE DILEMMA OF WHITE "PRIDE"

The following example is from an antiracism workshop at a large women's center that has been attempting antiracism change for a number of years. It is particularly useful because it is told by both a woman of color and a white woman, each involved in antiracism work, who have quite opposing perspectives of the same incident. During one exercise, called "Naming the Things That You Are Proud Of," the facilitator divided the participants into two groups, white women and women of color. Yasmin, a recently hired woman of color, describes her irritation at the exercise:

> There was an exercise—"Naming the Things That You Are Proud Of"— asking us to name the things that we were proud of having accomplished as a group. When people reported back, the white women had almost nothing. That made the women of color really angry. By you not putting anything, it shows that you are not aware of what you have. Although you think you have an analysis, ironically that analysis is actually minimizing the power that you have. *(interview transcript)*

Even when directly asked, the white women reported nothing—they sidestepped the question of examining their own histories and stories of "pride" and ethnicity. Yasmin sees this as a position of privilege. The white participants, in Yasmin's analysis, have the privilege of being able to distance themselves from their history and ethnicity, as well as the privilege to refuse to make themselves vulnerable in this exercise. Yet the white participants think that they are being antiracist precisely because, in refusing to participate in the exercise, they have refused to be proud of being white. Samantha, for instance, a white manager at the same organization, felt that the discussion was fruitful, and she was taken aback by the anger expressed by the women of color:

> We had a discussion about what makes us proud to be white, and a bunch of other things, which we had a very heated discussion around—and the women of color went off and talked about what made them proud to be women of color. A very loaded question. And so we decided that there was nothing that made us proud to be white, because . . . anyway. But, very, very, very good discussion. But women of color were really pissed off that white women couldn't come up with anything. And—imagine if we did come up with stuff! They would be saying, "How dare you take credit for stuff." *(interview transcript)*

Samantha's description shows that white women feel caught in the dichotomy of this exercise—how do they express feelings of pride without reinforcing racial superiority? "Naming the things you are proud of" puts women into a competition of knowledge and emotion about race and ethnicity, a competition that seems destined to fail—or perhaps to be "won" by the white participants who choose not to participate.

The exercise was perhaps meant to ethnicize whites or to counter the usual spectacle of women of color as ethnic resources. It failed to do either because the white participants chose not to make themselves vulnerable by treading into the dangerous territory of "white" identity and "white pride." The facilitators then failed to use the exercise as an opportunity to discuss whiteness, ethnic "pride," and the privilege inherent in being able to distance oneself from ethnicity.

"Naming things you are proud of" was perhaps also inspired by criticisms of "white guilt" which suggest that white participants' brooding on their own culpability can bog down discussion. Some writers have proposed that this focus on white guilt should be replaced by a "positive, proud, attractive antiracist white identity."[119] Sara Ahmed's biting commentary on the place of happiness in antiracism rejects this notion; she explicitly refutes the proposal that "antiracism resides in making whites happy or at least feeling positive about being white."[120] If we were to follow Sara Ahmed's critique, the white participants are right to refuse the possibility of a "positive white identity that makes the white subject feel good . . . about 'their' antiracism."

A dangerous strategy for all concerned, a focus on "white pride," particularly pride in white antiracism, means that racism becomes the province of some *other* "racist whites." This allows "progressive whites to be happy with themselves in the face of continued racism toward racialized others." As Ahmed suggests, in accepting white pride as a route to antiracism, they would be simply returning whiteness to its center. Clearly the white participants are aware of this jeopardy. And yet their refusal to participate in the "white pride" exercise ironically reflects a desire to instantiate their own identities—and perhaps their pride—as white antiracists.

Once again, the burden of being a teaching resource falls on non-white participants, who themselves learn nothing new about the construction of "white" or European culture from the perspective of white women. This discussion ends by merely highlighting that only non-white ethnicity is meant to be displayed and explored in these workshops, and that whiteness remains the invisible ethnic norm, supposedly with no stories to "uncover." In other words, the dead end of this exercise reinforces the wishful myth that whites are ignorant when it comes to race.

How might the white women have responded differently? What kinds of discussions of whiteness would avoid both a centering of happy white pride and a facile equivalence between white and non-white ethnicity? Is there a way to respond to this invitation to "pride" without falling into the escapism of the happy, positive white antiracism that Sara Ahmed critiques? Perhaps Samantha could have begun with a willingness to be vulnerable in discussions of whiteness. In that way she might have acknowledged the vulnerability of women of color as well as the privilege of her refusal to be vulnerable. Perhaps she could have begun with a willingness to express her critical thoughts on the notion of "pride." This line of inquiry might have led in some useful directions. Which sources of pride reflect privilege and exclusion, and which reflect challenges to relations of power? What might white women's stories of ethnicity and pride tell us about constructions of racial dominance and inferiority? It is the fear of revealing this knowledge that keeps Samantha and her colleagues quiet and in the safer place of ignorance and innocence.

The racial tensions between Métis writer and activist Maria Campbell and white actor Linda Griffiths, documented in *The Book of Jessica: A Theatrical Transformation*, mirror these difficulties of exploring knowledge of cultural histories and feelings of ethnic pride without exploring power relations of race. Campbell and Griffiths were estranged for years after finishing their play, *Jessica*, rich with the stories, spirituality, and history of Campbell's life and Métis ancestry.[121] A central tension arose during rehearsals when Campbell became infuriated that Linda Griffiths, who played the central Métis character, was eager to embrace Indigenous history and culture, yet content to be ignorant of her own Scottish and Welsh background. In conversation, Maria explains her dismay at Linda's ignorance:

> I started studying, reading all these books about the Scots and the Irish. . . . I found out that they had the same things, storytellers, music, sacred stones, mother earth, little people. They told me that when the British came they took the bagpipes away, banned them, because they knew that their music was sacred, gave them strength. . . . Then I think, "How could people who had been conquered in that way, come here and do exactly the same thing to Indians?" . . . It took me ages to realize that you didn't know about that stuff, and then I was appalled. . . . [H]ow could you be political without knowing your own stories?[122]

Here Maria Campbell links an understanding of one's history to an understanding of oppression. Like Yasmin, Campbell argues that these women are not only unaware of their own history, but are also in a position to place the burden of that knowledge on people of color. Linda Griffiths, however, responds to Campbell's critique by speaking about her own tremendous feelings of guilt, rather than by engaging Maria's emphasis on history:

> Maria, you have no idea what it's like to have what happened to Native people, the whole of it, finally hit you. . . . If you're Catholic and have any sense of guilt, justified or not, if guilt can ever be right, or make sense, then I was drowning in it. . . . Hard to stand up and say, "Oh yeah, well, six hundred years ago in Scotland my ancestors had a rough time too."[123]

Both the burden of sharing stories and the burden of understanding Linda's feelings fall on Maria.

In framing Indigenous people as the sole bearers of ethnic knowledge and cultural history, Linda Griffiths was also able to her to position herself as the arbiter of more "universal" values. Maria says to Linda,

> While you were being overwhelmed with my history and my oppression, you were making me feel like it was exclusively mine. I couldn't understand why you didn't know your own history, never mind the magic and power stuff. . . . At the same time, you . . . would talk about universal themes, and I would get so angry. "Universal," I'd think, "universal, what the fuck do you know about universal, when you think that we have a monopoly on oppression?"[124]

As the exchange between Maria Campbell and Linda Griffiths shows, the "other" is the bearer of a certain kind of racialized knowledge—while the knowledge of whites is imagined as universal and deracialized.

All of these accounts highlight that learning about race and diversity often means learning about people of color, often through the stories of participants of color. White participants, on the other hand, most often decline to contribute to the conversation, or are unable to produce the answers that facilitators desire.

David Bergner's account of recent antiracism workshops describes a similar impasse. In one small group activity, participants were asked to discuss, "What are some of the ways your race has shaped your life?" A white participant had difficulty answering the question. Bergner writes, "She struggled. She couldn't articulate much of anything about how she'd been shaped by being white."[125] Neither, for that matter, could Bergner himself answer in the manner expected by the facilitator.

Even if they do become more adept at answering these workshop questions, at reflecting on their privilege, and being introspective—which they likely will—it seems unlikely that their proficiency will get us closer to creating equitable workplace practices. It is true that these white participants sidestep their obligations in conversations about whiteness, but it is also true that there are few avenues for them to participate in ways that do not center their individual emotional responses or center white privilege.

The answer, however, is not to teach white participants how to become better at self-knowledge and self-reflection in group settings. Instead, all of these accounts highlight the limitations of any workshop practice that begins and ends with the individual experiences, knowledge acquisition, emotions, and identities of the participants.

KNOWLEDGE MARKS THE KNOWER

So how do this knowledge of race and racism mark the knowers? In the above accounts, white participants become identified as failed students who have not only been able to adequately undertake this educational project, this exercise of self-knowledge, but who may also be marked as having failed the antiracism project.

Overall, the educational approach to gaining knowledge of race and racism often reconfirms static associations between racial identity and lived experience. As Britzman and her colleagues argue in their examination of multicultural schooling, this approach is guided by a "mistaken faith in the stability of representations and language and in the obviousness of experience as the ground of truth."[126] The assumption, for example, is that people of color who speak in workshops or discussions of race represent stable identities that reflect a global experience, and that their stories will thus provide the most truthful knowledge. Not only may experience be established as a ground of truth in pedagogical attempts at discussing difference, but those with the most "authentic" experience can then also become a knowledge bank from which withdrawals may be made on demand.

Organizational discussions of antiracism can begin to echo the cultural celebrations of liberal multiculturalism to which they are often contrasted. In both antiracism and multicultural education there is a sense of planned authenticity in which display of a certain kind of difference becomes newly required[127] but also ensured through the structured activities of the workshop. In both cases, a "faulty" knowledge is addressed by the performance of scenes from people's lives. In both cases we see that, as Trinh Minh-ha suggests, the voice of difference can serve as a kind of entertainment or spectacle.[128] The literal display, "for all to see," of painful and intimate experiences is one example. Certainly, the theatricality of the slavery role-play rivals the cultural performances of multiculturalism. In this way, equity workshops can unintentionally echo the kind of multicultural ad campaigns that celebrate ethnic diversity. The confinements of representation in diversity workshops echo superficial celebrations in which people become synecdoches of "almond eyes," "exotic hairstyle," and "bronzed color."[129] While multicultural projects may circumscribe cultural characteristics and make them broadly representative of a community, we also need to be aware of similar tendencies in antiracism education. There is a parallel, for example, between multiculturalism's "positive images" and the tendency of antiracism education to limit Black histories to struggles against racism.[130]

The inevitable dismissals and denials also put people of color in the position of defending, reasserting, and reinforcing their identities as resources on racism. The focus begins and can remain on these individuals, the legitimacy of their stories, and by implication, the legitimacy of their identities. The use of experience as the basis of a newly required knowledge of racism may also be implicated in reproducing and creating new racial oppressions and identities. As in the "Naming the Things That You Are Proud Of" exercise and the exchange between Maria Campbell and Linda Griffiths, the telling of experience may circumscribe us, for example, as victims of racism or resources on racism. In other words, having to present our experiences as knowers of racism or as people of color produces and reproduces those categories. As Joan Scott suggests, descriptions of experience "take as self-evident the identities of those whose experience is being documented and thus naturalize the difference."[131]

As in antiracism workshops, these exchanges also underline the assumptions about the link between ignorance and racism, as well as assumptions about "better" knowledge and who should "know better." Maria assumes, because of Linda's and Paul's association with "political" theater, their university education, and their knowledge of their own histories, that they should "know better." Elly Bulkin, in her essay on racism and anti-Semitism, analyzes her own similar sentiments: "For Jewish women, the rage at the anti-Semitism of non-Jewish women of color sometimes seems far greater." She continues: "When, for instance, I am dyke-baited on my block by teenagers, white and Black, I am, in total defiance of logic, angrier at the Black kids than at the white ones: *they*, I mutter to myself, should *know better!*"[132]

The faith in knowledge as an antidote to racism marks women of color as either experts if they accept the invitation to dialogue, or as angry or indifferent if they reject the demand. Antiracism attempts are often bogged down by the way that angry or indifferent responses are linked to and fixed alongside racial identity, creating the stereotypical "angry woman of color." Anger against other women, anger against racism, indifference, or irritation at organizational efforts at antiracism, are clearly not embraced as part of the open sharing of emotion. Despite the entreaties to express one's feelings, certain expressions of emotion are acceptable; others are seen as pathological, dangerous, highlighting both the racialized representations of emotion and the emotional representations of race that can arise from feminist debates on antiracism. As organizations began to feel the presence of antiracist feminism in the 1990s, the "angry woman of color" also became a more persistent representation. As we saw in the previous chapter, the "angry woman of color" became a stand-in for the troubles of community organizations, as the media coverage of battles at Nellie's shelter demonstrated. In media and other accounts, anger often defines the representation of women of color and Black women fighting racial injustice.[133] This representation also draws its strength from the long-standing racial stereotyping of people of color as being less in control of their emotions and passions and therefore less fit to govern themselves. Several authors show how this representation of people of color has been used as a justification for practices and laws under colonial rule.[134]

Of course, there is no doubt that people of color do feel angry and upset about racism—certainly, several of my interviewees described anger as an inevitable part of fighting racism; they also expressed anger and bitterness toward white co-workers or board members who resisted antiracism critiques. At times this anger can erupt in open confrontation. In one organization, for example, there was an angry reaction, a "huge, huge fury," when the executive director made a highly unpopular hiring decision, employing a white woman as the first antiracism change coordinator. Marlene, a white woman active in antiracism efforts, describes the "terrible meeting" that followed, saying, "It was very hostile, it was very angry" *(interview transcript)*. But even these eruptions of angry feelings are clearly shaped by explicit concerns about avoiding the "angry woman of color" stereotype. While continual resistance to antiracism most often requires the continual containment of anger, this long-term containment can sometimes be punctuated by eruptions of quiet rage. Nina reflects on this pattern of anger in antiracism challenges:

We only show anger in extreme situations. . . . People usually try and be professional for a long time. But then, because there are certain blocks in the way, people end up saying things like, "Yeah, you are racist." . . . The same kinds of patterns show up. *(interview transcript)*

As Nina describes her anger, she takes pains to carefully preface her statement with the explanation that women of color activists "only show anger in extreme situations" and that they "usually try and be professional for a long time" *(interview transcript).*

Much of the time, however, the intensity of this anger is contained and controlled; activists remain quiet to "keep the peace," to "better" educate, to keep their jobs, and for a variety of other strategic reasons. Mimi's interview account, for example, discusses how she suppresses her intense anger toward a co-worker. Her co-worker ignores suggestions to integrate an antiracism perspective when counseling immigrant women, "because she thinks she is the expert on women's oppression of all kinds." Mimi declares, "It just enrages you." Yet her interactions with her colleagues remained, on the surface, courteous.

The open sharing that characterizes certain diversity workshops does not invite this anger. Nor should it. While I have taken pains to demonstrate that the invitation to share feelings is shaped by inequitable relations of race, my point is not that antiracism workshops should be encouraging *more* participants to share their feelings. My point is rather that when our diversity efforts emphasize knowledge about individuals and self-knowledge we very often produce and reproduce stereotypical categories of identity. These stereotypes in turn shape and limit our equity efforts.

For example, the persistent narrative that "women of color are always angry" or "don't care" is influential and limits future antiracism efforts. Consider the commentary of Samantha, a white senior manager of a large women's drop-in center. She is assessing the emotional aftermath of failed attempts at antiracism change in her organization:

Every time we come up against resistance, people shut down or drop out of the process, and just let it happen. . . . People don't understand the impact of when that happens. We all work really hard to come up with a decision, and four people say, "I don't care." Actually, that's not OK, it's not OK that you don't care, because you shouldn't be here if you don't care. *(interview transcript)*

Samantha's description demonstrates that an image of "women of color who don't care and shouldn't be here" has also grown out of these events. Their supposed lack of caring arises from emotional burnout; they may be cautious about or withdrawing from antiracism change because of past experience. But representing this as "lack of caring" contributes to racialized representations of both the failure of diversity efforts and of co-workers. The "women of color who don't care and shouldn't be here" then become a ready *explanation for* rather than a *symptom of* failure. Because of their supposedly inappropriate emotions, their supposed lack of caring, they become problems in and of themselves. Both their anger *and* their retreat are given as explanations for the failure of antiracism.

Similarly, Nina finds that after challenging racism at one organization, she has been branded as a "shit-disturber," rather than being labelled as antiracist, for example. She resents this representation of antiracism change and of herself—she resents the assumption that she raised critiques of racism with the intention of causing disruption:

They phoned me up and asked me if I would like to be on the board of [a women's organization]. And I said, "I'm burnt out, I was just on the board of [another women's organization]. Thank you, good-bye." But obviously something happened, because they said, "We heard you're a real shit-disturber." I said, "I'm not interested, I don't know what the hell you're asking me. I wasn't on the board of [the other organization] to be a shit-disturber, I wasn't doing that at [that organization] and I resent that." *(interview transcript)*

As Nina's story suggests, these representations may lead to what Susan Friedman calls the dead end of repetition, or a repetition of the primary scripts about race—denial, accusation, and confession.[135]

AUTHENTICITY AND IDENTITY

The significance given to the link between knowledge and identity is used to undermine antiracism activists in other ways. Consciousness-raising groups, struggles for diversity and representation, the use of caucuses, antiracism workshops—all are examples of ways in which these issues come to the foreground in organizations. Through antagonistic struggle over antiracism organizational change, political and racial identity can become a focus of resentment and conflict. Discussion of and resistance to antiracism can then become strongly tied to individuals and their identities and to a highly phenotypic discourse of "race." Mixed-race participants who have their authenticity called into question may also have their right to promote antiracism challenged. With evident pain, Carmen, who identifies as Black or as a person of color, describes the resistance from co-workers when she made several antiracism challenges:

> The final thing that [she] said, as if to wipe out everything I'd said, was "Well, Carmen, I don't think most people would consider you a woman of color." To wipe it out, as if to say, you don't know what you're talking about, you're just making it up. Or to say, "Well, people couldn't have been racist towards you because they don't think you're a woman of color." *(interview transcript)*

Because this organization's staff rejects Carmen's authenticity as a person of color, they have yet another basis on which to undermine and reject her antiracism challenge. As Razack observes, one's knowledge claims "can be easily dismissed as fake, inauthentic and non-feminist" when one fails to say what institutions want to hear.[136]

Challenges to these relationships between identity, knowledge, and experience are difficult. At an antiracism youth forum I coordinated with Indigenous youth, an adopted student withdrew from a session in tears. She felt that her inability to tell the same story of racism as her friends called into question her cultural and national identity. A focus on her individual identity and experience excluded her from participating in collective conversations about antiracism action relevant to her family and community.

But there are other possibilities. In the following example, Ginny refuses to be a part of the familiar "angry woman of color" story. In Ginny's account of a staff workshop, an antiracism facilitator attempts to frame the organizational dynamics by calling attention to and labeling Ginny's anger:

> The facilitator actually said to me, "I think you have a real fuck you attitude." And I said, "You're right, I do, and I actually have one towards you right now. . . . I resent being portrayed as the angry woman of color." And [my co-worker] Zahra also said to her, "I also find that really inappropriate." *(interview transcript)*

From the start, Ginny's emotions are framed as angry, belligerent, unproductive. But when she immediately names and directly subverts the facilitator's interpretation, Ginny undermines the force of this representation and changes the direction of the discussion.

If we were to closely analyze these representations, we might instead broaden the possibilities of changing them and the relations that produce them. It is evident that these representations of racial identity and emotion are neither static nor homogeneous. As narratives shaped through struggle, they are also continually challenged. For example, *Toronto Life*'s "angry women of color" article, described in chapter 2, also presented new opportunities for local, collective action. Letters to the editor, an organized demonstration, meetings with the editor, and media coverage of the demonstration not only challenged the representations of angry women of color, but also helped produce new images of antiracist feminists. As Butler advises, "the social categorizations that establish the vulnerability of the subject to language are themselves vulnerable to both psychic and historical change."[137]

CONCLUSIONS: FALLOUT AND RETREAT

Tracing those practices that emphasize equal sharing of personal experiences and emotions is crucial to understanding how racial identities and racial knowledge are represented inside organizations attempting change. Assumptions about how racism may be countered by better knowledge both support and are supported by these personalized interpretations of conflict-resolution, popular education, and consciousness-raising techniques. We see that "the personal is political" and its organizational expression, the consciousness-raising group, have a long and valued history that remains tenacious in contemporary practices of training, problem-solving, and conflict resolution, particularly with respect to equity and antiracism.

The result is that many approaches used to discuss racism or to forward diversity frame it as an individual, personal concern that requires education and reflection, rather than as a systemic problem requiring organizational solutions. Both acquiescence and challenges to these techniques are difficult. White participants may be expected to reflect on and share their experiences of being white or being racist. Non-white participants often become represented either as pedagogical resources or as angry or indifferent.

The emphasis on individual experience makes the inevitable dismissals and denials not only more painful but also more personal. Demands for disclosure can become intensely painful: my friend begins crying during one workshop; I wait until I get home. Critical race scholar Sherene Razack writes about how she finds herself "distressed to the point of tears" after one of her students leaves a seminar crying.[138] This has serious implications for any antiracism work in heterogeneous organizations. Because of these discouraging, draining, and painful encounters, many people of color drop out of and refuse to participate in mixed antiracism workshops. In interviews, activists consistently describe how the emotional stress is one of the primary limiting factors in continuing antiracism work.

These encounters sap a great deal of energy from vibrant change efforts; the emotional toll makes it impossible for many activists to continue working in their organizations—let alone on antiracism change. Phrases such as "burnt out," "in hiding," "in retreat" were used by those interviewed to describe the effects of failed antiracism efforts. The result is that many women retreat from social movements, the mainstream feminist movement, or from antiracism struggle. Sarah, a white senior manager at a women's drop-in, observed these long-lasting impacts after one particularly difficult organizational conflict: "I see women of color who I know, who were at [that organization], who are still hiding, almost." Carmen suggests that many women who are "burnt out" are returning to work in their own communities, rather than continue to advocate antiracism in mainstream feminist organizations:

> Everybody is just retreating into their own work. . . . Which, I can totally see why. The little bit that I've felt beat up trying to do that work, I can only imagine what it's like for women of color who have been really in there. . . . People who have really been struggling. I can see why they just want to go back and work in their communities. *(interview transcript)*

Audre Lorde shares this desire for retreat, saying that she had decided "never again" to speak to white women about racism, as that could be done by other white women "at far less emotional cost."[139] These incidents also emphasize that "sharing experiences" has different implications depending on local histories and power relations in an organization. For years, people may have felt compelled to be silent about ethnicity or racism in order to survive; a conversation about race and diversity means that suddenly this requisite silence coexists with a demand for disclosure. Benjamin observes that people of color who may have remained quiet in order to survive, economically and mentally, then become more vulnerable.[140] As one interviewee pointed out, the stakes of becoming involved in organizational antiracism efforts are high:

> You have to bare your soul, put your job on the line. . . . We knew we had
> to make a decision that we would be willing to lose our jobs. . . . Why
> should we be the ones that go? But in most situations, it is the women of
> color that get squeezed out. *(interview transcript)*

Perhaps these failures explain why these dynamics appear to be endlessly repeated. As Sarah complains, her organization has taken several
identical attempts at antiracism:

> We have done [antiracism] training already a couple of times. And so
> many of us who have been here for four or five years have already done
> some training. And it feels like Antiracism 101. *(interview transcript)*

As Benjamin has suggested, employers rarely expect "equity training/
training in diversity/ multicultural training" to generate the kind of radical change that antiracism and popular education espouse.[141] The focus
of training or conflict resolution is often weighted toward individual
transformation over organizational analysis.

For example, a women's center employee identifies the institutional
context that keeps discussion at a personal level:

> What happened was that things got named, but in a really personal way,
> so then the facilitator did a lot of conflict resolution. . . . What I find
> interesting is that [the facilitator] named the systemic stuff at [another
> women's organization], but then she lost her job. And maybe she had a
> few other experiences like that, where she realized that if you name the
> stuff, you lose the job. So when she got here, she kept things very per-
> sonal. And what happened then, it moved away from talking about the
> power differential between staff. *(interview transcript)*

In one women's drop-in center, the woman of color who first proposed hiring an antiracism facilitator was similarly disappointed:

> I hoped to have a change in programming, to address the needs of the
> women of color coming to the center, and for Denise [a white collective
> member] to have input in that decision-making. . . . For me the goal was
> to evaluate what we were doing, what was beneficial, and how we could
> change programming in a way that would help and reflect the women
> that came to the center. *(interview transcript)*

But, she says, she quickly realized that the facilitated meetings were not
designed to address organizational change. Similarly, the main outcome
of Pheterson's consciousness-raising project was simply to be "setting up
more consciousness-raising workshops."[142]

These organizational interpretations of "the personal is political"
help to explain the failures of some equity efforts. The resulting discussion techniques support a particular representation of antiracism: that
racism may be countered by changes in feelings and attitudes, and by
greater knowledge of personal experiences of racism. These techniques
also constitute racialized people as either the producers of that knowledge or recalcitrant obstacles to knowledge production. The apparently
contradictory relationship between an organization's avowed commitments to diversity and its sluggish progress can be explained in part
by pervasive techniques of emotional and personal disclosure and the
ways they support persistent constructions of racial knowledge and racial identities. Observing the emotional fallout of diversity workshops is,
in other words, a provocative starting point for understanding racialized
relations of affect, knowledge, and power.

ALTERNATIVES

What is the alternative to these literacy, contact, and therapeutic models? Several of the participants I interviewed point insistently to the way
forward. There are ways of building knowledge or transforming consciousness that may provide a reliable antidote to racism—collectively

creating our own strategies for local, systemic change, for example—but the conventional workshop approaches have not provided them. We must, as Dixon and colleagues suggest, shift the "prejudice-reduction model of change" toward "a collective action model of change, designed to ignite struggles" toward equity.[143] If it remains true to its original intent, a popular education approach provides a way for a community to create this collective model for change by drawing on its members' intimate knowledge of local practices and problems, and analyzing the conditions that produced those problems. This starting point of local, collective knowledge then allows people to work together to analyze the most effective sites, moments, and strategies for change in their organization. This is a very different kind of pedagogical project. Rather than focus on knowledge of others and self, we could collectively reflect on the principles and values that will guide strategies for change in our organization.[144]

4

Cry Me a River

And this white woman spent a lot of time bawling her eyes out during the meetings. So it was like [we] were the nasty women. And we were thinking, why is *she* crying? *We're* the ones who do all the shit work.

—Ginny *(interview transcript)*

T HE song "Cry Me a River" was at the top of the charts in 1955, but it has endured as a jazz standard and a popular idiom: "Now you say you're sorry / Well, you can cry me a river, cry me a river / I cried a river over you."[1]

Sung by countless jazz vocalists over the decades, its title has become a sarcastic retort: "Cry me a river," one says, when unimpressed by someone's misfortunes—especially misfortunes that seem minor compared to the troubles of others. The phrase is also an unfortunate echo of the emotional drama and tensions that arise when we talk about race. The lyrics to "Cry Me a River" evoke a key debate about the place of emotion in conversations about race. Are conversations about race and equity the appropriate place to reflect on one's shame, vulnerability, or empathy? Should we share our anger as it rises to the surface? Are antiracism workshops the place to disclose the feelings of discomfort and pain that people feel as they move through difficult conversations about

racism? Is the practice of "calling out," "cancelling," and publicly shaming people a constructive route to systemic change or merely cathartic?

The emotional temperature of conversations about race is high and
the rhetoric sharp. My interviewees used evocative language to describe
the tumultuous scene in meetings or workshops about antiracism: "She
was bawling her eyes out" or having a "freak out," they might say about
a white colleague who was reacting in defensive or emotional ways. But
quiet feelings of shame, empathy, or fear are also part of the roiling,
emotional undercurrents to any conversation about race. Some white
participants in antiracism workshops express hurt and anger on hearing
that they may contribute to or benefit from racism; they may feel deep
sadness, shock, and empathy on hearing stories of racism. Perhaps it is
the first time that they are hearing face-to-face, first-person accounts
of racist and colonial violence. However, the participants of color I interviewed are not impressed by these displays of emotion. "Why is *she*
crying?" her co-worker asks; why are we dealing with *her* tears now, she
wonders, when we are the ones who have been suffering all along? "Cry
me a river," we might paraphrase. "I cried a river over you."

Why *is* her co-worker crying?

These are not simply inconvenient or awkward moments. From angry
outbursts to therapeutic reflections, emotional preoccupations can dis-
arm and divert discussions about race. Resistant and defensive emotions
frequently stall dialogue and so become an obstacle to change efforts.
Anger, accusation, or "calling out" of co-workers or community members can become an additional dimension of antiracism debates. While
these public challenges of individuals can be an emotional release and
comfort to some, they also divert emotional energies away from systemic changes and precipitates emotional conflict. Many community
activists describe all these emotional moments as quagmires that drag
down the process of equity work. But, most importantly, too often our
efforts are shaped by these individualistic emotional interactions, when
they should be shaped by decolonial, antiracism values and collective
commitments to alternative practices.

Diversion and division are not the only concerns. Emotional displays also create a new locus of racialized tension. Emotional expression can itself become a site of contention and criticism in debates about race. Tears and anger become bound up with representations of racial privilege and racial stereotypes such as the "angry woman of color" and the "weeping white woman." The very act of a white person crying, for example, comes to represent the resistance of whites to antiracism, and therefore comes to represent racism itself.

In this chapter, I explore how and why open displays of emotion are at turns acceptable, desirable, contentious, and obstructive in conversations about race. Tracing the prevalence and tenacity of therapy and emotional connection as organizational practice, I demonstrate what therapeutic approaches constrain and what they produce during efforts at antiracism and diversity.

Discussions of race are too often motivated by individual psychic comfort and moral redemption—or what I refer to as "Feel-Good racial politics." But the expectation to share feelings, personal experience, and stories about racism—what I call the "Let's Talk" approach—heightens this affective climate. In the last chapter, I suggested that the Let's Talk approach has two modes, the popular education mode, which focuses on the experiences and stories of participants, and the therapy mode, which focuses on sharing and reflecting on emotions. While these two modes have much overlap and are often used simultaneously, in this chapter I focus on the therapy mode, exploring the long traditions of emotional disclosure, connection, and conflict resolution common to many feminist, collectivist, and not-for-profit organizations. I look closely at how the therapy mode encourages and shapes the emotional intensity and individualization of diversity efforts.

These practices carry weight precisely because they are articulated to values of social justice and community building. This explains why they continue to be tenacious and widespread as a form of problem-solving and conflict resolution. In turn, the open expression of emotions has become framed as an acceptable and even necessary part of antiracism efforts.

I begin this chapter by exploring the affective relations of race, suggesting why conversations about race evoke a gamut of feelings and emotional tensions, and documenting this range of disruptive emotional reactions described in my interviews. I then sketch the roots that give rise to the therapy mode in organizations, showing how psychosocial theories and collectivist values facilitate therapeutic approaches to discussion. The core of this chapter explores the myriad of ways that this therapeutic undercurrent limits, disrupts, or attenuates efforts at diversity and antiracism. As my interviews show, the therapy mode is rejected by antiracism activists, who both offer an alternative analysis of emotion and advocate an alternative focus on organizational practice.

AFFECTIVE RELATIONS OF RACE: WHY ARE CONVERSATIONS ABOUT RACE SO EMOTIONAL?

We must attend to both the impact of emotional responses that surround antiracism efforts as well as to the broader affective relations of these efforts. Some of these emotional responses are quite visible, easy to document, and obvious in their impact—the tears, defensive words, and so on. Less visible are the affective relations—the emotional threads that are always present in conversations about race, whether or not we are aware of them, and whether or not anyone in the room is crying, angry, or even aware of their own emotions. The author of *Feeling Power*, Megan Boler, asks, "How do socially- and culturally-constructed rules of emotion define identities, determine communities, and which bodies are permitted the privilege to express which emotions?"[2]

While I frequently use the term "emotions," it is a shorthand for these broader affective relations. Inspired by Sara Ahmed's concept of "affective economies," in her book *The Cultural Politics of Emotion*,[3] I am using the term "affective relations" not just as a synonym for emotions, but also as a way of highlighting the continual undercurrent of emotions in social life, the link between emotions and relations of power and knowledge. The term "affective relations" is particularly useful in bridging conventional distinctions between what is thought of as interior to us—the psyche, unconscious desires, inner feelings, thoughts—and what is thought of as exterior to us—outward emotional expressions and the social, cultural, and material relations that shape their meaning and value. This use of "affective relations" breaks down the distinctions among concepts such as psyche, emotions, feelings, affect, and social relations, and acknowledges that these are profoundly connected and mutually constitutive.

Emotions matter not just because they are obstructive, distracting, or annoying—although that is also relevant. They matter because of the ways they are valued and devalued, attached to gendered and racialized identities, and linked to notions of ethics, morality, and justice.

To repeat Megan Boler's questions, "How do socially- and culturally-constructed rules of emotion define identities, determine communities, and which bodies are permitted the privilege to express which emotions?" The affective relations of race are underscored by scholars who have highlighted the psychic investments in racial oppression.[4] Sociologist Cynthia Levine-Rasky notes that many critiques of whiteness miss the "profound emotional investment in the everyday practice of whiteness."[5]

In *The Emotional Politics of Racism*, Paula Ioanide shows that "emotional rewards and losses play a central role in shaping how and why people invest in racism, nativism, and imperialism in the United States." Public feelings about race, argues Ioanide, "are not simply individual sentiments, they have been essential to manufacturing consent."[6]

These are not just contemporary questions. Scholars have traced the emotional, moral, and psychic underpinnings of both racism and colonialism. In his book *Black Skin, White Masks*, psychiatrist Frantz Fanon argued that the Black-white relationship had become "a psychoexistential complex" and that only a psychoanalytical analysis "can lay bare the anomalies of affect that are responsible for [its] structure."[7] He hoped, he said, "by analyzing it to destroy it."[8] Leaving France to work as a psychiatrist in 1950s colonial Algeria, Fanon later observed first-hand the psychic effects and structure of colonialism.

These affective relations of race have also been relevant in social movements, particularly those dedicated to racial and social justice. The fight against slavery, for example, depended on whites cultivating feelings of sympathy, argues Amit Rai, feelings that in turn required and reinforced a position of superiority. While sympathy may now appear to be an outdated political sentiment, Rai demonstrates that notions of solidarity and sympathy continue to support unequal relations of power in global politics today.[9]

A GAMUT OF EMOTIONS: TEARS, TEARS, AND INDIGNANCE

Discussions about race and equity in organizations are often met with emotionality and emotional resistance. In my interviews, the most intense emotions seemed to arise when racism was discussed in meetings among staff or board members. As we saw in chapter 2, emotional reactions appear at all levels of activity surrounding antiracism: initiation, resistance, aftermath. Over and over, those I interviewed described how some of their white co-workers or board members became very emotional and agitated when antiracism criticisms were raised. Participants feel moved to express empathy, cry openly, give and receive emotional care, and express rage. White participants may speak in an emotional manner about their commitment, hope, solidarity, complicity, guilt, lack of complicity, failure to understand, disbelief, and hurt that they have been accused.

This emotional climate is one that surrounds and affects all participants. Although the conventions of public emotional expression mean that certain people will be more comfortable expressing emotion openly, these affective relations implicate all, even those who are silent. Participants of color also talk about feeling angry, withdrawn, despairing, or tearful, although it may not be as openly expressed. Anger and shame may be expressed by individuals, but it may also be directed *toward* individual co-workers and community members, often directing emotional energies away from systemic and organizational changes that are needed.

These observations are echoed by other studies. Sociologist Ruth Frankenberg, for example, tells the story of how white feminists like herself first reacted to antiracism criticism:

At worst—and it appeared from where I was standing that "worst" was much of the time—it seemed as though we white feminists had a limited repertoire of responses when we were charged with racism: confusion over accusations of racism; guilt over racism; anger over repeated criticism; dismissal; stasis. . . . Too often, I witnessed situations in which, as predominantly white feminist workplaces, classrooms, or organizations tried to move to more multiracial formats or agendas, the desire to work together rapidly deteriorated into painful, ugly processes in which racial tension and conflict actually seemed to get worse rather than better as the months went by.[10]

Gloria Anzaldúa elaborates on the gamut of emotion in her classroom discussions of antiracist feminism, describing the students' feelings of "confusion, helplessness, anger, guilt, fear of change and other insecurities."[11] Writing about the conflict at a Toronto feminist organization, one journalist recounts that reactions to accusations of racism "varied from sympathetic to ragingly defensive."[12]

The majority of emotional responses in my interviews fall under four key categories: empathy and tears, hurt and tears, defensiveness and tears, anger and indignance. I document each here, before moving to a closer analysis of the organizational context and effects of these emotional reactions.

Openly empathetic responses are common. Often these moments are accompanied by tears and broad expressions of the sadness, pain, and solidarity that people feel on learning about racism. In one interview narrative, a white woman comes to a woman of color caucus meeting and begins weeping as she expresses her empathy with the experiences of women of color. Samantha, a white woman involved in antiracism change in her organization, reflects on her own tearful reaction, saying: "One horrible incident makes me want to cry when I hear about it."

In most interview accounts, however, tears arise from feeling hurt, betrayed, or personally accused. In other words, when an issue of racism or equity is raised, some members of the organization may feel hurt or overwhelmed and begin to cry.

In other cases, tears support more confrontational responses to anti-racism. In one organization, staff members presented a document to the board that outlined organizational problems of racism. The result was a particularly acrimonious board meeting. Lynn describes the emotional aftermath: "And [one of the board members] was bawling her eyes out, and saying that she wasn't going to apologize for anything that she had done."

Similarly, Vijaya relates a number of confrontational and tearful exchanges about racism in feminist publishing:

And, we got into the interpersonal. . . . One or two white women had a freak-out session around the issue of race, and our rejecting a particular piece, or our comment around language.

[Can you remember what kinds of things they said or did?]

I've blocked it out . . . but I remember a woman crying. I remember women crying. . . . White women cry all the fucking time, and women of color never cry.

Finally, confrontational anger was a commonly described emotional response in my interview commentary. Megan Boler refers to this kind of anger as "defensive" or "indignant" anger[13]—a protectionist anger that arises when one's identity or beliefs are threatened. Vijaya, a woman of color with years of experience in feminist and nonprofit organizations, describes "the interpersonal responses to [challenges to] racism—like people's resistance, their hostility, and their indignancies." She says, "I think anywhere I've ever gone, it has been anger, and indignance: How can you call me racist?" Fiona Nicoll's university students in Australia similarly expressed sentiments that echo the familiar and angry "Are you calling me racist?"[14]

Notably, my interviewees used terms that describe immature and unwarranted anger. Rayna's description identifies these confrontational responses as typical:

> The indignant response, anger, the rage that turns into tears, the foot-stomping, temper tantrums, which are very typical responses. Every single organization that I have been in, every single one. So I realized that it wasn't about me . . . after a while [*laughter*]. (*interview transcript*)

Anzaldúa's commentary also highlights anger as a primary emotion that surfaces when racism is discussed. She recounts,

> At first, what erupted . . . was anger—anger from *mujeres*-of color, anger and guilt from whites, anger, frustration, and mixed feelings by Jewish-women [*sic*] who were caught in the middle . . . and anger and frustration on my part.[15]

The patterns described in my interviews echo what Charlotte Bunch refers to as "divisive reactions" to diversity in the women's movement.[16] Indeed, almost all of the "divisive reactions" that Bunch names are emotional: guilt, shame, withdrawal, hurt, resentment, and defensiveness.

Why have these kinds of responses been common, and why have they been considered acceptable, in some cases even expected? A key to understanding these responses is the influence of theories that represent open emotional expression as a progressive, political, or therapeutic act. In this way, emotions such as tears and anger may obstruct antiracism while appearing politically consistent with progressive values.

THE THERAPY MODE

The success of self-help books about interpersonal communication and the proliferation of talk show formats and reality TV based on increasingly intimate revelations of anguish is the most obvious manifestation of the influence of the therapy mode. In the context of family relationships and mental health, professional therapy and popular psychology have had increasing acceptability, popularity, and success. While the role of emotional expression in social life can be traced to a number of roots, it is the practice and discourse of psychotherapy, including the traditions of psychoanalysis, self-help literature, and popular psychology, that has had a powerful influence on how we think about and value practices of emotional expression.

In the context of diversity workshops, the therapy mode gains additional weight from its foundation in theories and practices that underlie feminist, community, and collectivist organizations. In community and feminist organizations, and in other spaces inspired by the ideals of new social movements, therapeutic discourse is actually strengthened by political and organizational ideals.

There are long-standing conventions of emotional disclosure, connection, therapy, and conflict resolution common to many feminist and collectivist organizations. In the previous chapter, I used the phrase Let's Talk to describe this powerfully influential approach, one that pushes us toward talk, personal experiences, confession, and the therapeutic as ideal routes to knowledge, self-knowledge, and connection. These practices carry weight precisely because they are articulated to values of social justice and community building, explaining why they continue to be tenacious and widespread as a form of problem-solving and conflict resolution. So widespread and tenacious, in fact, that the open expression of emotions has become framed as an acceptable and even necessary part of antiracism efforts. Practices such as consciousness-raising, therapy, and sharing experiences underlie modes of discussion in many organizations, particularly those inspired by collectivist, alternative, or egalitarian ideals. The inspiration can be traced to feminist theories that have framed open emotional expression as both *natural* and *political*.

In her book *Cold Intimacies*, which traces links between emotion and capitalism, sociologist Eva Illouz echoes the significance of both the therapy mode and feminism in understanding how emotional expression has become central to public spheres:

> While some argue that television and radio have been responsible for the sentimentalization of the public sphere, I suggest rather that it is therapy—joined with the language of economic accountability and with feminism—which has made emotions into micro public spheres, that is, domains of action submitted to a public gaze, regulated by procedures of speech and by values of equality and fairness.[17]

THEORIES OF EMOTION, ETHIC OF CARE, AND THERAPY

The tenacity of therapeutic practices in antiracism efforts can also be traced to broadly influential theories of emotion and care. Psychosocial theories about women's ethic of care and feminist psychoanalysis have shaped organizational practice and, consequently, conflict surrounding antiracism.

The observation that in Western thought a woman has been traditionally perceived as primarily emotional rather than rational, and therefore closer to nature,[18] has been taken up in various ways by feminist theory.[19] While radical feminist theories that confirm rather than challenge this essentialist framing of women have been widely criticized and discredited,[20] this perspective has nevertheless been broadly influential on popular discourse,[21] and in turn on community organizations more broadly. Since this stream of radical feminist thought identifies the technocratic and instrumental with the masculine, for example, it has helped to cultivate an ideal in which feminist and progressive community organizations should emphasize feeling, emotion, and the interpersonal.[22] Though it has a variety of roots, the idea that emotional expression and sensitivity is key to a more progressive organizational practice has become an enduring one.

Overall, feminist psychosocial theories have historically emphasized women's capacity for empathy and care as well as the political importance for women to celebrate these emotions. One of the most well-known is Carol Gilligan's study of women's "ethic of care."[23] Her central thesis is that women's moral reasoning is based on an ethic of caring for or taking care of others. According to Gilligan's analysis, "women not only define themselves in a context of human relationship, but also judge themselves in terms of their ability to care."[24] Gilligan's theories have been enormously popular, had considerable effect on popular discourses of emotion and morality,[25] and now continue to have profound impact on organizational practice and popular culture.[26]

It is a natural corollary, then, for this perspective to be integrated as a central feature of feminist practice. The feminist therapy mode provides the clearest example, one that has also become an enduring influence within community organizations and antiracism discussions and workshops.

Feminist therapy's emphasis on caring and nurturing has its roots in the predominant perspective of feminist psychosocial theories about empathy and care.[27] The "taking care" or "ethic of care" analysis has shaped much of feminist therapy's aims and perspectives.[28] In particular, feminist therapy modes advocate that women need to focus on taking care of themselves and each other, because they have been raised to take care only of others.[29]

The therapy mode we see in many organizations has grown out of the philosophy and aims of the feminist movement, both in North America and Britain.[30] In particular, feminist therapy is closely tied to the "the personal is political" ideology and seen as a natural expression of feminist goals and ways of doing things. Just as early feminism created spaces for women to "come together and meet to break the silence about their experiences," feminist therapy developed as a place to address the psychological dimension of these experiences of victimization.[31]

In addition, rage at domination and oppression has been an important part of the feminist movement; these emotions are said to have "empowered the second wave of feminism."[32] Both feminist practice and therapy have encouraged women to express their anger at oppression, not only "for instrumental purposes, but toward a larger project of claiming knowledge and identity."[33] So significant has this trend been that Burack refers to the "fervor of discovering and employing depths of rage, despair and hatred" in feminist organizing.[34]

In other words, a number of influential feminist theories and practices see the expression of women's emotions as universally beneficial and politically progressive.

EMOTION AS THE BASIS FOR COLLECTIVE ORGANIZATIONS

Of course, emotional debates about race are not limited to feminist organizations nor even to social movement contexts. However, the emotional climate of many social movements and other progressive spaces is further intensified by the political weight and history of the therapeutic ideals developed within the feminist movement.

I sketched a history of "the personal is political" in the previous chapter and showed how it has helped to cultivate the use of personal experience and feelings as a source of knowledge in antiracism and diversity workshops. Here I focus more closely on how "the personal is political," consciousness-raising, and feminist therapy have had profound effects in two related areas: forms of organization and modes of discussion. In both forms of organization and modes of discussion, we can see that emotional connection forms a significant foundation and everyday practice.

The grassroots and collective feminist organization, for example, has its roots in these ideals; Briskin[35] calls the collective feminist organization an "outgrowth" of "the personal is political." Its basic elements include collective organization, sharing of all tasks, consensus decision-making, and "emphasis on personal experience."[36] In reaction to the rationalist, hierarchical organization, these collectivist organizations have emphasized their personalized nature.[37] Rather than bureaucratic efficiency, it is consensus, solidarity, and egalitarianism that are favored.[38]

In building these collectivist organizations, it has been the goal of feminists to more strongly link personal relationships, communities, and work life with feminist philosophy. Costain, for example, has documented the importance of social aspects or personal relationships for keeping members of feminist organizations involved.[39]

However, it is important to note that, just as "the personal is political" is not unique to feminism, neither is this form of organization. A collectivist or egalitarian form of organizing that focuses on personal connection and mutual support is a form common to many spaces inspired by these ideals. A large majority of social-change groups cited social-emotional group support to be one of the specific goals of their groups.[40] Community organizers and social anarchist writers have also explicitly emphasized the personal aspects of social life as a part of their political philosophy: egalitarian human relationships and decentralized organizations are seen as key. Bookchin, for example, advocates the "affinity group," developed by Spanish anarchists in the 1920s, as a way for individuals and communities to recover "personal power over social life."[41] John Clark, in advocating the development of "small personalistic groups," argues that "there must be a practice of *psychosocial* transformation."[42] Similarly, Lustiger-Thaler distinguishes the Green Party from other environmental groups because of its focus on interpersonal process. For the Green Party, he says, the notion of process was itself a large part of the task of being political.[43] Clearly, close communities are a powerful aspect of many social movement organizations, reinforced by rituals of verbal and physical expressions of emotion and intimacy.

The open expression of emotions has been essential not only to feminist analysis and action, then,[44] but also to all spaces inspired by these new social movement ideals, including many educational spaces. In many of these feminist and "alternative" organizations, the sharing of feelings and personal experience has become prescriptive and normative. Emotion seen as more desirable than reason, expressing emotion is seen as both therapeutic *and* political. Sharing feeling is meant to be good for individuals, organizations, and the whole movement. To some extent, the open sharing of feelings is seen as a defining feature of the feminist, alternative, or collectivist organization.

For example, emotional rituals are seen as important to building social ties and solidarity. Many social movement communities are constructed not only on the basis of common social location, but also on a familial sense of connection and solidarity. A feminist or alternative community is typically idealized as one in which its members have caring feelings toward each other and share the intimacy of family members.[45] Sherryl Kleinman, in her ethnographic study of an alternative health organization, shows how intimate "solidarity-producing rituals" such as circles, hugs, and retreats were key to building a shared vision of community.[46] These organizational rituals reinforced this key idea:

> the idea that the organization was truly a community in which those who opened their hearts received others' appreciation. This too reinforced the staff members' sense of specialness, because they were part of this loving community.[47]

In other words, strong emotions can reinforce the idea of the alternative organization as a loving community—a family.

The focus on emotional needs is not only expected, but ritualized; both the therapeutic approach and the consciousness-raising group authorize a ritual confession of feelings. Cassell hints at the techniques of self-disclosure and self-presentation that are required in consciousness-raising meetings, noting that "those with previous movement experience have mastered the confessional mode, ritual phraseology, expected behaviors."[48]

Emotional disclosure is explicitly associated with empowering women and building feminist solidarity.[49] Display and use of emotion in social movement activism is in itself defined by many theorists as both feminine and feminist. If women depart from this compassionate role, then they may be described as "masculinist," in both activist and academic commentary.[50] Feminist organizations have also been described as having a distinct "emotion culture."[51] One national conference had several "vibes watchers"—women whose job it was to monitor the emotional climate and advise the participants when to take a deep breath, take a moment of silence, or scream.[52]

A feminist health clinic studied by Morgen had regular "feelings meetings" to air out the emotional "fallout" of their work, as well as interpersonal conflicts: e.g., "I'm getting hurt by your personal style."[53] Within feminist organizations such as drop-in centers or shelters whose aim it is to provide support for women in their experiences of oppression, therapy is also a significant aspect of the services offered, although most staff members are not professional therapists. In other words, there is a strong ethos and practice that frames open emotional expression as desirable not only for organizational and personal health, but also for political action. As Verta Taylor notes in her study of feminist organizations, "emotion is both a basis for defining oneself and a tool for change."[54]

ANTIRACISM AS THERAPY?

We can see that a number of strands come together to support open emotional expression as universally desirable and politically vital in many organizations: feminist theories of emotion, the conventions and prevalence of therapy, and the values of collectivist organizations.

However, just as scholars have shown that theories of women's oppression have been incorrectly universalized from white, middle-class women's experiences, so too must we recognize that feminist theories of emotion have led to an inaccurate universalization of the role of emotions in women's lives within collectivist organizations—particularly when it comes to antiracism efforts.

Observations of antiracism workshops reveal that, despite the dominant discourse of open emotional expression, this is no space of equal sharing. Instead, while participants of color are asked to share their feelings and experiences concerning racism, it is frequently white participants who openly express their emotions of fear, anger, and despair, and are supported in doing so by a strong tradition and practice of emotional expression and sharing.

My interviews show that the therapy mode has been particularly significant as a vehicle for the expression of white participants' "feelings" about racism in organizational or political discussions. As I showed in chapter 3, for example, consciousness-raising techniques of self-disclosure have been directly translated to discussions of racism. Maya tells how an antiracism workshop in her feminist collective was referred to as a "consciousness-raising session for white women." Antiracism workshops that use the consciousness-raising mode have provided white women, as Vron Ware observes,[55] a space for "working out feelings" about racism, a place to share their "guilt and fear."[56] For example, Ware describes a Manchester group, Women Against Racism and Fascism (WARF), who "advocated consciousness-raising in groups as a way of 'dealing with' what it called personal racism."[57] As she shows, white feminists have often used their formal discussions of racism for personal exploration, precisely because consciousness-raising provided them an explicitly feminist mode to do so.

Contemporary antiracism workshops continue this emotional trajectory. Robin DiAngelo, a sought-after facilitator, highlights emotionally focused tactics in her popular book *White Fragility* and in her own workshops. While DiAngelo also points to the obstructive emotional responses common to antiracism workshops, rather than moving away from an emotionally focused approach, she suggests a list of alternative emotions. Instead of fragile, defensive emotions, DiAngelo suggests, whites could try to "have very different feelings," feeling such as gratitude, excitement, guilt, and so on. These feelings, DiAngelo implies, could themselves produce different, better behaviors. She advocates that people focus on therapeutic practices such as "Reflection" and "Apology."[58]

Sherryl Kleinman's step-by-step description of conflict in Renewal, an alternative health organization, is illustrative of how the therapy mode is commonly used as a form of problem-solving and conflict resolution. Kleinman found that members were strongly encouraged to openly express their painful emotions as the most sincere and effective way to resolve a conflict: "Members' rules for self-disclosure fit with their idea that all conflict results from personal issues and uncomfortable feelings about oneself or others."[59] Within the organization's board meetings and retreats, the staff and board members worked to make sure that all conflict was dealt with through intimate personal interaction and explicitly emotional expression. Whenever there was any conflict or complaint, the organization's members were expected to express their feelings directly to another individual: "They expected the participant to talk in the first person, admit a 'negative' feeling (anger or fear), and address that thought or feeling directly to the person he or she had conflicts with."[60] At Renewal, says Kleinman, all interpretation of feelings was through a therapeutic mode. In fact, the therapeutic focus *reinforced* their view that they were an "alternative" organization.

This technique is echoed in many organizations attempting antiracism change. In formal meetings, informal discussions, and workshops, people of color are expected to confront, directly persuade, or "share" their feelings with whites in their workplaces or organizations. In my own experience with conflict resolution at my environmental organization, a hired facilitator asked me and my co-worker to each write down our concerns about the other, being careful to use only "I" statements, a standard technique (e.g., "I feel that you don't respect my skills"). In one organization I studied, the staff collective had come to an impasse after two women of color began to raise concerns about racism in the center's programming and division of labor. The response of the board was to hire an antiracism facilitator who used this same conflict-resolution or therapeutic mode. Ginny, one of the women of color I interviewed, complained that discussions of racism during these regular sessions therefore became focused on individual personalities and emotions, rather than on organizational change:

> She [the facilitator] turned it into a therapy session. She would say, "Ginny, it sounds like you think that Denise doesn't understand what you are trying to say." She basically did a personality test. I was supposed to be a visual person, whereas Denise was more of an oral person. *(interview transcript)*

Zahra, a co-worker of Ginny's, also shares her frustration with the therapeutic, Let's Talk approach of the antiracism facilitator. In particular, Zahra argued that the facilitator's focus on the emotional was overly therapeutic and irrelevant in a workplace discussion of organizational problems. "All she [the facilitator] talked about was, 'How do you feel, and how do you feel?'" *(interview transcript)*.

Shalini, a young woman of color working on short-term contract in an anti-violence advocacy group, describes a similar conflict-resolution tactic. At a board meeting, Shalini was taken aback by the racist attitudes of a board member toward programming for Black youth. She later raised her concerns with senior management. The director responded that she and the other woman of color involved in the organization should confront the offending board member directly. In other words, the response was a therapeutic form of conflict resolution, rather than strengthening organizational support for antiracism programming. Finally, the responsibility for dealing with this racist incident reverted to the woman of color with the most junior and precarious position, who was expected to initiate a personalized confrontation about racism. Incredulous, Shalini refused: "There was no way I should have to do that" *(interview transcript)*.

We can see that the therapeutic conflict-resolution mode continually reverts to personality, emotions, and personal style as explanations for racism. By mining the intimate and personal field, it hopes either to discover the roots of conflict or to smooth it over by teaching people how to talk to each other. Self-knowledge is an explicit goal, as is greater knowledge of "people skills." Yet we can see that these approaches also reproduce a certain knowledge of racism and therefore of suitable antiracism practice.

While the history of feminist theory and organizing gives particular weight to these discussions in feminist organizations, however, it also has enduring influence in any conversations about race and diversity. Many conversations or workshops about race and antiracism continue to use this emotionally based, personalized mode of connection and conflict resolution. Antiracism consultant Robin DiAngelo, for example, advocates the use of reflection and apology in her concluding chapter, "Where Do We Go From Here?"[61] She illustrates this by beginning the chapter with a personal story in which a Black co-worker makes her aware that she has been racist toward her during a meeting; DiAngelo meets with her and apologizes.[62] "After I had vented my feelings (embarrassment, guilt, shame, and regret," writes DiAngelo, "we did our best to identify how I had reinforced racism."[63] Yet we don't hear this story from the co-worker's perspective—and so the emotional labor of communicating with colleagues about their behavior, hearing their apology, and forgiving them are not acknowledged. While it is clear that these apologies can provide some emotional relief to the person apologizing and help smooth things over in the workplace, we rarely acknowledge the demands these personal apologies place on the listener. To be clear, I believe that apologies and making amends are important aspects of personal and professional relationships. However, DiAngelo's recommendation that white people "learn to apologize better for racism" must be interpreted through the lens of Feel-Good racial politics. These apologies are both ineffectual for antiracism organizational change and burdensome to those bearing the apologies and carrying the weight of forgiveness. Individual, emotionally based strategies such as learning to apologize better must be understood in the context of Feel-Good racial politics in which an apology is linked closely to the individualistic framing of racism, and the desire to feel good and forgiveness denotes a kind of racial innocence.

In other words, the "therapy mode" can both shape and authorize resistant responses to antiracism efforts. Discussing feelings and emotions provides a place for white participants to express their resistance, their guilt, their fears of change, or their anger that they are being challenged. The therapeutic approach and feminist theories of emotion help to frame this emotional disclosure as a natural, universal, and political response, rather than an expression of historical racial privilege.

Looking more closely at the commonly observed responses of some white participants in antiracism discussions, a pattern of nonformal techniques and rituals of emotion emerges. These techniques or rituals include:

- Crying and talking about how bad one feels about racism
- Confessions of white privilege
- Confrontational or resistant responses accompanied by tears or anger
- Taking care of white participants who are crying or emotionally distraught
- The apology as a route to forgiveness, repair, social and political connection, repair, bridging rifts, making amends, surmounting anger[64]

The influence of therapeutic practice and feminist theory shapes the responses of everyone who surrounds the tearful or angry participant. An emphasis in feminist organizations on "taking care" of each other and on the community organization as "family" burden these practices of emotional expression with political and normative weight. All participants become compelled to minister to emotional expressions, rather than to continue with discussion.

Yasmin, a feminist of color who observed the difficulties of antiracism efforts in a number of organizations, believes that these therapeutic conventions were a critical factor. The emotional reactions of white feminists facing antiracism criticism are, she argues, supported by the expectations women may have of their organization—the workplace—as a therapeutic space:

Over and over again, I noticed, in terms of emotion—is that people blur the lines between their workplace and the place of therapy, that the organization is going to give them therapy. *(interview transcript)*

She notes that, in this therapeutic space, focus immediately shifts from the concerns of women of color to white women's emotional needs. For example, in one women's service organization Yasmin raised concerns that the diversity of clients' needs was not being met. Her co-workers' responses, however, immediately centered on how Yasmin's criticism affected their own feelings, their own needs for emotional support. Yasmin surmises that the therapeutic environment of her feminist community organization shaped these reactions:

> There's a lot of room for, emphasis placed on, feelings. There isn't a lot of emphasis placed on being professional, working towards goals and objectives . . . there's so much room for accommodation [of personal feelings]. . . . There's this expectation, spoken and unspoken, that there's going to be a place for feelings, for people's personal needs. The thing that I saw over and over was that it was *employees* that were getting their needs met [rather than women coming to the center for help]. *(interview transcript)*

Ginny, a member of a women's drop-in center collective, also observes the obstructive effects that these therapeutic practices may have when antiracism concerns are raised. In this case, Ginny and a co-worker had criticized the lack of attention paid to the needs of women of color and immigrant women. They also pointed out the inequitable division of power and labor between white and non-white collective members, demonstrating that non-white collective members did a far greater share of administrative and financial work. As a result, Ginny found it particularly ironic that it was a white co-worker who began crying when she and her co-worker, both women of color, raised their concerns in collective meetings:

And this white woman spent a lot of time bawling her eyes out during the meetings. So it was like [we] were the nasty women. And we were thinking, why is *she* crying? *We're* the ones who do all the shit work . . .

[*Why was she crying?*]

Because her *feelings* were hurt. Because no matter what. . . . She would say verbally, "I understand the issues," but I still think that she just personalized everything. *(interview transcript)*

Ginny goes on to describe how her co-worker's tearful reaction extended over weeks and spilled over into her daily work. Ginny exclaims, "She was blubbering all the time. She would do it in the drop-in center!" Ginny's account demonstrates not only the intensity of emotional response, but also its potential effects on organizational work and on antiracism change:

We started talking about it outside of work, because it became very stressful. . . . Now we had opened this can of worms, and now we had to work with this woman. She would try and make us feel bad on a daily basis. She would come in looking like she had been bawling her eyes out all night, looking like a wreck, basically saying, "Don't talk to me about any of these issues, I can't handle it." And she was doing that all the time. *(interview transcript)*

The therapeutic and conflict-resolution framework of the original antiracism meeting allows the white co-worker to use her emotional distress to communicate not only resistance ("Don't talk to me about any of these issues") but also vulnerability ("I can't handle it") and reproach ("She would try to make us feel bad"). Describing her co-worker's tearful reaction, Ginny elaborates on this point: "I think a lot of her crying was out of just feeling sorry for herself, of losing power and control. But it was hurt feelings. I think she felt betrayed, because she just didn't

realize . . ." What effect do these affective relations have on representations of race, and on efforts at antiracism? Ginny finds that her white co-
worker's tears had the effect of positioning the women of color working
on antiracism as the problem, the cause of distress, and the "nasty" ones.

These interactions demonstrate that racial hierarchies shape not just
material privilege, but also cultural and emotional space. Who is more
comfortable crying, and why? Who bears the tears? In this interview
account, it is the white co-worker who spends days crying, although the
women of color have adequate cause for their own tears. As Ginny asks,
"Why is *she* crying? *We're* the ones who do all the shit work." Recall, for
example, Vijaya's statement "White women cry all the fucking time, and
women of color never cry." As Rose Baaba Folson observes in her commentary on the German feature film *Aimée & Jaguar*, the true story of a
love affair between a Nazi officer's wife and a Jewish woman, privilege allows some the luxury of "expressing grief, anger, frustration, just as they
come, whilst others need to suppress these emotions, to be expressed at
an appropriate time, or not at all."[65]

TAKING CARE

Carol Gilligan's finding that women "judge themselves in terms of their
ability to care" has made theories about women's ethic of care enormously popular, and to some extent self-fulfilling.[66] One outcome is that
care of the emotionally distraught can become paramount in many organizational discussions, diverting attention from antiracism itself. Several
interviewees said it was common for discussion to be halted as women
"took care" of a white colleague distressed by discussions of racism. Maya
describes how this dynamic of "taking care" unfolded in the antiracism
sessions at the women's publishing collective where she worked:

> It was incredibly painful. One of the meetings was supposed to happen
> in my home. And I had one of the white women come and accuse me of

being racist, and bawling her eyes out. And all of the white women taking care of her. It was horrific. *(interview transcript)*

Similarly, speaking of her experience in feminist organizing in Germany, Rose Baaba Folson says that when women of color decided to raise issues of race in the feminist movement or at feminist conferences, it was common for some white women to "break down" emotionally: "They would be having breakdowns. And then everything stops. And who is looking after who?"[67]

These events reflect a clear hierarchy that privileges emotion and care in feminist and alternative settings, one that is difficult to challenge without appearing to be unfeminist or uncommitted to the organization's values. Zahra describes how the emotional care of individual women coming to the women's center was always supposed to supersede her distress about their racist behavior. However, when she objected to this hierarchy of therapy before challenges to racism, her co-workers implied that she did not understand "women's issues":

Any sort of behavior was acceptable. So if someone screamed in my face, that was acceptable, because she's having a difficult time adjusting. So in the name of suffering, in the name of transition, behavior like that, hostility, anger which was expressed, racism, that was all secondary. And my inability to tolerate that, was a sign that I don't understand women's issues. I'm not with it. I'm too rushed. I don't want to give women space. This is a drop-in. We have to let things go really slowly, at women's individual pace. We can't rush anyone's progress. *(interview transcript)*

"Taking care" also means that emotional resistance to antiracism efforts receives undue space. For example, Samantha places a heavy emphasis on emotional care over organizational change, as she reflects on the hardship and "mourning" involved in challenging racism:

And, what [the facilitators] were saying, is that . . . change work is hard and new and different. And that we don't really know a lot about it. And, what she was saying, is that there is some mourning that has to take place. Change is also about loss. We need a chance to grieve. *(interview transcript)*

Carmen's description of organizing a feminist health conference reflects similar dynamics. Trying to integrate an antiracism perspective, she broadened the conference topics, added a woman of color caucus, diversified the list of speakers, and increased outreach to potential participants. However, Carmen met with a great deal of resistance from others in the organization. She recounts that Margaret, a senior staff member, was particularly worried about the emotional perils of antiracism:

Margaret said, "Well, it's like that really horrible thing that happened at the NAC meeting,[68] where a white woman went to the Women of Color Caucus and was horribly thrown out."

It was some [development organization] woman, who said, "I've lived in countries of people of color, so I should be allowed to be here." Anyway, so she got told to leave. Then she fought with people, and so then people got a bit firm and told her to get the fuck out of here, we're not wasting our time fighting with you. And so she was hurt, and she went and cried to all the white women.

So Margaret sympathized and said, "What a horrible thing, this poor woman, her feelings were hurt, I just don't want that happening at our conference." *(interview transcript)*

In other words, positive feelings are a priority for Margaret. The Feel-Good imperative in racial politics means both feeling food and feeling that one *is* good. Here the Feel-Good imperative means that a successful conference is successful if people have good feelings about doing good antiracism work, rather than risk having people being challenged about racism. Diane used the same measure when she made sure her co-worker Ginny knew "she made me feel bad." The centering of one person's emotions can, in other words, entirely sidetrack a systemic change program. As Nagel says in critiquing theories of women's ethic of care, "not all caring is always already good caring."[69]

CHOOSING BETWEEN "FAMILY" AND ANTIRACISM

When Diane confided her hurt feelings to Ginny, her confidences depended on an imagined, nurturing feminist community in which she could express and share her feelings with other women in a nonjudgmental environment. This notion of the social movement group as a family or community reinforces the conflicted place of emotional disclosure and care in antiracism discussion.

Consider Kleinman's analysis of why the substance of conflict was never addressed at Renewal, the alternative health community organization she studied:

> Participants weren't interested in using retreats to deal with divisions at Renewal; rather, they wanted retreats to make them feel that they constituted a special community, one in which they trusted each other enough to disclose anger, distrust, or hurt and cared enough about each other to endure the pain of personal confrontations.[70]

Further, those who revealed "risky" feelings, such as fear or anger, were rewarded with "hugs, nods and smiles."[71] As we saw earlier, the imagined community or family is often propped up in social movement organizations by rituals of emotion.

Yet these rituals of emotion and ideals of family can become a significant barrier to open discussions of antiracism. A focus on emotional expression and care works to buttress the organizational family, but also to keep it protected from concerns about race. When I asked Yasmin to reflect on the emotional reactions of her colleagues; she explains that ideals of protection and solidarity make it difficult to raise antiracism challenges:

[Why do you think they react that way?]

I think these organizations, like ones that are created as alternatives to mainstream organizations . . . there's kind of a protection . . . everyone is protecting each other, from the funders, who don't understand what we're doing. . . . So then, by naming your colleague as someone that could be doing something wrong, you're breaking an unspoken code. This is something I have just been thinking about, and have been talking about with [colleagues].

[Like breaking solidarity?]

Yeah. If you are a person of color, you have to decide, am I going to present this side of me or that. They are hoping by crying, that you'll say, "I'm so sorry, I won't bring it up again." Yeah, the anger happens next, when they see that you don't take it back, or say "There, there." *(interview transcript)*

Yasmin has to decide which "side" to present—the side that speaks openly about racism, or the side that protects the family and looks after her white sisters' feelings. Here the notion of "family" or community is maintained by its silence about racism—or more accurately, family intimacy is maintained by the comfort of some members and the silence of others. In this case, power relations of the family are shaped by racialized discourses that characterize some emotional expressions as worthy of care and other emotional expressions as disruptive. Who is expected to take care of whom in this family? Who counts as family?

Yasmin also shows that ironically the demand for personal disclosure coexists with a requirement for silence. Not every emotion, not everyone's pain, is freely expressed, openly acknowledged. Here we see that the power relations of race invert some of the emotional rituals of organizational family; for Yasmin to be family, she must remain silent.

For Ginny too, the notion of family is fraught with racial tensions. She had assumed that the framework of "family" meant that her colleagues would share the desire for a better, more diverse antiracist organization. She quickly became disillusioned when she and a co-worker raised antiracism challenges:

> Part of the way it works with these kinds of organizations like [this one] is that everybody's like, "We're a family"—there is that protection thing. So I think all of us went into it thinking that there would actually be changes. [Laughter] We were naive, we didn't think that there would be a backlash.
>
> *[So you were thinking of it as a family, where you have a general feeling that you're all working for the same thing.]*
>
> Yeah, exactly, you think, this will improve things. But, within a short time, you realize, it's not what I thought it was. *(interview transcript)*

As Ginny realizes, the sentiment of "family" is conditional on the invisibility of concerns about racism.

The imagined community or family that Ginny describes, and that Diane assumes when she confides in Ginny, is further supported by the dominance of feminist theories that position emotional expression and care as either characteristic of women or inherently positive and feminist. In the following story, we can see how these emotional rituals of family can effectively marginalize already marginalized newcomers—in this case, people of color. In her new job at a women's drop-in center, Zahra recounts the long, drawn-out, and emotional ritual that accompanied the resignation of the white woman she is replacing. Not only does their emotional ritual focus on the white woman's departure, the collective also neglects any ritual to welcome the new woman of color.

To her co-workers, it represents a family grieving, an important "process" in organizational life and a symbol of a feminist way of doing things. To her it is self-indulgent, contrary to the goals of this feminist organization, rather than integral:

> There's a literal mourning period that happened—and it's common in a lot of women's groups, when frontline staff leave, they do a lengthy closure. And this woman's closure was six weeks. Talk about dragging it on . . . it was just too much.

> [What did they do for six weeks?]

> Oh, cried every day, drank lots of coffee and tea from Second Cup—so never mind in terms of expenses, that's a whole different story. . . . The woman's going, time's up, let's move on. And I was seen as not being an in-touch person, with my feminine side, and so on.

> [Not in touch?]

> Many people said to me, I'm just being too . . . People said to me, that this process is important. People like [the facilitator] talk about grieving, loss as an important process. But there's never any talk about responsibility as an organization, if we sit here and cry for six weeks when other women's day-to-day lives are filled with shit. Do we need to add another burden to their lives—so that we as staff feel good that we will be missed? There was never that connection made. *(interview transcript)*

Once again, challenging the emotional rituals of family and solidarity is very difficult and risks censure. Those like Zahra who are reluctant to give generous space and time to emotional "process" may be seen as not progressive, not alternative, and not feminist enough, a criticism that also reinforces stereotypes of Asian and Muslim women.

Maya also highlights how the familial intimacy of collective organizations makes it feel that much more personal when resistance to antiracism does happen:

> But the interpersonal responses to challenges to racism—like people's resistance, their hostility, and their indignancies—I mean, when you're working with somebody forty hours a week, that can start to feel like family, that can start to feel very personal. *(interview transcript)*

THERAPY GOVERNS THE UNRULINESS OF ANTIRACISM

Many have described these tears and anger as "divisive,"[72] and certainly, as we have seen, therapeutic approaches can derail and disrupt efforts at antiracism and diversity. But ironically, the therapy mode can also work to calm, limit, and govern the unruliness of racism and antiracism.

For example, therapeutic approaches means that discussion of antiracism is often limited to expressing one's feelings about racism, or to exploring the associated emotional damage. The result is that discussion of change focuses only on existing, inequitable organizational practices, and the emotional trauma associated with them, rather than on future possibilities for change.

Samantha demonstrates how the language of therapy may also be used in the service of *defusing* antiracism criticism. Using therapeutic language, Samantha tells co-workers of color that they should "let go" of "old hurts" of racism:

> This has been hard, this has been a long history, this has been rough, we've had lots of starts and stops. People are pissed off about different things. Totally fair. . . . [But] *we need to let go of that*, because if we don't, we're not going to look forward. And, that's a hard thing, particularly if you're feeling particularly marginalized, in your life, in your work, in whatever. *Being able to hang on to old hurts is the only power you might*

have. And, so, I don't want to dishonor that, and say that there isn't reason to do that. But, partly, it feels now that we get to a place, and people say, "Oh yeah, yeah, that'll never happen," or "Yeah, you didn't do that in the past," or "Yeah but you fucked it up last time." *(interview transcript)*

Racism is interpreted and softened through therapeutic discourse: racism becomes "old hurts" that are only remembered because they are the "only power" marginalized women of color might have. At the same time, women of color are counseled that they "need to let go," need to forget their disappointments with previous failures of antiracism efforts because they are holding the organization back. The irony is that the therapeutic mode first encourages people to focus on individual emotions, but later those same participants, particularly participants of color, become targets of criticism when their emotional expressions are seen as unproductive for change.

The therapeutic mode is seen as a way of dealing with divisions, but it does so by sidestepping a discussion of the systemic causes that can lie at the root of these divisions, as well as the practical solutions for addressing these root causes. Instead, revealing the "deeper" cause, exposing the emotions that underlie conflict, becomes a goal in and of itself.

Sociologist Sherryl Kleinman describes a typical scene at a meeting of Renewal, the alternative health organization she studied.[73] Renewal offers a range of alternative health services and brings together the practitioners in a collective. In this excerpt, Jane has just challenged the validity of her co-worker Sarah's professional practice. A substantive debate about the very legitimacy of Sarah's work might be imminent. Instead, the collective members are concerned only with encouraging Sarah to express how she *feels* about Jane's criticism, rather than addressing anything substantive in Jane's reasonable concerns:

Members concentrated on teaching Sarah how to talk about her feelings rather than dealing with Jane's issue. How could they so easily ignore Jane's potentially threatening remarks? . . . From participants' perspective, they had dealt with the *hard* issue, getting Sarah to admit she felt hurt. Jane's issue . . . became the superficial issue that revealed the "deeper" one beneath.

And while Jane begins by challenging someone in a position of authority, she is pushed by the group not to explain her critique, but to instead express her own underlying emotions of vulnerability and fear. Says Kleinman, "Jane became a 'good' participant . . . she had few options for how she could express her feelings, at least if she wanted others to continue to like her."[74]

Thus, dealing with feelings and with interpersonal conflict is seen as the truly "hard" work. In this framework, a therapeutic breakthrough or emotional shift is akin to antiracism change. The commentary of Samantha, a white senior manager, demonstrates this:

The best thing that I've learned, is that this is hard. And this is probably about my own inexperience, but I guess what I take from it is that this is incredibly difficult stuff for everyone involved. It's certainly more difficult for women of color, but it's hard for everyone, because everyone is asked to look at their own shit, and their place in this, and sharing power. And how we do everything is on the table. And so, that's hard. But, I now know, that you can go through some really hard stuff and come out the other end. And if you don't know that, then it is far scarier. *(interview transcript)*

Yasmin comes up against this discourse when she tries to change programming to reflect the diversity of traditions, foods, and events of women coming to the women's center. She is met with tears or with requests to respect the hard, emotional work of change.

For me it was about taking staff resources and energy, and putting them into other functions, events, celebrations for other women in their home community, what's important to them, into honoring those traditions. . . . [But] there wasn't any change in program philosophy. . . . I was met with either tears, or "Too much change at one time is not good," or "These things take time."

[And people would actually be crying?]

A lot of it was about, well, [people felt] there was no appreciation: "You have to appreciate we've done this for several years, without you, and we've done a good job. How come you're coming in now, and saying this is not good, that is not good. You have criticism, but nothing positive to say." (interview transcript)

As these examples show, the therapeutic discourse can provide a means for obstructing antiracism organizational change. Cassell had similar findings in her study of consciousness-raising groups that help some participants to "resist, rather than initiate" changes. They can also, she found, be used as a "safety valve." In each of the cases she studied, she found that the groups "let off steam verbally without making revolutionary behavioral changes that might threaten the status quo."[75]

The tears or expressions of pain and dismay that can characterize white participants' reactions may also be encouraged by the allure of safety that the therapeutic space offers. For example, when subtle critiques of racism were raised in the women's center where Ginny worked, Diane, a white collective member confided her hurt feelings to her co-workers. Ginny relates, "And then she would come to us and say, 'So-and-so really made me feel bad today.' So then, by doing that she's saying to us, I don't want you to do that to me either."

Ginny and Diane were not friends—in fact, there were clearly tensions between them that escalated as Ginny began to challenge racism. Yet Diane's first reaction was to confide her hurt feelings to Ginny. Why? Emotional expression, connection, and mutual support are particularly valued in many community, alternative, and feminist organizations. For Denise, expressing how she felt to her co-worker was likely a natural, honorable—and strategic—response. Perhaps by sharing her emotions she is seeking support and comfort; perhaps she is seeking redemption or protection. However, Ginny's analysis reframes Diane's emotional sharing through an antiracism perspective: she sees her co-worker as using the therapeutic discourse of emotional disclosure and mutual emotional respect as a way of protecting herself from uncomfortable antiracism discussions.

Not that Diane's hurt feelings are insincere—some white women are so disturbed by criticisms of racism that they end by leaving the organization. In my interviews, there were descriptions of three such white women who "burnt out" or "broke down" and left their respective organizations after antiracism change was initiated. Of a fellow collective member, Vijaya says, "I'm sure that the white woman burnt out and had her breakdown partly as a result of not having her position of power as a white woman in the same way that she had in the organization before. I am sure that it was a complex issue for her, and impacted on her significantly, because she didn't have prior experience." While these emotional *impacts* are often genuine, the therapy mode provides legitimate space for the open expression of this pain—as well as an imperative to attend to their pain in a way that displaces organizational work on antiracism.

Challenging or berating a member of the community is another dimension of these familial relations. When a community member is chastised as oppressive or racist, this act of "calling out" is itself an emotional act. As sociologist Aliya Amarshi shows in her recent research on antiracist feminism, "calling out" others or publicly shaming them can be an *emotional salve* for the trauma of racism.[76] Ironically, "calling out" also becomes a Feel-Good strategy because it offers an outlet for both emotional pain and moral redress.

But quite often the practice of calling out or criticizing others focuses only on one-time, isolated acts of individuals and rarely suggests a focus of systemic change and transformation. And as Aliya Amarshi and Mario Vanegas have each shown, "calling out" white members of a community also exacerbates division and sectarianism.[77] Social media further intensify this focus on the individual, who is either censured as racist or lauded as a champion.

THERAPY AS THE GROUND FOR CONFLICT

Clearly, the imperative for emotional disclosure has been a point of tension in antiracism change and conflict. We have seen how demands for emotional disclosure becomes a site of conflict, and then an explicit target of criticism. The therapy mode, despite its strong popularity and influence in feminist and alternative organizations, is not seen as universally good. On the contrary, most of the women of color I interviewed criticize and even mock it. Maya's assertion that "white women cry all the fucking time, and women of color never cry" highlights how tears may have quite a different meaning for white women and for women of color in feminist organizations: tears for white women may offer a place of comfort and even distraction, while, as we have seen in chapter 3, emotional disclosure may be a place of vulnerability for women of color.

In other words, the therapy mode and related theories of emotion have become a significant ground of tension in antiracism discussions. One focus of critique is the universalist analysis of emotions. Feminist theories of emotion have, for example, generalized from the experience of white women in a conventional, heterosexual, nuclear middle-class family. Antiracism scholars such as Uma Narayan, Audre Lorde, and bell hooks have criticized theorists, such as Nancy Chodorow, who have used this conventional family mode as the basis for making general analyses of women and men's psychic development. Since mothering within a conventional family is the focus for these analyses, critics such as bell hooks have shown that they inaccurately universalize psychosocial relations.[78] Segal similarly notes that these modes "fail[s] to discuss how class and race (for example) impinge upon family life."[79]

Even individual therapy as treatment has become a target of antiracism criticism. Aida Hurtado notes that "ethnic and racial political movements in the United States fight vehemently against the use of therapeutic treatments that depoliticize and individualize their concerns."[80] She argues that this struggle against therapy reflects historical differences in the availability of therapeutic services and options to white women and women of color. Hurtado also argues the desire to project private sphere issues onto the public arena is not shared by women of color, in part because "they have not had the benefit of the economic conditions that underlie the public-private distinction."[81]

These tensions reflect competing theories of emotions, therapy, and their place in social and racial justice. The "free" expression of emotion and personal experience is not, in other words, equally beneficial for all. On the contrary, this sharing, which is meant, as we have seen, to build analysis, solidarity, and support, can make participants of color more vulnerable. Akua Benjamin notes, for example, how in workplace antiracism workshops, people of color who have previously remained silent now become highly vulnerable to backlash.[82] The public-private split, which "the personal is political" attempts to redress, is not necessarily one that participants of color want to remedy on an organizational level. Often those marginalized within an organization do not want to break down the barriers between public and private; on the contrary, they may want to maintain and reinforce those boundaries to circumvent the discussion of their private lives, clothes, background, recipes—and to counter the association between their personal identity and their politics. As we have seen in my interview transcripts, by focusing on personal feelings, "therapeutic" techniques not only obscure these power relations but can also block change.

The listening relationship can also be coercive. Himani Bannerji, for example, says she felt constrained to "have to" hear the confessions of her white female colleagues.[83] As noted earlier, Maya tells of an antiracism workshop in her feminist collective that was referred to as a "consciousness-raising session for white women." She is highly critical of this consciousness-raising technique, as it provided a space "where women disclosed their experiences of internalized dominance," a space, in other words, to express their previously undisclosed racist perspectives. Since a Let's Talk approach assumes equal speaking positions and a supportive, community context, there is an assumption that Maya will be hearing and speaking on the same terms as her co-workers. Yet she recalls this "consciousness-raising" as "brutal":

It was the most brutal and horrific experience, that I will never forget. . . . And incredibly eye-opening. . . . I mean . . . I don't even want to repeat some of the things I heard, because it is too painful. But I walked away really wounded from that experience, and vowed never again to ever participate. . . . My politicization around that form, consciousness-raising, grew from that experience. *(interview transcript)*

This supposedly equal space of sharing does not acknowledge the unbalanced relations of power. In her study of an alternative health organization, Sherryl Kleinman argues that these rituals of emotion actually reinforced gender inequality, since all conflicts were related to the individual psyche, rather than to power relations.[84]

The therapeutic convention to always use "I" to preface statements privileges personal feelings over collective sentiments and discourages people from naming broader, shared organizational problems. Kleinman's study found that, at Renewal, participants were always expected to use "I," not "we," when talking about feelings. The unfortunate effect was that "talking about *shared* problems of members of a social category was considered a cop-out." And yet, as Kleinman points out, the use of "we" was acceptable in expressions of solidarity; saying "we" was only unacceptable when it challenged the belief in "a community of equals."[85]

Another way of understanding these racialized categories of emotion is to recognize them as tensions between quite different strategies for antiracism change. When the women of color I interviewed criticize their white co-workers' emotional expressions, they are doing more than pointing the finger at individuals. They are challenging an approach to antiracism that allows personal feelings to supersede concrete discussions of organizational practice. The problem, Zahra elaborates, is that the therapy mode shapes the approach to antiracism change and allows personal feelings to become a self-indulgent distraction from the work at hand:

But despite the upfront problems that we articulated to [the facilitator], what she focused on was the feelings, and what she focused on was, "So what does this mean for you?" Well, it doesn't mean anything for me—it means the place is a fucking mess, and we have some problems. *(interview transcript)*

Zahra insists on remaking the facilitator's therapeutic question ("So what does this mean for *you*") into a collective, organizational analysis. Instead, she emphasizes that "*the place*" and "*we*" have problems. She upholds the importance of keeping feelings and therapy separate from her work:

If you want to know how I feel, well call me on the weekend. . . . If I want therapy, I'll go pay for it. All she [the facilitator] talked about was, "How do you feel, and how do you feel?" And neither of us were interested in talking about how we feel. We were more interested in working here and providing the service. Keep it work-related, and not keep it anything personal. *(interview transcript)*

Writers such as Kathy Ferguson have criticized the traditional bureaucracy as a "scientific organization of inequality," which projects forms of domination "onto an institutional arena that both rationalizes and maintains them."[86] Yet in Zahra's analysis, the conventional organizational bureaucracy *protects* her personal life and privacy, and ironically, *sustains* the integrity of her community work. For Zahra, the focus on process and feelings merely distracts attention from the more important work of the organization.

Contrast Zahra's fatigue with emotions—"ask me on the weekend"—with Samantha's emphasis on understanding and taking care of people's feelings. Rather than using these observations to suggest a polarized association of women of color with rational bureaucracy and white women with feelings, it is more useful to understand the apparent reason-emotion split as not only gendered but also racialized through the history of structural inequities in social movement organizations.

On one hand, we discern a mode which believes that a change in feelings and cognition is important, and on the other, a mode which believes that a change in behavior and practice is what really counts. For example, Sandra Bartky's interpretation of antiracism change focuses on emotional disclosure and transformation; she suggests that antiracism change aims at "the acquisition of greater skill in the exposure, and extirpation from one's psyche, of submerged attitudes of superiority or condescension."[87] Bartky speculates that feminists of color are asking white feminists to develop a "new" set of emotions:

> when feminists of color take white feminists to task for racial bias, I understand them to mean more than that white feminists acquire additional information. . . . What they are demanding from white women . . . I venture, is a knowing that . . . brings into being *new sympathies, new affects*, as well as new cognitions. . . . The demand, in a word, is for a knowing that has a *particular affective taste* [italics added].[88]

This entreaty for new emotions echoes the suggestion by author Robin DiAngelo with which we began this chapter—that to counter their fragile, defensive emotions in conversations about race, white participants should try to "have very different feelings."

Contrast Bartky's focus on the importance of emotion, however, with the following analysis by Ginny, who, like others I interviewed, observes that a focus on feelings blocks antiracism change efforts:

> When organizational change happens, the white women tell you, through their weeping, that they can't take it anymore. So what happens is, it gets to the point where you get this really superficial change, you put this thing up where you say that this is an antiracist center, and you supposedly have zero tolerance, and this and that and everything but then there's nothing that actually changes other than this thing. And that's what happened at [this organization]—it literally went up on the wall, and the staff wrote a thing that they're now antiracist, but then, so what? *(interview transcript)*

At Yasmin's organization, organizational change was similarly stalled. I asked her if it didn't seem that their workshop series was focused on "personal issues of racism, rather than antiracism organizational change." She responded, "Yeah, absolutely. There was some work to be done, a workplan, about how the organization was to change, all levels . . . but that was constantly delayed, and so it didn't happen. And when it did, it happened haphazardly."

Ginny illustrates what a different approach to change might look like. She managed to directly subvert the therapeutic process in her organization, naming it as the very reason for her intervention in the antiracism change process:

> We actually had a paid [antiracism] facilitator, and the time would be spent, at $80 or $180 an hour, talking about our feelings with our co-workers. And I finally started saying, "This is a waste of time. Is this a support group? I thought I was staff person. I don't want to be in a support group with you as a co-worker." *(interview transcript)*

Ginny complains that the organizational change process was directed by the focus on personal feelings: "What happened," she says, is that "things got named, but in a really personal way, so then the facilitator did a lot of conflict resolution . . . and what happened then, it moved away from talking about the power differential between staff." Fed up with the direction the antiracism sessions were going, Ginny spoke to the staff and made an intervention that proposed to speak directly to the programs, division of labor, and organizational practices that *she* sees as the focus of antiracism change. She and a co-worker also began to gather data on the racialized division of labor in the collective.

Yet, as we have seen earlier, the discourse of therapy is so pervasive that it is difficult to challenge without being perceived as cold or bureaucratic. Speaking of her experience in feminist organizing in Germany, an academic reflects on the complications of challenging the therapy mode: at first, she and her colleagues firmly asked white women to leave their emotional breakdowns at the door of feminist conferences and meetings. Later, however, they began to worry that they were "unfeeling":

> We finally said that, if you are going to break down, go see a psychiatrist. This is not the place. In smaller groups, seminars, we would say, "If you think you are going to break down, then this is not the place for you." But then we started to feel like we were going too much the other way . . . not caring about feelings, being unfeeling. *(interview transcript)*

CONCLUSION

According to interview accounts, the frequency, intensity, and damaging effects of emotional expressions mark them as a central issue for anti-racist activists. The emotional expressions are not only an obstacle to change, but also a source of frustration and resentment. These incidents also loom large in the accounts of antiracism, in the tensions among participants, and in the representations of those involved. While debates about race have reinforced the "angry woman of color" stereotype, they have also produced the stereotype of the tearful or guilty white woman. In these accounts is a clear image of the "tearful white woman" who cannot deal with antiracism: she is described as "bawling her eyes out," "freaking-out," "weeping," and "blubbering" when racism is raised.

Tearful and angry moments are not uncommon occurrences, but neither are they universal—there are many workshops and many participants that do become emotional. But even when emotions are not apparent, even when people do not feel upset, Feel-Good racial politics shape these workshop conversations. The tendency to focus on self-reflection, inner feelings, the sharing of feelings, and the cultivation of family feeling are all part of the affective relations of diversity workshops.

This focus on individual emotions, concerns, and grievances is not only a recurring feature of antiracism discussion, but is also a practice with strong historical impetus and normative weight. The practices of many organizations are strongly influenced by a foundation of feminist theories of emotion, therapy, conflict resolution, and consciousness-raising. Tracing the history of these practices allows us to also acknowledge their contingent and nonuniversal nature and to understand how they are shaped by relations of race.

The continuing influence of the therapy mode has had significant repercussions for antiracism efforts. It facilitates obstructive emotional responses, and also reframes, defuses, and personalizes antiracism analysis through the language of therapy and conflict resolution. One result of equity workshops based on the consciousness-raising model has been that "for many people it confirmed the importance of changing consciousness from within, rather than concentrating on external structures of power."[89]

The therapy mode has also become a sticking point in antiracism change efforts. In both Samantha's critique of "the women who don't care," which we heard in chapter 3, and in Maya's horror at the consciousness-raising session on racism, we can hear the profound conflict that centers around rituals of emotion. Particularly in the context of antiracism, these competing discourses of emotion become both a continual thread of friction and a clear focus of criticism. There is a clearly racialized rift between divergent practices of emotion in organizations.

Yet apparently contradictory analyses—Bartky's focus on therapy versus Ginny's emphasis on organizational change—are not irreconcilable. While Ginny bemoans the neglect of organizational change, she does not say she is opposed to whites developing, as Bartky says, "a new affective repertoire,"[90] as long as the focus of antiracism change is on organizational practices. We can perhaps imagine that these paths could be parallel, with the affective work being undertaken by people outside of the antiracism workshop. Developing a new affective repertoire might be exactly what is needed—as long as this project does not replace the substance of equity work. Any affective project, any project to examine and remake the affective relations of race, should not become simply a forum for expressing emotions.

Internal reflections and emotional explorations have their place—in therapeutic spaces. The angry targeting of individuals, the desire to hear stories of trauma, or the shaming of others—despite how emotionally satisfying these practices may be—undercut the ethos of racial and social justice.

Instead, we could explore alternative practices of emotion that would be more effective at undoing oppressive relations of race and identity. In Frankenberg's study of white women and race, one of the interview subjects reflects on the anger white women should feel about racism, including the effect of racism on their own lives. She asks a question we have not heard here: "What does it mean to take angry space as a white woman" when the issue is racism?[91] This is an invitation to refocus the anger or defensiveness someone might feel on being implicated in racism and to turn it toward racism itself.

Similarly, what would it mean to explore a collective anger at racism? Rather than feeling defensive anger that we have been implicated in racism, and rather than focusing our anger on individual co-workers, we could instead share a collective anger aimed toward collective action.

Ruth Frankenberg has suggested that "the personal is political" approaches might be recuperated to explore how racism shapes whites and their relationships with racial others.[92] Yet, as we have seen, there would have to be a drastic reordering of "the personal is political" discourse and its associated techniques of individually focused emotional expression. Any alternative possibilities require a rethinking of not only the practices of emotion in organizations, but also the historical relations of power that prompt emotional resistance to discussions of race and that encourage certain participants to openly express all their tears, anger, and despair.

The concept of Feel-Good racial politics, however, highlights not simply the links between emotion and race, but rather the links among emotion, morality, identity, and community in conversations about race. As we turn to examining the moral dimensions of these conversations, it will become even clearer that individual fear, shame, and desires for goodness too often shape the direction of equity and diversity efforts, when they should instead be shaped by decolonial visions, antiracism values, and collective commitments.

5

Innocence as Warfare

OR "YOU'RE SO GUILT-RIDDEN (YOU PROBABLY
THINK THIS CHAPTER IS ABOUT YOU)"

... in expressing shame about racism, then we are not racists, as
racists are shameless ...
—Sara Ahmed, "Declarations of Whiteness"

THERE is a brand of popular satire in which whites
attempting to be antiracist are portrayed as weak or
laughable—acquiescing to absurd and "politically correct" dimin-
ishments of their cultural traditions or driven by "liberal guilt"[1] to
obsequiously prop up people of color.[2] In political cartoons lampooning
"white guilt," whites are represented in subordinate or servile positions,
subordinate to their own guilt, to "political correctness," and to people
of color. Political cartoonist Jake Fuller used the caption "White liberal
guilt finds atonement" in his depiction of whites prostrating themselves
in front a political sign labeled "Obama." The "guilty whites" are shown
jubilantly proclaiming "I've been freed!"—presumably freed from their
burden of "guilt" by the election of the first US Black president.[3] This
kind of ridicule of "liberal guilt" and "political correctness" is a familiar
weapon of neoconservatism, used to recast equity initiatives as forms
of tyranny.[4,5] Concerns about historical inequities are ridiculed as

"politically correct" and oppressive, individuals clumsily reflecting on their own place in these historical inequities are satirized—and deeper discussions of political change are sidestepped. Humor about racial encounters, however, not only relieves racial uneasiness but also reveals it.[6] So the joke that "guilt-ridden" whites were responsible for the election of the first Black president of the United States[7] reflects an unease not only with his election but also with the relationship of whites in the US to histories of racism and antiracism.

One way of relieving this uneasiness is precisely through proclamations of innocence or guilt. Satirical treatments of white guilt are useful then, as they point us to the complex and contradictory arena of guilt, shame, and fear within which discussions of race and antiracism flounder. Ridicule of white guilt and political correctness is but a telling signpost for the paradoxical relationship among performances of guilt, shame, and innocence that complicate *any* discussion of race and equity, even the most well-meaning. In this chapter, I argue that the paradoxes of racial guilt not only complicate our discussions of race, they forestall, divert, and arrest meaningful changes to the ways we think about race. Looking closely at the narratives of morality that undergird inequitable relations of race, I show that the typical pattern of emotional responses to antiracism challenges—anger, fear, and tears—is in part produced by implied challenges to what counts as a good person, a good activist, and a good national citizen.

While ridicule of white guilt may be seen as its own proclamation of innocence, there are many more explicit declarations of innocence that arise in organizational and political debate. As I found in feminist, social movement, and educational spaces, indignant denials of racism, visceral expressions of deep shame and guilt about being implicated in racism, or fear and anxiety about being called racist are frequent responses to conversations about antiracism. Often visibly emotional expressions of guilt and claims of innocence are among the most visible landmarks of the subterranean affective and moral flux of well-meaning racial encounters. As the activists I interviewed describe, overt and subtle variations on the sentiments "You're calling me a racist?" or "I'm afraid I'll be called racist" are common responses to their efforts at antiracism. In other words, whether the goal is to ridicule antiracism, to embrace anti-racism, or to be seen as egalitarian and non-racist, we are often trading in currencies of innocence, guilt, shame, and fear. Indeed, the sneers and fears share a common terrain—the affective and moral terrain of all racial encounters.

In both political humor and political debate, representations of inno-cence and guilt also act as a fulcrum for resistance to antiracism—here innocence becomes a form of *warfare*. The term "warfare" signals the defensive and aggressive uses of innocence and guilt not only as protec-tion from accusations of racism, but also as deflection and manipulation. The "call-out culture" that has become pervasive in social movements and in social media is another manifestation of this form of warfare, in which individual guilt and innocence have become ammunition for full-scale battle and censure.

In gut-wrenching conversations about racism with Métis actor Maria Campbell, Linda Griffiths demonstrates that her own innocence can be used as both shield and weapon; her performance of innocence was, as Griffith acknowledges, a form of "warfare."[8] Similarly, as Jennifer Pierce shows in her study of white lawyers, representations of "white male in-nocence" fuel opposition to affirmative action because they allow law-yers to maintain their sense of their own benevolence.[9] Popular images of white male lawyers as racial advocates, such as the character of At-ticus Finch in *To Kill a Mockingbird* who defends a wrongly accused Black man in a Southern town, help support this representation of white lawyers as innocent—a representation that in turn disguises their more subtle opposition to measures aimed at challenging racism in workplace hiring.[10] Representations of innocence, then, not only shape conversa-tions about race, but also cloak and sanitize practices of resistance and manipulation.

A paradox of racial innocence, however, is that it is also secured by guilt, shame, and fear. As I showed in chapter 3, one of the paradoxical limitations of educational approaches to antiracism is that expressions of racial ignorance are created through an active epistemic process—racial "ignorance" rests on knowledge claims. Racial "ignorance" paradoxically requires the cultivation of certain kinds of racial knowledge. In this chapter, I highlight yet another paradoxical feature of conversations about race: people often demonstrate racial innocence through their emotional expressions of guilt and shame—a show of racial "innocence" can ironically require a cultivation of guilt. Bids for innocence often share a stage with remorse, guilt, anger, empathy, and shame. Indeed, the contradictory coexistence of guilt, shame, and fear with bids for innocence is precisely what distinguishes most efforts to talk about race. As Linda Griffith's description of her use of innocence as warfare demonstrates, expressions of remorse, guilt, empathy, and innocence in conversations about race can be highly performative—the performance of guilt secures innocence, the performance of innocence protects and deflects.

Social movements add an additional layer of moral imperative to these performances of racial innocence. A unique contradiction within social movement spaces is that while moral ideals such as egalitarianism and social justice are vital to building progressive communities, these can simultaneously be the foundations upon which antiracism change falters. The passionate commitments to social justice and the intimacy of activist communities mean that the challenges to moral identity that arise out of debates about racism are especially charged. As Mary Louise Fellows and Sherene Razack describe in their analysis of a fractious conference, feminist discussions often break down as women run a competitive "race to innocence"—each woman maintains an "emotional attachment to innocence" in the face of the other's oppression.[11] Debates about exclusionary practices within social movements, feminist, and community organizations become heightened not only by ideals of social justice but also by practices of self-reflexivity and therapy—an intensity that pushes conversations about race into preoccupations with morality and *self*.

Studies of moral regulation have often emphasized the significant role of the state in the social and legal control of morality, but there is less attention to the ways that social movements and community organizations have been both partners and participants in moral regulation. Community organizations may inadvertently or even actively support state moral regulation and nation building—Margaret Little, for example, shows that both state and community agencies are implicated in the moral regulation of single mothers through social assistance.[12] At the same time, social movements are also active in creating alternative social spaces with unique codes of morality that counter state aims. In this way, community organizations may find themselves aligned with state multiculturalism policy at the same time as they are actively committed to producing alternative, egalitarian, antiracist spaces.

It is these imagined moral communities, or "heterotopias" as Foucault called them,[13] that I am most interested in here. These heterotopias shape relations of race by supporting accounts of self that attest to a person's good character and good intentions. Within social movements, within educational spaces, and within nations that pride themselves on tolerance and equality, we can discern distinct moral accounts of self, or moral identities, accounts that disallow open discussions of what it might mean to be antiracist. In other words, organizational, national, imperial, and historical conventions of morality shape not only obviously resistant responses to discussing racism, they also shape the efforts of those actively working to challenge racism. The conflation of nonracism, innocence, and goodness prevent the meaningful excavation of the histories and everyday practices of racism.

Yet even as some activists move away from egalitarian ideals of nonracism and toward antiracism, they are often still mired in preoccupations of morality and self—moving toward deeper self-examination rather than toward organizational change. In particular, I show that some activists express their shift toward antiracism through a discourse of stepwise moral progression that remains framed by poles of purity and impurity. Many of the deadlocks of antiracism efforts can be traced to these foundering ruminations on morality and self. Indeed, antiracism efforts not only produce new organizational policy and practice, but also challenge moral and political accounts of self.

It becomes important to unearth not only moral narratives surrounding conversations about racism, but also to ask how we might change them. Is there a way to shift the centrality of this moral preoccupation? Do conversations about equity and diversity inevitably raise questions of morality and personal ethics? Tracing the construction and conflicts of imagined moral communities within feminist politics opens the possibility that we might move beyond the poles of innocence and evil that appear to currently structure responses to antiracism critique. I begin by tracing historical representations of white, innocent femininity and feminism, and then show how these are conjoined with the moral conventions of the contemporary feminist community. I then turn to the observations and reminiscences of antiracist feminists, tracing their emotions as they begin to have their goodness and fitness as feminists interrogated.

MORAL IDENTITY, RACE, AND THE HETEROTOPIA

The impulse to make the world a better place is a moral impulse. The desire to do good and the drive to fight injustice represent moral motivations and ethical practices that define the work of most activists, educators, community workers, development workers, and social workers. This impulse, however, is best understood not as an individual desire, but rather as part of the discursive and affective scaffold that has continues to prop up institutional and everyday practices of race, gender, imperialism, and morality. This entanglement of race, gender, imperialism, and morality is starkly evident in the study of the intimate arrangements of colonial life, for which scholars such as Ann Stoler are so well-known. Contemporary studies of white women's service, professional ,and feminist work have made careful analyses of these historically gendered and racialized constructions of morality.[14] Barbara Heron shows that the desire of white women from Canada to do development work in Africa is inextricable from the "enduring legacy of . . . middle-class women's moral role."[15] The women she interviewed, for example, typically said that their motivation to work in Africa was to "make myself better by doing something for someone somewhere."[16] Kerstin Roger, in her study of white women psychotherapists, argues that the "good fairy" image of white femininity still operates in powerful and professional ways.[17]

Notions of innocence have been historically important in securing the ongoing respectability of white women.[18] Historically gendered and racialized constructions of morality have been highlighted in studies of contemporary women's work in psychotherapy,[19] international development,[20] and teaching,[21] as well as in ongoing feminist debates,[22] demonstrating that nineteenth-century imperial constructions of a white, innocent femininity continue to structure white women's motivations and justifications.

This preoccupation with the ethical self and with innocence, while governed by common histories of racism, also varies across social spaces in its emotional, personal, and political content and weight. These imperial and contemporary images of benevolence, tolerance, and non-racism are more likely to be meaningful for women and men who engage in work for social change or in the "helping professions." The content of this gendered moral imperative has had contemporary nuances. While a number of organizations are still characterized by the model of helping the "less fortunate," newer social movements have also been characterized by the efforts to create egalitarian communities and nonhierarchical and consensual and expressive ways of working. However, Gada Mahrouse's work shows that the international solidarity activists' work in places such as Palestine is shaped not only by moral impulse but also by whiteness.[23] The moral impulse that continues to shape social movement and community organizing needs more such scrutiny.

Linking feminism and morality more directly, women's rights activists in the nineteenth century used anti-slavery discourse to "claim that theirs was a respectable moral cause"[24] After abolition, they continued to borrow the discourse while neglecting the cause and earlier connection to the plight of their Black "sisters." The turn-of-the-century moral reform movement, closely linked to first-wave feminism, echoed these constructions of femininity and gendered morality. The moral climate of these times meant that some women "were given the possibility of acquiring a relatively powerful identity as rescuers, reformers and even experts," says Valverde of these movements in Canada.[25] In other words, the role of moral leader and reformer allowed white feminists to attain respectability and status. Turn-of-the-century maternal feminism, for example, reproduced women as keepers of morality in the family and the nation.[26] In many ways, not only feminine but also *feminist* moral identities have been historically focused on benevolence and innocence. By helping the "less fortunate"—Blacks, immigrants, the "feeble-minded," and the poor[27]—these maternal feminists thereby constructed their own benevolence and innocence.

Here I use Foucault's concept of "heterotopias," or alternative moral orders, to demonstrate that the imagined moral community of feminism shapes white feminists' responses to antiracism. I suggest that there are shared understandings of morality—imagined moral communities or moral orders—that shape relations of race. I further argue that imagined moral communities such as feminism also construct "moral identities," or characterizations of self that attest to a person's good character and good intentions. Identities such as "feminist," Kleinman argues, may be called moral identities because they are particularly invested with moral significance.[28] For one thing, white feminists have often resisted antiracism discussions through nostalgic references to a pure and universal feminism. This imagined moral community and its historical conventions can shape resistant responses to antiracism, as well as those of white feminists active in antiracism work.

In other words, in the context of the feminist movement, or similar spaces concerned with social change, historically gendered representations of white innocence are also joined by ideals of a just community of caring people working for a more egalitarian world. Kevin Hetherington's historical discussion of heterotopia is helpful in understanding the moral significance of these imagined communities. In the "imagined community"[29] of universal feminism, for example, only certain political issues were historically marked as important to "all" women. While Anderson's notion of "imagined community" refers to nations, the conditions and practice of imagining a nation have striking echoes in the construction of solidarity and commonality in social movements. But social movements require not only a vision of a community of individuals, but also of shared ideas, morals, and ethics.

Kevin Hetherington, for example, explores the creation of an alternative moral order by the Freemasons, an exclusive men's social organization that thrived in eighteenth-century England.[30] Through their masonic lodges, the Freemasons created spaces of social solidarity, or alternative community, that symbolized a new moral order. Here, the masonic lodges themselves took on "symbolic and moral significance"—as an alternate moral space, freemasonry expressed humanistic ideals of fraternity, individual freedom, charity, and tolerance. Hetherington's description of the heterotopia as an "other" social space shaped by the desire of various groups for a new moral order, or "good place," is strikingly similar to the imagined, alternative community created by the feminist movement. As with any social movement, a common code of justice and ethics provides the foundational discourse for feminism. While the women's movement has had wide-ranging goals and tactics, shared ethics underlie this imagined community. Feminism's global sorority of women has many similarities to the Freemasons' fraternity. Of course, the women's movement is not a monolith. Yet it is clear that the feminist movement is an imagined social, political, and moral community—albeit one re-created and re-visioned in a variety of physical and imagined spaces. In their discussion of "moral politics," for example, Valverde and Weir argue that feminism provides an "alternative moral system."[31] Robin Morgan argues that, as a global sisterhood, women share not only a "common condition," but also "shared attitudes" and "a common world view."[32] It is a world view that has defined the goals of the movement—that has even defined what counts as a "women's issue." Feminist and "alternative" identities are, as we have seen, associated with anti-oppressive practices and lifestyles, and with an ethic of care, emotional self-expression, and egalitarianism.

This new imagined community cannot be separated from its historical roots. Just as in the first-wave women's movement, we find that the second-wave movement draws on representations of morality rooted in racist and imperial histories, even as it produces a distinct moral climate and community. In other words, just as first-wave feminism was shaped by the backdrop of imperialism and nation building, contemporary feminist communities have been similarly shaped by the historical and gendered organization of femininity and morality—however, they have also been shaped by contemporary feminist values. For social movement activists or those in "progressive" communities, national or cultural values of tolerance and multiculturalism, and imperial constructions of white bourgeois benevolence and respectability, are then also overlaid with newly theorized concerns for social justice, equity, and political integrity. Historical constructions of white innocent femininity are married to contemporary feminist ideals of political morality.

As we saw in chapter 2, the vociferous and public defense of prominent activist June Callwood centered around these very images of the good activist and the good nation. When a Black staff member read a letter outlining concerns of racism to the board of Nellie's Hostel, Callwood was quick to remind her of what she owed to the white women in the organization and demanded, "Are you the same woman we helped for over a year?"[33] The staff member's reply—"You want me on my knees forever"—rejects Callwood's call to gratitude. In one woman's call to gratitude, and the other's rejection of indebtedness, is the play of "good" and "evil" that surrounds any discussion of racism. If one is generous, helpful, and committed, the taint of racism is unthinkable.

MORAL IDENTITY AND ETHICAL SELVES

Hetherington's discussion of how individuals are shaped by a "good place" such as freemasonry is also relevant to social movements. He notes that the making of the "good place" is about creating a space not only for the perfection of society, but also the individual within it. Freemasonry was notable for its production not only of a new moral order but also a new individual and collective identity. The Freemason lodge, for example, "served as the space for the transformation of identity, from isolated stranger to trustworthy brother."[34] In other words, the ethical practices of trust, tolerance, and fraternity shaped ethical *selves*.

In social movements, or those social spaces that are organized around alternative social justice, distinct organizational rituals, discourses, and shared values also produce local moral identities. The aim of moral reform movements of the turn of the century was precisely to create moral subjects.[35] Kleinman uses the term "moral identity" to refer to

> an identity that people invest with moral significance; our belief in ourselves as good people depends on whether we think our actions and reactions are consistent with that identity. By this definition, any identity that testifies to a person's good character can be a moral identity, such as mother, Christian, breadwinner, or feminist.[36]

All moral identities, as Margaret Walker says, are "produced by and in these histories of specific relationship."[37] Because of the organized effort to create a new sense of justice and new ethical practices, social movement identities have a heightened moral significance. Thus, just as the freemason's identity becomes morally significant when he becomes brother to all freemasons, the feminist's identity becomes morally significant when she becomes sister to all women. Contemporary social movements have had a particular investment in the production of ethical selves. "The personal is political," for example, gives us the sense that we might create a more just world through the practice of ethical self-regulation. This used to be referred to in activist circles as "political correctness,"[38] or behavior "which adheres to a movement's morality and hastens its goals."[39] Early uses of the phrase "political correctness" among the left implied an alignment of personal lifestyle and actions with one's political beliefs.[40]

However, Yasmin's story reminds us that this imagined "alternative" identity is not shared by all feminists. A Muslim woman newly hired at a women's agency, she described "my fear of being seen as not feminist." Yasmin was conscious that her home and community life were quite different from those of the women with whom she worked, and did not fit the local interpretations of "feminist." She said both staff and clients in the organization judged whether her lifestyle was "alternative"[41] enough—she was "very aware of how I was constantly being challenged in who I was, as an individual."

In other words, not all participate equally in this moral community. Benedict Anderson reminds us that the making of a nation or community requires not only imagining sameness and communion but also forgetting difference and oppression. The ideas of community are conjured, Anderson says, because "regardless of the actual inequality and exploitation that may prevail in each, the nation is always conceived as a deep, horizontal comradeship."[42] He quotes Ernest Renan: "Or l'essence d'une nation est que tous le individus aient beaucoup de chose en commun, et aussi que tous aient oublié bien des choses," which we can roughly translate as: "The essence of a nation is that all the individuals have many things in common, and have also forgotten a good many things."[43]

The forgetting of difference has also been a central problem for social movements. It has been possible to imagine solidarity and sisterhood among all women only because relations of power and anger among women have been "forgotten." Imagining the good feminist requires similar omissions. We need to ask new questions about the ethical subject of feminism: Who is "good," or seen as good? How is "good" defined? Who is good to whom? Does good feminist mean good white feminist? In other words, how might feminist moral identity have been shaped by race and class relations? After all, not everyone measures up to the community's moral scrutiny. Describing her co-workers, Yasmin reminds us of the omissions in the imagining of the just, alternative identity:

> it gave the programming a certain slant, this alternative, totally isolated world that we lived in . . . everything they embodied was this alternative way of being. "I'm not going to drink tap water," "I'm going to send my child to an alternative school." And it went on and on. So if you live that sort of life, you present that, that's the only thing you know, and that's what you feed to the people you know. So in some ways, it prevented certain people from feeling comfortable here too. *(interview transcript)*

In Yasmin's account, the "alternative" identity is imagined by and includes only her professional white colleagues. In other words, this moral identity is premised on racialized and classed conceptions of justice and gender. The moral community, or heterotopia, that her co-workers imagine is a place that Yasmin is neither invited to imagine nor desires to imagine.

NON-RACIST IDENTITY

Another aspect of this feminist moral community that absents Yasmin and other women of color is its implicit non-racism. If we were to roughly codify ethical discourses about race in feminist politics, we might refer to them as "non-racist" and "antiracist."[44] Here, I focus on the predominant "non-racist" discourse. Notably, this non-racist discourse fits neatly with a broader liberalist discourse that frames racism as acts done by bad or ignorant individuals and ameliorated through education. As a historically humanist project, feminism, like liberal democratic nations, is imagined as inherently egalitarian and inherently non-racist. In other words, non-racist moral discourse therefore expresses antiracism not as an active political project, but as an inherent egalitarianism. However, this broader liberal discourse is joined with a feminist vision of radical democracy and revolution. Vron Ware argues that this implicit belief was a tenet of British feminism in the 1980s, one that stood in the way of antiracism activism: "To begin with, there was almost an assumption among many women that as feminism was a progressive, even revolutionary force, it contained within it an auto-matic antiracism position."[45] One newspaper columnist writing about racial conflict among feminists asks rhetorically, "Surely feminism, a movement based on equality, has always been implicitly anti-racist?"[46] Feminism is, in this representation, always already a place of good indi-viduals, just practices, egalitarian relations, and revolutionary goals.

In that imagining of shared non-racist values, or rather in that forget-ting of conflicting values, is the seed of clashes around antiracism. Of course, racism does not originate with these conflicting moral visions. However, the struggle by some white feminists and feminist organizations to maintain an ethical face can become an impediment to meaningful antiracism analysis and change. My interviews and my review of feminist media suggests that white feminists see non-racism or antiracism as inte-gral to their political identity *as feminists* or *as activists*, or as community workers—as people working toward a more just world. This political con-text explains why being seen as non-racist or antiracist is more likely to be a highly emotional concern for activists or community workers, and more likely to be crucial to their moral identity or sense of self.

Kleinman's study of moral identity shows how the struggle to main-tain an "alternative" identity can ironically hamper social change. In the alternative health organization Kleinman studied, the members' sense of self-worth was dependent on their belief that they were "doing some-thing different," that they were truly alternative. However, Kleinman says, their deep investment in this alternative moral identity "kept them from seeing how their behaviors contradicted their ideals."[47] In other words, as Kleinman suggests, moral identity both fosters and impedes social change. We may act in ways that are contrary to our principles, but deny or ignore those behaviors, "because doing so preserves a cherished moral identity."[48] As Kleinman argues, "we become so invested in our beliefs as radicals or 'good people' that we cannot see the reactionary or hurtful consequences of our behaviors."[49] Frankenberg, in speaking of her growing awareness of antiracist feminism, says, "Because we were basically well-meaning individuals, the idea of being part of the problem of racism was genuinely shocking to us."[50]

"YOU'RE CALLING ME A RACIST?": EMOTION AND MORALITY

So what happens when this non-racist identity is challenged? W. E. B. Du Bois highlighted not only the "moral satisfaction" among whites compelled to do good for Blacks, but also the emotional shifts that follow when their good deeds are not appreciated:

> The first minor note is struck, all unconsciously, by those worthy souls in whom consciousness of high descent brings burning desire to spread the gift abroad—the obligation of nobility to the ignoble. Such sense of duty assumes two things: a real possession of the heritage and its frank appreciation by the humble-born. So long, then, as humble black folk, voluble with thanks, receive barrels of old clothes from lordly and generous whites, there is much mental peace and moral satisfaction. But when the black man begins to dispute the white man's title to certain alleged bequests of the Fathers in wage and position, authority and training; and when his attitude toward charity is sullen anger rather than humble jollity; when he insists on his human right to swagger and swear and waste—then the spell is suddenly broken.[51]

An understanding of the individual and psychic aspects of moral regulation gives us new insight into the emotional resistance to antiracism in feminist communities. Experiments in creating a new social order, a social movement, create not only spaces of new ethics, but also new emotions. Historical analyses of the ethical and emotional climate of fraternity parallel that of sisterhood:

Fraternity had a very strong emotional content, uniting something like the sentiments of kinship, friendship and love in the heightened atmosphere of something like a religion. Hence—as in freemasonry—it also had a very strong ethical content.[52]

Similarly, social movements produce moral climates that become emotional spaces for the production of ethical selves. For example, in Kleinman's study, members of an "alternative" health organization used emotional rituals to reinforce their "alternative" moral community and identity.[53] Rituals of emotional expression and confession have been equally important in building feminist moral identity, particularly in organizations that draw on the consciousness-raising model. There is a clear link between ethical and emotional practices in shaping the imagined progressive communities.

It is no wonder, then, that the crisis of moral identity elicits certain kinds of emotions: empathy, guilt, fear, denial, anger. Reactions range from what Narayan describes as "honest bafflement"[54] to anger when one's moral identity is challenged. The two key ways of directly challenging an antiracism criticism are anger or sarcasm, both of which attack the speaker. "How can you call me racist?" is a common angry and indignant reaction. Similarly, when their tolerant self-image is challenged, Essed found that it is common for Dutch whites to become "very emotional." She contrasts this to her US sample where, because the subject of racism was not as morally charged, denial of racism was more direct, without the strong emotions and "emotional blackmail" that were common in the Netherlands.

Perhaps because there is so much at stake—not only one's sense of goodness and sense of self, but also one's political identity, one's career as activist or service worker—these denials and defenses are not only couched in personal ethical terms, but are also emotional. We see that white women's emotional reactions are not only regulated through feminist therapy, but also undergirded by a deep desire for a sense of innocence and by feelings of betrayal that innocence has been disrupted. That disruption is represented as a betrayal of community—of sisterhood.

An understanding of how moral identity is troubled by antiracism challenges helps us to understand why discussion becomes centered on who is and is not a racist, rather than on personnel, decision-making, or programming. The possibility of being touched by the "evil" associated with the "racist" identity calls up deep emotions—fear, anger, despair. If one's identity as feminist, as woman, as Canadian, as liberal, rests on being tolerant and just, then antiracism challenges profoundly unsettle that foundation. Here, as elsewhere, whites direct their anger at those who have disturbed that imagined identity. Their anger erupts out of indignance that their goodness and non-racism should be questioned. For example, the defensive reactions that accompanied antiracism change in a local feminist community organization are described by Samantha, a white manager: "Oh, lots of defensiveness, definitely, 'That's not racism,' or 'I can't believe you think that.' Or, 'She didn't mean that.' Or, 'I'm not racist.' You certainly heard that a lot" *(interview transcript)*. In my interviews this is a strikingly common description. Catherine, a white executive director of a women's agency, describes the kinds of reactions she sees as she begins to broach antiracism as an organizational issue—"I'm not prejudiced, I've never discriminated against anybody in my life" *(interview transcript)*.

Some white feminists also describe feeling terrified that their moral accounts of self will be challenged. Minnie Bruce Pratt speaks of the "clutch of fear around my heart," the "terror" she feels on being "found out" as a white person who has "wronged others" and is about to be "punished." Ruth Frankenberg's story of confronting antiracist feminism echoes these feelings: "And the issue was also terrifying, in the sense that we constantly felt that at any second we might err again with respect to racism, that we didn't know the rules."[55] She and her white feminist friends were terrified, she says, of "not being able to 'get it right.'" Not only are these exchanges and stories highly personalized, but they also invoke the identity of "racist" and, more to the point, of "not-racist." We can hear in the resistance to antiracism not only an egalitarian non-racist discourse, but also a strong protestation of innocence.

When it comes to discussing racism, the moral terrain of the feminist movement can take on a dramatic tenor: the non-racist must be not just good, but also innocent and pure. That desire for innocence underlies many conflicts around difference in feminist fora. Fellows and Razack[56] describe several feminist roundtables in which they were participants and show how the presumption of innocence—this "belief that we are uninvolved in subordinating others"[57]—underlies the deep fracture that opens when feminists talk about race. As Fellows and Razack suggest, contemporary relations between white and non-white feminists have been shaped by a history of imperial benevolence on the part of white women. It has been white women who have "extended a hand" to women of color, in their positions as respectable missionaries, educators, and models of civilization.[58] This same dynamic has played out in the women's movement, as white women have worked to make their movement "inclusive." When women of color begin to criticize those very efforts, begin to make their demands, that same racialized relationship of benevolence cannot be sustained. Kerstin Roger for example, shows that when the white psychotherapist can no longer constitute herself as helper, it disrupts "a central practice that white women engage in to negotiate their respectability both within patriarchy and imperialism."[59]

Ginny's commentary echoes Fellows and Razack's analysis. Reflecting on some of the common reactions to antiracism that she has experienced in community organizations, she suggests that the resistance comes from a deep incredulity that the women feel about being implicated in any oppressive practice:

> I think a lot of time the white women that are in power, they don't actually think of themselves as having power, they think of themselves as victims, as women, so that when they're told that they've done something to hurt somebody, they just can't believe it. "Me? But I'm the one who've been a victim all my life. I went through . . . de da de da de . . ." *(interview transcript)*

As I have argued, this profound belief in non-complicity can be linked to the moral climate of feminist politics. Ellen Rooney argues that the very concept of sisterhood expresses a "longing for innocence."[60] Rooney's reference to the longing for innocence and the "interest each of us has in her own innocence" suggests a key critique of the moral climate of social movement politics. As the fiction of women's unity that has been challenged, the women's movement has become a place where the non-racist image of goodness has been severely shaken. Kiké Roach argues that these investments shaped politics at a national women's organization: "I think that most white women think, 'Accept me as I am, I'm a good person, I'm involved in this social justice issue,' but racism can be very subtle and deeply embedded."[61]

When this innocent, "alternative" identity is challenged, emotional and resistant responses spill forth. Denial and resistance to any antiracism effort then becomes centered around personal defense. "Racist" is seen not as a political analysis, organizational problem, or even as an insult, but as a definition of character, one in conflict with a movement's and an individual's moral and political identity—"How can you call me racist?" For some progressive organizations and individuals, "racist" is seen as an attack on goodness rather than as political analysis. As Catherine, the white manager, says, the personal defense can supersede a political analysis: "And so to get to the analytical understanding, or acceptance of racism, there's a lot of resistance. There's people who say, "I'm feeling attacked"" (interview transcript).

Not surprisingly, these kinds of responses to organizational change efforts are often couched in terms of good versus evil—the good person versus the evil racist. In the following description, a woman of color reflects on the typical reaction to antiracism challenges in organizations where she has worked: "So, it goes to the core of themselves, 'I am bad, [if] you are calling me racist; how can you? I have a vision of myself as good.' Well, no one is saying you're bad. This is something that needs changing" (interview transcript).

Samantha, a white manager active in antiracism efforts, elaborates on the good-versus-evil framework of responses to antiracism change in her organization: "People are so afraid, that people are going to get sued, or you're going to be labelled racist, and therefore evil, and you can never change" *(interview transcript)*. Samantha's references to "evil" highlight the discourse of original sin around matters of race. In both of my interview excerpts above, ironic references to the immutability of a "racist" identity are notable. One woman notes that suggestions of racism "go to the core" of a woman's identity; Samantha says it is assumed that "you can never change." It is clear that racism is seen by many as being an internal, fixed quality. Ruth Frankenberg's study of race in white women's lives found similar references to racism as a personal sin, or "original sin."[62] (On the other hand, one of her interview subjects excuses her aunt for saying a racial epithet because she is such a good, kind person; her aunt's racist language is "overridden by her essential goodness.")[63] While the possibility of redemption seems scarce, it is at the same time the only savior. Because "racist" is described as a personal trait, rather than practice or relation of power, the possibility for change is also located within the individual.

In turn, protestations of innocence appear to be used as a way of tempering white women's feelings of desolation, as well as protecting themselves from anger and criticism by women of color. For example, Yasmin describes a typical reaction by some white women who were challenged that they had not contributed to an antiracism workshop exercise. That, Yasmin says, "just led to tears on the part of the white women . . . and blah, blah . . . things like, 'I've tried really hard to see where I've come from, and who I've oppressed as a white woman'" *(interview transcript)*. One can hear the anxiety that their endeavors to be good antiracist activists should be recognized. Clearly, as activists endeavor to maintain this ethical, nonracist face, their resistance to antiracism can become quite emotional.

EMPATHY

According to interview accounts, some white women openly demonstrate their remorse and empathy when they come face to face with the everyday meaning of racism for women of color. We can see that, like anger, expressions of empathy and care help to construct and maintain self-image of the good feminist. In feminist moral philosophy, displaying empathy and care for the other is generally characterized as a desirable expression of the caring and political connection among women, as well as of egalitarian relations. In fact, feminist philosophers have argued for the importance of empathy in working across difference, as it is seen as central to moral judgement about oppression.[64]

Ironically, this is precisely why the expression of empathy and sympathy can become problematic in organizational settings: empathic expressions often revolve around an individual's moral self-image, rather than organizational change. In the context of feminist psychotherapy, Kerstin Roger argues that empathy reinforces the notion of the universally kind, helping white woman.[65] For example, Nina tells the story of her organization, one in turmoil over accusations of racism. One of the white board members shows up at the women of color caucus meeting to voice her support, but instead speaks about herself and cries. Nina recalls:

> She came to the women of color caucus, and then she just talked about herself. . . . And she started crying, she was bawling her eyes out in fact, and saying, "It's terrible, I don't know how you guys stand it." *(interview transcript)*

This white board member clearly sought out a space to quite publicly display her revulsion of racism, even as the same self-preoccupation left her unwilling to actually do anything to support antiracism change. Her public display of revulsion—"I don't know how you guys stand it"—was also a necessary display of her inherent antiracism, her inherent goodness.

Describing the emotional reactions in her classroom, Gloria Anzaldúa says one white woman in her class had "tears streaming down her face" as they spoke about racism and antiracist feminism.[66]

Unfortunately, the expression of empathy and pain in these examples often centers on the speaker's own emotional needs. This intense emotion requires response, energy, care from other participants, sometimes the people of color.

Himani Bannerji, in her recollections of antiracism discussions, writes that empathic expressions are meant to show that whites are "doing good" to people of color. Thus it is empathy, "rather than questions, criticisms and politics," that emanates from her colleagues.[67]

> And sitting there, hearing claims about sharing "experience," having empathy, a nausea rose in me. Why do they, I thought, only talk about racism as understanding us, doing good to "us"?[68]

Contrary to the arguments of many feminist philosophers, these displays of empathy are clearly not helpful but offensive. Here we see that empathy about racism implies that the problem belongs to people of color and requires only the sympathetic feelings of white co-workers—it emphasizes, in other words, the unequal relations of power. In the context of feminist discussions of racism, displays of empathetic feelings also reinforce the "goodness" in being a feminist—they show that one is highly sensitive to injustice.

TRAUMA

In earlier chapters, I used the concept of "trauma"[69] to help explain both the effects on people of color engaged in antiracism struggle and the responses of whites confronting these antiracism challenges. Here, I am interested in more closely exploring the trauma white women and men display on learning the "difficult knowledge"[70] that their self-image as just activists, good feminists, alternative folks, and tolerant national citizens may be suspect.

Deborah Britzman argues that the trauma of learning "difficult knowledge"—knowledge of ethnic hatred and social violence—leads to a crisis of the self, what we might also call a crisis of moral identity or of the good self-image. This crisis of self, Britzman shows, also leads to a profound resistance to learn. She uses the term "passion for ignorance" for the refusal to learn from these traumatic moments, a passion we have certainly seen in accounts of white feminists' angry and tearful diversions.[71]

Shoshana Felman's psychoanalytic take on the trauma her students experience on hearing Holocaust stories is helpful in understanding the intensity and limits of white feminists' emotional responses.[72] Her descriptions of her students' panic, anxiety, anger, and tremendous "need to talk" echo the reactions of some of these activists on confronting stories of racism and their own complicity. Of course, the trauma of learning about the Holocaust comes from confronting existential questions about death, life, and relationships. Nevertheless, the pedagogy of confronting antiracism has clear parallels to Felman's classroom; the trauma of facing questions of morality, complicity, or oppression is surely common to both pedagogical encounters.

We see that the refusals of some activists to confront concerns about racism, their "passion for ignorance," stem from a refusal to face certain questions of morality and complicity. The resulting emotional reactions are echoed in Dori Laub's analysis of trauma. He outlines the kinds of defensive emotions that people use to fend off the upheaval—the pedagogical opportunity—of confronting the difficult knowledge of genocide:

- A sense of total paralysis.
- A sense of outrage and anger unwittingly directed at the victim.
- A flood of awe and fear; we endow the survivor with a kind of sanctity, both to pay our tribute to him and to keep him at a distance, to avoid the intimacy entailed in knowing. . . .

- Hyperemotionality, which superficially looks like compassion and caring. The testifier is simply flooded, drowned, and lost in the listener's defensive affectivity.[73]

As we have seen, the resistance to learning about racism is suffused with similar refusals. In feminist contexts, however, these preoccupations are also shaped by the unique ethical questions associated with an imagined feminist heterotopia, by practices of emotional disclosure, and even by colonial histories of white femininity. The crisis of self that Britzman, Felman, and Laub discuss is colored by these histories of community organizations.

Recall Nina's fellow board member who comes to the caucus to "bawl her eyes out." She has experienced the trauma both of learning about racism from the perspective of women of color and of having her moral identity challenged. She is feeling, as Felman and Laub predict, a tremendous "need to talk," a "hyperemotionality" that helps her deal with that upheaval. As we saw in chapter 4, feminist contexts also provide a political climate that allows her to openly display her empathy, and to receive care and understanding for her emotionality. Here we see that this display, like other empathetic displays, also allows her to superficially maintain a caring, non-racist moral identity.

Britzman's analysis similarly explains the aggression and the discounting of experience and of history that result when the non-racist self-image is challenged:

varying forms of aggression also can be staged as the self struggles for elusive mastery through strategies such as the discounting of an experience as having anything to do with the self and the freezing of events in a history that has no present.[74]

Judith Butler's use of Freud's concept of melancholia or mourning is also relevant to the trauma of learning difficult knowledge.[75] Melancholia or mourning is defined as the sorrow at the loss of a person or ideal—here, the loss of the ideal of a just, non-racist feminist community and identity. Minnie Bruce Pratt, for example, highlights the feeling of loss that a deeper acknowledgment of racial privilege brings: "When we begin to understand that we have benefitted, for no good reason, from the lives and work of others . . . we do experience a loss: our self-respect."[76]

One of the expressions of this loss is melancholia and the "shameless voicing of self-beratement in front of others."[77] Thus melancholia becomes a form of narcissism: "I revile myself and rehabilitate the other. . . . I refuse to speak to or of the other, but I speak voluminously about myself."[78] Once again, we hear Felman and Laub's description of a tremendous and emotional "need to talk." The white woman's melancholic performance in Nina's quote has similar tones—"She came to the women of color caucus, but then she just talked about herself." We might suggest that through her tears she berates herself for the loss of the ideal of the non-racist feminist. In Butler's attempt to break down the categories of "inner" psychic life versus "exterior" social life, she also argues that these psychic dramas are structured by social relations—in other words, forms of social power emerge that regulate what losses can and cannot be grieved. Who is allowed to grieve for which losses? In discussions of racial privilege, it appears that it is white women's expression of grief that is privileged, comfortable, and even respectable.

INNOCENCE AS "WARFARE"

While we may interpret these emotional reactions as the traumatic effects of learning racial privilege, we must also acknowledge that they are also *strategic* responses. Protestations of innocence, empathy, expressions of loss, are not only posttraumatic, they are also used as a way of tempering feelings of desolation and as a form of protection from anger and criticism. There can be no clearer illustration of "innocence" as strategic and performative than in playwright Linda Griffiths's self-described use of innocence as "warfare." In collaborating on the play

Jessica, based on Campbell's Métis ancestry, Linda Griffiths persistently mines the depths of Campbell's Métis history, thereby drawing her anger.[79] Griffiths describes how she uses her innocent face to not only shield herself from Campbell's anger, but also to obtain the information she needs, manipulating Maria Campbell into sharing deeper and more emotional insights into her life as a Métis woman. Innocence was, Griffiths says, "my only protection" against what she saw as Maria Campbell's resentment:

> It was the only way I could protect myself, with innocence, niceness. I just couldn't figure out why anyone would want to get mad at someone who was trying so hard. . . . What would have happened if I'd fought you? Then you could have . . . quit the whole thing . . . but you couldn't fight what I was putting out. Like a blank page staring at you. . . . My only protection was my innocence, my little white hand on your arm—Maria, why are you angry? Why don't you like me?—hating myself for the smile on my face.[80]

The face of innocence not only protected Griffiths from Campbell's anger, it made Campbell herself more vulnerable. For Griffiths is successful. Maria Campbell explains that it is Linda Griffiths's innocent facade, her smile, her "glassy stare," her "stupid Virgin face" that both infuriated her and compelled her to give Griffiths what she wanted—the painful details of her experience and history as a Métis woman.[81]

Griffiths's performance of "innocence" protects her against Maria's anger—anger at Griffiths's privilege and presumption. Griffiths's face of niceness—the "Virgin face"—also protects her own sense of innocence and goodness. Like the women in Yasmin's organization who proclaimed, "I've tried really hard to see where I've come from as a white woman," Linda uses her innocence to portray herself as "someone who was trying so hard." In simultaneously mobilizing her racial and class privilege and her femininity, Griffiths's innocence is a kind of "warfare":

But you did talk to her, that girl with the smile. For some reason you gave her what you couldn't give anyone else, not lovers, family, children, community. And somewhere I know that little white hand was buried in your guts, saying, "Give it to me, I know where to put it, trust me." You'd never have survived in suburbia, you didn't understand that kind of warfare, that kind of warrior, the one in a pink dress and Mary Janes.[82]

Yet even as Linda Griffiths acknowledges the privilege associated with her "white hand," she now remakes herself as a protector of Campbell, who "didn't understand that kind of warfare." Linda attributes the effectiveness of her innocence to Campbell's supposed lack of cultural knowledge about white middle-class femininity. On the contrary, Campbell's commentary shows that she well recognizes the pretense to innocence as both a weapon and effect of war; however, the power of its respectability is so great, a power she associates with the Church and the Virgin Mary, that she has few weapons with which to fight back:

You don't know what a love/hate relationship it's been with you, you don't know. You'd stand there with this smile on your face, just stand there wanting more. So innocent, so nice. Like a bloody virgin being raped by all these men and you didn't even know it. . . . And you just wanted me to give you more. You didn't know anything. And I would get so angry. I'd see you and I'd see the Catholic Church.[83]

SHIFTS IN MORAL IDENTITY, STEPS TOWARD ANTIRACISM

Yet neither moral community nor identity maintain a static non-racist frame. The social context of feminism and non-racism have also been continually shifting. As Margaret Walker points out, "communities of people who hold each other morally accountable reconfigure over time [their] shared understandings."[84]

Over the last two decades, an antiracism ethical discourse has evolved after years of challenges and writing by women of color who argued for an integrative antiracism perspective.[85] There have been accompanying shifts in the imagined moral community, and in what makes a good feminist. For example, a new ethical practice that grew out of these shifts is the prefacing of commentary with a statement of social location: "I am a white, middle-class heterosexual urban woman."[86]

Outlining a genealogy of ethics, Foucault argues that modern ethical practices have focused primarily on self-examination and "self-decipherment," the goal being "transformations" of the self.[87] These ethical practices of self-decipherment and transformation of self also describe the route of some activists moving toward antiracism. Here I show that some of these women become mired in self-examination and deliberations on morality and salvation.[88]

When interpreted as personalized ethical practice, antiracism has often come to mean the self-examination, declaration, and regulation of an individual's racist beliefs. In this model, antiracism practice is seen as providing a key to the self. We might call this a personalized antiracism ethic. In the 1980s, for example, many white feminists began writing self-reflective accounts of their racial histories and antiracism journeys. Two of the most well-known of these are Minnie Bruce Pratt's essay "Identity: Skin Blood Heart"[89] and Mab Segrest's *My Mama's Dead Squirrel*.[90] Pratt, for example, argues that to regain the self-respect lost in becoming aware of racial privilege, "we need to find new ways to be *in* the world, those very actions a way of creating a positive self."[91] In Ruth Frankenberg's study, the "race-cognizant" white feminists focused on their personal identity, practices, and behaviors when asked about race. For many of them, the idea of "practicing your antiracism"—in other words, "the personal is political"—had become an ethical yardstick. This focus on self-examination and personal "process" is apparent when one of these white feminists talks about confronting the racism expressed by her old friends, but remarks, "I think it's someone's own process to go through."[92]

However, this ethical self-transformation is still framed by the poles of good versus evil, newly interpreted as the fraudulent non-racist versus the authentic antiracist. Those newly involved in antiracism clearly struggle with their own place on this moral and political trajectory. Having started with a non-racist self-image, as they move toward a more systemic understanding of racism, they must also shift their understandings of moral community and self. Yet these shifts are not straightforward. These are unsettled and discontinuous states for both individuals and organizations. Let's look again at Catherine's full description of some of the other white women in her organization:

> There's people who say, "I'm feeling attacked. Why am I being attacked? I'm not racist, I'm not prejudiced . . . I've never discriminated against anybody in my life." *So you're at that stage.*

Catherine's reference to "that stage" highlights the variability of responses to antiracism over time. It also signals the extended and predictable stages many white feminists move through as they learn about antiracism. The stages in this discourse of moral progression might be characterized as follows:

1. Being color-blind, being unaware of color and race.
2. Becoming aware that racism is a problem, and being committed to your own non-racism.
3. Becoming aware of your own racism, and feeling terrible about it.
4. Being able to accept and live with the fact that you might be racist, rather than fearing it.

Mab Segrest uses much the same language of moral progression to speak about the disorienting process of finding a new basis for her identity as a white Southern woman. She also describes the process as having four stages—beginning with total unawareness of privilege and moving, finally, toward connection with other women:

> First, I am so racist, class-privileged, Christian that I don't even realize it, but assume that I am naturally wonderful. . . . Then I begin to see the

false status that I get from my race and class and Christian privilege. And as soon as I do, I begin to see lies everywhere, and everywhere my own responsibility, my own complicity. . . . As I begin to feel what slavery did to Black people, I look up and see—God, we killed the Indians too. Then I hit the third stage of intense self-hatred. . . . I think the reason why white women avoid their racism . . . and can act so weird around women of color is because deep down we are afraid that this third level is all that there is . . . that we will end up stuck in despair. . . . But I believe that underneath there is another level, a self that longs for wholeness and connection.[93]

Contained within these moral progressions are both the non-racist ethic and personalized antiracism ethic. As the political and moral climate of an organization and a movement shift, individuals also move slowly and erratically between these apparent poles. Again, Britzman's discussion of the pedagogy of "difficult knowledge" is helpful. She confirms that learning difficult knowledge can be an inconstant process:

the psychic time of learning [is] one in which the confronted self vacillates, sometimes violently, sometimes passively, sometimes imperceptibly and sometimes shockingly, between resistance as symptom and the working through of resistance.[94]

It is important to remember that, for feminist activists, this learning is going on within a social movement and organizational context. As activists learn about racial privilege, the context of a changing moral order adds another unsettled layer. Since the mid-1980s, the broader climate of social movement politics has shifted away from non-racism, and the imagined moral community is increasingly fragmented. For those in the process of shifting their ethical self-image, the non-racist self-image no longer makes sense to them, but the antiracism ethic is still hazy within the larger feminist community. People hover between two unattainable poles.

These unsteady moments of uncertainty mark the journey between two cloudy and unreachable spaces of purity—"non-racist" and "antiracist." This unsteadiness—what Felman calls the vicissitudes of learning[95]—explains the haziness of the transition between "non-racist" and "antiracist." If we follow Samantha, a white senior manager working on antiracism change, we can see the movement from non-racist to antiracist ethical self-image is both ambivalent and highly personalized. As we saw in chapter 4, Samantha struggles with understanding the daily experience of racism. If we look again at her reflections, we can trace not only her evolving emotional responses but also the shift in how she thinks about herself in relation to people of color and racism:

> I can't imagine what it is like. I can hear people's stories that tell me a bit of what it's like. But I'm not dealing with it. Because one horrible incident makes me want to cry, when I hear about it. But, then think about, if you had a life like that, each incident is just the accumulation of that experience—I can't even begin to imagine what it's like to be in that place. (*interview transcript*)

As Samantha struggles toward understanding racism, she falls into the expected, tearful empathetic response. As we have seen, outpourings of expressions of empathy are common in this initial non-racist stage of ethical practice. Deborah Britzman also describes empathy as a first step in dealing with the difficult knowledge of others: "initially the learner attaches to the experience of the other by way of wondering what she or he would have done had such an event occurred in her or his own life."[96] However, Britzman notes that "this experiment in empathy" can not only provoke resistance but also "impedes an understanding of the differences between the learner's knowledge and the knowledge of the other."[97]

Thus, at the same time as Samantha expresses her empathy, she also appears to acknowledge the disjuncture of knowledges that Britzman highlights. She explicitly recognizes the difference between hearing or crying about racism—which only "tell[s] me a bit of what it's like"—and actually experiencing racism day-to-day. She also openly struggles with the apparent impossibility of empathy: "I can't even begin to imagine what it's like to be in that place."

However Samantha's journey is still expressed as a personal moral progression. Even when Samantha discusses her organization, she describes progress on antiracism in terms of individuals' ethical shifts. For example, Samantha describes what she sees as the next "big step" in her organization: getting to the point where people are able to hear the word "racism" without instant refusal or fear.

> I think that we got to the place where . . . we were working on discussions, and "let's just talk about racism, what does it look like here," getting to the point where we could sit at a table anywhere in the agency and say "racism" and people wouldn't run. . . . I think that is a really big step. And it is hard to acknowledge. And it's critical. *(interview transcript)*

According to Samantha's account, her co-workers' moves away from a non-racist self-image are significant. She contrasts this stage to the earlier fear and terror that discussions of race evoked. We can see how, within the four-step model of moral progression, talking openly about racism is indeed "a big step." Certainly, this shift allows—at least in Samantha's organization—new kinds of discussions and conversations about racism. Her reference to the "big step" indicates that this shifting moral discourse and antiracism organizational change may be mutually formative. In other words, as the organizational climate moves away from a non-racist framework, her co-workers are able to discuss antiracism change.

This shift is reflected on an organizational and social movement level as well; Samantha told me that her organization did shift its focus from multiculturalism to antiracism and also created an antiracism policy that recognizes its own place in the relations of racism.

However, the moral narrative is still individualized, and so are the organizational discussions. In both Samantha's and Catherine's comments, antiracism progression is measured by the personal growth of individuals. Getting to the point where even the word "racism" can be spoken without other women "running" is seen by Samantha as a major turning point for this organization. In contrast, the women of color I spoke to generally identify this stage—"let's just talk about racism"—as stagnation, and even a frustrating full stop. Yet Samantha identifies it as "a really big step," perhaps because she recognizes her own personal ethical transition in this organizational shift away from non-racist discourse.

As we have seen, Samantha teeters between these stages, particularly ambivalent about the last one. For example, in describing the "defensiveness" in her organization when discussions about racism first arose, Samantha reflects on her own fear, saying, "I was more afraid of being called racist than anything else." She shifts from seeing "racist" as anathema to seeing "racist" as part of her progressive identity:

> Throughout the agency . . . [there was] I think real fear, of being called racist. . . . [I]t is hard for me to reflect back on where I was then, but I am sure that's where I was too. I was more afraid of being called racist than anything else. And now, if someone were to say that, I would say, you're probably right. *(interview transcript)*

We can hear the tension she feels between these two moral poles, these two "stages" in moral progression: "And now, if someone were to [call me racist], I would say, you're probably right." The individualized discourse of moral progression makes a broader antiracism analysis difficult. So she becomes stuck between the two poles: if she were to say instead, "I am racist," to her colleagues or to the woman of color interviewing her, she risks criticisms that she is complacent about being racist. If she were to outright deny being racist, she knows she would be stuck in an unacceptable ethical position.

Despite the ambiguity of her position, Samantha's commentary shows that the focus on self-examination of one's personal antiracism practice leads ultimately to a "once was lost, now am found" narrative. As in *Amazing Grace*, the slave trader's song from which this phrase is drawn,

Samantha's redemption comes from a turning point of personal salvation. In other words, the narratives of purity and impurity remain from non-racist discourse. Instead of racist versus innocent, however, the poles of purity and impurity in commentaries such as Samantha's are described as knowledge versus ignorance. For example, in her reflection on how racism can be perpetuated in the routine "way we've always done things," Catherine, another white manager, contrasts herself to others who have not reached her stage of understanding. She says, "And even I—'even I'—after a lot of years of experience, I can find myself doing things a certain way, just because they've always been done that way" *(interview transcript)*.

Catherine's commentary shows that a personalized antiracism ethical discourse contains a new yardstick for measuring others: it is the self-made antiracist who is good, other white co-workers who are not good enough. Thus the narrative of Catherine's shift toward antiracism is described in distant relation to her less enlightened white co-workers. However, Catherine also catches herself perpetuating this dichotomy: in an ironic aside she even mocks her herself. With the parenthetical and wry repetition of the phrase "even I," she indicates that she is ruefully aware of her own tendency to present herself as morally superior. Here self-deprecation works to signal her awareness that she has slipped back into her older ways of thinking, and that she is aware of the irony of this back-sliding. Catherine clearly feels that she should acknowledge that she is *aware* that she is not above racism. In fact, this is the moral stage that she is trying to achieve—what I have coined as the fourth stage, or being able to accept and live with the fact that you might be racist, rather than fearing it. Yet her slip shows that the old familiar dichotomy, between thinking of herself as "pure" and others as racist, the re-creation of poles of individual good and evil, ironically still underlies her transition. Once again, racism and antiracism become framed as personal moral traits, even as Catherine analyzes broader patterns of organizational practice.

Also supporting this discourse of moral progression are discourses of emotional self-care and therapy. So in explaining why it is important to examine oneself in antiracism discussions, Samantha also highlights the emotional benefits:

> It's like doing any of your own work—it's really scary to look at the ghosts in your own closet. But if you know that by looking at them you're going to feel better, then you are more likely to look at them than just trying to keep the door shut. *(interview transcript)*

In other words, we attempt to extirpate our racist beliefs because we will know ourselves better and "feel better." Certainly we see that some activists express their emotions about racism using the language of therapy and liberalism; however, these sentiments are also redisciplined through a desire for self-decipherment and ethical self-transformation. The individually focused progress toward a new antiracist moral identity is advocated in the language of self-contemplation and self-care.

SALVATION

In this muddy arena of moral uncertainty, antiracism caucuses, task forces, experts, facilitators, and antiracism policy can take on particular moral significance and moral authority. If one is failing in the task of self-contemplation, one may look for someone else to provide an easier route to salvation. Samantha reflects on the deference staff and board members have toward the new antiracism task force in her organization:

> Like if someone says, "the [antiracism] task force says this," people go, "*Ohhh* . . ." I think partly it's that we don't really know all the answers. So, if someone thinks they know the answers, that's great. *(interview transcript)*

In Yasmin's organization, her co-workers' desires for moral guidance and salvation is even more strikingly expressed in their awe of the well-known Black antiracism consultant from the US whom her organization wants to hire:

She's seen as an expert, and . . . people take her word as the goddess' word. . . . There was this awe surrounding her. There would be this hesitation, by all three women, to even phone her. There was this reverence about her—"What are we going to say to her?" . . . I just really thought that was bizarre, that people were all tongue-tied at the thought of her. . . . Phone her up, she's charging us $1,000 a day, you can damn well think of something to say!

It was like suddenly, she was this catalyst of change, just as Martin Luther King was. You could make that parallel: this great woman was going to make change for us. And I think that was the problem, that there was this dependence on her already, before they even phoned her.

[She was going to make things right.]

Right. *(interview transcript)*

Both goddess and "godsend," the antiracism consultant appears to inspire the emotional and religious reverence of a spiritual leader, of a great civil rights leader. Without a clear moral guide to antiracism behavior, people look for guidance, even a savior. Yasmin's description of lost sheep looking for moral guidance suggests a moral community in transition, uncertain of its new parameters, ethical practices, and language, and preferring to follow rather than to act. People then pin impossible expectations for "solving the problem" on a brief visit by an antiracism facilitator.

Yasmin's language also recalls Laub's description of the self-protective awe, fear, and sanctity with which people endow the teller of genocide.[98] Laub suggests this response allows people to put distance between themselves and difficult knowledge. In Yasmin's organization, by constructing a sacred image of moral superiority, those struggling with a new understanding of racism can distance themselves from their responsibility for ethical decisions and action. Once again, this moral preoccupation can structure antiracism change efforts: in looking for the savior, organizational hopes and energies are focused on the outside expert, and on outside facilitation and consultation as a solution.

CONCLUSIONS

Like the heterotopia of which Hetherington writes, feminism as a modern, humanist project produced a new ethical subject and social order, a new moral community. However, as we saw in the rocky history of antiracism in the feminist movement, a crisis arises when people realize that the imagined utopic community, or the "transparent community of beautiful souls,"[99] is neither possible nor universally desired.

One reaction to this crisis has been to reassert and refine its moral boundaries. Wendy Brown's discussion of social movements facing the loss of universal visions is apt: "It is when the telos of the good vanishes but the yearning for it remains that morality appears to dissolve into moralism in politics."[100] This "moralism" presents itself in various forms, as we saw in angry or nostalgic attempts to recuperate a universal "core" of a movement, at other times in attempts to maintain the image of a just, non-racist activist and "basically well-meaning individual."[101] One's own moral account may rely on a self-image of being a good non-racist. In tracing the narratives of activists in various stages of refusal, it becomes clear that not only imperial histories of innocent white femininity, but also historical constructions of a just, egalitarian community underlie their emotional protestations of innocence. In the context of antiracism discussion, the result is a range of emotional reactions that deflect and protect. We have seen, in conversations between Linda Griffiths and Maria Campbell for example, that this innocent face is also used as "warfare," a way of battling and forestalling criticism from women of color.

However, not all activists coming face-to-face with antiracism challenges react to the "difficult knowledge" of racial privilege with emotional refusals. Those active in antiracism work also struggle to find their own place in it. However, in their desire to remain ethical feminists, they too may become trapped in an attempt to redefine the moral narrative of feminist identity. As they try to leave the non-racist ethic behind, they may construct a personalized antiracism ethic, one that also relies on narratives of impurity and purity. This ethic implicitly relies on a discourse of moral progression, one that requires either self-examination, utterances of purification, or salvation by others. As the political and moral climate of their movement shifts toward antiracism, these individuals, and often the organizations they run, can become stalled as they vacillate between these apparent moral poles.

Yet why not be introspective about racialized ideas and practices, and thereby become a "better" person? The "attention to the ways racism shaped white experiences, attitudes and world view" that Frankenberg[102] found only in the white feminists in her sample is important, she believes. According to Samantha, this approach did result in big steps toward antiracism change in her organization. As her co-workers talked about racism, their attitudes shifted—one could "say racism and people wouldn't run." Her organization also drafted an antiracism policy and created an antiracism committee.

However, personal accounts of ethical practice that are framed around poles of purity and impurity in turn shape the kinds of antiracism organizational debates and actions that are possible. Samantha recognizes that this "big step" was also a resting place where organizational structure was not even addressed; the expected changes did not flow from that "place." Says Samantha: "So, we got to that place. But what happened, was that nothing happened because we weren't working on the structural stuff" *(interview transcript)*. Even the final stages of moral progression still stop short of confronting antiracism organizational change. In other words, practices of self-examination and self-improvement may shift the moral and ethical climate, and may facilitate ant-racism initiatives, but lead to limited organizational change. Liberalist discourses that frame racism as done by bad people and extirpated by confession dictate an individual "solution." Within social movements, these broader discourses are joined by local ethical practices and interpreted within moral communities that tie the personal to the political, and non-racism to political goodness and fitness.

ALTERNATIVES

But does antiracism inevitably raise questions of individual morality and personal ethics? Could we not imagine discussions of racism as collective political and social analyses rather than individual preoccupations with morality? On one hand, these preoccupations seem unavoidable in social movements directed by a moral code to not oppress others—to act, in fact, to challenge oppression. One of the white feminist activists whom Frankenberg interviewed provides a simple example. In trying to move outside the poles of complicity versus non-complicity, this woman reflects that it is important to finally admit, "Well, yeah, our hearts are in the right place, but it's still not coming together," and to discuss why.[103] She too sees this as a moral obligation, yet her response to her feelings of guilt and confusion differs from earlier examples. She is more interested in why antiracism change is not happening, and less in her own moral acceptability.

Certainly many activists do not frame antiracism as a question of innocence versus sin, and some openly criticize this approach. Ruth Frankenberg found that this is particularly true of much older feminists involved in early antiracism struggles, from the 1940s on. Frankenberg shows that the historical context of race-blindness, which necessitates white women's soul-searching in the first place, has not shaped older activists' responses. For example, Marjorie, a former civil rights activist in her seventies, refers disparagingly to "soul-searching" approaches to antiracism, saying acerbically, "You can do it endlessly and it makes you feel *so* good."[104] In the following exchange, Ruth Frankenberg responds to Marjorie's criticism by trying to explain to her the importance of "the personal is political." It is worth quoting at length, noting where Marjorie interrupts and challenges Frankenberg.[105]

RF: I guess one of the things about the women's movement that I think is real important is the relationship between personal and political life, and the whole notion that, if you live in a particular kind of social structure, you don't just inhabit it, but it also shapes who you are. And that . . .

MARJORIE: . . . so that we have to also try to shape that structure . . .

RF: Mhm. We have to shape the structure, but we also have to recognize that as agents we are already shaped by the structure that we're trying to change.

MARJORIE: Yeah, but if we're conscious of that, can't we turn around and reshape the structure that distorted us into a form we don't like?

RF: Mhm. Definitely, I mean, that's the thing that we have to do.

MARJORIE: I don't think we've come up with the formula on that yet, and I don't know that there is any.

RF: So I suppose for me that's the reason for "soul searching," is to make us into better, more capable activists, in relation to the structure.

MARJORIE: Yeah. The only reason I'm a bit caustic about it is, it can develop into an endless pastime that leads to nothing. And yet you can wallow in your discoveries of your inner self. Without doing a damn thing about it. But the converse—of being politically active in any kind of a program and not recognizing the contradictions or the limitations of self in it, or the distorted ego satisfactions that we're indulging—is equally weak. It can be devastating.

Many workshop and consciousness-raising approaches have taught us to "know better," feel better, and be better people. Yet in addition to knowing more and feeling better, we might want to think better and do better. Marjorie's counter-commentary shows that there are alternatives to these moral preoccupations—a "third" way that starts with the goal of systemic antiracism change, yet still acknowledges the individual preoccupations that may impede that work. There are certainly examples of ethical practices that are not based on deep psychological or moral self-examination, but operate on the level of practical advice, shared criticism among colleagues, and handy "tips," as Valverde and White-Mair argue in their study of Alcoholics Anonymous meetings.[106] The primary practices of AA's twelve-step programs are ethical techniques—practices aimed at changing the self, one's own desires and habits. While this is an effective practice for AA meetings that operate outside of one's everyday work and community context, there are better sites for ethical self-transformation than board meetings, staff meetings, and antiracism workshops. It should also be noted that while the AA program cultivates these ethical practices within a collective framework, broader structural factors are not a significant part of the change process. Equity work cannot parallel this approach of ethical tips and practices.

In other words, antiracism organizational change must step outside the seesaw of purity versus corruption. Beginning with a focus on political analysis and action, rather than with nostalgic moral visions of a united community or attempts at ethical self-transformation might better avoid the pitfalls we have seen here. Sandra Bartky suggests that antiracist feminist change aims at a transformation of self.[107] I would argue that antiracism efforts might better aim at an unbalancing of historical links between racism and the poles of innocence versus evil, knowledge versus ignorance.

Rather than framing it as "natural" to escape from bad feelings, rather than emphasizing the naturalness of escape, we could embrace feeling bad. Can feeling bad ever be good? Alexis Shotwell suggests that "a certain kind of feeling bad" might be desirable. Taken together with Sara Ahmed's critique of the happiness imperative, this suggestion gives us an ample push to not necessarily embrace negative affect, but to avoid avoiding bad feelings. Sharon Sullivan, in her study of whiteness and morality, *Good White People*, offers another kind of escape—that of self-love and spirituality.[108] It is perhaps apropos that a profound challenge to racism might require us to valorize feeling bad. And yet to valorize feeling bad veers close to the territory of self-beratement, of trafficking in and dueling with guilt and innocence. Is there a way to balance both these practices, to gather together these unnecessarily dichotomous approaches, to temper the polarized gulf between happiness and guilt, innocence and hate, and to reconcile both love and bad feelings in the service of diversity or social justice? I am not arguing that we should simply shift the practice of self-beratement to self-love, but I am suggesting that we explore how these two poles of "feeling bad" and "feeling good" can coexist, converse, or come closer together.

First, we must unsettle the impulse toward Feel-Good racial politics that focuses on not only feeling good, or on psychic comfort, but also on feeling that we are good people.

Ultimately, equity work must be a political project, a project that focuses on real-world practices, rather than simply a project of self-knowledge or self-love.

6

#BlackoutTuesday

SOCIAL MEDIA AS ANTIRACISM?

If you asked marginalised communities how best to address discrimination, it's unlikely they'll say that they want to be physically protected via popular hashtags.
—Osman Farouki, Sydney resident, on #IllRideWithYou

SOCIAL media are perfect vehicles for Feel-Good racial politics. With only the slightest movement of one's thumb, one can make global gestures that look good and feel good, but which may accomplish little. The problem does not lie with any particular medium; social media have become vital to building networks of activists. Nor is it helpful to dismiss or ridicule those who want to do good by showing support for the right cause. It is, however, crucial to ask questions about what the Feel-Good impulse produces.

When racial virtue becomes the driver for social media campaigns, what are the outcomes? What kinds of change might be produced when people are focused on easy acts that make them feel good, rather than on more complex and more collective negotiations? The Feel-Good impulse can not only sideline more meaningful, systemic changes, but also, as I show in this chapter, cultivate unintended harms. Elsewhere in this book I have looked at the Feel-Good racial politics inside organizations;

here I look at the Feel-Good racial politics within social media. I conclude that, whether in social media, social movements, or organizations, strategies for change should start with the more mundane work of looking closely at local practices and histories, rather than with expressing one's emotions and morality.

The #BlackoutTuesday campaign of the spring of 2020 is a poignant reminder of these pitfalls. In the midst of Black Lives Matter protests in the spring of 2020, two women working in the music industry, Brianna Agyemang and Jamila Thomas, asked people to post a black square on their Instagram, Twitter, and other social media accounts on Tuesday, June 2. The aim of the campaign, which eventually came to be known as #BlackoutTuesday, was to call attention to how the music industry had marginalized Black artists.[1]

In a moment when so many people were wondering how to demonstrate their outrage at the murder of George Floyd, the act of posting a black square gave millions of people the answer to that question. Hugely popular, the #BlackoutTuesday campaign filled the social media universe with endless black squares; 14.6 million people had posted a black square on Instagram before midday.[2]

However, the campaign also echoed the many rote declarations supporting racial justice that filled social media, news media, and email in the spring of 2020.[3] Comedian Julie Nolke satirizes this aspect of #BlackoutTuesday in a self-deprecating skit in which she expresses astonishment that racism is still a problem, despite the activism of 2020: "But . . . presumably things are better? Because we all . . . Because *I posted a black square!*" she declares emphatically.[4] In other words, #BlackoutTuesday quickly became a conspicuous reminder of the pitfalls of well-intentioned avowals that easily substitute for meaningful change.

By temporarily taking over social media channels, the #BlackoutTuesday campaign also unintentionally obscured the activities of the Black Lives Matter network. To demonstrate their support, many people added the hashtag "#BlackLivesMatter" to their Blackout Tuesday posts, causing their black square to show up on the Black Lives Matter social media channel as well. As a result, the Black Lives Matter social media channels, usually dedicated to organizing work, became overwhelmed with Black Tuesday posts. The crucial feed of activist exchange became swamped with a sea of unending, empty, blank squares, preventing community members from communicating with each other. Several activists began to plead for people to stop using the Black Lives Matter hashtag. As one activist tweeted, "it feels dangerous . . . because once you click on the BLM hashtag you're directed to an overflow of black images, instead of other more useful content people could look at for information."[5]

#BlackoutTuesday reminds us of the unintended consequences of Feel-Good racial politics. When our driving motivation of antiracism initiatives is the desire to be seen as good or as not racist, the outcomes for racial justice and equity can be ineffective and even damaging. In some cases, Feel-Good racial politics sustain expensive and inadequate practices such as therapeutic diversity training, as I have shown in previous chapters. In other cases, Feel-Good racial politics may lead to obstructive or distracting practices, as in the case of #BlackoutTuesday.

"I'LL RIDE WITH YOU"

The #IllRideWithYou campaign, in which people volunteered to keep Muslim commuters safe, is another instructive example of Feel-Good racial politics on social media. In 2014, a lone gunman claiming allegiance to Islamic extremists took several hostages at a Sydney café. Anti-Muslim attacks, already on the rise in the previous year,[6] increased immediately after the siege.[7] In the days that followed, the right-wing Australian Defence League targeted the Muslim community, threatening to converge on a Sydney suburb that is home to many of Australia's half a million Muslims.[8]

In response, local resident Rachel Jacobs posted a long story on her Facebook page about seeing a woman take off her hijab as she got off the bus, presumably because she feared racist violence. Jacobs wrote that she ran after the woman and said, "Put it back on and I'll walk with you."

The woman hugged her for a minute and then left. Rachel Jacob's story inspired an international mini-movement on social media. Australians and people around the world pledged to accompany Muslims during their daily commute, with the intention of keeping them safe from racist violence. The hashtag #IllRideWithYou was born, quickly becoming a hugely successful Twitter campaign.[9] It spread like wildfire. There were there were 150,000 #IllRideWithYou tweets in just four hours, and the movement grew rapidly across the globe, with 300,000 tweets over the first two days, according to Twitter Australia.[10]

The movement was not only widespread, it was also enduring.[11] After a 2015 attack in France by two gunmen avenging a magazine's satires of the prophet Mohamed, the hashtags #VoyageAvecMoi ("travel with me") and #IllRideWithYou once again appeared on Twitter.[12]

The campaign was also echoed in a cartoon vignette, entitled "What to Do if You Are Witnessing Islamophobic Harassment: A bystander's guide to helping a person who is being targeted," that began circulating widely on social media in 2017. It showed a man verbally harassing a Muslim woman on public transit, and advised the bystander to strike up a bland conversation with the person targeted and to completely ignore, rather than confront, the attacker.[13] The cartoon was then used as a 2017 poster campaign by the city of Boston.

Was the "I'll Ride with You" campaign effective? Did any commuters take protection from the strangers with an "I'll Ride with You" note pinned to their shoulder bags? Did the campaign curb racist violence? Apparently not. Sydney resident Osman Farouki said that, despite repeated callouts, he was "unable to find a single Muslim who took up the offer to ride with anyone."[14]

It is not surprising that #IllRideWithYou did not, despite appearances, offer practical support to Muslim communities or challenge the substance of anti-Muslim racism. For one, it was an initiative that, as Farouki points out, grew without any engagement from the Muslim community. After all, he continues dryly, "if you asked marginalized communities how best to address discrimination, it's unlikely they'll say that they want to be physically protected via popular hashtags."

One might argue that these campaigns are an inspiring example of how people can come together to speak out against reactionary xenophobia, parlaying their own privilege to protect individuals. Unfortunately, the quick impulse to do good by posting a message prevented people from having more detailed conversations about how to prevent racial violence on the street. The result is that nobody questioned the assumption that walking with a white person would prevent racial violence. Yet the commuters who volunteered likely have little experience with challenging racism; in practice, the presence of a white ally may do very little to discourage it. Perhaps, never having experienced it, most of the people who tweeted their support had little idea of what it means to be racially harassed on the street, of the relationship between verbal and physical violence, and of what they might do to challenge it. The Muslim residents who declined the help of fellow commuters may have been thinking—"You believe you are invincible, you think you can protect me. That is only because you have never walked with me before." The attacks documented by the Muslim Legal Defense Fund and the Islamophobia Register include people kicking a stroller, spitting, yelling verbal abuse, and grabbing a woman's hijab. Would the company of a stranger protect anyone against these kinds of verbal or physical attacks?

The #IllRideWithYou campaigns attracted so much attention because it feels good to stand up against racism, it feels particularly good to help individuals in need, and it appears to be an easy, low-risk act to do so by walking with someone. But these campaigns not only neglected to acknowledge that the consequences of intervention can be dangerous, they also failed to explore better and safer approaches than individual intervention by commuters. Two men in Portland were killed when they spoke to a man who was verbally harassing Muslim women on a commuter train.[15] Street and transit harassment can quickly escalate to physical violence. Not long ago, I saw someone being verbally harassed on a subway train; I moved toward them to call out, but the interaction rapidly escalated and one of the harassers attempted a physical assault with a hammer. I pulled the emergency brake and alarm, and they fled when the doors opened. It is unlikely that striking up an innocuous conversation with the targeted person, as recommended by the "I'll Ride with You" poster, would have been possible or helpful. Lecia Brooks, outreach director for the Southern Poverty Law Center, which runs workshops on how to intervene in street harassment, argues that the posters should have included "a note of caution" and information about safety.[16]

Imagining that one might fight racism through the simple act of helping out an individual is a powerful notion. Perhaps it is not coincidental that the story Rachel Jacobs told on Facebook was revealed to be partially fabricated; Jacobs later shared that the narrative in which she speaks to and embraces the stranger who removed her hijab was an imagined one.[17] This imagined individual act then became reframed as a national and international act of unity. #IllRideWithYou, while on the surface an individual, practical measure, became a celebration of pride in national and even global unity and goodness, celebrations of the generous antiracist spirit of the Australian and global community. As Jacobs said, "social media showed me good people can create their own avalanche of kindness."[18] She herself was also overwhelmed with thanks from around the world for her compassionate gesture. The self-congratulatory tone of the #IllRideWithYou tweets did prompt one person to admonish others that "standing up to racism is just baseline decency," not something to celebrate with pride. Still, the #IllRideWithYou campaign became another demonstration of Feel-Good racial politics, which props up *sentiments* of tolerance and antiracism, rather than substantively challenges antiracism.

The Feel-Good motivations of #IllRideWithYou become more evident when seen against the backdrop of recent anti-migrant campaigns in Australia. The "I'll Ride with You" hashtag may be seen, in this context, as the expression of a desire to repudiate a history of xenophobia and racism, rather than as a practical measure to challenge it. Only months before the Sydney siege, an anti-migrant marketing campaign, "Operation Sovereign Border," was launched by the Australian government. It featured a poster and video with the enormous phrase "NO WAY: You will not make Australia home." Given that the #IllRideWithYou campaign was running alongside an official Australian campaign to discourage outsiders, it is perhaps even less surprising that Muslim commuters did not take advantage of the offers of random strangers.

#IllRideWithYou is but one example of social media campaigns that echo the long-standing moral and emotional preoccupations with innocence and individual redemption which I highlighted in chapter 5. It is these moral and emotional preoccupations that explain how energy and resources become directed toward poster campaigns about how individual commuters should act during racist harassment, rather than on strategizing more broadly about racist harassment.

A hashtag or isolated moment of connection on a subway does little to touch widespread, institutional, and deep-seated practices of racism. I am reminded of the strategies I was taught as a young woman to fend off sexual assault—strategies that encouraged women to adjust our own behaviors. I took all this advice to heart: I was told to "walk briskly and look powerful, walk under the streetlights, keep keys ready to use as a weapon, and yell 'fire' if attacked." But strategies to challenge sexual assault have shifted since then. There is now greater emphasis on institutional responsibilities, strengthening the position of girls and women, creating a culture of mutual consent, and defining and reinforcing appropriate consensual behavior. In much the same way, strategies for intervening in racist practices fall short when we focus on fending off isolated moments of aggression. We need to also be analyzing, in a locally and temporally specific way, how to intervene in the broadest iterations and most systemic foundations of racism. Social media can and should be an integral part of those strategies, as long as we are mindful of the tendency toward Feel-Good approaches to antiracism.

CALLOUT CULTURE

I've argued throughout this book that equity efforts stall when we frame racism as a personal trait and moral flaw. Social media debates exacerbate this tendency, often focusing on individuals as culprits and cultivating images of evil racists as exceptional cases, rather than acknowledging racism as the mundane practice it so often is. The case of Amy Cooper, the infamous dog-walker in Central Park who called 911 during an argument with a Black bird-watcher illustrates this tendency.[19] Discussed on social media as the shocking acts of one loathsome woman, she and the incident were represented as exceptional. A Black man asked Amy Cooper to leash her dog and she called 911 to complain that "an African-American man is threatening me": yet as abhorrent as such actions appear, these kinds of incidents are not singular. Just weeks later, Amy Cooper's actions were echoed by an Ottawa woman who called 911 to complain about a Black man taking a break while walking on a nature trail. The woman insisted that the young man move off a bridge so that she could cross at a safe physical distance during the COVID-19 pandemic. When he correctly pointed out that no matter where he moved on the trail, she would have to pass by him at the same, safe distance, she called 911 and told police that a Black man was intimidating her.[20] The similarity of these two incidents is not coincidental, but part of a continuum of anti-Black racism and violence. Yet these everyday moments appear in social media as extreme acts of unstable or immoral individuals, instead of as integral to the ecosystem of morality and race.

The social media spotlight, or "calling out," of these individuals also help many people feel vindicated. They may feel that justice is being done, and that racist people are getting justly punished. To paraphrase one of my graduate students, "I love callout culture; it makes me feel good to see somebody racist called out, when there are no other avenues for accountability." However, there is also a corollary: if they are guilty, then I am innocent. Everyone who has escaped being "called out" also feels more virtuous. Few of the over forty million viewers of Amy Cooper's video would admit they might have done or felt the same thing. Instead, the incident and the person become spectacles viewed from afar, with little connection to the long history and ubiquity of anti-Black racism.

Social media callouts also further cultivate superficial declarations of antiracism as a moral position, rather than as a practice. As Erin Aubry Kaplan wrote, "Everyone's an Antiracist. Now What?[21] The murder of George Floyd sparked a global movement against anti-Black violence, one in which everyone suddenly seemed to be declaring an antiracism ethic. Indeed, those who didn't explicitly make a statement on social media were chastised. As I wrote in chapter 5, much diversity work cultivates an antiracist ethic that echoes the personalized ethics of Alcoholics Anonymous. It does so at the cost of working toward systemic organizational change. The ethical frameworks cultivated on social media are not only personalized, but also polarized. We hear an echo of this polarized ethical framework in the popular book *How to Be an Antiracist*, which suggests that we have one of two positions available to us: either one is racist or one is an antiracist.[22] Author Ibram Kendi's aim is, I believe, to highlight that there is no ethically acceptable neutral position. Having only two positions available, however, antiracist and racist, reinforces the notion that the "racist" is both an individual and marginal identity rather than a way of describing ordinary practices. Cultivating these stark dichotomies for individuals makes it difficult to have the down-to-earth conversations about everyday racism that will lead us to practical solutions rather than to personal identifications.

7

Why Is Antiracism Elusive?
(Try This Instead)

THE ACT APPROACH TO CHANGE

I BEGAN this book with the following questions: Why is antiracism, decolonization, and equity so elusive? Why is it that, whether in well-meaning workplaces or community organizations, race and diversity continue to be emotional hotspots? Why, despite decades of antiracism workshops and equity policies, has it often been difficult to make meaningful progress, even in spaces dedicated to social justice? In this chapter, I summarize the answer to these questions. But I also offer a practical approach to organizational equity, decolonization, and antiracism. There is no ready-made, one-size-fits-all manual or toolkit for this work. Instead of an ideal model for antiracism, equity, and diversity work, this chapter will offer a broad framework for collective, systemic organizational analysis and practical change that I call ACT.

THE EMOTIONAL AND MORAL ROADBLOCKS

As I have shown in this book, whether in global social media debates or in small community groups, the desire to feel good and appear good forestalls meaningful work to change systemic practices.

Of course, there has also been much progress, enthusiasm, and energy directed toward equity work over the last several decades. Yet too many of these efforts have been uneven and sometimes contradictory. My research shows that antiracism efforts have been marked by frustrating contradiction: both energetic and anemic, both enthusiastic and ambivalent. Tracing the fitful efforts of several organizations, I suggest that the movement toward antiracism and equity can be characterized as a composite picture of energetic progress, insubstantial organizational responses, and recalcitrant opposition.

There have been profoundly important turning points in community organizations, schools, and universities. Many have moved toward more diverse leadership and membership, and these efforts have continued with renewed optimism amid a new wave of racial justice efforts. Yet overall, movement toward equity in organizations over the last few decades has been slower than we might have expected or hoped. Whether the goal is hiring for equity and diversity, working toward reconciliation and decolonization, integrating critical decolonial and antiracist knowledge into curricula, conferences, policies, and publications, or providing appropriate services for various communities, the record shows that many organizations have stumbled or stalled. It is a longstanding tension within social movements that even organizations whose broader goals include equity and social justice nevertheless must confront exclusions and inequities among their own members.[1] Not only have concrete changes been slow to come, but even preliminary discussions about racism and equity are often painful, bitter, and unhelpful.

Analyzing the emotional tenor of such discussions also helps us understand their unsatisfactory progress. In Philomena Essed's study of everyday racism in the Netherlands, people of color reported emotional denial by whites when racism was raised in casual social and workplace discussions.[2] While Essed's study was twenty years ago, we nevertheless continue to observe this dynamic. My interviewees too often faced the incredulous question, "You're calling me a racist?" While the denial may be more subtle and far less vocal than this, forms of emotional and personalized denial, disbelief, or minimizing of concerns about racism and equity continue to be common in discussions today, traceable to the image many people have of themselves as tolerant and non-racist.

But this kind of denial, although it is highlighted in the title of this book, is only one part of the emotional and moral landscape of racial encounters. In the organizations that I've studied and in the spaces that I work, I've observed that even within a group of people deeply committed to equity, antiracism, and decolonization, the focus of change nevertheless remains on the individual and the self. The emotional weight of this focus is profound. Many people are afraid of being seen as racist, and still others are deeply invested in being seen as antiracist. We are so keenly aware of the volatile and emotional nature of any discussions about race that we often hold back on *all* critical discussions of racism, for fear that someone may think we are calling them racist. This is a legitimate fear, because the desire to be seen as antiracist is widespread in these spaces, and yet being antiracist is interpreted as an individual ethic and identity. As a result, our organizational discussions often struggle to make analytical critiques that venture beyond individuals, blame, and raw feelings, and that lean instead toward concrete strategies and everyday practices that address root causes of ongoing inequities.

The egalitarian or collectivist history of many organizations can ironically sustain this heightened emotional and moral landscape. One of the striking aspects of social movements and community organizations is the range of practices aimed at shaping community and self. Groups use a range of practices for knowledge production and emotional expression to represent ourselves as deserving or upstanding members of a community, to define the boundaries of a community, to achieve its goals, and to resolve conflict in a community. All these practices help to constitute and maintain imagined egalitarian communities and ethical selves. In this book I've shown that these techniques, drawn from conflict resolution, popular education, and consciousness-raising, can at times also sustain inequitable relations of race. For example, I argue that a Let's Talk approach too often shapes pedagogical strategy, so that knowledge about race is drawn from the personal stories or experiences of people of color, constituting people of color as either resources for personal and emotional explorations of racism—or, if they refuse that role, as obstacles to dialogue. While an egalitarian concept of knowledge and education is the underlying principle of these workshops, in practice this pedagogical strategy can become not an egalitarian exchange, but a one-way corrective for a supposed "ignorance" of racism. Antiracism sessions may invite mutual sharing of all parties, but often have vague therapeutic or conflict-resolution practices that offer neither emotional relief nor practical change. A common approach over the last thirty years, today the Let's Talk strategy remains familiar in public institutions. One university, for example, recently held "listening sessions" to respond to an incident of anti-Black racism toward a student.[3]

In some organizations, there is a strong prescriptive emphasis on open emotional expression and its importance in building knowledge and solidarity. White participants may then feel freer to express their empathy, sadness, anger, and other emotional responses when the topic of racism is raised, responses that often distract or deflect. Discussions of inequity often become overly focused on the supposed emotional and interpersonal causes of racism, rather than on its broader histories. Antiracism analysis then becomes reframed and defused through therapeutic technique: white participants may dwell on their empathetic feelings, on personality differences, or on how emotions and "old hurts" are preventing open discussion and change, and so on. The notion that emotion is always positive, useful, and beneficial to our work in organizations has rarely been contested; in the context of unequal relations of race, however, open displays and deep analyses of emotion are frequently distractions from concrete antiracism change.

The social space of community organizations, nonprofits, and social movements adds an additional layer of moral complexity to emotional conversations about race and equity. Because of their focus on collectivist values of collaboration and equity, these organizations often work to cultivate a social space or "good place," one that is shaped by the desire for a new moral order defined by a common code of justice, values, and ethics.[4] In many progressive organizations, the shared ethics that underlie this imagined community include "the personal is political," an anti-oppressive personal and political practice, an ethic of care, emotional self-expression, egalitarianism, and so on.

Within this imagined heterotopia, several things can happen when the fact of racist exclusion is raised. The first is a rush to reassert and refine its moral boundaries, to assert its purity or to protect its integrity, a trajectory we have seen within the feminist movement. The second is an effort to adjust the moral parameters of the community by declaring a new antiracist position or identity. In shifting toward a new antiracist identity, educational and therapeutic strategies often take prominence. Not surprisingly, the transformation of self can then become a focus of antiracism change. Hetherington notes that the making of the "good place" is about creating a space not only for the perfection of society, but also the individual within it.[5] "The personal is political," for example, gives us the sense that we might create a more just world through the practice of ethical self-regulation.

Antiracism has too often been a personal moral preoccupation, accompanied by practices aimed at greater self-knowledge that will produce a better ethical subject. White activists can then become concerned either with their own salvation, or with their own status as saviors of Indigenous and Black folks and people of color—both focus on shaping moral identity rather than on changing practices. This moral journey toward salvation typically begins with assertions of non-racism and ends with acknowledging one's own racism. Too often, however, these moral preoccupations with becoming an antiracist person sidestep concrete changes in organizational practice. Recall that Samantha, a white senior manager, said that she used "to be more afraid of being called racist than anything else," but now sees herself as having progressed to the point where she could acknowledge that she was. Yet at both of these stages, the concern remained with improving and understanding the self, a preoccupation that makes it difficult for organizational change to progress. Samantha reflects that "moving outside of oneself" is hard to do. This, she suggests, is why antiracist change is so difficult in her organization:

> I mean, mostly we're asking people to move outside of themselves. I mean, I think that's gotta be true for all of us. Certainly for white people who never have to. But, trying to see beyond our own experience, is what we're saying. And, I think that's really hard for white people to do. *(interview transcript)*

For Samantha, "moving outside of ourselves" simply means cultivating empathy, understanding the experiences of our co-workers, of others. If, as Samantha suggests, the big accomplishment of antiracism workshops is "for white people to move" toward empathy, then what hope do we have of moving from soul-searching to systemic change? Emotional evolution is a worthy and time-consuming personal goal; however, it should not be the primary goal of equity work in organizations.

This book argues that several factors come together to stall antiracism change:

- Feel-Good racial politics in which conversations about race are shaped by concerns with psychic comfort and morality
- The characterization of racism as a personal trait and moral flaw
- The emphasis on dialogue and therapy as a route to equity
- A history of self-examination as an ethical practice

These factors have moved organizations more toward individual education and reflection rather than toward analysis of their own histories and practices. These broader tendencies often intersect with several features common to collectivist social spaces:

- Profound investments in a universal vision of equity
- Attachment to one's moral identity as progressive and anti-oppressive
- An assumption that social movements are inherently egalitarian spaces
- A strong sense of familial and emotional community
- Well-established practices designed to express emotion and shape community

While we see some of these tendencies across a variety of organizations, they are particularly well-rooted in organizations inspired by progressive social movement ideals. It's important to acknowledge that progressive organizations are usually beginning from a place of collective commitment to equity and antiracism. However, those commitments are harder to implement when they are diverted to emotional resistance, self-reflection, and sharing feelings.

Workshops continue to be the go-to response when corporate or public organizations attempt to address concerns about racism and diversity. In many cases, diversity training is mandatory. It is a solution that often arrives readily packaged and delivered by external diversity consultants or by the equity office of a large organization. Antiracism and diversity workshops have only increased in popularity in recent years, making diversity consulting a multimillion-dollar industry. They even caught the attention and ire of former president Donald Trump, prompting him to ban any antiracism workshops by federal contractors.[6]

Workshops and books such as these were in particularly high demand after the global Black Lives Matter protests of May of 2020 prompted so many more corporations to take public action. Yet the approach of these workshops appears to remain focused on the individual, either through standardized training, conflict resolution, or reflection. For example, author and facilitator Robyn DiAngelo teaches workshop participants that racism is systemic and historical; disappointingly, however, the solutions

she proposes at the end of her book remain in the realm of the therapeutic. Turning to the last chapter of her book *White Fragility*, "Where
Do We Go from Here," I hoped to find suggestions for how to move toward institutional and systemic change. Instead it focuses on individual
repair and emotions. Indeed, the author begins the chapter with a story
about how she has learned to apologize better when she makes a racist
misstep with a co-worker. She then offers a list of alternative emotional
responses; instead of fragile, defensive emotions, whites could try to
"have very different feelings"—here she lists gratitude, excitement, guilt.
D'Angelo suggests that these feelings could lead to different behaviors as
well. Instead of systemic or organizational strategies for change, the final
chapter of *White Fragility* advocates that people focus on therapeutic
practices such as "Reflection," "Apology," "Listening," and so on.[7]

There is no doubt that apologies, talking, and connection can help
us clarify a problem and help us build trust and community. These are
otherwise important endeavors—building better relationships with our
friends, family members, and communities is vital to the vision of an
egalitarian community. Nothing in this book should be interpreted as
being opposed to emotions or to therapeutic practices per se. On the
contrary, emotional self-management and a degree of empathy are key
to building positive working relationships in teams, which is in turn key
to working collectively against racism.

But these practices should not be an end goal. If listening or reflection
is not accompanied by problem-solving that challenges the underlying
practices that produce exclusion, it may serve to sustain it. Too often
the implication of Let's Talk approaches is that if average white folks
taking these workshops acknowledge that they are racist, listen, reflect,
and apologize appropriately, racial justice will be served. Unfortunately,
people can become quite good at reflecting, apologizing, and listening,
without changing much in terms of social justice, diversity, antiracism,
inclusion, and equity.

Solutions that require us only to reach deep into ourselves are attractive and appealing. Tactics that ask us for inward reflection dovetail well

with the self-help and therapeutic undercurrent common to so many aspects of our lives, one that continually moves us to relentlessly pursue personal development. Even if one were to accept this as a reasonable workplace practice (as opposed to a personal practice), it would need to be succeeded by concrete and systemic organizational changes; too often, however, it is the first and only step. Recall Aruna, one of a few teachers of color at her school, who had to read a book on racism and share their feelings about it in a mandatory workshop. Although irked, Aruna, as noted before, tried to be generous in her assessment of the initiative: "I guess they feel that introspection is the first step. But I don't think that there is going to be a step 2 or step 3." I recently attended a seminar on "inclusive leadership" that took the same limited approach: The first step toward inclusive leadership, said the speaker, is to be aware of our own biases. The second is to have empathy, and the third is to be vulnerable. In this model of inclusive leadership, however, the entire focus remains limited to one's own self and one's own emotions.[8]

In her book *Cold Intimacies: The Making of Emotional Capitalism*, Eva Illouz argues that the therapeutic narrative has such wide cultural resonance precisely because it "makes one responsible for one's psychic well-being, yet does that by removing any notion of moral fault."[9] It is through therapeutic work on the self, Illouz observes, that "modern subjects experience themselves as being most morally and socially competent."[10] As one professor asks of her university colleagues, why do they "only talk about racism as understanding us, doing good to 'us'"? Why, Bannerji wonders, do they prefer to express empathy and their desire to do good, "rather than questions, criticisms and politics."[11]

Unfortunately, there are often not many avenues for equity work in most organizations. Outside of the standard training workshop, the alternative avenues focus on conflict resolution and complaint. The equity policies and practices of most organizations direct people to complaints procedures that often center on resolving conflict between individuals. Sara Ahmed argues that we should acknowledge "Complaint as Diversity Work," suggesting that complaints *are* the substance of diversity work, and that "complaints are what we have to do to dismantle the structures that do not accommodate us."[12] As a systematic practice of change, however, using an organization's grievance or complaint process not only falls short, it is also almost inevitably a frustrating and painful path for the individuals who attempt it. Complaints and grievance procedures tend to funnel systemic problems into discrete and individual instances of harm. Remedies then also focus on the individuals involved, often through conflict resolution or training, rather than on prevention. Sara Ahmed's book *Complaint!* demonstrates that while complaints do identify harassment within universities, they are also heavily constrained by institutional procedure and culture and rarely lead to satisfactory outcomes. As Ahmed's colleagues write about their complaint work, "These complaints often did not sound like us: we had such a narrow channel in which to describe what happened to us."[13]

The ideal that individuals can challenge harassment and injustice by standing up and speaking out nevertheless remains a worthy one. It is not a notion that should be abandoned, but it will be far more effective in the context of collective analysis and collaborative and systemic redress.

WHAT CAN WE DO? ACT FOR CHANGE

Rather than individual complaint as the mode of intervention, we should lean toward a collective and broader scope of action. Collective energy and vision should be focused less on channeling complaints and more on transforming the conditions that produce complaints. We could also cultivate a broader collective responsibility for equity in our organizations, rather than locating that responsibility with an equity consultant, equity office, or the same group of people. Communities committed to working on equity and antiracism need other approaches besides Let's Talk workshops, diversity training, conflict resolution, and complaints, ones that do not focus primarily on individuals, their experiences, knowledge, and sentiments.

There are three directions for equity work that do offer promise for organizations—concrete practices, ethical and affective shifts, and community relationships:

- Concrete Practices: Focus on analyzing taken-for-granted practices and histories, and use this analysis to rethink and transform the familiar ways of doing things. How do we as an organization or community represent who we are, create and share ideas, distribute resources, bring people together, bring in new people, and get our day-to-day work done?
- Ethical and Affective Shifts: Cultivate an ethical shift, away from valuing self-examination and self-improvement and toward collective responsibility to act for racial justice.
- Community Relationships: Develop affective communities[14] and friendships that not only work toward antiracism and equity but also practice those values within everyday relationships. Shift our ethical and emotional preoccupations from individual reform and education to creating ethical and affective communities that can better support thoughtful equity work.

Working toward more equitable communities will need creative efforts that work across these three intersecting areas of work: concrete practices, ethical and affective shifts, and community relationships. In this chapter, I focus primarily on the first area, concrete practices. I offer my ACT framework as a way of beginning to think about local analysis and the transformation of concrete practices.

HOW TO ACT FOR EQUITY: ASK, COLLABORATE, TAKE ACTION

The ACT framework is designed to support collaborative and systemic work toward equity in organizations. It advocates the following three key steps: Ask questions about the root of the problem. Collaborate and craft solutions. Take at least one small action now.

A: Ask questions and analyze.

Ask how did we get here, how did this happen, how big a problem is this? Analyze practices. Pinpoint problems and obstacles.

C: Collaborate and craft solutions and a vision.

Collaborate and consider solutions to the problems you've identified. Imagine alternatives to the way we've always done things. Craft alternate practices and visions. How could things be different? What everyday practices could we change, what new ones could we create? This is the "problem-solving" phase.

T: Take one small action now.

What small action can we take right now? The action must address the roots of the problem and the solutions that we identified in the first two ACT steps. Drawing directly on our own analysis, vision, and problem-solving, we should make a commitment to take at least one small, effective action as soon as possible. The point of this step is to recognize that meaningful change relies on shifts in practices and resources. Seemingly small actions—in areas such as data gathering, mentorship, leadership, workload and space allocation, recruitment and hiring criteria and practices, course content, news stories, exhibitions, conferences, anthologies—can have broader and lasting impacts.

These three steps should ideally begin from a place of collective commitment to shared values. If an organization does not begin with some degree of intentional commitment to equity, decolonization, and antiracism, at least on the part of leaders or core members, more inner reflection and therapeutic conversation is unlikely to produce it. This work should arise not simply from abstract, universal ideals, but also from commitments to change within our own communities.

A: ASK QUESTIONS AND ANALYZE

While other people's success stories are inspiring, they should not be taken as an ideal roadmap to equity to be closely followed. Instead, efforts at decolonization, equity, and antiracism need to begin with an analysis that is focused on an organization's location, its goals, and its particular history and practices. A working group or a workshop could begin this analysis by asking any of these questions, or by formulating its own questions focused on obstacles to equity, conditions for equity, and new approaches:

- Describe, document, analyze the nature and origin of the inequities we are trying to address. Where do the problems lie? Do we have data or documentation on longstanding inequities in our programs, leadership, budget allocations, hiring, recruitment, outreach, services, curriculum, benefits, and other practices? Here we should be interested not just in analyzing statistics about demographic diversity, but also in reviewing our services, curriculum, community events, and so on, to assess whether they reflect our values of equity and diversity. We should also ask why these inequities exist: How are historical relations of power reproducing inequities and lack of diversity? If we don't have the documentation we need, can we begin to document and gather our own data, and, for example, use it to guide hiring decisions?[15] Alternatively, could we look at documentation and data from other institutions?
- Do we have routine procedures for making decisions, or do we rely on informal relationships and instincts? Where are the areas where we lack a systematic policy and criteria to make decisions, and instead rely on informal connections and personal feelings? It is often in these informal processes that bias and "the way we've always done things" can reproduce inequities.
- Do we include competence and commitments to antiracism and equity in our criteria when evaluating programs, people, or prospective new members and hires?
- If we have a systemic policy that addresses racism or inequity, do we have concrete goals attached to it? Do these concrete goals policy take into account diversity, equity, workload, and everyday lived realities? Do we monitor and keep records of our progress? Of which strategies that have proven effective in the past?

- If we have an equity policy, are we using it? Is it doing what we want it to do? Does the policy align with our intention or values? Do we need to change the policy?
- Are we being mostly *reactive*—responding after instances of racism, sexism, and harassment have already occurred?
- How might we be proactive? Explore ways to cultivate an environment that would prevent these instances. Ask instead, how did this conflict or concern arise and how might we prevent it in future?
- What remedies have we used in the past? Do we tend to rely on remedies such as apology and conflict resolution between individuals, or are we also looking for systemic, forward-thinking solutions? Review policies so that they include systemic analysis and solutions.
- How do equity and diversity issues come to the attention of decision-makers? Is it through complaints and grievances? Review this history and create proactive strategies for monitoring progress on equity issues before they get to the grievance stage.

C: COLLABORATE AND CRAFT SOLUTIONS AND A VISION

This could be the task for a different kind of equity workshop. Ongoing collective, practical, and systemic equity analysis is detailed and difficult work and is exactly the kind of collaborative problem-solving that would be ideal for a focused workshop. We could be redirecting the large amounts of money, time, and emotional energy spent on generalized anti-bias workshops to this locally specific and detailed work. An effective organizational workshop would instead be an opportunity to collaborate in taking our organization to another place, rather than an opportunity for individuals to reflect and train. In other words, an organizational workshop is most effective when we are using it to undertake work that engages us deeply in the tasks of reframing and remaking how we do things as an organization, rather than using workshops to listen, absorb information, reflect, and talk about our experiences and feelings. There is a place for that work, but in and of itself it will not and has not helped us move toward equity, decolonization, and antiracism.

A workshop could, for example, bring an organization together to produce an equity analysis of recruitment and hiring (or service delivery, curriculum, scholarships, research funding, or any area of practice). In this scenario, rather than educate the participants, a workshop facilitator's role is to guide the analysis, identify gaps in data, and ask the necessary questions. A facilitator might point to successful models of equitable hiring practices,[16] but the analysis of how to apply this to our own space still needs to be local. Who works in our organization and at what level? How are we doing when measured against the standard criteria for equity? Are there other measures of equity we might want to apply, such as analyzing the position of Black and Indigenous employees rather than using a general category such as "racialized"? How can we promote equity through all employment practices, including job descriptions,[17] recruitment,[18] retention, interviewing, orientation, evaluation, awards, training, and mentorship. Can we break down each of these steps further into precise practices? To cultivate widespread shifts, we need to analyze and shift everyday practices.

Imagine if instead of being a place for individual learning and reflection, the antiracism or equity workshop could be recuperated into a space for collaboration and collective problem-solving. Instead of focusing on individual "biases" and emotions, workshops could focus on analyzing taken-for-granted practices and creating new practices. As Musa al-Gharbi suggests, diversity training should be focused not on avoiding conflict, "but on helping people . . . collaborate *despite* eventual (essentially, inevitable) disagreements."[19]

We can then begin the more difficult work of looking closely at the precise practices that reproduce our daily activities, allocate resources, and create knowledges. New practices must also respond to the specificities and histories of our own space and places. Where possible, new practices should be developed in collaborative ways. Finally, our practices must continue to evolve.

An equity workshop should be a place to get this work done. Reflection and analysis are always vital to this work—but on what should we be reflecting? A workshop that has organizational or systemic change as its goal should avoid a focus on inner reflection, or on the sharing of feelings and experiences. Instead, by reflecting on the spaces where they work or live, equity workshop participants could work together to:

- Pinpoint systemic practices that reproduce inequality or racial violence.
- Uncover where existing equitable policies and equitable practices are being circumvented.
- Creatively and collaboratively generate new practices in key areas where change needs to happen. This may mean new practices in recruitment, evaluation, and program delivery, or new content, curriculum, services, products, and so on.
- Focus more on changing practices and less on processing emotions and knowledge. This is the case even when we are discussing knowledge creation, research, and curriculum. Even here, we can focus on deepening practices of research community and curriculum development, rather than on the usual workshops that aim to transfer generic knowledge or cultivate self-knowledge.
- Discuss strategies and action plans to undertake new practices in the immediate and short term, even if the first steps are small.
- Discuss the desired outcomes of these action plans, that is, how will we know whether our actions have made a difference?
- Document and share the new framework in accessible ways so that ongoing implementation is not dependent on particular individuals and can maintain continuity even when leadership changes.

Rather than having stand-alone sessions on "diversity issues," which implicitly frame diversity-related competencies as something separate from, or in addition to, one's general work responsibilities, diversity-related training should be well-integrated with other forms of training.[20]

Could we use this approach—precise analysis of local practices—to redirect the Feel-Good campaigns such as #IllRideWithYou and #Black-outTuesday? Instead of tweeting an offer to ride the subway, a genuine and potent effort to stop street violence requires us to bring together people who live in those communities, who plan and run transit, urban spaces, and schools, to create and implement comprehensive, collective, long-term anti-harassment measures. Might we be able to similarly re-think the practice of social media censure aimed at individuals, and shift that mass of emotional energy toward positive change?

T: TAKE ONE SMALL ACTION NOW—A FEW INSPIRATIONS

What small action can we take right now that addresses the roots of the problem and the solutions that we identified in the first two ACT steps? I use the word "small" to describe these actions not because these are trivial in impact, but because I want to emphasize that even seemingly small actions can have widespread effects that outlast anti-bias training.

Not just any small step counts toward the ACT approach. After all, many organizations are taking small actions on equity and diversity—holding workshops, lectures, posting a policy, and so on—but often these actions are neither effective nor respond directly to local concerns.

To be effective, actions must arise from our own local analysis of problems and solutions. There are two important intentions of my exhortation to "Take One Small Action Now." The first is to favor practical action, however small, over inner reflection and conventional training. The second is to favor actions that respond directly to the analysis that we carried out in the first two ACT steps: identifying problems and imagining solutions.

For example, gathering information and data specific to our own communities is often an important foundation not only for analyzing inequities but also for catalyzing and sustaining change. I was inspired, for example, by the story told to me by a woman of color who subverted the therapeutic antiracism workshops in her organization. She and another woman of color became fed up with the facilitator's focus on feelings and interpersonal facilitation and instead decided to create their own intervention by gathering data on the inequitable and racialized division of labor in their collective. The data showed that, contrary to being an equal collective, women of color were doing the majority of day-to-day administrative and maintenance tasks, while the white members of the collective did policy and management tasks such as grant proposal writing. My own institution, OCAD University, undertook a similar study a few years ago, aimed at gathering data on the racial diversity of our faculty members. Not surprisingly, the study showed that, while our students represent considerable racial diversity, the faculty did not. The combined weight of stark data and the accompanying recommendations of the presidential task force[21] created to redress this imbalance have helped to focus and direct hiring efforts. Over the last few years, the university has made intentional and successful efforts to shift these figures, hiring two clusters of Indigenous faculty and a cluster of Black faculty. Commitments to hiring Indigenous and Black faculty as a group or cluster, as OCAD University has done, require more funds and time up front, but also help to cultivate an intellectual community of collaboration, advocacy, and mutual support, and must be followed by consistent support and mentorship—another area for potential small actions. As my colleague Dori Tunstall argues in her book *Decolonizing Design*,[22] organizations must reallocate their limited resources to decolonization, particularly if we are to correct the serious underrepresentation of faculty members. As Tunstall points out, in these challenging fiscal times, our university's successful efforts to hire Indigenous and Black faculty members and faculty of color, efforts to create a position for a senior Indigenous academic leader, and many other decolonization initiatives only came about by making new priorities for existing funds, rather than finding new funds.

In my own work as a dean at OCAD University, one of my goals is to analyze our taken-for-granted ways of doing things and to rethink and transform the familiar and mundane practices that can perpetuate inequities in workload, recruitment, hiring, tenure, mentorship, working conditions, and allocation of resources. It is not enough to proclaim that we are working to create a university that reflects the diversity of our students. It is not enough to post job ads that state that "we prioritize equity-seeking candidates," as organizations have done for many years. Instead, we have to consider all the practices associated with hiring: How do we describe and frame the key requirements of a position? How do we recruit, interview, assess candidates, and create hiring criteria that are explicitly linked to our goals of decolonization and equity? This requires a very intentional shift in how we look at applications, evaluate candidates, and structure interviews and questions. We need to intentionally look at each of these hiring practices and ask ourselves in each moment of the process—how might we use these practices to redress the historical imbalance in training and employment opportunities? For example, I've made it our standard practice to do a first round of short teaching presentations and brief interviews with an initial large pool of candidates, prioritizing underrepresented applicants. This gives junior applicants with less experience a chance to demonstrate their often tremendous potential and capacity to teach and research. We also write job criteria and interview questions that help us to assess how candidates consider equity, decolonization, and antiracism in their teaching and research practice. This approach has been successful in beginning to redress the imbalance in our faculty complement and in developing a global and decolonial framework for our curriculum by bringing in a greater diversity of scholars and scholarship. I have also tried to support and retain these newly hired junior faculty through one-on-one mentorship, micro research and publication grants, cultivating research and social community, and early adjustments to workload. Small actions perhaps, but nevertheless more effective and more long-lasting than scheduling an anti-bias training workshop or listening session. One might argue that a workshop or a "listening session," a typical response to an incidence of racism, also counts as a small step; I would argue, however, that this kind of workshop has not arisen from a local and collaborative analysis that asks, "What action can we take right now that addresses the root of the problem?" Instead of a "listening session" or training to address a moment of conflict or racism, let's ask instead—what are some of the root causes of this incident, and what small step might we take to begin to address this in a more precise way? Shifting some of our energies away from conflict resolution, we might instead focus energies on changing the conditions from which those conflicts arise.

There are many examples of institutional diversity, equity, and inclusion models (DEI or EDI) that are beginning to integrate these kinds of practice-based analyses and actions, integrating new, clearly defined, and concrete projects of support and development.[23] While most diversity and equity plans continue to foreground conventional equity training, we are beginning to see equity and diversity plans that also include concrete, small-scale, practical, and systemic changes to the usual way of teaching, developing curricula and hiring, supporting, and retaining Indigenous and Black students and students of color. While University of Colorado's action plan,[24] for example, does reiterate standard approaches such as training, listening sessions, and general promises to focus on equity—it also asserts that the first mandate of the equity committee is to "identify proven practices that will advance equity and cultivate a culture of belonging," a shift in language and intent from many other equity efforts.

Since the conventional DEI model is already in place in so many institutions, shifting these plans toward more precise practice-based analysis and action, and away from the generic call for training, is an attainable goal within the reach of any institution committed to a different way of approaching equity and antiracism.

Collective art, design, and creative research projects are another, entirely different, form of intervention, one that pushes us to reimagine our public spaces, communities, and intellectual landscapes. At my own university, students in our Creative Writing program came together after the murder of George Floyd to create a public art installation. The installation used large traffic signs to broadcast provocative and poignant statements such as "Emergence from Emergency," "Black Joy Radiance Forever," and "Black Lives Matter, Not a Trend," making a bold intervention in the visual and cultural landscape of a busy urban space and joining arts education to racial justice—a very different kind of "antiracism workshop."

We need to collaborate and craft meaningful responses to racism that are not based on familiar Feel-Good and redemptive narratives. While preoccupations with one's moral identities and innocence have clearly been harmful to the cause of racial justice, it does not mean that we should abandon ethical conversations. Instead, we should rethink and reaffirm collective ethical commitments to racial justice, continually linking them to the broader projects of sustainability and equity. Michael Young shows that the movement for the abolition of slavery was able to grow only when Christian conceptions of sin began to shift, leading to a new sense of optimism in the ability of people to perfect themselves[25] and to become more moral people by standing against injustice. Young argues that these collective concerns with becoming better people "provided a form and purpose to extensive social movements."[26] In our own historical moment, racial justice will also require ethical shifts. As organizations and institutions, however, our ethical commitments should focus more closely on collective transformation and relationships, rather than on individual missteps.

At the start of this book, I told the story of two men who walked into a coffee shop for a meeting and came out in handcuffs. In response to the ensuing controversy over this now well-known incident, Starbucks closed all its stores across the US for an antiracism workshop. This grand gesture cost Starbucks $12 million. It signaled commitment through large expenditures of money and the emotional contributions of staff.

But even if these antiracism workshops somehow altered the hearts and minds of their employees and opened their eyes to racism, would that awareness prevent someone from calling the police? Perhaps—but perhaps not. As I argued in chapter 3, the line between knowledge and conduct is tenuous. Even if people remember and retain the knowledge

Images from web page for
*Emergence from Emergencies—
Black Realities*, a series of
public installations by OCAD
University students at stackt
Market, Toronto, presented by
the OCAD U Creative Writ-
ing Program, July 7–21, 2020.
Curators: Creative Writing
chair Prof. Catherine Black and
poet and instructor Ian Keteku.
Participating student-artists:
Jennifer Kasiama, Leaf Watson,
Meighan Morson, Ehiko Odeh,
and Chris Markland.

from a single afternoon workshop, many other factors shape their conduct. It is a highly unreliable strategy.

Let's imagine another strategy. Communities could work together to have public conversations about gathering spaces such as coffee shops, campuses, and parks: How do we share them, keep them safe for *everyone* in them, and shift practices and resources toward antiracist relationships among communities, local businesses and institutions, and police? While Starbucks' antiracism workshops received a great deal attention, the company also took another less expensive and more effective action—the creation of a new policy that allows customers to sit in any of their coffee shops without ordering. These policies should ideally arise from community-based conversations about public space and policing. Shifting urban bylaws and policing practice would then require businesses to have precise protocols to guide store employees about when and how to ask for help. The same strategy should apply to college campuses, where Black students are more likely to be stopped and scrutinized by campus security.[27] What employees think or feel about racism or about themselves would then be less relevant in decision-making.

In other words: focus on collective and concrete practice rather than inward sentiment or "racial literacy." This approach is vital if we want to see change, rather than just hope for change.

Rather than turn away from emotions, we must shift where we direct our emotional energies.

Climate action offers a potential framing for approaching an issue that is emotionally charged and laden with feelings of anxiety, sadness, and fear. A 2021 global survey of youth and young adults showed that almost 60 percent felt extremely worried about the climate crisis, and 45 percent said these feelings affected their daily functioning.[28] The responses to youth do not necessarily address climate change, however, but rather their emotions about it, echoing the Let's Talk approach of diversity workshops: in "climate emotions conversations," for example, participants speak of their grief, terror, rage, shock, betrayal, guilt, and alienation about the climate crisis.[29]

Margaret Klein Salamon, psychologist and director of the Climate Climate Emergency Fund, rightly asks, "But how do we turn this pain into action?" Her answer is to channel these feelings and "pour them into disruptive protest and nonviolent direct action." Not only would we be working for climate justice, Salamon argues that taking action on climate change would also benefit mental health.

Working toward racial justice and decolonization similarly requires moving from emotional trauma to building affective communities,[30] close working relationships, new ethical commitments, and passionate movements for change.

Conventional equity and diversity strategies need to be rethought but with the awareness that there isn't a single model or correct path toward racial justice, reconciliation, or decolonization. On the contrary, I have tried to show that when people are preoccupied with representing themselves as on the correct and moral path, the journey becomes directed to the self rather than toward racial justice. It would be better to acknowledge that, in this landscape of racial politics, our only way toward racial justice is through a maze of unmarked trails in a changing terrain. These trails do not form a golden path of redemption, but rather a mundane set of pedestrian walkways on which we might imagine guiding each other through our missteps. The key to finding our way is neither to pretend that we have a reliable roadmap nor to remain seated while we contemplate a challenging journey. The key is to continually remind each other that the journey cannot remain a solitary or inward one.

I am optimistic that these approaches will take us beyond feeling and talking and toward alliances of people committed to thinking and doing. Let's continue to move from inner reflection to collectively rethinking our practices and remaking our spaces.

ACKNOWLEDGMENTS

THERE is a convention that the author of a book receives all the formal credit for creating it; only the author's name appears on the cover. A film poster might spotlight the director or the actor, but the long list of credits acknowledges all the talented artists, musicians, and technicians that worked on it, the people of the town where it was filmed, the story that inspired it, and so on. In comparison, these acknowledgements, summoned at the end of a long writing process, will inevitably fall short in breadth, detail, and precision.

I hope I can make up for this lack in precision by expressing the depth of my gratitude and love to all those who supported me through the years of producing this work. Thank you to those who inspired it, who contributed their words, interviews, and scholarship, who repeatedly offered comments and edits, who offered intellectual companionship, solidarity, friendship, love. Thank you to those who were patient with my preoccupation and absences from family and social life. Thank you to those students, friends, colleagues, and even faraway activists and scholars who write to tell me that this work is valuable and needs to be shared.

You all know who you are, but allow me to highlight a few individuals—a very partial list of all those who have helped me to create this book.

Thanks to my dear friends who believed in me, supported me, fed me, and have been writing companions over the years. To name but a few, thanks to Pippa Domville, Neil Mclaughlin, June Larkin, Antonio Michael Downing, David Szablowski, Jeannie Samuel, Catherine Grant, Stacey DePass, Lina Cino, Sara Porter, Sara Marlowe, Jonathan Hodge, Margot Francis, Cynthia Wright, Mary-Jo Nadeau, Minelle Mahtani, Ben Barnes, Adonis Huggins, writing companions, Rick Roberts, Gokboru Tanydiz, Vinh Nguyen, my neighbors Eduardo and Gaby, who always look out for me, and my steadfast neighborhood book club members. Thanks to my family for many years of support and love, including Usha, Muni, Vinita, Anita, Anil, Zack, Timm, Ram and Rolf in Norway, my extended family in India, and so many others.

Raising my children as a solo parent has been my proudest accomplishment but, as many parents know, parenting is so often tinged with the sense that we are falling short, with never enough time to offer our children. It was difficult for me and for my kids that I was often saying to them—"I'll have more time once this book is done, I promise," but they never said so or complained. Maya and Navin: thank you both for your love and patience, and for never saying, "Isn't that book done yet?"

The foundation of this book stretches back to my work as an activist, and to my days as a graduate student: here I want to acknowledge dear friends and fellow activists in the environmental movement, Andrea Ritchie, Andrea Imada, Sheree Wells, Ann Chu, community radio co-hosts at CKLN, friends at Saugeen First Nation including former chief Darlene Ritchie, Saugeen Nation Citizen's Coalition, Saugeen Employee Association, and many friends and inspiring scholars at the University of Toronto and OISE, including Mariana Valverde, Roxana Ng, Sherene Razack, Dorothy Smith, Kari Dehli, and Deborah Britzman, and the Faculty of Environmental Studies at York University, including dian merino, Leesa Fawcett, and many others.

My PhD, MA, and thesis students in the Sociology Department at Queen's University have been a source of intellectual vibrance, solidarity, and yes, pride—Marsha Rampersaud, Melissa Forcione, Sylvia Grills, Vanessa Watts, Jennifer Matsunaga, Sylvia Bawa, Rachel Chan, Rachel Alter, Rui Hou, Erica Spink, Mandy Veenstra, to name only a few—if you have an eye on any of these folks, you'll understand my praise. These students and those in my graduate seminars in Research Methods and in Transnational Theories of Race, Gender and Sexuality, and in my undergraduate seminars in Race, Gender and Nation, in Sociology of the Body, and in my Social Justice Practicum, have always inspired me; they have also taken up the ideas in this book and applied them in a myriad of ways.

Thank you to all my colleagues at Queen's University in the Sociology, Gender Studies, and Cultural Studies, who offered support, friendship, and intellectual inspiration, including Lisa Kerr, Roseanne Currarino, Anastasia Riehl, David Murakami-Wood, Jeffrey McNairn, Alana Butler, Yolande Bouka, Elliot Paul, Abbie Bakan, Sammi King, Katherine McKittrick, and Margaret Little, to name but a few.

To all my colleagues at OCAD University: being embraced by a new community that is committed to the practice of equity, social justice, and decolonization, and that genuinely and generously supports my own work in this area, has been a true gift. It has been a challenge to balance this writing with academic leadership at OCAD U, but that challenge is outweighed by the strong sense of community, values, solidarity, and potential for change. There are too many to name here, but thanks especially to Alia Weston, Charles Reeve, Caroline Langill, Ashok Mathur, Elizabeth Clydesdale, Ana Serrano, Tony White, Stephen Foster, the chairs, faculty, and staff of the Faculty of Arts and Science (FAS), and many, many others.

And of course, thank you to the reviewers of this manuscript who offered both generous praise and careful critique, to Cynthia Lauer, Plum Publishing Development Services, for extensive publication support, and to the folks at NYU Press, notably Ilene Kalish, Executive Editor, Social Sciences, for keenly guiding me throughout.

NOTES

PREFACE

1 Yasmin Alibhai-Brown, "Meghan Markle and Prince Harry: Can the Royal Wedding Change Centuries of Racism and Classism in Britain?," *Newsweek*, May 11, 2018, www.newsweek.com.

2 Erin Vanderhoof, "Why Meghan and Harry's Revelations about Racism within the Royal Family Were So Devastating," *Vanity Fair*, March 8, 2021, www.vanityfair.com.

3 Stephen Bates and Richard Norton-Taylor, "Video Nasty: Prince Harry Faces Racism Inquiry over Footage of 'Paki' Remark," *The Guardian*, January 12, 2009, www.theguardian.com.

4 Oluwaseun Matiluko, "The Meaning of Meghan Markle," *That's What She Said Magazine*, December 13, 2017, https://twssmagazine.com.

5 Laurel Wamsley, "Buckingham Palace Responds to Allegations in Harry and Meghan's Oprah Interview," National Public Radio, March 9, 2021, www.npr.org.

6 BBC News, "Slave Trader Statue Torn Down in Bristol Anti-racism Protest," June 7, 2020, www.bbc.com; Claire Selvin, "Toppled Statue of Slave Trader Goes on View in Bristol, Generating Controversy," *Art News*, June 8, 2021, www.artnews.com.

7 Merope Mills, "Rasta Poet Publicly Rejects His OBE," *The Guardian*, November 27, 2003, www.theguardian.com.

8 Alibhai-Brown, "Meghan and Harry."

9 Nicole Wilson, "'I Like My Baby Heir with Baby Hair and Afros': Black Majesty and the Fault-Lines of Colonialism," *Women's Studies International Forum* (2021): 84.

10 Dani Di Placido, "Piers Morgan Has a Public Tantrum over Prince Harry and Meghan's Interview with Oprah Winfrey," *Forbes*, March 9, 2021, www.forbes.com.

11 DiAngelo, *White Fragility*.

12 Dobbin and Kalev, "Why Doesn't Diversity Training Work?"

CHAPTER 1. THE FEEL-GOOD POLITICS OF RACE

Epigraph: From the transcript of one of many confidential, open-ended interviews with community-based workers and activists; names and details have been changed in this book to protect the identity of interviewees. "Rayna" identifies herself as a woman of color, a writer, and a community activist.

1 CIVQS, "National Black Lives Matter Poll," June 18, 2020, https://civiqs.com.

2 Government of Canada, "Statement of Apology to Former Students of Indian Residential Schools," June 11, 2008, www.rcaanc-cirnac.gc.ca; CBC Archives, "Government Apologizes for Residential Schools in 2008," June 25, 2018, www.cbc.ca.

3 Chang et al., "The Mixed Effects"; Kalev and Dobbin, "Best Practices or Best Guesses?

4 In her book *Respectably Queer*, Jane Ward studied community organizations that, despite a reputation for diversity, fail to achieve profound change.

5 Thomas, *Diversity Regimes*.

6 Ben Miller, "It's Time to Worry about College Enrollment Declines among Black Students," Center for American Progress, September 28, 2020, www.american-progress.org.

7 Thomas, *Diversity Regimes*, chap. 6.

8 Matt Stevens, "Starbucks CEO Apologies after the Arrest of Two Black Men," *New York Times*, April 15, 2018, www.nytimes.com.

9 Melissa DePino, Twitter post, April 13, 2018, https://twitter.com/missydepino (since deleted). Also see Melissa DePino, "Why I Tweeted the Starbucks Arrest Video," CNN Opinion, April 16, 2018, www.cnn.com.

10 Rachel Abrams, Tiffany Hsu, and John Eligon, "Starbucks's Tall Order: Tackle Systemic Racism in 4 Hours," *New York Times*, May 28, 2018, www.nytimes.com.

11 Jonah Engel Bromwich, "Sephora Will Shut Down for an Hour of Diversity Training Tomorrow," *New York Times*, June 4, 2019, https://www.nytimes.com; Devika Krishna Kumar, "Sephora Plans Day of Diversity Training at All U.S. Stores after Security Called on Singer SZA," *Global News*, June 2, 2019, https://globalnews.ca.

12 Frank Dobbin, *Inventing Equal Opportunity* (New Brunswick, NJ: Princeton University Press, 2009); Dobbin and Kalev, "Why Doesn't Diversity Training Work?"

13 Fair and Impartial Policing LLC, "Agreement for the Provision of Fair and Impartial Public Safety: A Science-Based Perspective for the Police Department of the City of New York," PIN 0561800001298, December 13, 2017, https://int.nyt.com/data/documenthelper/82-fair-policing-contract-produce/68a8bf346ec3c8dc560c/optimized/full.pdf#page=1.

14 Eberhardt, *Biased*.

15 Eberhardt, *Biased*.

16 Parker, "Stanford Big Data."

17 Ward, *Respectably Queer*.

18 Chang et al., "Mixed Effects"; Kalev, Dobbin, and Kelly, "Best Practices?"; Dobbin and Kalev, "Why Diversity Programs Fail."

19 Dobbin and Kalev, "Why Doesn't Diversity Training Work?," 48.

20 Al Baker, "Confronting Implicit Bias in the New York Police Department," *New York Times*, July 15, 2018, www.nytimes.com.

21 M. Duguid and M. C. Thomas-Hunt, "Condoning Stereotyping? How Awareness of Stereotyping Prevalence Impacts Expression of Stereotypes," *Journal of Applied Psychology* 100, no. 2 (2015): 343–359, doi:10.1037/a0037908.

22 Ritchie, *Invisible No More*; Maynard, *Policing Black Lives*.

23 Alexander, *New Jim Crow*; Gilmore, *Golden Gulag*, 201.

24 "The establishment and operation of residential schools were a central element of this policy, which can best be described as 'cultural genocide.'" Truth and Reconciliation Commission of Canada, "Honouring the Truth, Reconciling for the Future: Summary of the Final Report of the Truth and Reconciliation Commission of Canada," 2015, www.trc.ca. Also see Matsunaga, "Limits of 'Truth and Reconciliation'"; J. Matsunaga, D. Long, A. Gracey, and L. Maracle, "CRS Symposium on Reconciling Indigenous-Settler Relations in Canada: Whose Voice Counts?," *Canadian Review of Sociology* 53, no. 4 (2016): 457–460, doi:10.1111/cars.12126.

25 Abu-Laban and Bakan, *Israel, Palestine*.

26 DiAngelo, *White Fragility*, 2.

27 For the most part, the women I interviewed used the terms "women of color" and "white women" to describe themselves and others, and I have continued to use these terms. The term "white" homogenizes a great deal of differences in ethnicity, class, and status; however, the people I interviewed use "white" not to describe physical appearance nor to refer to a political or individual identity, but as a way of referring to structural locations and histories associated with socially constructed racial categories. I have also continued to use the term "people of color" throughout the book, a category that is comprised of Indigenous people, Black people, and other people of color, rather than the more recent acronyms such as IBPOC or BIPOC, because these shorthands are not known universally and continue to change.

28 The women I interviewed worked in a wide variety of organizations, including national advocacy groups, feminist publishers, environmental groups, and women's services; most women were involved as activists and staff in more than one group simultaneously.

29 I use pseudonyms and alter identifying details when quoting from the interviews. The organizations are local, national, or international and based in Toronto.

30 CIVIQS, "National Black Lives Matter Survey Results," April 25, 2017–January 7, 2023, https://civiqs.com.

31 Monmouth University Polling Institute, "National: Protestors' Anger Justified Even If Actions May Not Be," poll conducted June 2, 2020, www.monmouth.edu.

32 Chang et al., "Mixed Effects"; Kalev et al., "Best Practices?"

33 For a history of corporate diversity policy and training, see Dobbin, *Inventing Equal Opportunity*, 200.

34 Tina Shah Paikeday, "Positioning Your Chief Diversity Officer for Top Performance," June 2021, Russell Reynolds Associates, www.russellreynolds.com; Leo Charbonneau, "Most Universities Report Having Equity Diversity and Inclusion Plans but Challenges Remain," *University Affairs*, November 2019, www.universityaffairs.ca; Leslie Davis and Richard Fry, "College Faculty Have Become More

Racially and Ethnically Diverse, but Remain Far Less So Than Students," Pew Research Center, July 31, 2019, www.pewresearch.org.

35 National Center for Education Statistics. *Digest of Education Statistics 2019*, https://nces.ed.gov.

36 Michael Nietzel, "Diversity Gains at Big Ten Universities Don't Include Black Students," *Forbes*, September 2021. www.forbes.com.

37 Jeanne Sahadi, "After Years of Talking about Diversity, the Number of Black Leaders at U.S. Companies Is Still Dismal," CNN, June 2020, www.cnn.com; Jared Council, "Record Number of Black CEOs Will Lead S&P 500 Companies," *Forbes*, March 2023, www.forbes.com.

38 Seung-Hwan Jeong, Ann Mooney, Yangyang Zhang, and Timothy J. Quigley, "How Do Investors Really React to the Appointment of Black CEOs?: A Comment on Gligor et al. 2021," *Strategic Management Journal* 44, no. 7 (2023): 1733–1752.

39 Ben Miller, "It's Time to Worry about College Enrollment Declines among Black Students," Center for American Progress, September 28, 2020, www.american-progress.org; Andrew Howard Nichols, "Segregation Forever? The Continued Underrepresentation of Black and Latino Undergraduates at the Nation's 101 Most Selective Public Colleges and Universities," Education Trust, July 2020, https://edtrust.org.

40 Oyin Adedoyin, "What Happened to Black Enrollment?," *Chronicle of Higher Education*, August 2022, www.chronicle.com.

41 Andrew Howard Nichols, "'Segregation Forever?': The Continued Underrepresentation of Black and Latino Undergraduates at the Nation's 101 Most Selective Public Colleges and Universities," Education Trust, July 21, 2020, https://edtrust.org.

42 Nietzel, "Gains Don't Include Black Students."

43 Nietzel, "Gains Don't Include Black Students."

44 Universities Canada, "Equity, Diversity and Inclusion at a Canadian University: Report on the 2019 National Survey," www.univcan.ca.

45 Tina Shah Paikeday, "Positioning your Chief Diversity Officer for Top Performance," Russell Reynolds Associates, June 2021, www.russellreynolds.com.

46 Henry Report, Queen's University; Presidential Task Force on Underrepresentation, OCAD University; www.univcan.ca; Henry et al., *Equity Myth*; Cukier et al. *Racialized Leaders*; Henry and Tator, *Racism in the Canadian University*.

47 Thomas, *Diversity Regimes*, chap. 1.

48 Thomas, *Diversity Regimes*, chap. 1.

49 Hate Crime Statistics, "2013 Uniform Crime Report," Washington, DC: US Department of Justice, Federal Bureau of Investigation, December 2014. www.fbi.gov.

50 Federal Bureau of Investigation, "2018 Hate Crime Statistics," https://ucr.fbi.gov.

51 National Center for Educational Statistics, "Hate Crime Incidents at Postsecondary Institutions," https://nces.ed.gov.

52 Greg Moreau, "Police-Reported Hate Crime in Canada, 2019," Canadian Centre for Justice and Community Safety Statistics, March 2021, www150.statcan.gc.ca.

53 DeMarcus A. Jenkins, Antar A. Tichavakunda, and Justin A. Coles, "The Second ID: Critical Race Counterstories of Campus Police Interactions with Black Men at Historically White Institutions," *Race Ethnicity and Education* 24, no. 2 (March 4, 2021): 149–66, doi:10.1080/13613324.2020.1753672.

54 Elizabeth L. Paluck and Donald P. Green, "Prejudice Reduction: What Works? A Critical Look at Evidence from the Field and the Laboratory," *Annual Review of Psychology* 60 (2009): 339–367.

55 C. A. George Mwangi, R. Thelamour, I. Ezeofor, and A. Carpenter, "'Black Elephant in the Room:' Black Students Contextualizing Campus Racial Climate within U.S. Racial Climate," *Journal of College Student Development* 59 (2018): 456–474, doi: 10.1353/csd.2018.0042; Paluck and Green, "Prejudice Reducation," 60; Nietzel, "Diversity Gains."

56 Ahmed, *On Being Included*.

57 Ward, *Respectably Queer*.

58 Ward, *White Normativity*; Ahmed, *On Being Included*; Khan, "Whiteness of Green."

59 Ahmed, *On Being Included*, 175.

60 Ward, *White Normativity*; Ahmed, *On Being Included*; Khan, "Whiteness of Green."

61 Russo, "Between Speech," 44.

62 Ward, *White Normativity*.

63 Ward, *White Normativity*.

64 Greensmith, "Desiring Diversity," 57.

65 Ward, *Respectably Queer*.

66 Ward, *Respectably Queer*.

67 Phillip Atiba Goff, personal communication; Goff, Steele, and Davies, "Space between Us."

68 Vorauer and Sasaki, "Liberation or Constraint?"

69 Apfelbaum et al., "Racial Color Blindness."

70 Jacques Gallant, "Law Society Scraps Key Diversity Initiative," *Toronto Star*, September 11, 2019, www.thestar.com; Paola Loriggio, "Ontario Law Society Revokes Rule Requiring Members to Commit to Diversity," *Global News*, September 2019, https://globalnews.ca.

71 "Atticus has become something of a folk hero in legal circles and is treated almost as if he were an actual person," says Alice Petry, *On Harper Lee*, xxiii.

72 In 2014, the name Atticus rose to occupy spot 370 in boys' most popular names in the US, perhaps spurred by a number of celebrities who have named their children Atticus (Garber, "My Atticus"). In the UK, the popularity of the name Atticus has also risen in recent years, becoming the most popular literary boys' name (Chitra Ramaswamy, "What Happens Now to the People and Businesses Named after Atticus Finch?," *The Guardian*, July 13, 2015, www.theguardian.com).

73 Dahlia Lithwick writes, "It's almost a cliché to say that Atticus Finch is one's legal hero, like saying you like good chocolate or high thread count sheets. Still, I am one of many thousands of people who probably would not have gone to law school were it not for the fictional hero of Harper Lee's *To Kill a Mockingbird*." In Lithwick, "My Legal Hero."

74 Chakrabarti, "*Mockingbird* Made Me a Lawyer."

75 Harper Lee, *Go Set a Watchman*. Marketed as a sequel to *To Kill a Mockingbird*, *Go Set a Watchman* was in fact Harper Lee's first book manuscript. It is set years after *To Kill a Mockingbird* when Scout, the child in *To Kill a Mockingbird*, is an adult. Harper Lee submitted it to publishers in 1957, but was asked to revise it. See Michiko Kakutani, "*Go Set a Watchman* Gives Atticus a Dark Side," *New York Times*, July 10, 2015, www.nytimes.com.

76 Maloney and Stevens, "Harper Lee's Father."

77 Ricker-Wilson relates her experience of teaching the novel to a class of white and black students; while the white students found it a positive experience, the experience was more mixed for black students, who also found it demoralizing. Ricker-Wilson, "Mockingbird Becomes an Albatross."

78 Katie Reilly, "Read Hilary Clinton's 'Basket of Deplorables' Remarks about Donald Trump Supporters," *Time*, September 10, 2016, https://time.com.

79 "Video of Hilary Clinton Meeting with Black Lives Matter Activists," August 19, 2015, www.democracynow.org.

80 Hilary Clinton, "U.S. Presidential Debate," Politico.com, October 2016, www.politico.com.

81 Goldberg, *Threat of Race*, 343.

82 Razack, "Simple Logic."

83 For example, Goff, Steele, and Davies, "Space between Us."

84 Ian Burkitt suggests that emotions are "expressions between people and not expressions of something contained inside a single person." See Burkitt, "Social Relationships," 40. See also Ahmed, *Cultural Politics of Emotion*; Spencer, Walby, and Hunt, *Emotions Matter*.

85 For example, Arlie Hochschild introduced the concept of "emotional labor." See Hochschild, *Second Shift*, and Hochschild, *Managed Heart*. Also see Bendelow and Williams, *Emotions in Social Life*; Spencer, Walby, and Hunt, *Emotions Matter*.

86 Ahmed, *Cultural Politics*, 12.

87 Weisman, "Being and Doing"; Weisman, *Showing Remorse*.

88 Bonilla-Silva, "Feeling Race."

89 Similar concepts include Sara Ahmed's term "affective economies" in *The Cultural Politics of Emotion*, or Paula Ioanide's "emotional economies" in *The Emotional Politics of Racism*. For a review of affect theory and the myriad of ways that scholars have theorized affect and emotion, see Seigworth and Gregg, "Inventory."

90 Foucault, "Genealogy of Ethics."

91 Levine-Rasky, *Whiteness Fractured*, 153.

92 For example, see Ferguson, *Feminist Case against Bureaucracy*; Putnam and Mumby, "Myth of Rationality"; Boler, *Feeling Power*.

93 Putnam and Mumby, "Organizations, Emotion," 55.

94 Stoler, *Carnal Knowledge*; Stoler, *Education of Desire*; Roediger, *Wages of Whiteness*; Said, *Orientalism*; Fanon, *Black Skin, White Masks*, 10; Rai, *Rule of Sympathy*.

95 Nagel, *Race, Ethnicity, and Sexuality*.

96 Stoler, *Carnal Knowledge*; Stoler, *Education of Desire*.

97 Mahrouse, *Conflicted Commitments*; Heron, *Desire for Development*.

98 Bonilla-Silva and Dietrich, "Sweet Enchantment." See also Essed, *Understanding Everyday Racism*.

99 Sociologist Eduardo Bonilla-Silva uses the phrase "racism without racists" to describe this social trend. Bonilla-Silva, *Racism without Racists*. The evocative term "racism without racists" aptly describes how it is that racial discrimination is perpetuated even when and in part because people do not think of themselves as racist and imagine that racism has disappeared.

100 Kubota, et al., "Price of Racial Bias."

101 M. Bertrand and S. Mullainathan, "Are Emily and Greg More Employable than Lakisha and Jamal? A Field Experiment on Labor Market Discrimination," *American Economic Review* 94, no. 4 (2004): 991–1013; F. McGinnity and P. D. Lunn, "Measuring Discrimination Facing Ethnic Minority Job Applicants: An Irish Experiment," *Work, Employment & Society* 25, no. 4 (2001): 693–708, doi:10.1177/0950017011419722.

102 Dowd, "Public and Academic."

103 Ioanide, *Emotional Politics of Racism*.

104 Foucault, *Power/Knowledge*, 97; Foucault, *History of Sexuality, Vol. 1*, 90. Despite Foucault's methodological focus on local practices, he also stresses that power regimes have also been integrated into "global or macrostrategies of domination." See Foucault, *History of Sexuality, Vol. 1*, 158–159.

105 See Barrett, *Politics of Truth*. In "Foucault and the Tyranny of Greece," for example, Mark Poster remarks on a conspicuous absence in Foucault's work of discussion about the affective nuances of sexual relations (cited in Barrett, *Politics of Truth*).

106 Foucault noted, for example, that the work of historians has dramatically changed as a result of recognizing "it was also possible to write the history of feelings, behavior and the body." In Kritzman, *Michel Foucault*, 104, cited in Barrett, *Politics of Truth*.

107 Foucault, "Genealogy of Ethics," 238.

108 Stoler, *Carnal Knowledge*; Stoler, *Education of Desire*.

109 Ruth Frankenberg's study of whiteness, *White Women, Race Matters*, for example, defines it as "a set of locations that are historically, socially, politically, and culturally produced and . . . linked to unfolding relations of domination."

110 Du Bois, "Souls of White Folk," 32.

111 Goldberg, *Racist Culture*, 39.

112 Goldberg, *Racist Culture*, 23; Dudley and Novak, *Wild Man Within*.

113 Goldberg, *Racist Culture*, 22.

114 Dyer, *White*.

115 Dyer's example is the 1949 film *Beyond the Forest*, in which Bette Davis plays an evil murderer and adulterer with long jet-black hair who gradually adopts the dress of the Indigenous woman who cleans her home.

116 Dyer, *White*, 65.

117 Ware, *Beyond the Pale*.

118 Valverde, *Age of Light*.

119 Stoler, *Education of Desire*, 130.

120 Demanded by the small white colonial settler community in 1920s Papua, the White Women's Protection Ordinance of Papua (www.paclii.org), which made the sexual assault of "European" women punishable by death, is but one piece of colonial legislation that cemented these representations. The territory of Papua was a British colony administered by Australia. For a discussion of this legislation, see Inglis, *White Women's Protection Ordinance*.

121 Stoler, *Education of Desire*; Dyer, *White*; Valverde, *Age of Light*; Enloe, *Bananas, Beaches and Bases*; Razack, *Looking White People in the Eye*.

122 Fellows and Razack, "Race to Innocence," 1; Heron, *Desire for Development*; Roger, "Fairy Fictions."

123 Roger, "Fairy Fictions."

124 Heron, *Desire for Development*.

125 Schick, "By Virtue of Being White," 310.

126 Fellows and Razack, "Race to Innocence."

127 Heron, *Desire for Development*, 102.

128 Roger, "Fairy Fictions."

129 Applebaum in *Being White, Being Good* explores "white complicity" as a moral question. Mab Segrest's memoir explored her own moral complicities with racism, evocatively detailing her own moral and psychic journey as a white woman growing up in the South.

130 Segrest, *Memoir*. See also Sullivan, *Good White People*.

131 Young, *Bearing Witness*.

132 Kouchaki, "Vicarious Moral Licensing." Also see Krumm and Corning, "Who Believes Us?"; Monin and Miller, "Moral Credentials."

133 Bonilla-Silva, *Racism without Racists*.

134 Razack, "Simple Logic."

135 Schick, "By Virtue of Being White," 310.

136 Essed, *Everyday Racism*.

137 Wetherell and Potter, *Language of Racism*.

138 Bonilla-Silva, *Racism without Racists*.

139 Pierce, *Racing for Innocence*, 9.

140 Sullivan, *Good White People*.

141 Sullivan, *Good White People*, 4.

142 Sullivan, *Good White People*; Pierce, *Racing for Innocence*.

143 Sullivan and Tuana, *Race and the Epistemologies*; Mills, "White Ignorance."

144 Also referred to as "white racial literacy." DiAngelo, *What Does It Mean?*;
     DiAngelo, *Developing White Racial Literacy* (New York: Peter Lang, 2012).

145 Lani Guinier, "From Racial Liberalism to Racial Literacy: Brown V. Board of
     Education and the Interest-Divergence Dilemma," *Journal of American History* 91,
     no. 1 (2004): 92–118.

146 Guinier, "From Racial Liberalism."

147 Kevin J. Harrelson, "White Racial Literacy and Racial Dexterity," *Educational
     Theory* 71, no. 2 (2021): 203–221.

148 Gordon Allport, *The Nature of Prejudice* (Boston: Addison-Wesley, 1954).

149 Denis, "Contact Theory"; Amir, "Contact Hypothesis."

150 Denis, "Contact Theory."

151 Bullard, *Confronting Environmental Racism*.

152 Roger Keil, "Green Work Alliances: The Political Economy of Social Ecology,"
     Studies in Political Economy 44, no. 1 (1994): 7–38, doi:
     10.1080/19187033.1994.11675380.

153 Also see Barbara Lynch's comparison of Latino environmental discourses with
     mainstream environmentalism in Lynch, "Garden and the Sea."

154 Khan, "Whiteness of Green."

155 Mariana Valverde's study of Alcoholics Anonymous, for example, shows that its
     primary practices can be described as ethical techniques—practices aimed at
     changing the self, one's own desires and habits—as opposed to medical or
     psychological. See Valverde, "One Day at a Time."

156 For empirical assessments of the various aspects of Michels's "iron law of
     oligarchy," see Herbert Kitschelt's study of ecology parties, "The Medium Is the
     Message," and Lipset, Trow, and Coleman, *Union Democracy*, on the American
     printers' union.

157 Gilroy, *There Ain't No Black*, 21.

158 See Roediger, *Wages of Whiteness*, and Saxton, *Rise and Fall*, for historical
     analyses of whiteness and the working class.

159 Roediger, *Wages of Whiteness*, 8.

160 See Phizacklea and Miles, "British Trade Union Movement," and Frager,
     Sweatshop Strife, for examinations of racism in early labor movement struggles.

161 See Giddings, *When and Where*; Davis, *Women, Race and Class*; Valverde, *Age of
     Light*.

162 *Women's Journal* was the journal of the Women's Christian Temperance Union of
     Canada (WCTU) (quoted in Valverde, "Mother of the Race," 17).

163 See, for example, Evans, *Tidal Wave*; Bullard, *Confronting Environmental Racism*;
     Grills, "Should the Rainbow?"

164 Awwad et al. *Disrupting Queer Inclusion*; Grills, "Should the Rainbow?"; Bhanji, "Trans/scriptions"; Morgensen, *Spaces between Us*.
165 Sylvia Grills, "Should the Rainbow?," 6.
166 Halcli, "AIDS, Anger, and Activism"; Patton, *Inventing AIDS*.
167 Martinez, "Where Was the Color?"
168 Martinez, "Where Was the Color?"
169 Dei, *Anti-racism Education*, 66.
170 For details of antiracist feminist struggles in the US, see Breines, *Trouble between Us*.
171 Breines, *Trouble between Us*; Sudbury, *Other Kinds of Dreams*.
172 National Action Committee on the Status of Women (NAC).
173 Breines, *Trouble between Us*; L. Sarick, "NAC to Vote for More than a President/ NAC Has Fallen into the 'Skin Trap,' Critic Says," *Globe and Mail*, June 15, 1996, A1.
174 Farah Stockman, "Women's March on Washington Opens Contentious Dialogue on Race," *New York Times*, January 9, 2017, www.nytimes.com; Karen Grisby Bates, "Race and Feminism: Women's March Recalls the Touchy History," National Public Radio, January 21, 2017, www.npr.org; Riggs, *Psychic Life of Racism*.
175 Carby, "White Women Listen!"
176 Russo, "Without Our Lives"; Lugones and Spelman, "Have We Got a Theory!"; Narayan, "Working Together"; Lorde, "Letter to Mary Daly."
177 Exceptions include Egan, Gardner, and Persad, "Politics of Transformation."
178 Sarah Schwartz, "Map: Where Critical Race Theory Is Under Attack," *Education Week*, June 11, 2021, www.edweek.org.
179 Foucault, *Discipline and Punish*.
180 Dreyfus and Rabinow, *Michel Foucault*, 118.
181 Brown, "Moralism as Anti-politics," 20.
182 Taylor, *From #BlackLivesMatter*, 190.

CHAPTER 2. "NOSTALGIA FOR A WORLD WE NEVER KNEW"
1 Carby, "White Women Listen!," 212–235.
2 Carby, "White Women Listen!"; hooks, "Ain't I a Woman"; Moraga and Anzaldúa, *This Bridge Called My Back*.
3 Breines, *Trouble between Us*, 7.
4 Damien Riggs, "Introduction," *The Psychic Life of Racism*, 5.
5 BoardSource, *Leading with Intent*.
6 Kelly LeRoux, "The Effects of Descriptive Representation on Nonprofits' Civic Intermediary Roles: A Test of the Racial Mismatch Hypothesis in the Social Services Sector," *Nonprofit and Voluntary Sector Quarterly* 38, no. 5 (2009): 741–760; Callander, Holt, and Newman, "Gay Racism," 3. Also see Keith Boykin (*One More River to Cross*), who observed that the largest gay rights organizations based in Washington, DC, had almost entirely white staff.

7 Grills, "Should the Rainbow?," 1.
8 LeRoux, "Effects of Descriptive Representation."
9 Many of the events I discuss took place in Toronto, but either received national media coverage or involved national organizations.
10 Statistics Canada, "Census Data 2016," www12.statcan.gc.ca.
11 Canadian Research Institute for the Advancement of Women (hereafter CRIAW), *Looking for Change*. See also Aggarwal, "Continuing on the Ground."
12 Callander, Holt, and Newman, "Gay Racism."
13 Todd Gitlin, "After the Failed Faiths: Beyond Individualism, Marxism, and Multiculturalism," *World Policy Journal* 12, no. 1 (1995): 66.
14 Gitlin, *Twilight of Common Dreams*. See also Gitlin, "Rise of Identity Politics."
15 Gitlin, "Failed Faiths," 68.
16 Gitlin, "Failed Faiths," 68.
17 Moraga and Anzaldúa, *This Bridge Called My Back*.
18 Nila Gupta, personal communication to author, 1996.
19 Landsberg, "Feminists Must Learn."
20 Rebick, *Ten Thousand Roses*, 254.
21 Bannerji, *Returning the Gaze*, xiii.
22 Cernetig, "Feminist Conference Disrupted."
23 Carby, "White Women Listen!," 111.
24 Bannerji, *Returning the Gaze*.
25 Giddings, *When and Where*; Evans, *Tidal Wave*; Sudbury, *Other Kinds of Dreams*; Breines, *Trouble between Us*.
26 Backhouse and Flaherty's anthology on the North American women's movement includes an important section on racism and feminism. The section includes three articles: Arun Mukherjee's "A House Divided: Women of Color and American Feminist Theory," Mariana Valverde's "Racism and Anti-racism in Feminist Teaching and Research," and Glenda Simms's "Beyond the White Veil."
27 Vickers et al.'s book on NAC, *Politics as if Women Mattered*, does look at internal challenges and change, but conflict surrounding antiracist change is a peripheral topic. There have been few historical examinations of Canadian social movements that trace the development of antiracist concerns. *Scratching the Surface*, Dua's and Robertson's review of the development of antiracist feminism, is an important contribution. However, it deals primarily with conceptual directions in antiracist feminism rather than the story of organizations and internal battles.
28 Nadeau, "Troubling Herstory," 6.
29 The International Women's Day/March 8th Coalition brought together women's groups in Toronto on an annual basis to organize events for International Women's Day.
30 See Gabriel and Scott's analysis of developments at the Women's Press of Toronto.
31 Scott, *Gender and Politics*, 6.
32 Alonso, "Effects of Truth," 37, 40.

33 Foucault referred to his genealogical method of examining history to understand present social relations as a "history of the present."

34 See, for example, Giddings's *When and Where I Enter* on the first- and second-wave US women's movement. Carol Bacchi, Angus McLaren, and Mariana Valverde have all written on Canadian first-wave feminism.

35 Ware, *Beyond the Pale*, 109.

36 The "first wave" of the women's movement refers to the period of the late nineteenth and early twentieth centuries during which a central focus of the movement was women's suffrage, or the right to vote. The first-wave women's movement also included organizations, such as the Women's Christian Temperance Union, that were more focused on fighting for the prohibition of alcohol, for moral regulation, and for child and family welfare.

37 Giddings, *When and Where*.

38 Valverde, "Racial Poison," 39.

39 Valverde, "Mother of the Race."

40 Valverde, "Racial Poison," 37. See also Valverde, *Age of Light*.

41 Giddings, *When and Where*, 119.

42 In addition, Dua and Robertson shows that we may also define a period of antiracist feminism from 1850 to 1970 in which Indigenous women, Black women, Japanese Canadian women, and South Asian women were active in struggles against racism that were excluded from the first-wave women's movement.

43 This battle is well-detailed by Ware, *Beyond the Pale*, 169–224; see also Giddings, *When and Where*, chapter 5.

44 Paula Giddings, "A Noble Endeavor: Ida B. Wells-Barnett and Suffrage," Women's Suffrage Centennial Commission (WSCC), April 1, 2020, www.nps.gov; see also Giddings, "Missing in Action."

45 Giddings, *When and Where*, 123.

46 Angela Davis, a philosophy professor and activist, was arrested and imprisoned in August 1970 on suspicion of involvement with a courthouse shooting, prompting a campaign to "Free Angela Davis." She was acquitted of all charges in June 1972.

47 Giddings, *When and Where*, 305.

48 Sara Evans, in her book *Personal Politics*, details the links between the civil rights movement and the women's movement of the late 1960s.

49 Beins, *Liberation in Print*.

50 A Toronto-based national feminist newspaper, *Broadside* was published monthly for a decade, between 1979 and 1989, and was the site for intense debates about antiracism and feminism.

51 In September 1981, the national feminist monthly *Kinesis* published what may be the first article in the Canadian feminist press on racism and feminism, "The Politics of Visibility: Addressing Third World Concerns," by Maylynn Woo and Prabha Khosla. The authors, who referred to themselves as non-white feminists and Third World women, wrote that there was a "political stagnation" in the

women's movement, and that white feminists had to "confront their own racism"—they argued feminism had come to a "turning point." See Woo and Khosla, "Politics of Visibility," 16.

52 Angela Davis, bell hooks, Gloria Joseph, Gloria Anzaldúa, Cherríe Moraga, Hazel Carby, Valerie Amos, and Pratibha Parmar also had international influence.

53 It is important to note that while recorded critiques of the feminist movement and its integration of antiracist analysis were still scant in the early 1980s, antiracist feminist activism was significant even in the 1970s—concerns included police violence and immigration policy. See Dua and Robertson, *Scratching the Surface*; Carty, "Combining Our Efforts."

54 Egan, Gardner, and Persad, "Politics of Transformation," 37.

55 Weir, "Anti-racist Feminist Pedagogy," 19.

56 Gupta and Silvera, "Never Lost," 5.

57 Bannerji, *Returning the Gaze*, xii.

58 Bannerji, *Returning the Gaze*, xii.

59 Valverde, "Letter to the Editorial Collective," 3.

60 For a fuller discussion of debate on this issue following IWD in 1983, see Abdo, "Gender and Politics"; Gotlieb, "What About Us?"

61 Both O'Brien and Forman were at the Ontario Institute for Studies in Education (OISE) at the University of Toronto, and associated with the Women's Research and Resource Center there.

62 O'Brien and Forman, "Letter to the Editorial Collective," 3.

63 Landau, "Letter to the Broadside Editorial Collective," 3.

64 Ware, *Beyond the Pale*, 26.

65 Lenon and Dryden, "Introduction," 9.

66 Mukherjee, "A Four-Hundred Year Old Woman," 25.

67 Anderson, *Imagined Communities*, 6.

68 Morgan, *Sisterhood Is Powerful*, 4.

69 Rebick, *Ten Thousand Roses*, 254.

70 Similarly, activist and scholar Todd Gitlin has positioned himself as a keeper of the left against the dilutions of identity politics. Gitlin's book, *The Twilight of Common Dreams*, laments the ways that organizing on the basis of gender, race, or identity politics has eroded the unity and central goals of the left. See Young, "Complexities of Coalition," for a critique of Gitlin's argument.

71 Brown, "Moralism as Anti-politics," 28.

72 Breines, *Trouble between Us*, 9.

73 Breines, *Trouble between Us*, 10.

74 Erikson, "Notes on Trauma," 187.

75 At the Women's Resource Educational Center of the Ontario Institute for Studies in Education (OISE).

76 Cynthia Wright, personal communication to author, 2002; Mariana Valverde, personal communication to author, 2002.

77 These categories of feminism are outlined in detail in Alison Jaggar's book *Feminist Politics and Human Nature*. Generally speaking, radical feminism focuses on the universal oppression of women, while socialist feminism marries an analysis of gender oppression to other social relations, particularly class. Liberal feminism focuses on gender equality through reforms of existing institutions.

78 Mariana Valverde, "Letter to the Editorial Collective." It is important to note that, while Valverde's letter contrasts the issue of sexuality with that of race, the many women of color lesbians at the forefront of antiracist feminism did important work to integrate these issues. To name only a fraction of the most prominent in the US, there were Audre Lorde and Barbara Smith, and in Toronto, Makeda Silvera and Dionne Brand.

79 International Women's Day Committee, "Letter to the Editorial Collective."

80 *Broadside* Collective, "Broadside and Beyond."

81 Lowenberger, "IWD."

82 Quoted in Egan, Gardner, and Persad, "Politics of Transformation," 38.

83 Egan, Gardner, and Persad, "Politics of Transformation," 39.

84 Egan, Gardner, and Persad, "Politics of Transformation," 39.

85 *Broadside* Collective, "No to Racism."

86 Quoted in Egan, Gardner, and Persad, "Politics of Transformation," 44.

87 Refers only to periodicals and articles catalogued in the *Canadian Feminist Periodicals Index*.

88 Weir, "Anti-racist Feminist Pedagogy," 22.

89 Weir, "Anti-racist Feminist Pedagogy," 22.

90 *Broadside* Collective, "Broadside and Beyond."

91 *Broadside* Collective, "Broadside and Beyond."

92 NAC, "NAC Organizational Review Document," 3.

93 Vickers, Rankin, and Appelle, *As If Women Mattered*.

94 Lesbian Writing and Publishing Collective, *Dykeversions*.

95 In part, the committee was concerned with stories that appropriated or exoticized the voice and style of other cultures. See Cole, "Writing Out Racism"; Stasiulis, "Authentic Voice."

96 See Cole, "Writing Out Racism"; Stasiulis, "Authentic Voice"; Philip, "Gut Issues in Babylon"; Fung, "Working Through Cultural Appropriation." As a result of the broken contracts, the Writer's Union of Canada advised its members not to deal with the Women's Press. Within the Writer's Union, subsequent polarized debate about racism and publishing led to the formation of the Committee on Racism in Writing & Publishing. See "Writing Authentic Voice," *Fuse* 1, no. 1/2 (1990): 1–15.

97 Margie Wolfe later founded Second Story Press with other ex-collective members who did not support the new direction of Women's Press.

98 Others have commented that the conflict was less about racism than it was about the struggle for power among white women controlling Women's Press (Philip

1989; Interview transcripts). However, I am not concerned with imputing "true" motive, but rather with understanding the nature of the debate and how it shaped antiracist feminism.

99 See Henry et al., *Color of Democracy*, 163, for a fuller discussion of events inside Nellie's.

100 Freedman, "White Woman's Burden," 76.

101 Dewar, "Wrongful Dismissal."

102 Rose, "Trouble at Nellie's."

103 Peter Gzowski, host of CBC show *Morningside*, on-air comment, 1992.

104 Quoted in Douglas, "Checking In," 6.

105 Freedman, "White Woman's Burden."

106 Freedman, "White Woman's Burden," 40, 84.

107 See Richer and Weir's anthology *Beyond Political Correctness* for historical detail on this phenomenon in Canada. Weir quotes Ruth Perry ("Historically Correct," *Women's Review of Books*, February 1, 1992) as the best source on the origin of the phrase "politically correct." Perry suggests that the phrase was first used in the Black Power and New Left movements of the 1960s, and was taken from the English translation of Mao Tse-tung's "On the Correct Handling of Contradictions among the People," published in 1966.

108 Dewar, "Wrongful Dismissal."

109 Freedman, "White Woman's Burden."

110 Callwood was also featured on the cover of *Quota*, a lesbian monthly, accompanied by the headline "Who's Minding the Store?" (See Douglas, "Checking In," 6). Other articles focusing on Callwood include a full-page spread in the *Globe and Mail* (Rose, "Trouble at Nellie's"; Paris, "Unsaid Words on Racism").

111 Dewar, "Wrongful Dismissal."

112 Thorsell, "Question of the Pot."

113 See, for example, letters to the editor of *Toronto Life*, May 1991, 14, 18. The majority were supportive of the Women of Color Coalition and included letters from feminist leaders such as Judy Rebick and Phyllis Berck, chair of LEAF (Women's Legal Education and Action Fund). See also Loucas, "Commentary," 3. Others praised the magazine for its courageous stand in this time of political correctness: see Berger, "Flimsy Case against Callwood"; McMullen, "Callwood's Tactful Abilities."

114 Ilves, "Letter to the Editor."

115 Mayes, "Racism Remains."

116 For example, NAC's internal conflict over whether to endorse the book *Our Little Secret*, which became framed as a fight between women of color and lesbian women, became the topic of media coverage.

117 Paris, "Unsaid Words on Racism."

118 Berton, "If Callwood Is a Racist."

119 See Nadeau, "Who Is Canadian Now?," for an analysis of backlash against Sunera Thobani after 9/11.

120 "The White Man's Burden," originally published in 1899 (accessed at www.kipling-society.co.uk), referred to the role of the US in the Philippines. Another example of its latter-day usage is a radio interview on the reconstruction of Afghanistan in which a political scientist quoted Kipling's poem and commented that "the problem with imperialism is that no one ever says thank you." As illustration, he cited the role of the British in Egypt (CBC, *This Morning*, October 15, 2001).

121 Henry et al., *Color of Democracy*.

122 Henry et al., *Color of Democracy*, 37.

123 Henry et al., *Color of Democracy*, 34.

124 Henry et al., *Color of Democracy*, 35.

125 Douglas, "Checking In," 6.

126 Strauss, "Politically Correct 'n' Ridiculous."

127 Freedman, "White Woman's Burden."

128 Brown, "Not outside the Range."

129 Caruth, *Trauma*, vii.

130 Lucas et al., "Changing the Politics," 3. This article was written by five women representing local groups in Toronto: Salome Lucas from Women Working with Immigrant Women, Judy Vashti Persad of the Cross Cultural Communications Center, Gillian Morton of Toronto's Socialist Feminist Action, Sunita Albuquerque of the South Asian Women's Group, and Nada el Yassir of the Palestinian Women's Association.

131 Helen Armstrong, "Planning for Women's Day Fragmented," *NOW Magazine*, March 4, 1991.

132 Landsberg, "Feminists Must Learn."

133 In 1995, the Canadian government introduced a $975 head tax on all immigrants entering the country. NAC, along with many other groups, argued that this was a regressive and discriminatory tax that disproportionately limited the immigration of those from the Third World, people of color, women, women of color, and poor women.

134 Henry et al., *Color of Democracy*.

135 CRIAW, *Looking for Change*.

136 United Way of Greater Toronto, *Action, Access, Diversity!*

137 BoardSource, *Leading with Intent*; M. Kim, "Representation and Diversity, Advocacy, and Nonprofit Arts Organizations," *Nonprofit and Voluntary Sector Quarterly* 47, no. 1 (2018): 49–71. See also Devor, "Face of Nonprofit Boards"; McCambridge, "Disturbing Lack"; Taylor, "State of Diversity"; Tempel, "Nonprofits Have a Spotty Record"; Thurman, "Nonprofits Don't Really Care."

138 Callander, Holt, and Newman, "Gay Racism."

139 CRIAW, *Looking for Change*.

140 CRIAW, *Looking for Change*, 22.

141 CRIAW, *Looking for Change*, 22.

142 In her article "Why Identity Politics Is Not the Answer," Irshad Manji quotes briefly from her interview with Joanne St. Lewis about the "organizational racism that forced St. Lewis from . . . her post."

143 Aggarwal quoted in Angela Robertson, "Continuing on the Ground," 312.

144 For example, the United Way of Greater Toronto published a booklet called *Action, Access and Diversity: A Guide to Multicultural/Anti-racist Change for Social Service Agencies*, and began to require agencies it funded to develop a multicultural/antiracist policy and plan. See also Ward, *Respectably Queer*.

145 CRIAW, *Looking for Change*, 22.

146 CRIAW, *Looking for Change*, 23.

147 CRIAW, *Looking for Change*, 23.

148 Pastrana, "The Intersectional Imagination," 223.

CHAPTER 3. "LET'S TALK, CRY A LITTLE, AND LEARN ABOUT EACH OTHER"

1 Kyle Westaway, "20 Books for 2020: A Reading List on Race in America," *Forbes*, June 4, 2020, www.forbes.com.

2 The Anti-Racism Secretariat was initiated when the New Democratic Party (NDP) won the elections for Ontario's provincial government in 1990. With its traditionally strong links to labor organizations, the NDP is the most "left-leaning" of the major political parties in Canada and has governed several provinces.

3 Bergner, "White Fragility Is Everywhere."

4 For example, see Ward, *Respectably Queer*, 37; Scott, "Creating Partnerships."

5 Dobbin and Kalev, "Why Doesn't Diversity Training Work?"

6 Friedman, "Beyond White and Other," 5.

7 Razack, "Storytelling"; Benjamin, "Critiquing"; Ellsworth, "Why Doesn't This?"

8 Sarah Schwartz, "Map: Where Critical Race Theory Is Under Attack," *Education Week*, June 11, 2021, www.edweek.org.

9 I draw on observations concerning twelve antiracist workshops, numerous organizational meetings, interviews with women active in antiracism, and reviews of antiracist education training manuals. I have observed, as participant or facilitator, five of these workshops or workshop series. These workshops or meetings are discrete but sometimes regular events, and their goal may be to raise awareness, reduce conflict, or initiate change.

10 Bergner, "White Fragility Is Everywhere."

11 Kleinman, *Opposing Ambitions*.

12 Ward, *Respectably Queer*, 92.

13 Ontario Ministry of Education and Training, *Resource Guide*.

14 Ontario Ministry of Education and Training, *Resource Guide*.

15 Ontario Ministry of Education and Training, *Resource Guide*.

16 Originally applied by anthropologist Claude Lévi-Strauss to theorize how people remake cultural meanings. See Claude Lévi-Strauss, *The Savage Mind* (Paris: Librairie Plon, 1962).

17 Bergner, "White Fragility Is Everywhere."

18 Sullivan and Tuana, *Race and Ignorance*, 2.

19 M. A. Forcione, "(Un)settling Education: Navigating Québec Curriculum, Settler-Indigenous Dynamics, and Possibilities for Local Elementary and Secondary Teaching," PhD diss., Queen's University, 2022.

20 Mills, *Racial Contract*.

21 C. W. Mills and S. Vucetic, "Race, Liberalism, and Global Justice: Interview with Charles W. Mills," *International Politics Review* 9 (2021): 155–170, doi:10.1057/s41312-021-00085-2.

22 Robyn Moore, "Resolving the Tensions between White People's Active Investment in Racial Inequality and White Ignorance: A Response to Marzia Milazzo," *Journal of Applied Philosophy* 36, no. 2 (2019): 257–267; Mills, "White Ignorance."

23 See, for example, Marilyn Frye, *The Politics of Reality: Essays in Feminist Theory* (Berkeley, CA: Crossing Press, 1983), for her analysis of ignorance of racism and racialized communities with respect to feminist politics.

24 Alcoff, "Epistemologies of Ignorance," 47.

25 Goldberg, *Racist Culture*, 5.

26 Dreyfus and Rabinow, *Michel Foucault*, 175.

27 Goldberg, *Racist Culture*, 117.

28 Short, "Prejudice Reduction," 164.

29 Cynthia Wright, personal communication to author, November 2001. Activist responses to the attacks on the World Trade Centre and on Afghanistan on and after September 11, 2001, continued to reflect this closely held idea. In particular, some campus and community fora supported the popular belief that a fuller knowledge of Muslim communities, or of racist attitudes, would lead to more fruitful strategy. Two local examples from the fall of 2001 are a University of Toronto film series about Islamic religion and culture, and an attempt to run an antiracist workshop during a community forum on US military action in Afghanistan.

30 Goldberg, *Racist Culture*, 4.

31 Sullivan, *Good White People*.

32 Allport, *Nature of Prejudice*.

33 Fiona Kate Barlow, Stefania Paolini, Anne Pedersen, Matthew J. Hornsey, Helena R. M. Radke, Jake Harwood, Mark Rubin, and Chris G. Sibley, "The Contact Caveat: Negative Contact Predicts Increased Prejudice More than Positive Contact Predicts Reduced Prejudice," *Personality & Social Psychology Bulletin* 38, no. 12 (2012): 1629–1643.

34 Yves Dejaeghere, Marc Hooghe, and Ellen Claes, "Do Ethnically Diverse Schools Reduce Ethnocentrism? A Two-Year Panel Study among Majority Group Late

Adolescents in Belgian Schools," *International Journal of Intercultural Relations* 36, no. 1 (2012): 108–117.

35 Denis, "Contact Theory."

36 Troyna and Hatcher, *Racism in Children's Lives*; Amir, *Contact Hypothesis*; Cook, "Interpersonal and Attitudinal."

37 Durrheim, Jacobs, and Dixon, "Explaining the Paradoxical Effects."

38 Durrheim, Jacobs, and Dixon, "Explaining the Paradoxical Effects," 703.

39 Dixon, Durrheim, and Tredoux, "Beyond the Optimal," 703; Dixon et al., "Beyond Prejudice"; Dixon and McKeown, "Negative Contact."

40 DiAngelo, *What Does It Mean?*

41 Kevin J. Harrelson, "White Racial Literacy and Racial Dexterity," *Educational Theory* 71, no. 2 (2021): 203–221.

42 Elizabeth Harris, "People Are Marching against Racism. They're Also Reading about It," *New York Times*, June 5, 2020, www.nytimes.com; Elizabeth Harris, "Books on Race Filled Best-Seller Lists Last Year: Publishers Took Notice," *New York Times*, August 15, 2021, www.nytimes.com.

43 Gordon W. Allport, *The Resolution of Intergroup Tensions; A Critical Appraisal of Methods* (New York: National Conference of Christians and Jews, 1952), 6.

44 Britzman, "Ordeal of Knowledge," 127, 128.

45 Goldberg, *Racist Culture*, 184, 208.

46 Truth and Reconciliation Commission of Canada, "Honouring the Truth: Reconciling for the Future," Summary of the Final Report of the Truth and Reconciliation Commission, 2015, https://ehprnh2mwo3.exactdn.com/wp-content/uploads/2021/01/Executive_Summary_English_Web.pdf.

47 Assembly of First Nations, "Years after Release of TRC Report, Most Canadians Want Accelerated Action to Remedy Damage Done by Residential School System, Says Poll," June 15, 2021, www.afn.ca.

48 Government of Canada, "Statement of Apology to Former Students of Indian Residential Schools," June 11, 2008, www.rcaanc-cirnac.gc.ca; CBC Archives, "Government Apologizes for Residential Schools in 2008," June 25, 2018, www.cbc.ca.

49 "Emotional economies that are attached to race and sexuality . . . have the unique ability to foreclose people's cognitive receptivity." Ioanide, *Emotional Politics*, 2.

50 DiAngelo, *White Fragility*, 147.

51 Puar, *Terrorist Assemblages*, 166.

52 Proponents of the contact hypothesis also set a number of conditions for beneficial contact, primarily "group equality and egalitarian inter-group association" (Short, "Prejudice Reduction," 162).

53 Including, for example, collectively run enterprises and certain academic environments.

54 Marx, *German Ideology*, 90.

55 Jaggar, *Feminist Politics*, 232.

56 Clark, *Anarchist Moment*.

57 Kropotkin, *Mutual Aid*.

58 Kropotkin, *Mutual Aid*, 296.

59 Of course, Kropotkin's *Mutual Aid* was written almost a century before our use of the word "personal" was irrevocably changed by "the personal is political." In Kropotkin's writing, "mutual aid" implied the "feeling" or "instinct" that was communal *as opposed to* personal. In his analysis, individual self-interest and love were seen as "personal" and therefore separate from anarchist principles of mutual aid.

60 Ferree and Hess, *Controversy and Coalition*, 34.

61 Ferree and Hess, *Controversy and Coalition*, 35.

62 Ferree and Hess, *Controversy and Coalition*.

63 Redstockings, "The Redstockings Manifesto," July 7, 1969, www.redstockings.org.

64 Ferree and Hess, *Controversy and Coalition*, 72.

65 Adamson, Briskin, and McPhail, *Feminist Organizing for Change*.

66 Adamson, Briskin, and McPhail, *Feminist Organizing for Change*, 198.

67 Adamson, Briskin, and McPhail, *Feminist Organizing for Change*, 214.

68 Brown, *Not outside the Range*, 109.

69 Briskin, "Feminist Practice," 30.

70 Adamson, Briskin, and McPhail, *Feminist Organizing for Change*, 236.

71 Ferree and Hess, *Controversy and Coalition*.

72 Lustiger-Thaler, "Afterword," 184.

73 Briskin, "Feminist Practice," 27.

74 Donovan, *Feminist Theory*, 85.

75 Jagger, *Feminist Politics*, 333.

76 For example, Jagger cites Marx, who in "The Eighteenth Brumaire of Louis Bonaparte" (Marx and Engels, *Selected Works*, 171) describes nineteenth-century French peasants who shared a relation to production. However, their isolation from each other prevented them from developing a shared political community and purpose.

77 Conventional education is often referred to by critics as "banking" education, whereby knowledge is deposited into students and later withdrawn through interrogation or examination.

78 Freire, *Pedagogy of the Oppressed*.

79 Arnold and Burke, *Popular Education Handbook*; Arnold et al., *A New Weave*; Arnold et al., *Educating for a Change*.

80 Weiler, *Women Teaching for Change*.

81 Barndt, *Naming the Moment*; Arnold, *Educating for a Change*; GATT-Fly, *Ah-Hah*.

82 Razack, "Storytelling," 35.

83 Razack, "Storytelling," 63.

84 Critical antiracist writings and struggles have helped inspire the conception and growth of antiracist education as part of regular schooling (Dei, "Challenges";

McCaskell, *Anti-racist Education*; McCarthy and Crichlow, *Race, Identity*; McCarthy, *Race and Curriculum*; McCarthy, "Politics of Culture"; Troyna and Carrington, *Education, Racism and Reform*; Thomas, "Anti-racist Education"). In turn, these proposals for antiracist education, and their increasing implementation, have contributed a framework, techniques, and impetus for antiracist workshops in a variety of organizations.

85   Dei, "Challenges," 47.

86   McCarthy and Crichlow, *Race, Identity and Representation*; Dei, "Challenges"; Dei, *Anti-racist Education*.

87   Cassell, *Group Called Women*, 17.

88   Adamson, Briskin, and McPhail, *Feminist Organizing for Change*, 241.

89   Adamson, Briskin, and McPhail, *Feminist Organizing for Change*, 45.

90   Carey, "Personal Is Political," 5.

91   Briskin, "Feminist Practice."

92   Carey, "Personal Is Political."

93   Ware, *Beyond the Pale*.

94   Pheterson, *Alliances Between Women*.

95   Ward, *Respectably Queer*, 38.

96   Ward, *Respectably Queer*, 39.

97   Dreyfus and Rabinow, *Michel Foucault*, 175.

98   Foucault, *History of Sexuality, Vol. 1*, 58.

99   Foucault, *History of Sexuality, Vol. 1*, 58.

100 Moore, "On Talk Shows."

101 Moore, "On Talk Shows."

102 Razack, "Storytelling," 67.

103 Ellsworth, "Why Doesn't This?"

104 Razack, "Storytelling," 63.

105 Anzaldúa, *Making Face*, xx.

106 Carty, "Women's Studies," 15.

107 Valverde, "Experience and Truth-Telling," 68–69.

108 Goldberg, *Racist Culture*.

109 Gurnah, *Politics of Racism*, 7.

110 McCaskell, *Anti-racist Education*, 256.

111 Briskin, "Feminist Practice."

112 Razack, "Storytelling."

113 Sleeter, How White Teachers.

114 Smith, *Conceptual Practices*, 26.

115 This incident in a Pennsylvania school was reported as "mock slave lesson prompts an outcry by pupil's parents," *New York Times*, January 22, 1993, A7, and was related by Deborah Britzman in her seminar "Inventing Sex, Race and Gender," Ontario Institute for Studies in Education, February 1993.

116 Also see Essed, *Understanding Everyday Racism*, 5; van Dijk, *Elite Discourse*.

117 Ontario Ministry of Education and Training, *Resource Guide*.

118 Razack, "Storytelling," 66.

119 Joe Kincheloe and Shirley Steinberg, "Addressing the Crisis of Whiteness: Reconfiguring White Identity in a Pedagogy of Whiteness," in *White Reign: Deploying Whiteness in America*, ed. Joe L. Kincheloe, Shirley R. Steinberg, Nelson M. Rodriguez, and Ronald E. Chennault (New York: St. Martin's Press, 1998), 2. Quoted in Ahmed, *On Being Included*.

120 Ahmed, *On Being Included*, 169.

121 *Jessica* had successful runs across Canada in the mid-1980s and won a number of awards, including the 1986 Dora Mavor Moore Award for Outstanding New Play.

122 Griffiths and Campbell, *Book of Jessica*, 36.

123 Griffiths and Campbell, *Book of Jessica*, 36.

124 Griffiths and Campbell, *Book of Jessica*, 35.

125 Bergner, "White Fragility Is Everywhere."

126 Britzman, "Ordeal of Knowledge," 189.

127 Trinh, *Woman, Native*, 89.

128 Trinh, *Woman, Native*, 88.

129 My translation. The billboards, posters, and television ads appeared throughout Québec starting in May 1995. One poster depicts a child's face with the caption "Les yeux en amande"; another says "Le teint basané" under a photo of a smiling young woman; another shows a young man with "La coiffure exotique" (see Barlow, *Divided Colors*, 26).

130 Rattansi, *Changing the Subject*, 33.

131 Scott, "Experience," 25.

132 Bulkin, "Hard Ground," 150 (italics added to the phrase "know better").

133 Modern stereotypes of the African American woman as domineering and emasculating have also had historical significance, as in the 1965 Moynihan Report.

134 Enloe, *Bananas, Beaches and Bases*; Stoler, *Education of Desire*; Goldberg, *Racist Culture*.

135 Friedman, *Beyond White*.

136 Razack, "Simple Logic," 48.

137 Butler, *Psychic Life of Power*, 21.

138 Razack, "Storytelling," 64.

139 Lorde, "An Open Letter," 97.

140 Benjamin, "Critiquing Anti-racist Consultancy."

141 Benjamin, "Critiquing Anti-racist Consultancy"; Rosezelle, "Critiquing Anti-racist Consultancy"; Gurnah, *Politics of Racism*; Rezai-Rashti, *Multicultural Education*.

142 Pheterson, *Alliances*, 171.

143 Dixon et al., "Beyond Prejudice."

144 Smith, *Conceptual Practices*.

CHAPTER 4. CRY ME A RIVER

1 "Cry Me a River" was written by Arthur Hamilton for Ella Fitzgerald in 1953 but was first sung and made famous by Julie London in 1955. https://www.youtube.com/watch?v=DXg6UB9Qk00.

2 Megan Boler, "From 'Feminist Politics of Emotions' to the 'Affective Turn,'" interview by Michalinos Zembylas, *Methodological Advances in Research on Emotion and Education* (2016): 26, doi:10.1007/978-3-319-29049-2_2. Also see Boler, *Feeling Power*.

3 Ahmed, *Cultural Politics of Emotion*.

4 See, for example, Kleinman, *Opposing Ambitions*; Morgen, "Best of Times."

5 Levine-Rasky, *Whiteness Fractured*, 153.

6 Ioanide, *Emotional Politics*, 1.

7 Fanon, *Black Skin, White Masks*, 12.

8 Fanon, *Black Skin, White Masks*, 12.

9 Rai, *Rule of Sympathy*.

10 Frankenberg, *White Women*, 2.

11 Anzaldúa, *Making Face*, 44.

12 Landsberg, "Callwood Furor."

13 Boler, *Feeling Power*.

14 Nicoll, "Are You Calling Me a Racist?"

15 Anzaldúa, *Making Face*, xx.

16 Bunch, "Making Common Cause," 53.

17 Illouz, *Cold Intimacies*, 37.

18 Ortner, "Is Female to Male?"

19 This emphasis on feeling and intuition is also common to some ecofeminist writers and some strands of ecofeminist theory. See Mallory, "What's in a Name?"

20 Jaggar, *Feminist Politics*, 381.

21 Celebrations of women's earth-based spirituality, of "the goddess," and of shared ritual as a basis for political practice have been particularly influential. Different versions of ecofeminism are articulated in Judith Plant, ed., *Healing the Wounds: The Promise of Ecofeminism* (Gabriola Island, BC: New Society, 1989).

22 Jaggar, *Feminist Politics*, 115.

23 Gilligan, *In a Different Voice*.

24 Gilligan, *In a Different Voice*, 117.

25 See Nagel, "Critical Theory Meets," 307–326; Burack, *Problem of the Passions*. Gilligan was even voted Woman of the Year in 1984 by *Ms.* magazine, indicating her broad significance in popular feminist discussions and feminist politics.

26 Feminist object relations theory has, for example, made significant contributions to alternative analyzes within philosophy, anthropology, education, and sociology. See Burack, *Problem of the Passions*, 111.

27 Segal, *Is the Future Female?*, 138. Segal notes that the feminist therapy movement has been "directly informed" by object-relations theory.

28 Eichenbaum and Orbach, *Outside In.*
29 Roger, "Fairy Fictions," 138; Laidlaw and Malmo, *Healing Voices*; Eichenbaum and Orbach, *Outside In.*
30 Roger, "Fairy Fictions," 138.
31 Roger, "Fairy Fictions," 137; Laidlaw and Malmo, *Healing Voices.*
32 Burack, *Problem of the Passions*, 112.
33 Burack, *Problem of the Passions*, 112; Roger, "Fairy Fictions."
34 Burack, *Problem of the Passions*, 3.
36 Adamson, Briskin, and McPhail, *Feminist Organizing for Change*, 236.
37 Ferree and Hess, *Controversy and Coalition.*
38 Ferree and Hess, *Controversy and Coalition.*
39 Costain, *Inviting Women's Rebellion.*
40 Wittig, "Local Networks." In peace organizations, as Edwards and Oskamp ("Antinuclear War Activism") emphasize, social ties are key to explaining why peace workers remain active. Similarly, Gomes ("Rewards and Stresses") found that social aspects or personal relationships were important for keeping members of grassroots organizations involved.
41 Bookchin, *Toward an Ecological Society*, 47.
42 Clark, *Anarchist Moment*, 28–31.
43 Lustiger-Thaler, "Afterword."
44 Burack, *Problem of the Passions.*
45 Taylor, "Watching for Vibes."
46 Kleinman, *Opposing Ambitions*, 71.
47 Kleinman, *Opposing Ambitions*, 71.
48 Cassell, *Group Called Women*, 36.
49 The emphasis on emotional disclosure and care is not limited to feminism; its breadth and depth across social movements gives a clue to its tenacity. The idea that emotion makes our organizations better is accepted across a number of organizations, social movements, and disciplines (Wittig, "Local Networks").
50 For example, both Sherryl Kleinman's (*Opposing Ambitions*) study of the health movement and Joni Seager's (*Earthfollies*) study of the environmental movement analyze the emotional as radical, feminine, and therefore feminist, while the rational or unemotional is seen as conventional, "masculinist," and therefore detrimental.
51 Taylor, "Watching for Vibes."
52 Taylor, "Watching for Vibes."
53 Morgen, "Best of Times," 245.
54 Taylor, "Watching for Vibes," 230.
55 Ware, *Beyond the Pale.*
56 Pheterson in Mukherjee, "Four-Hundred-Year-Old Woman," 171.
57 Ware, *Beyond the Pale*, 18.
58 DiAngelo, *White Fragility*, 141.

59 Kleinman, *Opposing Ambitions*, 75.
60 Kleinman, *Opposing Ambitions*, 75.
61 DiAngelo lists reflection and apology as behaviors that we could undertake if we "transformed our racial paradigm." *White Fragility*, 141.
62 DiAngelo, *White Fragility*, 139–140.
63 DiAngelo, *White Fragility*, 145.
64 For example, DiAngelo, *White Fragility*, describes in detail her apology for a racist misstep and prescribes it as a form of repair and a form of antiracism. See pages 140-141.
65 Rose Baaba Folson, email communication to steering committee members of the Centre for the Study of Media and Culture in Education, OISE, University of Toronto, January 2001.
66 Gilligan, *In a Different Voice*, 17.
67 Rose Baaba Folson, personal communication to author, University of Toronto, October 2001.
68 Annual General Meeting of the National Action Committee on the Status of Women.
69 Nagel, "Critical Theory."
70 Kleinman, *Opposing Ambitions*, 78.
71 Kleinman, *Opposing Ambitions*, 21, 72.
72 Rose Baaba Folson, personal communication to author, University of Toronto, October 2001.
73 Kleinman, *Opposing Ambitions*.
74 Kleinman, *Opposing Ambitions*, 78.
75 Cassell, *Group Called Women*, 52.
76 Aliya Amarshi, "From Pain to Power: A Socio-psychological Investigation of Anti-racist Feminist Ressentiment," PhD diss., York University, 2018.
77 Venegas, "Between Community."
78 hooks, *Feminist Theory*, 140.
79 Segal, *Is the Future Female?*, 141.
80 Hurtado, *Color of Privilege*, 19.
81 Hurtado, *Color of Privilege*, 18.
82 Benjamin, "Critiquing Anti-racist Consultancy," 28.
83 Bannerji, "Introducing Racism."
84 Kleinman, *Opposing Ambitions*.
85 Kleinman, *Opposing Ambitions*, 80.
86 Kathy Ferguson, *Feminist Case*, 7.
87 Bartky, "Sympathy and Solidarity," 179.
88 Bartky, "Sympathy and Solidarity," 179.
89 Ware, *Beyond the Pale*, 18.
90 Bartky, "Sympathy and Solidarity," 181.
91 Frankenberg, *White Women*, 175.

92 Frankenberg's interpretation of the role of "the personal is political" in *White Women, Race Matters* (167) differs from my own: she says that those women who have this perspective because of their contact with feminism are also able to understand the social structure of race, not just personal prejudice, in contrast to the race-blind women, who see themselves only in individual terms.

CHAPTER 5. INNOCENCE AS WARFARE

Chapter subtitle: This subtitle echoes Eve Kosofsky Sedgwick's chapter "Paranoid Reading and Reparative Reading, or, You're So Paranoid, You Probably Think This Essay Is about You" in her book *Touching Feeling*, which in turn references Carly Simon's clever hit song of 1972, "You're So Vain (You Probably Think This Song Is about You)."

1 Ellison, "Short History."

2 A 2008 political cartoon showed Obama walking on water, propped up by "white liberal guilt." Mike Lester, *Centre Daily Times*, State College, Pennsylvania, April 15, 2008. A joke popular after the 2008 election of Barack Obama as the first Black president of the United States asked, "How many white people voted for Obama?" and answered, "A lot of guilt-ridden ones." Both examples are discussed by Sharon Sullivan in *Good White People*.

3 The author of the blog *Stuff White People Do* writes that he receives many complaints by readers who accuse him of promoting "white guilt." This cartoon was sent to him by one of these critics, and is depicted there: http://stuffwhitepeopledo.blogspot.ca/2010/02/dismiss-those-who-point-out-racism-for.html, accessed November 7, 2014.

4 Richer and Weir, *Beyond Political Correctness*, 3. Lorna Weir analyzes how political correctness became appropriated by neoconservatives beginning in the 1990s. See Weir, "PC Then and Now."

5 Jonathan Chait attacks "political correctness" in his article "Not a Very P.C. Thing to Say," *New York Magazine*, January 27, 2015, http://nymag.com. Also see Alex Parenee's response, "Punch-Drunk Johnathan Chait Takes on the Entire Internet," *Gawker*, January 2015, http://gawker.com.

6 Freud, *Jokes and the Unconscious*; Atluri, "Lighten Up?" Hartigan, "What Are You Laughing At?," also argues that racial humor reveals implicit cultural knowledge about race.

7 "White liberal guilt" is not only the target of jokes, it is also has been blamed for the paucity of Obama jokes. See April MacIntyre, "D. L. Hughley: 'White Liberal Guilt' Keeps Obama Jokes at Bay," *Monsters and Critics*, August 22, 2008, www.monstersandcritics.com, accessed October 29, 2014.

8 Griffiths and Campbell, *Book of Jessica*, 71, 73.

9 Pierce, *Racing for Innocence*.

10 Pierce, *Racing for Innocence*.

11 Fellows and Razack, "Race to Innocence," 1.

12 See, for example, Margaret Little's study of the moral regulation of single mothers through social assistance, "Manhunts and Bingo Blabs"; Valverde, *Age of Light*. Margaret Little also shows that community organizations were significant participants in advocating and administering the Ontario Mother's Allowance in her study "The Blurring of Boundaries."

13 Foucault, "Of Other Spaces."

14 Fellows and Razack, "Race to Innocence"; Heron, "Desire for Development"; Roger, "Fairy Fictions."

15 Heron, "Desire for Development," 86.

16 Heron, "Desire for Development," 102.

17 Roger, "Fairy Fictions."

18 Roger, "Fairy Fictions."

19 Roger, "Fairy Fictions."

20 Heron, "Desire for Development."

21 Schick, "By Virtue of Being White," 310.

22 Fellows and Razack, "Race to Innocence."

23 Mahrouse, *Conflicted Commitments*.

24 Ware, *Beyond the Pale*, 108.

25 Valverde, *Age of Light*, 29.

26 Valverde, "Mother of the Race."

27 Valverde, *Age of Light*.

28 Kleinman, *Opposing Ambitions*, 5.

29 Benedict Anderson's concept is used to explain the nation as an imagined political community in which members do not know each other, but share "the image of their communion" (*Imagined Communities*, 6). It is an idea that translates well to any form of collectivity.

30 Hetherington, *Badlands*.

31 Valverde and Weir, "Struggles of the Immoral," 33.

32 Morgan, *Sisterhood Is Global*, 4.

33 Freedman, "White Woman's Burden," 76.

34 Hetherington, *Badlands*, 97.

35 Valverde, *Age of Light*, 28.

36 Kleinman, *Opposing Ambitions*, 5.

37 Walker, "Picking Up Pieces," 69.

38 This meaning of "politically correct" has been caricatured and remade by many conservative writers. For a discussion of this "anti-PC" discourse, see Richer and Weir, *Beyond Political Correctness*.

39 Dimen, "Politically Correct?," 139.

40 See Weir, "PC Then and Now."

41 In her study of a health organization, Kleinman also uses the term "alternative" for this identity, one based in egalitarianism and in challenging conventional authority (*Opposing Ambitions*, 5). Although a variety of labels are used, and the

specific attributes are varied, many social movement identities, including feminist, share these traits (see Carroll and Ratner, "Master Frames").

42 Anderson, *Imagined Communities*, 7.

43 Anderson, *Imagined Communities*, 6.

44 There are a number of ways to conceptualize race and racism in terms of morality and ethical practices; these two are predominant in feminist literature and in my interviews.

45 Ware, *Beyond the Pale*, 18.

46 Lynda Hurst, "Feminism's Fault Lines," *Toronto Star*, November 28, 1992, D1, D4.

47 Kleinman, *Opposing Ambitions*, 11.

48 Kleinman, *Opposing Ambitions*, 11.

49 Kleinman, *Opposing Ambitions*, 11.

50 Frankenberg, *White Women*, 3.

51 W. E. B. Du Bois, *Darkwater: Voices from within the Veil* (New York: Harcourt, Brace and Howe, 1920), 32. Accessed at http://solomon.soth.alexanderstreet.com.proxy.queensu.ca.

52 Hobsbawm, *Age of Capital*, 472, quoted in Hetherington, *Badlands*, 101.

53 Kleinman, *Opposing Ambitions*.

54 Narayan, "Working Together across Difference," 41.

55 Frankenberg, *White Women*, 3.

56 Fellows and Razack, *Race to Innocence*.

57 Razack, *Looking White People in the Eye*, 14.

58 Enloe, *Bananas, Beaches and Bases*.

59 Roger, "Fairy Fictions," 129.

60 Rooney, "Commentary."

61 Roach and Rebick, *Politically Speaking*, 112.

62 Frankenberg, *White Women*, 173.

63 Frankenberg, *White Women*, 146.

64 Bartky, "Sympathy and Solidarity"; Meyers, "Emotion and Heterodox"; Dean quoted in Nagel, "Critical Theory."

65 Roger, "Fairy Fictions."

66 Anzaldúa, *Making Face*, xx.

67 Bannerji, "Racism, Sexism, Knowledge," 11.

68 Bannerji, "Racism, Sexism, Knowledge," 10.

69 I am using trauma both in its literal sense as the original "blow" or impact itself, as well as to refer to the effects of an event on an individual's psyche (or on the individuals in a community). This is a commonly accepted usage, although the clinically correct term to refer to the *effects* of trauma is "posttraumatic stress."

70 Britzman, *Lost Subjects*, 119.

71 Silin, *Sex, Death*.

72 Felman, "Education and Crisis."

73 Laub, "Bearing Witness," 72–73.

74   Britzman, *Lost Subjects*, 119.
75   Butler, *Psychic Life of Power*.
76   Pratt, "Identity," 42.
77   Butler, *Psychic Life of Power*, 181.
78   Butler, *Psychic Life of Power*, 183.
79   Griffiths and Campbell, *Book of Jessica*.
80   Griffiths and Campbell, *Book of Jessica*, 70.
81   Griffiths and Campbell, *Book of Jessica*, 71.
82   Griffiths and Campbell, *Book of Jessica*, 73.
83   Griffiths and Campbell, *Book of Jessica*, 70.
84   Walker, "Picking Up Pieces," 71.
85   For further discussion of this history, see chapter 2 of this volume; also see Dua and Robertson, *Scratching the Surface*.
86   For further discussion of the history of this practice, see Adams ("There's No Place," 22), who argues that "together we ascribed a moral significance to our individual litanies of oppression."
87   Foucault, *History of Sexuality, Vol. 2*, 29.
88   Once again, we see parallels with the moral reform movement whose regulation of morality entailed control over the innermost self, "which a century ago included not only 'the soul,' but also what we now call the emotions" (Valverde, *Age of Light*, 28).
89   Pratt, "Identity."
90   Segrest, *My Mama's Dead Squirrel*.
91   Pratt, "Identity," 42.
92   Frankenberg, *White Women*, 166.
93   Segrest, *My Mama's Dead Squirrel*, 171.
94   Britzman, *Lost Subjects*, 119.
95   Felman, "Education and Crisis."
96   Britzman, *Lost Subjects*, 119.
97   Britzman, *Lost Subjects*, 118.
98   Laub, "Bearing Witness."
99   Mariana Valverde, email communication, March 2002.
100 Brown, "Moralism as Anti-politics," 28.
101 Frankenberg, *White Women*, 3.
102 Frankenberg, *White Women*, 159.
103 Frankenberg, *White Women*, 175.
104 Frankenberg, *White Women*, 177.
105 Frankenberg, *White Women*, 178.
106 Mariana Valverde and Kimberly White-Mair, "'One Day at a Time' and Other Slogans for Everyday Life: The Ethical Practices of Alcoholics Anonymous," *Sociology* 33, no. 2 (2016): 393–410.
107 Bartky, "Sympathy and Solidarity."
108 Sullivan, *Good White People*.

CHAPTER 6. #BLACKOUTTUESDAY

Epigraph: Osman Farouki, "Sydney Siege: Australia's Muslims Need Much More than #IllRideWithYou's Hollow Symbolism," *The Independent*, December 16, 2014, www.independent.co.uk.

1 Melinda Locker, "Social Media Posts Honouring Blackout Tuesday with the Hashtag #Black Lives Matter Draw Criticism from Protesters," *Time*, June 2, 2020, https://time.com.

2 Jessica Bursztysnky and Sarah Whitten, "Instagram Users Flood the App with Millions of Blackout Tuesday Posts," *CNBC*, June 2, 2020, www.cnbc.com.

3 Jolynna Sinanan, "Blackout Tuesday: The Black Square Is a Symbol of Activism for Non-Activists," *The Conversation*, June 4, 2020, https://theconversation.com.

4 Julie Nolke, "Explaining the Pandemic to My Past Self, Part 3" (video skit), https://www.youtube.com/watch?v=Pbdk_lBCxJk.

5 @atothebed, June 2, 2020, https://twitter.com/atothebed/status/1267706564716216322.

6 Heath Ashton, "Dozens of Anti-Muslim Attacks as Islamic Leaders Warn of Community Fear," *Sydney Morning Herald*, October 9, 2014, www.smh.com.au.

7 Jane Wardell, "Sydney Siege Sparks 'I'll Ride with You' Campaign for Worried Muslims," *Reuters*, December 14, 2014, www.reuters.com.

8 Adam Chandler, "The Roots of #IllRideWithYou," *The Atlantic*, December 15, 2014, www.theatlantic.com.

9 Husna Haq, "Why #IllRideWithYou Worked and Other Muslim Hashtags Didn't," *Christian Science Monitor*, December 15, 2014, www.csmonitor.com.

10 Ruth Alexander, "Sydney Cafe: Australians Say to Muslims 'I'll Ride with You,'" *BBC Trending*, December 15, 2014, www.bbc.com.

11 Michael Kaplan, "Toronto #IllRideWithYou Offers Muslims in Canada Travel Companions," *International Business Times*, November 20, 2015, www.ibtimes.com.

12 "Charlie Hebdo: Des Hashtags contre l'Islamophobie," January 8, *L'Express*, 2015, https://www.lexpress.fr.

13 Camila Domonoske, "Boston Launches Anti-Islamophobia Poster Campaign," *National Public Radio*, July 18, 2017, https://www.npr.org; Tovia Smith, "New Campaign Teaches How to Help When a Muslim Is Harassed," *National Public Radio*, August 1, 2017, www.npr.org.

14 Osman Farouki, "Sydney Siege: Australia's Muslims Need Much More than #Illridewithyou's Hollow Symbolism," *The Independent*, December 16, 2014, www.independent.co.uk.

15 Phil Helsel and Shamar Walters, "Two Bystanders Slain on Portland Train Called Heroes," *NBC News*, May 27, 2017, www.nbcnews.com.

16 Smith, "New Campaign."

17 "#illridewithyou Story Didn't Happen as First Claimed," *BBC Newsbeat*, December 18, 2014, www.bbc.co.uk.

18 Rachel Jacobs, "How I'll Ride with You Began with Rachel Jacobs' Experience on a Brisbane Train," *Brisbane Times*, December 16, 2014, www.brisbanetimes.com.au.

19 Jan Ransom, "Amy Cooper Faces Charges after Calling Police on Black Birdwatcher," *New York Times*, July 6, 2020, www.nytimes.com; Sarah Maslin Nir, "How Two Lives Collided in Central Park, Rattling the Nation," *New York Times*, July 14, 2020, www.nytimes.com.

20 Idil Musa, "Ottawa Police Apologize for Handling of 911 Call about Black Man in Barrhaven Park," CBC News, July 10, 2020, www.cbc.ca.

21 Erin Aubry Kaplan, "Everyone's an Anti-racist. Now What?," *New York Times*, July 6, 2020, www.nytimes.com.

22 Kendi, *How to Be an Antiracist*.

CHAPTER 7. WHY IS ANTIRACISM ELUSIVE? (TRY THIS INSTEAD)

1 See Mitchell, "Building"; Ward, *Respectably Queer*; Greensmith, "Desiring Diversity."

2 Essed, *Understanding Everyday Racism*. Other researchers confirm that it is common for whites to deny racism by casting it as extreme behavior or a characteristic belonging to unknown others. For example, several of the white women Frankenberg (1993) interviewed denied racist events by constructing racism as sinful behavior practiced only by evil people.

3 E. S. Lawson, "Anti-Black Racism on the Sidelines: The Limits of Listening Sessions to Address Institutional Racism at Canadian Universities," *Canadian Review of Sociology* 57, no. 3 (2020): 491–494, doi:10.1111/cars.12296.

4 Hetherington, *Badlands*.

5 Hetherington, *Badlands*.

6 White House, "Executive Order on Combatting Race and Sex Stereotyping," September 22, 2020, www.whitehouse.gov.

7 DiAngelo, *White Fragility*, 141.

8 Scheherzade Rana, "Mindfulness for Inclusive Leadership," OISE Alumni Leadership Series, January 26, 2022.

9 Illouz, *Cold Intimacies*, 55.

10 Illouz, *Cold Intimacies*, 56.

11 Bannerji, "Racism, Sexism, Knowledge," 10, 11.

12 Ahmed, "Complaint as Diversity Work."

13 Leila Whitley, Tiffany Page, and Alice Corble, "Collective Conclusions," in Ahmed, *Complaint!*, 268.

14 Gandhi, *Affective Communities*.

15 Ninan Abraham, Associate Dean, Equity and Diversity, Faculty of Science, University of British Columbia, personal communication.

16 Özlem Sensoy and Robin DiAngelo, "'We Are All for Diversity, but . . .': How Faculty Hiring Committees Reproduce Whiteness and Practical Suggestions for How They Can Change," *Harvard Educational Review* 87, no. 4 (2017): 557–580.

17 Annette Henry, "'We Especially Welcome Applications from Members of Visible Minority Groups': Reflections on Race, Gender and Life at Three Universities," *Race Ethnicity and Education* 18, no. 5 (2015): 589–610, doi:10.1080/13613324.2015.1 023787.

18 Musa al-Gharbi, "'Diversity Training' Doesn't Work. This Might," Heterodox Academy, December 29, 2020, https://heterodoxacademy.org.

19 al-Gharbi, "'Diversity Training' Doesn't Work."

20 al-Gharbi, "'Diversity Training' Doesn't Work."

21 Ontario College of Art and Design University (OCADU), "Presidential Task Force on the Under-representation of Racialized and Indigenous Faculty and Staff: Report and Recommendations," 2017, https://www.ocadu.ca.

22 Tunstall, *Decolonizing*.

23 Emily Carr University of Art and Design, "EDI Action Plan," Vancouver, 2021, www.ecuad.ca.

24 Regents of the University of Colorado, 2022, "Commitments for Action—Establishing an Equity Task Force," www.ucdenver.edu. See also similar efforts at the University of Texas at Austin, which has produced a plan for equitable hiring that begins with the first stages of recruitment: "Inclusive Search and Recruitment Toolkit," Office of the Chancellor; "Commitments for Action," Office for Inclusion and Equity, University of Texas at Austin.

25 Young, *Bearing Witness*.

26 Young, *Bearing Witness*, 25.

27 DeMarcus A. Jenkins, Antar A. Tichavakunda, and Justin A. Coles, "The Second ID: Critical Race Counterstories of Campus Police Interactions with Black Men at Historically White Institutions," *Race, Ethnicity, and Education* 24, no. 2 (March 4, 2021): 149–166, doi:10.1080/13613324.2020.1753672; Kristine Phillips and Rachel Siegel, "Starbucks: You Don't Have to Buy Coffee to Sit in Our Cafes or Use Our Restrooms," *Washington Post*, May 20, 2018, www.washingtonpost.com.

28 Caroline Hickman, Elizabeth Marks, Panu Pihkala, Susan Clayton, R. Eric Lewandowski, Elouise E Mayall, Britt Wray, Catriona Mellor, and Lise van Susteren, "Climate Anxiety in Children and Young People and Their Beliefs about Government Responses to Climate Change: A Global Survey," *Lancet Planetary Health*, 2021, www.thelancet.com.

29 Margaret Klein Salamon, "If You're Anxious about the Climate, Try This," *New York Times*, May 1, 2022, www.nytimes.com.

30 Gandhi, *Affective Communities*.

BIBLIOGRAPHY

Abdo, Nahla. "Race, Gender and Politics: The Struggle of Arab Women in Canada." In *And Still We Rise: Feminist Political Mobilizing in Contemporary Canada*, edited by Linda Carty. Toronto: Women's Press, 1993.

Abu-Laban, Yasmeen, and Abigail Bakan. *Israel, Palestine and the Politics of Race Exploring Identity and Power in a Global Context*. New York: I.B. Tauris, 2019.

Adams, Mary Louise. "There's No Place Like Home: On the Place of Identity in Feminist Politics." *Feminist Review* 31 (1989): 22–33.

Adamson, Nancy, Linda Briskin, and Margaret McPhail. *Feminist Organizing for Change: The Contemporary Women's Movement in Canada*. Toronto: Oxford University Press, 1988.

Aggarwal, Pramilla. Quoted in Angela Robertson, "Continuing on the Ground: Feminists of Color Discuss Organizing." In *Scratching the Surface: Canadian Anti-racist Feminist Thought*, edited by Enakshi Dua and Angela Robertson. Toronto: Women's Press, 1999.

Ahmad, Fawzia. "The 'R' Word That Kills." *Canadian Woman Studies* 14, no. 2 (1994): 46.

Ahmed, Sara. *Complaint!* Durham, NC: Duke University Press, 2021.

———. "Complaint as Diversity Work." feministkilljoys (blog), November 2017. https://feministkilljoys.com.

———. *On Being Included: Racism and Diversity in Institutional Life*. Durham, NC: Duke University Press, 2012.

———. *The Cultural Politics of Emotion*. Edinburgh: Edinburgh University Press, 2004.

———. "Declarations of Whiteness: The Non-performativity of Anti-racism." *Borderlands* 3, no. 2 (2004).

Albrecht, Lisa, and Rose Brewer, eds. *Bridges of Power: Women's Multicultural Alliances*. Gabriola Island, BC: New Society Publishers, 1990.

Alcoff, Linda. "Epistemologies of Ignorance: Three Types." In *Race and Epistemologies of Ignorance*, edited by Shannon Sullivan and Nancy Tuana. Albany: SUNY Press, 2007.

Alexander, Michelle. *The New Jim Crow: Mass Incarceration in the Age of Colorblindness*. New York: New Press, 2010.

Alexander, Sally, and Anna Davin. "Feminist History." *History Workshop Journal* 1 (1976): 4–6.

Allen, Carol, and Judy Persad. "Fighting Racism and Sexism Together." Keynote Speech to International Women's Day rally, Toronto, 1987. Toronto: International Women's

Day Committee. Reprinted in *Feminists Organizing for Change: The Contemporary Women's Movement in Canada*, edited by N. Adamson, L. Briskin, and M. McPhail. Toronto: Oxford University Press, 1987.

Allen, Robert. *Reluctant Reformers*. Washington, DC: Howard University Press, 1977.

Allport, Gordon. *The Nature of Prejudice*. Cambridge, MA: Perseus Books, 1954.

Alonso, Ana María. "The Effects of Truth: Re-Presentations of the Past and the Imagining of Community." *Journal of Historical Sociology* 1, no. 1 (1988).

Amarshi, Aliya. "A Frommian Perspective on the Problem of Feminist *Ressentiment*." *Fromm Forum* 20 (2016): 50–55.

American Psychiatric Association. *Diagnostic and Statistical Manual III*. Washington, DC: American Psychiatric Association, 1987.

Amir, Yehuda. "Contact Hypothesis in Ethnic Relations." In *The Handbook of Interethnic Coexistence*, edited by Eugene Weiner, 162–181. New York: Continuum Publishing, 1998.

Amos, Valerie, and Pratibha Parmar. "Challenging Imperial Feminism." *Feminist Review* 17 (1984): 3–19.

Anderson, Benedict. *Imagined Communities: Reflections on the Origin and Spread of Nationalism*. New York: Verso, 1992.

Anthias, Floya, and Nira Yuval-Davis. "Contextualizing Feminism: Gender, Ethnic and Class Divisions." In *Defining Women*, edited by Linda McDowell and Rosemary Pringle, 107–117. Cambridge: Polity, 1992.

Anzaldúa, Gloria, ed. *Making Face, Making Soul: Creative and Critical Perspectives by Feminists of Color*. San Francisco: Aunt Lute Books, 1990.

Apfelbaum, Evan P., Michael I. Norton, and Samuel R. Sommers. "Racial Color Blindness: Emergence, Practice, and Implications." *Current Directions in Psychological Science* 21, no. 3 (2012): 205–209.

Applebaum, Barbara. *Being White, Being Good: White Complicity, White Moral Responsibility and Social Justice Pedagogy*. Lanham, MD: Lexington Books, 2010.

Armstrong, Helen. "Planning for Women's Day Fragmented." *NOW*, March 4, 1993.

Arnold, Gretchen. "Dilemmas of Feminist Coalitions: Collective Identity and Strategic Effectiveness in the Battered Women's Movement." In *Feminist Organizations: Harvest of the Women's Movement*, edited by Myra Marx Ferree and Patricia Yancey Martin, 276–290. Philadelphia: Temple University Press, 1995.

Arnold, Rick. *Educating for a Change*. Toronto: Between the Lines Press, 1991.

Arnold, Rick, Deborah Barndt, and Bev Burke. *A New Weave: Popular Education in Canada and Central America*. Toronto: Ontario Institute for Studies in Education, 1985.

Arnold, Rick, and Bev Burke. *A Popular Education Handbook: An Educational Experience Taken from Central America and Adopted to the Canadian Context*. Toronto: Ontario Institute for Studies in Education, 1983.

Atluri, Tara. "Lighten Up?! Humour, Race and Da Off Colour Joke of Ali G." *Media, Culture & Society* 31, no. 2 (2009): 197–214.

Awwad, Julian, Suzanne Lenon, and OmiSoore H. Dryden, *Disrupting Queer Inclusion: Canadian Homonationalisms and the Politics of Belonging*. Vancouver: UBC Press, 2016.

Backhouse, Constance, and David Flaherty, eds. *Challenging Times: The Women's Movement in Canada and the United States*. Montreal: McGill-Queen's University Press, 1992.

Baines, Donna. "Everyday Practices of Race, Class and Gender." PhD diss., University of Toronto, 1998.

Bannerji, Himani, ed. *Returning the Gaze: Essays on Racism, Feminism and Politics*. Toronto: Sister Vision Press, 1993.

———. "Racism, Sexism, Knowledge and the Academy. Re:turning the Gaze." *Resources for Feminist Research* 20, no. 3/4 (1992): 5–11.

———. "But Who Speaks for Us? Experience and Agency in Conventional Feminist Paradigms." In *Unsettling Relations: The University as a Site of Feminist Struggles*, edited by H. Bannerji, L. Carty, K. Dehli, S. Heald, and K. McKenna. Toronto: Women's Press, 1991.

———. "Introducing Racism: Notes towards an Anti-racist Feminism." *Resources for Feminist Research* 16, no. 1 (1987): 10–12.

Barlow, J. "The Divided Colors of Nationalism." *This* 29, no. 3 (1995): 26–29.

Barndt, Deborah. *Naming the Moment: Political Analysis for Action*. Toronto: Jesuit Centre, 1989.

Barnoff, Lisa. "Moving beyond Words: Implementing Anti-oppression Practice in Feminist Social Service Agencies." PhD diss. proposal, OISE University of Toronto, 2000.

Barrett, Michele. *The Politics of Truth: From Marx to Foucault*. Cambridge: Polity, 1991.

Bartky, Sandra. "Sympathy and Solidarity: On a Tightrope with Scheler." In *Feminists Rethink the Self*, edited by Diana Tietjens Meyers. Boulder, CO: Westview Press, 1997.

Bear, Shirley, and the Tobique Women's Group. "You Can't Change the Indian Act?" In *Women and Social Change: Feminist Activism in Canada*, edited by Jeri Dawn Wine and Janice Ristock. Toronto: James Lorimer, 1991.

Beeson, Diane. "The Relevance of Analysis of Emotions to Macro Economic Change: A Response to Concerns regarding Scheff's Work." *Sociological Perspectives* 40, no. 4 (1997): 537–551.

Beins, Agatha. *Liberation in Print: Feminist Periodicals and Social Movement Identity*. Athens: University of Georgia Press, 2017.

Belenky, Mary Field, Blythe McVicker Clinchy, Nancy Rule Goldberger, and Jill Mattuck Tarule. *Women's Way of Knowing*. New York: Basic Books, 1986.

Bell, Shannon. "More Than a Rhetorical War." *Broadside*, June 1983.

Bendelow, Gillian, and Simon J. Williams, eds. *Emotions in Social Life: Critical Themes and Contemporary Issues*. New York: Routledge, 1998.

Benjamin, Akua. "Critiquing Anti-racist Consultancy." Presentation at Making the Links: Anti-racism and Feminism, Canadian Research Institute for the Advancement of Women (CRIAW), Toronto, November 13–15, 1992.

Berck, Phyllis. "Naming Racism Is First Essential Step. Letter to the Editor." *Toronto Star*, December 17, 1992.

Berger, Phillip. "A Flimsy Case against June Callwood." *Toronto Star*, September 11, 1992.

Bergner, Daniel. "White Fragility Is Everywhere. But Does Anti-racism Training Work?" *New York Times Magazine*, June 6, 2020.

Berry, Sally. "Letter from the Women's Therapy Centre Study Group." *m/f* 3 (1979): 111. Quoted in Segal, *Is the Future Female?*

Berton, Pierre. "If Callwood Is a Racist Then So Are We All." *Toronto Star*, May 23, 1992.

Bettencourt, B., G. Dillman, and N. Wollman. "The Intragroup Dynamics of Maintaining a Successful Grassroots Organization: A Case Study." *Journal of Social Issues* 52, no. 1 (1996): 169–185.

Bhabha, Homi. Untitled conference presentation. In *Critical Fictions: The Politics of Imaginative Writing*, edited by P. Mariani, 62–65. Seattle: Bay Press, 1991.

Bhanji, Nael. "Trans/scriptions: Homing Desires, (Trans)Sexual Citizenship and Racialized Bodies." In *The Transgender Studies Reader* 2, edited by S. Stryker and A. Aizura. New York: Routledge, 2013.

Blee, Kathleen. "Women in the 1920s' Ku Klux Klan Movement." *Feminist Studies* 17, no. 1 (1991): 57–77.

Bleyer, Peter. "Coalitions of Social Movements as Agencies for Social Change: The Action Canada Network." In *Organizing Dissent*, edited by William Carroll, 102–117. Toronto: Garamond Press.

BoardSource. "Leading with Intent: 2017 National Index of Nonprofit Board Practices." https://leadingwithintent.org.

Boler, Megan. *Feeling Power: Emotions and Education*. New York: Routledge, 1999.

Bonilla-Silva, Eduardo. "Feeling Race: Theorizing the Racial Economy of Emotions." Presidential Address to ASA, 2018. *American Sociological Review* 84, no. 1 (2019): 1–25. doi:10.1177/0003122418816958.

———. *Racism without Racists: Color-Blind Racism and the Persistence of Racial Inequality in the United States*. Lanham, MD: Rowan & Littlefield, 2003.

Bonilla-Silva, Eduardo, and David Dietrich. "The Sweet Enchantment of Color-Blind Racism in Obamerica." *Annals of the American Academy of Political and Social Science* 634 (March 2011): 190–206.

Bookchin, Murray. *Toward an Ecological Society*. Montreal: Black Rose Books, 1988.

Boykin, Keith. *One More River to Cross: Black and Gay in America*. New York: Anchor, 1996.

Breines, Winifred. *The Trouble between Us: An Uneasy History of White and Black Women in the Feminist Movement*. New York: Oxford University Press, 2006.

Briskin, Linda. "Feminist Practice: A New Approach to Evaluating Feminist Strategy." In *Women and Social Change: Feminist Activism in Canada*, edited by Jeri Wine and Janice Ristock. Toronto: James Lorimer, 1991.

———. "Identity Politics and the Hierarchy of Oppression: A Comment." *Feminist Review* 35 (1990): 102–108.

Britzman, Deborah. *Lost Subjects, Contested Objects: Toward a Psychoanalytic Inquiry of Learning.* Albany: SUNY Press, 1998.

———. "The Ordeal of Knowledge: Rethinking the Possibilities of Multicultural Education." *Review of Education* 15 (1993): 123–135.

Britzman, D., K. Santiago-Valles, G. Jimenez-Munoz, and L. Lamash. "Slips That Show and Tell: Fashioning Multiculture as a Problem of Representation." In *Race, Identity and Representation in Education,* edited by C. McCarthy and W. Crichlow, 188–199. New York: Routledge, 1993.

Broadside Collective. "Broadside and Beyond" (editorial). *Broadside,* August/September 1989.

———. "No to Racism" (editorial). *Broadside,* March 1986.

Brown, Laura. "Not outside the Range: One Feminist Perspective on Psychic Trauma." In *Trauma: Explorations in Memory,* edited by Cathy Caruth. Baltimore: Johns Hopkins University Press, 1995.

Brown, Reva. "Emotions in Organizations." *Journal of Applied Behavioral Science* 33, no. 2 (1997): 247–262.

Brown, Wendy. "Moralism as Anti-politics." In *Politics Out of History,* edited by Wendy Brown. Princeton, NJ: Princeton University Press, 2001.

———. "Politics without Banisters: Genealogical Politics in Nietzsche and Foucault." In *Politics Out of History,* edited by Wendy Brown. Princeton, NJ: Princeton University Press, 2001.

Bulkin, Elly. "Hard Ground: Jewish Identity, Racism, and Anti-Semitism." In *Yours in Struggle,* edited by E. Bulkin, M. B. Pratt, and B. Smith. Ithaca, NY: Firebrand Books, 1984.

Bullard, Robert D., ed. *Confronting Environmental Racism.* Boston: South End Press, 1993.

Bunch, Charlotte. "Making Common Cause: Diversity and Coalitions." In *Bridges of Power: Women's Multicultural Alliances,* edited by Lisa Albrecht and Rose Brewer. Gabriola Island, BC: New Society Publishers, 1990.

Burack, Cynthia. *The Problem of the Passions: Feminism, Psychoanalysis and Social Theory.* New York: New York University Press, 1994.

Burkitt, Ian. "Social Relationships and Emotions." *Sociology* 31, no. 1 (1996): 39–55.

Butler, Judith. *The Psychic Life of Power: Theories in Subjection.* Stanford, CA: Stanford University Press, 1997.

Callander, Denton, Martin Holt, and Christy Newman. "Gay Racism." In *The Psychic Life of Racism in Gay Men's Communities,* edited by D. Riggs. New York: Lexington Books.

Callwood, June. "Struggling in a River of Distrust and Cynicism." *Toronto Star,* June 28, 1992.

Canadian Research Institute for the Advancement of Women (CRIAW). *Looking for Change: A Documentation of National Women's Organizations Working towards*

Inclusion and Diversity. Ottawa: Canadian Research Institute for the Advancement of Women, 1995.

Canel, Eduardo. "New Social Movement Theory and Resource Mobilization: The Need for Integration." In *Organizing Dissent*, edited by William Carroll. Toronto: Garamond Press, 1992.

Canning, Kathleen. "Feminist History after the Linguistic Turn: Historicizing Discourse and Experience." *Signs* 19, no. 2 (Winter 1994): 368–404.

Carby, Hazel. "White Women Listen! Black Feminism and the Boundaries of Sisterhood." In *The Empire Strikes Back*, edited by Centre for Contemporary Cultural Studies. London: Hutchinson, 1983.

Carey, Patricia. "Personal Is Political." *Canadian Women's Studies* 11, no. 2 (1980).

Carroll, William, and Robert Ratner. "Master Frames and Counter-hegemony: Political Sensibilities in Contemporary Social Movements." *Canadian Review of Sociology and Anthropology* 33, no. 4 (1996): 407–435.

Carty, Linda. "Combining Our Efforts: Making Feminism Relevant." In *And Still We Rise: Feminist Political Mobilizing in Contemporary Canada*, edited by Linda Carty. Toronto: Women's Press, 1993.

——. "Women's Studies in Canada: A Discourse and Praxis of Education." *Resources for Feminist Research* 20, no. 3/4 (1992): 12–18.

Carty, Linda, and Dionne Brand. "Visible Minority Women: A Creation of the Canadian State." *Resources for Feminist Research* 17, no. 3 (1989): 39–40.

Caruth, Cathy, ed. *Trauma: Explorations in Memory*. Baltimore: Johns Hopkins University Press, 1995.

Cassell, Joan. *A Group Called Women: Sisterhood and Symbolism in the Feminist Movement*. New York: David McKay Company, 1977.

Cernetig, Miro. "Feminist Conference Disrupted by Fracas: Poetry Reading Ends in Shouting Match." *Globe and Mail*, May 13, 1991.

Chakrabarti, Shami. "*To Kill A Mockingbird* Made Me a Lawyer." *The Guardian*, July 11, 2015.

Chang, Edward H., Katherine L. Milkman, Dena M. Gromet, Robert W. Rebele, Cade Massey, Angela L. Duckworth, and Adam M. Grant. "The Mixed Effects of Online Diversity Training." *Proceedings of the National Academy of Sciences* 116, no. 16 (April 16, 2019): 7778–7783.

Chater, Nancy. "Unexamined History Repeats Itself. Race and Class in the Canadian Reproductive Rights Movement." *Fireweed* 33 (Summer 1991): 44–60.

Chodorow, Nancy. *The Reproduction of Mothering: Psychoanalysis and the Sociology of Gender*. Berkeley: University of California Press, 1978.

Clark, John. *The Anarchist Moment: Reflections on Culture, Nature and Power*. Montreal: Black Rose Books, 1984.

Cockburn, Cynthia. *In the Way of Women*. Ithaca, NY: Cornell University Press, 1990.

——. *Brothers: Male Dominance and Technological Change*. London: Pluto Press, 1983.

Cole, Susan. "Writing Out Racism." *NOW*, March 23, 1989.

Collins, Patricia Hill. *Black Feminist Thought: Knowledge, Consciousness, and the Politics of Empowerment.* Boston: Unwin Hyman, 1990.

Cook, S. W. "Interpersonal and Attitudinal Outcomes in Cooperating Interracial Groups." *Journal of Research and Development in Education* 12 (1978): 97–113.

Corrigan, Philip. "On Moral Regulation: Some Preliminary Remarks." *Sociological Review* 29, no. 2 (1981).

Costain, A. *Inviting Women's Rebellion: A Political Process Interpretation of the Women's Movement.* Baltimore: Johns Hopkins University Press, 1992.

Cukier W., P. Adamu, C. Wall-Andrews, and M. Elmi. "Racialized Leaders Leading Canadian Universities." *Educational Management Administration & Leadership* 49, no. 4 (2021): 565–583. doi:10.1177/17411432211001363.

Davis, Angela. *Women, Race and Class.* New York: Vintage Books, 1983.

Dean, Jodi. "Critical Theory Meets the Ethic of Care: Engendering Social Justice and Social Identities." *Social Theory and Practice* 23, no. 2 (1997). Quoted in M. Nagel, "Critical Theory."

Dei, George J. Sefa. "Race and Defence: The Politics of Denial and Affirmation." Paper presented at the Congress of Social Sciences and Humanities, Ottawa, 1998.

———. *Anti-racism Education: Theory and Practice.* Halifax: Fernwood Publishing, 1996.

———. "The Challenges of Anti-racist Education in Canada." *Canadian Ethnic Studies* 25, no. 2 (1993): 36–51.

Denis, Jeffrey S. "Contact Theory in a Small-Town Settler-Colonial Context: The Reproduction of Laissez-Faire Racism in Indigenous-White Canadian Relations." *American Sociological Review* 80, no. 1 (2015): 218–242.

Devor, Tivoni. "The Face of Nonprofit Boards: A Network Problem." *Nonprofit Quarterly*, March 4, 2015. https://nonprofitquarterly.org.

Dewar, Elaine. "Wrongful Dismissal." *Toronto Life*, March 1993.

DiAngelo, Robin. *White Fragility.* Boston: Beacon Press, 2018.

———. *What Does It Mean to Be White? Developing White Racial Literacy.* New York: Peter Lang, 2012.

Dimen, M. "Politically Correct? Politically Incorrect?" In *Pleasure and Danger: Exploring Female Sexuality*, edited by C. S. Vance, 138–148. Boston: Routledge & Kegan Paul, 1984.

Dinnerstein, Dorothy. *The Mermaid and the Minotaur: Sexual Arrangements and Human Malaise.* New York: Harper & Row, 1977.

Dixon, John, Kevin Durrheim, and Colin Tredoux. "Beyond the Optimal Contact Strategy: A Reality Check for the Contact Hypothesis." *American Psychologist* 60, no. 7 (2005): 697–711.

Dixon, John, Mark Levine, Steve Reicher, and Kevin Durrheim. "Beyond Prejudice: Are Negative Evaluations the Problem and Is Getting Us to Like One Another More the Solution?" *Behavioral and Brain Sciences* 35, no. 6 (2012): 411–425.

Dixon, John, and Shelley McKeown. "Negative Contact, Collective Action, and Social Change: Critical Reflections, Technological Advances, and New Directions." *Journal of Social Issues* 77, no. 1 (March 1, 2021): 242–257. doi:10.1111/josi.12429.

Dobbin, Frank, and Alexandra Kalev. "Why Doesn't Diversity Training Work? The Challenge for Industry and Academia." *Anthropology Now* 10, no. 2 (May 4, 2018): 48–55. doi:10.1080/19428200.2018.1493182.

———, "Why Diversity Programs Fail and What Works Better." *Harvard Business Review* 94 (2016): 52–60.

Donovan, Josephine. *Feminist Theory.* New York: Frederick Ungar. Quoted in Adamson, Briskin, and McPhail, Feminist Organizing for Change.

Douglas, Catherine. "Checking In: June Callwood Talks about Her Feelings, Her Faults, and the Failing of Feminist Groups Struggling with Issues of Racism." *Quota*, April 1993.

Dowd, Jeffrey. "Public and Academic Questions on Race: The Problem with Racial Controversies." *Sociological Forum* 29, no. 2 (2014): 496–502.

Doyle, R., and L. Visano. "Access to Health and Social Services for Members of Diverse Cultural and Racial Groups." Reports 1 and 2. Toronto: Social Planning Council of Metropolitan Toronto, 1987.

Dreyfus, Hubert L., and Paul Rabinow. *Michel Foucault: Beyond Structuralism and Hermeneutics.* Chicago: University of Chicago Press, 1983.

Driedger, Leo. "Immigrant/Ethnic/Racial Segregation: Canadian Big Three and Prairie Metropolitan Comparison." *Canadian Journal of Sociology* 24, no. 4 (1999): 484–509.

Dua, Enakshi, and Angela Robertson, eds. *Scratching the Surface: Canadian Anti-racist Feminist Thought.* Toronto: Women's Press, 1999.

Du Bois, W. E. B. "The Souls of White Folk." In *Darkwater: Voices from within the Veil.* New York: Harcourt, Brace and Howe, 1920.

Dudley, Edward, and Maximillian E. Novak, eds. *The Wild Man Within: An Image from the Renaissance to Romanticism.* Pittsburgh: University of Pittsburgh Press, 1972.

Durrheim, Kevin, Nicola Jacobs, and John Dixon. "Explaining the Paradoxical Effects of Intergroup Contact: Paternalistic Relations and System Justification in Domestic Labor in South Africa." *International Journal of Intercultural Relations* 41 (2014): 150–164.

Dyer, Richard. *White.* New York: Routledge, 1997.

Eberhardt, Jennifer L. *Biased: Uncovering the Hidden Prejudice That Shapes What We See, Think, and Do.* New York: Penguin Books, 2020.

Edwards, C., and S. Oskamp. "Components of Antinuclear War Activism." *Basic and Applied Social Psychology* 13 (1992): 217–230.

Egan, Carolyn, Linda Gardner, and Judy Persad. "The Politics of Transformation: Struggles with Race, Class and Sexuality in the March 8th Coalition." In *Social Movements/Social Change*, edited by Cunningham, Frank, Sue Findlay, Marlene Kadar, Alan Lennon and Ed Silva. Toronto: Between the Lines, 1988.

Eichenbaum, Luise, and Susie Orbach. *Outside In, Inside Out.* Harmondsworth: Penguin, 1982.

Ellison, Julie. "A Short History of Liberal Guilt." *Critical Inquiry* 22, no. 2 (1996): 344–371.

Ellsworth, Elizabeth. "Why Doesn't This Feel Empowering? Working Through the Repressive Myths of Critical Pedagogy." *Harvard Educational Review* 59 (1989): 297–324.

el Sadawi, Nawal, Fatima Mernissi, and Mallica Vajarathon. "A Critical Look at the Wellesley Conference." *Quest* 4, no. 2 (1978).

Enloe, Cynthia. *Bananas, Beaches and Bases: Making Feminist Sense of International Politics*. London: Pandora Press, 1989.

Erikson, Kai. "Notes on Trauma and Community." In *Trauma: Explorations in Memory*, edited by Cathy Caruth. Baltimore: Johns Hopkins University Press, 1995.

Essed, Philomena. *Understanding Everyday Racism*. London: Sage, 1991.

Evans, Sara. *Tidal Wave: How Women Changed America at Century's End*. New York: Free Press, 2003.

———. *Personal Politics: The Roots of Women's Liberation in the Civil Rights Movement and the New Left*. New York: Vintage Books, 1980.

Fanon, Frantz. 1967. *Black Skin, White Masks*. New York: Grove Press.

Fellows, M., and S. Razack. "The Race to Innocence: Confronting Hierarchical Relations among Women." *Journal of Gender, Race and Justice* 1 (1998): 335–352.

Felman, Shoshana. "Education and Crisis, or the Vicissitudes of Teaching." In *Testimony: Crises of Witnessing in Literature, Psychoanalysis and History*, edited by S. Felman and D. Laub. New York: Routledge, 1992.

Ferguson, Kathy. *The Feminist Case against Bureaucracy*. Philadelphia: Temple University Press, 1984.

Ferree, Myra, and Beth Hess. *Controversy and Coalition: The New Feminist Movement across Three Decades of Change*. Boston: Twayne Publishers, 1994.

Ferree, Myra Marx, and Patricia Yancey Martin, eds. *Feminist Organizations: Harvest of the Women's Movement*. Philadelphia: Temple University Press, 1995.

Fineman, Stephen. "An Emotion Agenda." In *Emotions in Organizations*, edited by S. Fineman. London: Sage, 1993.

———, ed. *Emotions in Organizations*. London: Sage, 1993.

Foner, Philip. *Organized Labor and the Black Worker*. Chicago: Haymarket Books, 1976.

Forman, W., and L. Slapp. "Preventing Burnout." In *Working for Peace*, edited by N. Wollman. San Luis Obispo, CA: Impact Publishers, 1985. Quoted in Bettencourt, Dillman, and Wollman, "Intragroup Dynamics."

Foucault, Michel. "Questions of Method." In *The Foucault Effect: Studies in Governmentality*, edited by G. Burchell, C. Gordon, and P. Miller. Chicago: University of Chicago Press, 1991.

———. *The History of Sexuality, Volume 1: The Will to Knowledge*. New York: Random House, 1990.

———. "Of Other Spaces." *Diacritics* 16, no. 1 (1986): 22–27.

———. *The History of Sexuality, Volume 2: The Use of Pleasure*. New York: Pantheon, 1985.

———. "Nietzsche, Genealogy, History." In *Foucault*, edited by Paul Rabinow. New York: Pantheon Books, 1984.

———. "On the Genealogy of Ethics." In *Michel Foucault: Beyond Structuralism and Hermeneutics*, edited by H. Dreyfus and P. Rabinow. Chicago: University of Chicago Press, 1983.

———. "The Subject and Power." In *Michel Foucault: Beyond Structuralism and Hermeneutics*, edited by H. Dreyfus and P. Rabinow. Chicago: University of Chicago Press, 1983.

———. *Power/Knowledge: Selected Interviews and Other Writings, 1972–1977*, edited by Colin Gordon. New York: Pantheon Books, 1980.

———. *Discipline and Punish: The Birth of the Prison*. New York: Random House, 1979.

———. *Archaeology of Knowledge*. London: Routledge, 1972.

Frager, Ruth. *Sweatshop Strife: Class, Ethnicity and Gender in the Jewish Labor Movement of Toronto, 1900–1939*. Toronto: University of Toronto Press, 1992.

Francis, Margot. "Unsettling Sights: Artists Re-imagine the Nation." PhD diss., University of Toronto, 2002.

Frankenberg, Ruth, ed. *Displacing Whiteness: Essays in Social and Cultural Criticism*. Durham, NC: Duke University Press, 1997.

———. *White Women, Race Matters: The Social Construction of Whiteness*. Minneapolis: University of Minnesota Press, 1993.

Freedland, Michael. "I'm the Only Journalist Alive to Have Interviewed Harper Lee—and It's All Thanks to Gregory Peck." *The Guardian*, July 13, 2015.

Freedman, A. "White Woman's Burden." *Saturday Night*, April 1993.

Freire, Paolo. *Pedagogy of the Oppressed*. Harmondsworth: Penguin, 1972.

Freud, Sigmund. *Jokes and their Relation to the Unconscious*. New York: Penguin, 1976.

Friedersdorf, Conor. "Police Brutality and the Role That Whiteness Plays." *The Atlantic*, May 22, 2015.

Friedman, Susan. "Beyond White and Other: Relationality and Narratives of Race in Feminist Discourse." *Signs* 21, no. 1 (1995): 1–49.

Fung, Richard. "Working Through Cultural Appropriation." *Fuse* 16, no. 5/6 (1993): 16–24.

Gabriel, Chris, and Katherine Scott. "Women's Press at Twenty." In *And Still We Rise: Feminist Political Mobilizing in Contemporary Canada*, edited by Linda Carty. Toronto: Women's Press, 1993.

Game, Ann. "Sociology's Emotions." *Canadian Review of Sociology and Anthropology* 34, no. 4 (1995): 385–399.

Gandhi, Leela. *Affective Communities: Anticolonial Thought, Fin-de-Siècle Radicalism, and the Politics of Friendship*. Durham, NC: Duke University Press, 2006.

Garber, Megan. "My Atticus." *The Atlantic*, July 15, 2015.

Gates, Henry Louis, Jr. "Multicultural Madness." *Tikkun*, November/December 1991.

GATT-Fly. *Ah-Hah: A New Approach to Popular Education*. Toronto: Between the Lines, 1983.

Giddings, Paula. "Missing in Action: Ida B. Wells, the NAACP, and the Historical Record." *Meridians* 1, no. 2 (2001): 1–17.

———. *When and Where I Enter: The Impact of Black Women on Race and Sex in America*. New York: William Morrow, 1984.

Gilligan, Carol. *In a Different Voice: Psychological Theory and Women's Development*. Cambridge, MA: Harvard University Press, 1982.

Gilmore, Ruth. *Golden Gulag: Prisons, Surplus, Crisis, and Opposition in Globalizing California*. Berkeley: University of California Press, 2016.

Gilroy, Paul. *There Ain't No Black in the Union Jack*. London: Hutchinson, 1987.

Gitlin, Todd. "After the Failed Faiths: Beyond Individualism, Marxism, and Multiculturalism." *World Policy Journal* 12, no. 1 (1995): 61–68.

———. *The Twilight of Common Dreams: Why America Is Wracked by Culture Wars*. New York: Metropolitan, 1995.

———. "The Rise of Identity Politics." *Dissent*, Spring 1993.

Goff, Phillip Atiba, Claude M. Steele, and Paul G. Davies. "The Space between Us: Stereotype Threat and Distance in Interracial Contexts." *Journal of Personality and Social Psychology* 94, no. 1 (2009): 91–107.

Goffman, Erving. *Interaction Ritual: Essays on Face-to-Face Behavior*. Chicago: Aldine, 1967.

———. *The Presentation of Self in Everyday Life*. Garden City, NY: Doubleday, 1959.

Goldberg, David. *The Threat of Race: Reflections on Racial Neoliberalism*. Malden, MA: Blackwell, 2009.

———. *Racist Culture: Philosophy and the Politics of Meaning*. Cambridge: Basil Blackwell, 1993.

Gomes, M. "The Rewards and Stresses of Social Change: A Qualitative Study of Peace Activists." *Journal of Humanistic Psychology* 32 (1992): 134–146.

Goodwin, Jeff, James M. Jasper, and Francesca Polletta, eds. *Passionate Politics: Emotions and Social Movements*. Chicago: University of Chicago Press, 2001.

Gordon, Deborah. "Racism and the White Women's Movement: An Interview with Esmerelda Thornhill." *Breaking the Silence* 4, no. 1 (1985).

Gotlieb, Amy. "What About Us? Organizing Inclusively in the National Action Committee on the Status of Women." In *And Still We Rise: Feminist Political Mobilizing in Contemporary Canada*, edited by Linda Carty. Toronto: Women's Press, 1993.

Green, Marlene, Barb Thomas, and Venier Wong. "Letter to the Editor." *Toronto Life*, May 1993.

Greensmith, Cameron. "Desiring Diversity: The Limits of White Settler Multiculturalism in Queer Organizations." *Studies in Ethnicity and Nationalism* 18, no. 1 (2018): 57–77.

Griffiths, Linda, and Maria Campbell. *The Book of Jessica: A Theatrical Transformation*. Toronto: Playwrights Canada Press, 1999.

Grills, Sylvia. "Should the Rainbow Have Black and Brown Stripes? (Anti)-racism and Coalitions in Toronto's Rainbow Community." PhD diss., Queen's University, 2020.

Gunning, Isabelle. "Arrogant Perception, World Travelling and Multicultural Feminism: The Case of Female Genital Surgeries." *Columbia Human Rights Law Review* 2 (Summer 1992): 189–248.

Gupta, Nila, and Makeda Silvera. "Editorial: We Were Never Lost." *Fireweed* 16 (Spring 1983): 5–7.

Gurnah, Ahmed. "The Politics of Racism Awareness Training." *Critical Social Policy* 4, no. 11, (September 1984): 6–20.

Halcli, Abigail. "AIDS, Anger, and Activism: ACT UP as a Social Movement Organization." In *Waves of Protest: Social Movements Since the Sixties*, edited by Jo Freeman and Victoria Johnson, 135–150. Lanham, MD: Rowman & Littlefield, 1999.

Hall, Lisa Kahaleole Chang. "Bitches in Solitude: Identity Politics and the Lesbian Community." In *Sisters, Sexperts, Queers: Beyond the Lesbian Nation*, edited by Arlene Stein, 218–229. New York: Plume, 1993.

Hall, Stuart. "Introduction: Who Needs Identity?" In *Questions of Cultural Identity*, edited by Stuart Hall and Paul du Gay. London: Sage, 1996.

———. "Cultural Studies and Its Theoretical Legacies." In *Cultural Studies*, edited by L. Grossberg, C. Nelson, and P. A. Treichler. New York: Routledge, 1992.

———. "New Ethnicities." In *Race, Culture, Difference*, edited by J. Donald and A. Rattansi. London: Sage, 1992.

———. "Ethnicity: Identity and Difference." *Radical America* 23, no. 4 (Summer 1989): 9–20.

Hampton, Jaqueline. "Destructive Campaign Fans Flames of Racism." *Toronto Star*, September 11, 1992.

Haraway, Donna. "A Manifesto for Cyborgs: Science, Technology and Socialist Feminism in the 1980s." In *Feminism/Postmodernism*, edited by Linda Nicholson. New York: Routledge, 1990.

Harper, Helen. "Danger at the Borders: The Response of High School Girls to Feminist Writing Practices." PhD diss., University of Toronto, 1995.

Hartigan, John. "What Are You Laughing At? Assessing the 'Racial" in U.S. Public Discourse." *Transforming Anthropology* 17, no. 1 (2009): 1–4.

Heberle, Rudolf. *Social Movements: An Introduction to Political Sociology*. New York: Appleton Croft, 1951.

Henry, Frances, Enakshi Dua, Carl E. James, Audrey Kobayashi, Peter Li, Howard Ramos, and Malinda S. Smith. *The Equity Myth: Racialization and Indigeneity at Canadian Universities*. Vancouver: University of British Columbia Press, 2017.

Henry, Frances, Carol Tator, Winston Mattis, and Tim Rees. *The Color of Democracy: Racism in Canadian Society*. Toronto: Harcourt Brace, 1995.

Heron, Barbara. "Desire for Development: The Education of White Women as Development Workers." PhD diss., University of Toronto, 1999.

Hetherington, Kevin. *The Badlands of Modernity: Heterotopia and Social Ordering*. New York: Routledge, 1997.

Hill, Herbert. *Race and Ethnicity in Organized Labor*. Madison: University of Wisconsin Press, 1987.

Hobsbawm, Thomas. *The Age of Capital: 1848–1875*. New York: Charles Scribner's, 1975.

Hochschild, Arlie. *The Second Shift: Working Parents and the Revolution at Home*. New York: Viking, 1989.

———. *The Managed Heart: Commercialization of Human Feeling*. Berkeley: University of California Press, 1983.

hooks, bell. *Black Looks: Race and Representation*. Toronto: Between the Lines, 1992.

———. *Feminist Theory from Margin to Center*. Boston: South End Press, 1985.

———. *Ain't I a Woman: Black Women and Feminism*. Boston: South End Press, 1983.

Hou, Feng, and T. R. Balakrishnan. "The Integration of Visible Minorities in Contemporary Canadian Society." *Canadian Journal of Sociology* 21 (1996): 307–336.

Howell, Phillip. "Afterword: Remapping the Terrain of Moral Regulation." *Journal of Historical Geography* 42 (2013): 193–202.

Hurtado, Aida. *The Color of Privilege: Three Blasphemies on Race and Feminism*. Ann Arbor: University of Michigan Press, 1996.

Iacovetta, Franca, and Mariana Valverde, eds. *Gender Conflicts: New Essays in Women's History*. Toronto: University of Toronto Press, 1992.

Illouz, Eva. *Cold Intimacies: The Making of Emotional Capitalism*. Cambridge: Polity, 2007.

Ilves, Juta. "Letter to the Editor." *Toronto Life*, May 1993.

International Women's Day Committee, Toronto. "Letter to the Editorial Collective." *Broadside*, May 1983.

Inglis, Amirah. *The White Women's Protection Ordinance: Sexual Anxiety and Politics in Papua*. London: Sussex University Press, 1975.

Ioanide, Paula. *Emotional Politics of Racism: How Feelings Trump Facts in an Era of Colorblindness*. Stanford, CA: Stanford University Press, 2015.

Jaggar, Alison. *Feminist Politics and Human Nature*. Lanham, MD: Rowman & Littlefield, 1983.

Jaggar, Alison, and Susan Bordo, eds. *Gender/Body/Knowledge: Feminist Reconstructions of Being and Knowing*. New Brunswick, NJ: Rutgers University Press, 1989.

Jakobsen, Janet. *Working Alliances and the Politics of Difference: Diversity and Feminist Ethics*. Bloomington: Indiana University Press, 1998.

Jakubowicz, A. "The Celebration of (Moderate) Diversity in a Racist Society: Multiculturalism and Education in Australia." *Discourse* 8, no. 2 (1988): 37–75.

James, N. "Emotional Labor: Skill and Work in the Social Regulation of Feeling." *Sociological Review* 37, no. 1 (1989): 15–42.

Joseph, Gloria. *Common Difference: Conflicts in Black and White Feminist Perspectives*. Boston: South End Press, 1981.

Kalev A., F. Dobbin, and E. Kelly. "Best Practices or Best Guesses? Assessing the Efficacy of Corporate Affirmative Action and Diversity Policies." *American Sociological Review* 71 (2006): 589–617.

Kendi, Ibram X. *How to Be an Antiracist*. New York: Random House, 2019.

Khan, Sharmeen. "The Whiteness of Green." *Antithesis* 11, no. 1 (2004): 6–9.

Kinsmen, Gary. "Managing AIDS Organizing: 'Consultation,' 'Partnership,' and the National AIDS Strategy." In *Organizing Dissent*, edited by William Carroll, 215–231. Toronto: Garamond Press, 1992.

Kirby, Sandra, and McKenna, Kate. *Experience, Research, Social Change: Methods from the Margins*. Toronto: Garamond Press, 1989.

Kitschelt, Herbert. "The Medium Is the Message: Democracy and Oligarchy in Belgian Ecology Parties." In *Green Politics One*, edited by Wolfgang Rudig. Edinburgh: Edinburgh University Press, 1990.

Kleinman, Sherryl. *Opposing Ambitions: Gender and Identity in an Alternative Organization*. Chicago: University of Chicago Press, 1996.

Kleinman, Sherryl, and Martha Copp. *Emotions and Fieldwork*. Newbury Park, CA: Sage, 1993.

Kouchaki, Maryam. "Vicarious Moral Licensing: The Influence of Others' Past Moral Actions on Moral Behavior." *Journal of Personality and Social Psychology* 101, no. 4 (2011), 702–715. doi:10.1037/a0024552.

Kritzman, Lawrence, ed. *Michel Foucault: Politics, Philosophy, Culture*. New York: Routledge, 1988.

Kropotkin, Peter. *Mutual Aid: A Factor of Evolution*. Montreal: Black Rose Books, 1989 [1902].

Krumm, Angela, and Alexandra Corning. "Who Believes Us When We Try to Conceal Our Prejudices? The Effectiveness of Moral Credentials with In-Groups versus Out-Groups." *Journal of Social Psychology* 148, no. 6 (2018): 689–710. doi:10.3200/SOCP.148.6.689-710.

Kubota, J. T., J. Li, E. Bar–David, M. R. Banaji, and E. A. Phelps. "The Price of Racial Bias: Intergroup Negotiations in the Ultimatum Game." *Psychological Science* 24, no. 12 (2013): 2498–2504. doi:10.1177/0956797613496435.

Laclau, Ernesto, and Chantal Mouffe. *Hegemony and Socialist Strategy: Towards a Radical Democratic Politics*. London: Verso, 1985.

Laidlaw, Toni Ann, and Cheryl Malmo. *Healing Voices: Feminist Approaches to Therapy with Women*. San Francisco: Jossey-Bass, 1990.

Landau, Reva. "Letter to the Broadside Editorial Collective." *Broadside*, May 1983.

Landsberg, Michele. "Callwood Furor Masks Real Racism Struggle at Nellie's." *Toronto Star*, July 18, 1992.

———. "Feminists Must Learn to Share the Power." *Toronto Star*, May 1992.

Laub, Dori. "Bearing Witness, or the Vicissitudes of Listening." In *Testimony: Crises of Witnessing in Literature, Psychoanalysis and History*, edited by S. Felman and D. Laub. New York: Routledge, 1992.

Lawson, E. S. "Anti-Black Racism on the Sidelines: The Limits of Listening Sessions to Address Institutional Racism at Canadian Universities." *Canadian Review of Sociology* 57, no. 3 (2020): 491–494. doi:10.1111/cars.12296.

Leah, Ronnie. "Do You Call Me Sister?" In *Scratching the Surface: Canadian Anti-racist Feminist Thought*, edited by Enakshi Dua and A. Robertson. Toronto: Women's Press, 1999.

Lee, Harper. *Go Set a Watchman*. New York: HarperCollins, 2015.

———. *To Kill a Mockingbird*. Philadelphia: J. B. Lippincott & Co., 1960.

Lenon, Suzanne, and OmiSoore H. Dryden. "Introduction: Interventions, Iterations, and Interrogations That Disturb the (Homo)Nation." In *Disrupting Queer Inclusion: Canadian Homonationalisms and the Politics of Belonging*, edited by O. H. Dryden and S. Lenon, 3–18. Vancouver: UBC Press, 2015.

Lensmire, Timothy J. "Ambivalent White Racial Identities: Fear and an Elusive Innocence." *Race Ethnicity and Education* 13, no. 2 (2010): 159–117.

Lesbian Writing and Publishing Collective, eds. *Dykeversions*. Toronto: Women's Press, 1986.

Levine-Rasky, Cynthia. *Whiteness Fractured*. New York: Routledge, 2013.

Leys, Colin, and Marguerite Mendell. *Culture and Social Change: Social Movements in Quebec and Ontario*. Montreal: Black Rose, 1992.

Lipset, Seymour M., Martin A. Trow, and James S. Coleman. *Union Democracy*. New York: Free Press, 1956.

Lithwick, Dahlia. "My Legal Hero: Atticus Finch." *The Guardian*, September 1, 2010.

Little, Margaret. "A Fit and Proper Person: The Moral Regulation of Single Mothers in Ontario, 1920–1940." In *Gendered Pasts: Historical Essays on Masculinity and Femininity*, edited by K. McPherson, C. Morgan, and N. M. Forestell. Oxford: Oxford University Press, 1999.

———. "The Blurring of Boundaries: Private and Public Welfare for Single Mothers in Ontario." *Studies in Political Economy* 47 (1995): 89–109.

———. "Manhunts and Bingo Blabs: The Moral Regulation of Ontario Single Mothers." *Canadian Journal of Sociology* 19, no. 3 (1994): 233–247.

Lorde, Audre. "An Open Letter to Mary Daly." In *This Bridge Called My Back*, edited by Cherríe Moraga and Gloria Anzaldúa, 94–97. New York: Kitchen Table, 1983.

Lotringer, Sylvere, ed. *Foucault Live: Interviews 1966–1984*. New York: Semiotext(e). Quoted in Sawicki, "Foucault, Feminism."

Lowenberger, Lois. "IWD: Lip Service to Feminism." *Broadside*, April 1983.

Loucas, Salome. Commentary. *Cross Cultural Communication Centre Newsletter* xxi, no. 9, October 3, 1992.

Lucas, Salome, Judy Persad, Gillian Morton, Sunita Albequerque, and Nada El Yassir. "Changing the Politics of the Women's Movement." *Resources for Feminist Research* 20, no. 1/2 (1991).

Lugones, Maria, and Elizabeth Spelman. "Have We Got a Theory for You! Feminist Theory, Cultural Imperialism and the Demand for 'The Woman's Voice.'" *Women's Studies International Forum* 6, no. 6 (1983): 573–581.

Lustiger-Thaler, Henri. "Afterword." In *Political Arrangements, Power and the City*, edited by H. Lustiger-Thaler. Montreal: Black Rose Books, 1992.

Lynch, Barbara. "The Garden and the Sea: U.S. Latino Environmental Discourses and Mainstream Environmentalism." *Social Problems* 40, no. 1 (1993): 108–124.

MacIntyre, April. "D. L. Hughley: 'White Liberal Guilt Keeps Obama Jokes at Bay.'" *Monsters and Critics*, August 22, 2008.

MacKenzie, Laurie, and Sue Kirk. "What Is Radical Feminist Counselling?" Centre for Women's Studies and Services, San Diego, no date. Quoted in Jaggar 1983, 279.

Mackey, Eva. *House of Difference: Cultural Politics and National Identity in Canada.* Toronto: University of Toronto Press, 2002.

Madison, Kelly. "Legitimation Crisis and Containment: The Anti-Racist-White-Hero." *Critical Studies in Mass Communication* 16, no. 4 (1999): 399–416.

Mahrouse, Gada. *Conflicted Commitments: Race, Privilege and Power in Transnational Solidarity Activism.* Montreal: McGill University Press, 2014.

Mallory, C. "What's in a Name? In Defense of Ecofeminism (Not Ecological Feminisms, Feminist Ecology, or Gender and the Environment): Or Why Ecofeminism Need Not Be Ecofeminine—but So What if It Is?" *Ethics and the Environment* 23, no. 2 (2018): 11–35. doi:10.2979/ethicsenviro.23.2.03.

Maloney, Jennifer, and Laura Stevens. "Harper Lee's Father, Inspiration for Atticus Finch, Changed His Views on Segregation: *Go Set a Watchman*'s Depiction of Atticus Finch Has Prompted Dismay among Many Awaiting the Book's Release." *Wall Street Journal*, July 11, 2015.

Manji, Irshad. "Why Identity Politics Is Not the Answer." *Herizons*, Spring 1997.

Marchand, Phillip. "Callwood Denounces Bullying by Self-Defined Weak." *Toronto Star*, June 21, 1993.

Martinez, Elizabeth "Betita." "Where Was the Color in Seattle? Looking for Reasons Why the Great Battle Was So White." *ColorLines* 3, no. 1 (Spring 2000): 141–148.

Marx, Karl. "German Ideology." Excerpted in *Karl Marx: Selected Writings in Sociology and Social Philosophy*, edited by T. Bottomore and M. Rubel. Harmondsworth. New York: Penguin Books, 1986 [1854].

Matsunaga, Jennifer. "Limits of 'Truth and Reconciliation': The Effects of Compensation on Stories about Residential Schools and Japanese Canadian Internment." PhD diss., Queen's University, 2018.

Mawhinney, Janet. "Giving Up the Ghost: Disrupting the (Re)Production of White Privilege in Anti-racist Pedagogy and Organizational Change." Master's thesis, University of Toronto, 1998.

Mayes, Alison. "Racism Remains Feminist Groups' Dirty Laundry." *Toronto Star*, October 23, 1992.

Maynard, Robin. *Policing Black Lives*. Black Point, NS: Fernwood Press, 2017.

Maynard, Steven. "When Queer Is Not Enough: Identity and Politics." *Fuse* 15, no. 1/2 (1991): 14–18.

McCambridge, Ruth. "The Disturbing Lack of Diversity and Will in Environmental Nonprofits." *Nonprofit Quarterly*, July 30, 2014. https://nonprofitquarterly.org.

McCarthy, Cameron. "The Politics of Culture: Multicultural Education after the Content Debate." *Discourse* 14, no. 2 (1994): 1–16.

———. *Race and Curriculum: Social Inequality and the Theories and Politics of Difference in Contemporary Research on Schooling.* London: Falmer Press, 1990.

McCarthy, Cameron, and Warren Crichlow, eds. *Race, Identity and Representation in Education.* New York: Routledge, 1993.

McCaskell, Tim. "Anti-racist Education and Practice in the School System." In *Beyond Political Correctness: Toward the Inclusive University,* edited by S. Richer and L. Weir, 253–272. Toronto: University of Toronto Press. 1995.

McClintock, Anne. *Imperial Leather: Gender and Sexuality in the Colonial Conquest.* New York: Routledge, 1995.

McLaren, Angus. *Our Own Master Race: Eugenics in Canada, 1885–1945.* Toronto: University of Toronto Press, 2016.

McLaren, Margaret. "Foucault and the Subject of Feminism." *Social Theory and Practice* 23, no. 1 (1997).

McLeod, Keith. "Multiculturalism and the Concept of a Non-racial Society: A Perspective on Teacher Education." *Orbit* 25, no. 2 (1994): 18–25.

McMullen, Ross. "Callwood's Tactful Abilities Are a Marvel." *Toronto Star,* June 8, 1992.

Mercer, Kobena. "1968: Periodizing Postmodern Politics and Identity." In *Welcome to the Jungle: New Positions in Black Cultural Studies.* London: Routledge, 1994.

———. "Welcome to the Jungle: Identity and Diversity in Postmodern Politics." In *Identity, Community, Culture, Difference,* edited by Johnathan Rutherford. London: Lawrence Wishart, 1990.

Meyers, Diana. "Emotion and Heterodox Moral Perception: An Essay in Moral Social Psychology." In *Feminists Rethink the Self,* edited by D. Meyers. Boulder, CO: Westview Press, 1997.

———, ed. *Feminists Rethink the Self.* Boulder, CO: Westview Press, 1997.

Michels, Robert. *Political Parties: A Sociological Study of the Oligarchical Tendencies of Modern Democracies.* New York: Dover Publications, 1959 [1911].

Michels, W. "Race into Culture." *Critical Inquiry,* Summer 1992.

Miles, Robert. *Racism.* London: Routledge, 1989.

Mills, Charles W. "White Ignorance." In *Race and Epistemologies of Ignorance,* edited by S. Sullivan and N. Tuana, 13–38. Albany: SUNY Press, 2007.

———. *The Racial Contract.* Ithaca, NY: Cornell University Press, 1999.

Mitchell, Juliet. *Woman's Estate.* Harmondsworth: Penguin, 1971. Quoted in Segal, *Is the Future Female?*

Mitchell, Maurice. "Building Resilient Organizations." *The Forge,* November 29, 2022. https://forgeorganizing.org.

Mohanty, Chandra. "Cartographies of Struggle: Third World Women and the Politics of Feminism." In *Third World Women and the Politics of Feminism,* edited by C. Mohanty, A. Russo, and L. Torres. Bloomington: Indiana University Press, 1991.

Monin, Benoit, and Dale Miller. "Moral Credentials and the Expression of Prejudice." *Journal of Personality and Social Psychology* 81, no. 1 (2001): 33–43. doi:10.1037/0022-3514.81.1.33.

Moore, Basil. "The Prejudice Thesis and the De-politicization of Racism." *Discourse* 14, no. 1 (1993): 52.

Moore, Suzanne. "On Talk Shows the Democracy of Pain Reigns Supreme: We May Not All Be Famous, but We Have All Suffered." *New Statesman*, February 12, 1999.

Moraga, Cherríe, and Gloria Anzaldúa, eds. *This Bridge Called My Back: Writings by Radical Women of Color*. New York: Kitchen Table Press, 1983.

Morgan, Robin, ed. *Sisterhood Is Global: The International Women's Movement Anthology*. New York: Anchor Books, 1984.

Morgen, Sandra. "It Was the Best of Times, It Was the Worst of Times: Emotional Discourse in the Work Cultures of Feminist Health Clinics." In *Feminist Organizations: Harvest of the Women's Movement*, edited by Myra Marx Ferree and Patricia Yancey Martin. Philadelphia: Temple University Press, 1995.

Morgensen, Scott. *Spaces between Us: Queer Settler Colonialism and Indigenous Decolonization*. Minneapolis: University of Minnesota Press, 2011.

Morrison, Toni. *Playing in the Dark: Whiteness and the Literary Imagination*. Boston: Harvard University Press, 1992.

Mukherjee, Bharati. "A Four-Hundred-Year-Old Woman." In *Critical Fictions: The Politics of Imaginative Writing*, edited by P. Mariani, 24–28. Seattle: Bay Press, 1991.

Mumby, D., and L. Putnam. "The Politics of Emotion: A Feminist Reading of Bounded Rationality." *Academy of Management Review* 17, no. 3 (1992): 465–486.

Murray, V., P. Bradshaw, and J. Wolpin. "Power in and around Non-profit Boards: A Neglected Dimension of Governance." *Non-profit Management and Leadership* 3, no. 2 (1992): 165–182.

NAC. NAC Organizational Review Document. National Action Committee on the Status of Women, 1988.

Nadeau, Mary-Jo. "Troubling Herstory: Unsettling White Multiculturalism in Canadian Feminism." *Canadian Woman Studies* 27, no. 2/3 (2009): 6.

———. "Who Is Canadian Now? Feminism and the Politics of Nation after September 11." *Atlantis* 27, no. 1 (September 22, 2002).

Nagel, Joanne. *Race, Ethnicity, and Sexuality: Intimate Intersections, Forbidden Frontiers*. Oxford: Oxford University Press, 2003.

Nagel, Mechthild. "Critical Theory Meets the Ethic of Care: Engendering Social Justice and Social Identities." *Social Theory and Practice* 23, no. 2 (1997): 307–326.

Narayan, Uma. "Cross-Cultural Connections, Border-Crossings, and 'Death by Culture': Thinking about Dowry-Murders in India and Domestic Violence Murders in the United States." In *Dislocating Cultures: Identities, Traditions and Third World Feminism*, edited by U. Narayan. New York: Routledge, 1997.

———. "Working Together across Difference: Some Considerations on Emotions and Political Practice." *Hypatia* 3 no. 2 (1988): 31–47.

Newman, Katherine. "Incipient Bureaucracy: The Development of Hierarchy in Egalitarian Organizations." In *Hierarchy and Society: Anthropological Perspectives on
Bureaucracy*, edited by G. Britan and R. Cohen. Philadelphia: Institute for the Study
of Human Issues, 1980.

Ng, Roxana. "Integrating the Personal, Professional, Cultural, and Spiritual in the
Academy." Paper presented at the American Educational Research Association Annual Meeting, Montreal, 1999.

———. "Multiculturalism as Ideology: A Textual Accomplishment." Paper presented at
the American Anthropological Association Annual Meeting, San Francisco, 1992.

———. "Finding Our Voices: Reflections on Immigrant Women's Organizing." In
Women and Social Change: Feminist Activism in Canada, edited by Jeri Wine and
Janice Ristock. Toronto: James Lorimer, 1991.

———. "Sexism, Racism and Canadian Nationalism." In *Race, Class, Gender: Bonds and
Barriers*, edited by J. Vorst. Toronto: University of Toronto Press, 1991.

———. "Teaching against the Grain: Contradictions for Minority Teachers." In *Women
and Education*, edited by J. Gaskell and A. McLaren. Calgary: Detselig Enterprises,
1991.

———. "Racism, Sexism and Visible Minority Immigrant Women in Canada." *Zeitschrift
der Gesellschaft fur Kanada–Studien* 10, no. 2 (1990).

———. *The Politics of Community Services: Immigrant Women, Class and State*. Toronto:
Garamond Press, 1988.

Ng, Roxana, Elizabeth Kwan, and Baukje Miedema. "State Funding and Immigrant
Services: The Experience of an Immigrant Women's Group of the Maritimes." *Canadian Review of Social Policy* 27 (1991): 49–57.

Nicoll, Fiona. "Are You Calling Me a Racist? Teaching Critical Whiteness Theory in Indigenous Sovereignty." *Borderlands e-journal* 3, no. 2 (2015). www.borderlands.net.au.

O'Brien, Mary, and Frieda Forman. "Letter to the Editorial Collective." *Broadside*,
April 1983.

Ontario Ministry of Education and Training. *The Resource Guide for Anti-racist and
Ethnocultural Equity Education, JK–Grade 9*. Toronto: Ontario Ministry of Education and Training, 1994.

Ortner, Sherry. "Is Female to Male as Nature Is to Culture?" In *Woman Culture &
Society*, edited by M. Rosaldo and L. Lamphere. Stanford, CA: Stanford University
Press, 1974.

Paris, Erna. "Unsaid Words on Racism." *Globe and Mail*, July 21, 1992.

Parker, Clifton B. "Stanford Big Data Study Finds Racial Disparities in Oakland, Calif.,
Police Behavior, Offers Solutions." *Stanford News*, June 15, 2016. https://news.stan-
ford.edu.

Parkin, Wendy. "The Public and the Private: Gender, Sexuality and Emotion." In *Emotions in Organizations*, edited by S. Fineman. London: Sage, 1993.

Pastrana, Antonio. "The Intersectional Imagination: What Do Lesbian and Gay Leaders of Color Have to Do with It?" *Race, Gender & Class* 13, no. 3/4 (2006): 218–238.

Patton, Cindy. *Inventing AIDS*. New York: Routledge, 1990.

Perry, Ruth. "Historically Correct." *Women's Review of Books*, February 1, 1992.

Petry, Alice, ed. *On Harper Lee: Essays and Reflections*. Knoxville: University of Tennessee Press, 2007.

Pheterson, Gail. "Alliances between Women: Overcoming Internalized Oppression and Internalized Domination." In *Reconstructing the Academy: Women's Education and Women's Studies*, edited by Elizabeth Minnich, Jean O'Barr, and Rachel Rosenfeld. Chicago: University of Chicago Press, 1988.

Philip, M. NourbeSe. "Gut Issues in Babylon: Racism and Anti-racism in the Arts." *Fuse* 12, no. 5 (April/May 1989): 12–26.

Phizacklea, A., and R. Miles. "The British Trade Union Movement and Racism." In *The Manufacture of Disadvantage*, edited by G. Lee and R. Loveridge. Buckingham: Open University Press, 1987.

Pierce, Jennifer L. *Racing for Innocence: Whiteness, Gender and the Backlash against Affirmative Action*. Stanford, CA: Stanford University Press, 2012.

Pon, Madge. "Like a Chinese Puzzle: The Construction of Chinese Masculinity." In *Gender and History in Canada*, edited by Joy Parr and Mark Rosenfeld. Mississauga, ON: Copp Clark, 1996.

Poster, Mark. "Foucault and the Problem of Self-Constitution." In *Foucault and the Critique of Institutions*, edited by John Caputo and Mark Young. University Park: Pennsylvania State University Press, 1993.

———. "Foucault and the Tyranny of Greece." In *Foucault: A Critical Reader*, edited by David Hoy. Oxford: Basil Blackwell, 1986.

Pratt, Minnie Bruce. "Identity: Skin/Blood/Heart." In *Yours in Struggle*, edited by E. Bulkin, B. Smith, and M. B. Pratt. New York: Longhaul Press, 1984.

Pringle, Rosemary. *Secretaries Talk*. London: Verso, 1989.

Probyn, Elspeth. "True Voices and Real People: The 'Problem' of the Autobiographical in Cultural Studies." In *Relocating Cultural Studies: Developments in Theory and Research*, edited by V. Blundell, J. Sheperd, and I. Taylor. New York: Routledge, 1993.

Puar, Jasbir. *Terrorist Assemblages: Homonationalism in Queer Times*. Durham, NC: Duke University Press, 2007.

Putnam, Linda, and Dennis Mumby. "Organizations, Emotion and the Myth of Rationality." In *Emotions in Organizations*, edited by S. Fineman. London: Sage, 1993.

Rafaeli, A. "When Cashiers Meet Customers: An Analysis of the Role of Supermarket Cashiers." *Academy of Management Journal* 32 (1989): 245–273.

Rafaeli, A., and R. I. Sutton. "Busy Stores and Demanding Customers: How Do They Affect the Display of Positive Emotion?" *Academy of Management Journal* 33 (1990): 623–637.

———. "Expression of Emotion as Part of the Work Role." *Academy of Management Journal* 12 (1987): 23–33.

Rai, Amit. *Rule of Sympathy: Sentiment, Race, and Power, 1750–1850*. New York: Palgrave, 2002.

Ramaswamy, Chitra. "What Happens Now to All the People and Businesses Named after Atticus Finch?" *The Guardian*, July 13, 2015.

Ramazanoglu, Caroline. "Ethnocentrism and Socialist-Feminist Theory: A Response to Barrett and McIntosh." *Feminist Review* 22 (1986): 82.

Rattansi, Ali. "Changing the Subject? Racism, Culture and Education." In *Race, Culture and Difference*, edited by J. Donald and A. Rattansi, 11–47. London: Sage, 1992.

Razack, Sherene. "Simple Logic: Race, the Identity Documents Rule, and the Story of a Nation Besieged and Betrayed." *Journal of Law and Social Policy* 15 (2000): 181–209. https://digitalcommons.osgoode.yorku.ca.

———. "Your Place or Mine? Transnational Feminist Collaboration." In *Anti-racist Feminism: Critical Race and Gender Studies*, edited by Agnes Calliste and George Dei. Halifax: Fernwood Publishing, 2000.

———. "Making Canada White: Law and the Policing of Bodies of Color in the 1990s." *Canadian Journal of Law and Society* 14, no. 1 (1999): 159–184.

———. *Looking White People in the Eye*. Toronto: University of Toronto Press, 1998.

———. "Storytelling for Social Change." *Gender and Education* 5, no. 1 (1993): 55–70.

Rebick, Judy. *Ten Thousand Roses: The Making of a Feminist Revolution*. Toronto: Penguin Canada, 2005.

Reinharz, Shulamit. "Experiential Analysis: A Contribution to Feminist Research." In *Theories of Women's Studies*, edited by G. Bowles and R. Klein. London: Routledge & Kegan Paul, 1983.

Rezai-Rashti, G. 1989. "Multicultural Education, Anti-racist Education and Critical Pedagogy: Reflections on Every Day's Practice." Unpublished paper.

Richer, Stephen, and Lorna Weir, eds. *Beyond Political Correctness: Toward the Inclusive University*. Toronto: University of Toronto Press, 1992.

Ricker-Wilson, Carol. "When the Mockingbird Becomes an Albatross: Reading and Resistance in the Language Arts Classroom." *English Journal* 87, no. 3 (1998): 67–72.

Riggs, Damien W., ed. *The Psychic Life of Racism in Gay Men's Communities*. New York: Lexington Books, 2017.

Ristock, Janice. "Feminist Collectives: The Struggles and Contradictions in Our Quest for a Uniquely Feminist Structure." In *Women and Social Change: Feminist Activism in Canada*, edited by Jeri Wine and Janice Ristock. Toronto: James Lorimer, 1991.

Ritchie, Andrea. *Invisible No More: Police Violence against Black Women and Women of Color*. Boston: Beacon Press, 2017.

Roach, Kiké, and Judy Rebick. *Politically Speaking*. Madeira Park, BC: Douglas & McIntyre, 1996.

Roediger, David. *The Wages of Whiteness: Race and the Making of the American Working Class*. London: Verso, 1991.

Roger, Kerstin. "Fairy Fictions: White Women as Professional Helpers." PhD diss., University of Toronto, Ontario Institute for Studies in Education, 1998.

Roman, Leslie. "White Is a Color! White Defensiveness, Postmodernism and Anti-racist Pedagogy." In *Race, Identity and Representation in Education*, edited by C. McCarthy and W. Crichlow, 71–88. New York: Routledge, 1993.

Rooney, Ellen. "Commentary: What's to Be Done?" In *Coming to Terms: Feminism, Theory and Politics*, edited by Elizabeth Weed. New York: Routledge, 1989.

Root, Maria. "A Model for Understanding Variations in the Experience of Trauma and their Sequelae." Paper presented at the Eighth Advanced Feminist Therapy Institute, Banff, 1989. Quoted in L. Brown, "Not outside the Range."

Rose, Barbara Wade. "Trouble at Nellie's: Race and Feminism." *Globe and Mail*, May 9, 1992.

Rosezelle, P. "Critiquing Anti-racist Consultancy." Presented at the conference for the Canadian Research Institute for the Advancement of Women, Toronto, November 13–15, 1992.

Rowles, M. "Solidarity and Diversity: B.C.'s Summer Institute for Union Women." *Our Times*, March 18–20, 1995.

Russo, Ann. "Between Speech and Silence: Reflections on Accountability." In *Silence, Power, Feminism: Reflections at the Edges of Sound*, edited by Sheena Malhotra and Aimee Carillo Rowe. New York: Palgrave Macmillan, 2013.

———. "We Cannot Live without Our Lives: White Women, Anti-racism and Feminism." In *Third World Women and the Politics of Feminism*, edited by Chandra Mohanty, Ann Russo, and Lourdes Torres. Bloomington: Indiana University Press, 1991.

Said, Edward. *Orientalism*. New York: Vintage Books, 1979.

Sandoval, Cheyla. "U.S. Third World Feminism: The Theory and Method of Opposi-tional Consciousness in the Postmodern World." *Genders* 10 (Spring 1991): 1–24.

San Martin, Ruth, and Lisa Barnoff. "Let Them Howl: The Operations of Imperial Subjectivity and the Politics of Race in One Feminist Organization." *Atlantis: A Women's Studies Journal* 29, no. 1 (2004): 77–84.

———. "Let Them Howl: A Discursive Analysis of Racism in Feminist Organizations." Unpublished manuscript, 2001.

Sardar, Ziauddin. "The Rise of the Voyeur." *New Statesman*, November 6, 2000.

Sarick, L. "NAC to Vote for More than a President—NAC Has Fallen into the 'Skin Trap,' Critic Says." *Globe and Mail*, June 15, 1996.

Sawicki, Jana. "Foucault, Feminism, and Questions of Identity." In *Cambridge Compan-ion to Foucault*, edited by Gary Gutting. Cambridge: Cambridge University Press, 1994.

Saxton, Alexander. *The Rise and Fall of the White Republic*. London: Verso, 1990.

Scheff, Thomas. "1996 Presidential Address: A Vision of Sociology." *Sociological Per-spectives* 40, no. 4 (1997): 529–536.

———. *Bloody Revenge: Emotion, Nationalism and War*. Chicago: University of Chicago Press, 1994.

———. *Discourse, Emotion and Social Structure*. Chicago: University of Chicago Press, 1990.

Schick, Carol. "By Virtue of Being White: Racialized Identity Formation and the Implications for Anti-racist Pedagogy." PhD diss., University of Toronto, Ontario Institute for Studies in Education, 1998.

Scott, Ellen. "Creating Partnerships for Change: Alliances and Betrayals in the Racial Politics of Two Feminist Organizations." *Gender & Society* 12, no. 4 (1999): 400–423.

Scott, Joan. "Experience." In *Feminists Theorize the Political*, edited by J. Butler and J. Scott, 22–40. New York: Routledge, 1992.

———. *Gender and the Politics of History.* New York: Columbia University Press, 1988.

Seager, Joanne. *Earthfollies.* New York: Routledge, 1993.

Sedgwick, Eve Kosofsky. *Touching Feeling.* Durham, NC: Duke University Press, 2003.

Segal, Lynn. *Is the Future Female? Troubled Thoughts on Contemporary Feminism.* London: Virago, 1987.

Segrest, Mab. *Memoir of a Race Traitor.* Cambridge, MA: South End Press, 1994.

———. *My Mama's Dead Squirrel: Lesbian Essays on Southern Culture.* Ithaca, NY: Firebrand Books, 1985.

Seidman, S. "Postmodern Anxiety: The Politics of Epistemology." *Sociological Theory* 9 (1991): 180–190.

Seigworth, Gregory J., and Melissa Gregg. "An Inventory of Shimmers." In *The Affect Theory Reader*, edited by Gregory J. Seigworth and Melissa Gregg. Durham, NC: Duke University Press, 2010.

Sheth, Anita, and Amita Handa. "A Jewel in the Frown: Striking Accord between Indian Feminists." In *Returning the Gaze: Essays on Racism, Feminism and Politics*, edited by Himani Bannerji. Toronto: Sister Vision Press, 1993.

Short, Geoffrey. "Prejudice Reduction in Schools: The Value of Inter-racial Contact." *British Journal of Sociology of Education* 14, no. 2 (1993): 159–168.

———. "Combatting Anti-Semitism: A Dilemma for Anti-racist Education." *British Journal of Educational Studies* 34, no. 1 (1991): 33–44.

Shotwell, Alexis. *Knowing Otherwise: Race, Gender and Implicit Understanding.* University Park: Pennsylvania State University Press, 2011.

Sibley, David. *Geographies of Exclusion: Society and Difference in the West.* London: Routledge, 1995.

Silin, Jonathan. *Sex, Death, and the Education of Children: Our Passion for Ignorance in the Age of AIDS.* New York: Teachers College Press, 1995.

Sleeter, Christine. "How White Teachers Construct Race." In *Race, Identity and Representation in Education*, edited by C. McCarthy and W. Crichlow, 157–171. New York: Routledge, 1993.

Smith, Dorothy. *The Conceptual Practices of Power: A Feminist Sociology of Knowledge.* Toronto: University of Toronto Press, 1990.

———. *The Everyday World as Problematic: A Feminist Sociology.* Toronto: University of Toronto Press, 1987.

Spencer, Dale, Kevin Walby, and Alan Hunt, eds. *Emotions Matter: A Relational Approach to Emotions.* Toronto: University of Toronto Press, 2012.

Srivastava, Sarita. "Song and Dance? The Performance of Anti-racist Workshops." *Canadian Review of Sociology and Anthropology* 33, no. 3 (1996): 292–315.

———. "Voyeurism and Vulnerability: Critiquing the Power Relations of Anti-racist Education." *Canadian Woman Studies* 14, no. 2 (1994): 105–109.

Stamp, Paddy. "Educational Prescriptions." Unpublished research paper. Centre of Criminology, University of Toronto, 2001.

Stasiulis, Daiva. "Authentic Voice: Anti-racist Politics in Canadian Feminist Publishing and Literary Production." In *Feminism and the Politics of Difference*, edited by Sneja Gunew and Anna Yeatman. Halifax: Fernwood, 1993.

Stoler, Ann. *Carnal Knowledge and Imperial Power: Race and the Intimate in Colonial Rule*. Berkeley: University of California Press, 2002.

———. *Race and the Education of Desire: Foucault's History of Sexuality and the Colonial Order of Things*. Durham, NC: Duke University Press, 1995.

Strauss, S. "Politically Correct 'n' Ridiculous." *Toronto Sun*, May 18, 1992.

Sudbury, Julia. *Other Kinds of Dreams: Black Women's Organisations and the Politics of Transformation*. New York: Routledge, 1999.

Sullivan, Shannon. *Good White People: The Problem with Middle-Class White Anti-racism* Albany: SUNY Press, 2014.

Sullivan, Shannon, and Nancy Tuana. *Race and Epistemologies of Ignorance*. Albany: SUNY Press, 2007.

Sutton R. W., and A. Rafaeli. "Untangling the Relationship between Displayed Emotions and Organizational Sales: The Case of Convenience Stores." *Academy of Management Journal* 31 (1988): 461–487.

Tator, Frances, and Carol Tator, eds. *Racism in the Canadian University: Demanding Social Justice, Inclusion, and Equity*. Toronto: University of Toronto Press, 2009.

Taylor, Dorceta. "The State of Diversity in Environmental Organizations: Mainstream NGOs." Report prepared for Green 2.0. 2014. https://diversegreen.org.

Taylor, Keeanga–Yamahtta. *From #BlackLivesMatter to Black Liberation*. Chicago: Haymarket Books, 2016.

Taylor, Verta. "Watching for Vibes: Bringing Emotions into the Study of Feminist Organizations." In *Feminist Organizations: Harvest of the Women's Movement*, edited by Myra Marx Ferree and Patricia Yancey Martin, 223–233. Philadelphia: Temple University Press, 1995.

Tempel, E. "Nonprofits Have a Spotty Record on Diversity." *Nonprofit Times*, February 2007. www.thenonprofittimes.com .

Thomas, B. "Anti-racist Education: A Response to Manicom." In *Breaking the Mosaic: Ethnic Identities in Canadian Schooling*, edited by J. Young. Toronto: Garamond Press, 1987.

Thomas, James. *Diversity Regimes: Why Talk Is Not Enough to Fix Racial Inequality at Universities*. New Brunswick, NJ: Rutgers University Press, 2020.

Thorsell, William. "A Question of the Pot Calling the Kettle White?" (editorial). *Globe and Mail*, May 23, 1992.

Thurman, Rosetta. "Nonprofits Don't Really Care about Diversity." *Stanford Social Innovation Review*, May 18, 2011. http://ssir.org.

Toronto Coalition Against Racism (TCAR). *Solidarity Not Scapegoating: A Tabloid of the Toronto Coalition Against Racism*. Toronto: TCAR, 1994.

Touraine, Alain. "Beyond Social Movements?" *Theory, Culture & Society* 9 (1992): 125–145.

Trinh, T. Minh–ha. *Woman, Native, Other*. Bloomington: Indiana University Press, 1988.

Tronto, Joan. "What Can Feminists Learn about Morality from Caring?" In *Gender/Body/Knowledge: Feminist Reconstructions of Being and Knowing*, edited by A. Jagger and S. Bordo, 172–87. New Brunswick, NJ: Rutgers University Press, 1989.

———. "Beyond Gender Differences to a Theory of Care." *Signs* 12, no. 4 (1987): 644–663.

Trotz, Alissa. "Transnational Feminist Organizing." Guest lecture to Introduction to Women's Studies class, New College, University of Toronto, March 26, 2002.

Troyna, Barry. *Racism and Education: Research Perspectives*. Buckingham: Open University Press, 1993.

———. "Beyond Multiculturalism: Towards the Enactment of Anti-racist Education in Policy, Provision and Pedagogy." *Oxford Review of Education* 13, no. 3 (1987): 307–320.

Troyna, Barry, and Bruce Carrington. *Education, Racism and Reform*. New York: Routledge, 1990.

Troyna, Barry, and Richard Hatcher. *Racism in Children's Lives: A Study of Mainly-White Primary Schools*. London: Routledge, 1992.

Troyna Barry, and Jenna Williams. *Racism, Education and the State: The Racialisation of Education Policy*. Beckenham: Croom Helm, 1986.

Trudeau, P. E. "Federal Multicultural Policy." *House of Commons Debates*, October 8, 1971. *Hansard*, 8545–8548. Reprinted in *Immigration and the Rise of Multiculturalism*, edited by Howard Palmer, 135–137. Toronto: Copp Clark, 1975.

Tunstall, Elizabeth (Dori). *Decolonizing Design: A Cultural Justice Guidebook*. Cambridge, MA: MIT Press, 2023.

United Way of Greater Toronto. *Action, Access, Diversity! A Guide to Multicultural/Anti-racist Organizational Change for Social Service Agencies*. Toronto: United Way, 1991.

Valverde, Mariana. "Experience and Truth Telling in a Post-humanist World: A Foucauldian Contribution to Feminist Ethical Reflections." In *Feminism and the Final Foucault*, edited by Dianna Taylor and Karen Vintges. Chicago: University of Illinois Press, 2004.

———. "Racial Poison: Drink, Male Vice and Degeneration in First-Wave Feminism." In *Women's Suffrage in the British Empire*, edited by Ian Fletcher, Laura Mayhall, and Phillipa Levine. London: Routledge, 2000.

———. "'One Day at a Time' and Other Slogans for Everyday Life: The Ethical Practices of Alcoholics Anonymous." *Sociology* 33, no. 2 (1999): 393–410.

———. "'When the Mother of the Race Is Free': Race, Reproduction, and Sexuality in First-Wave Feminism." In *Gender Conflicts: New Essays in Women's History*, edited by Franca Iacovetta and Mariana Valverde. Toronto: University of Toronto Press, 1992.

———. *The Age of Light, Soap and Water: Moral Reform in English Canada, 1885–1935*. Toronto: McClelland & Stewart, 1991.

———. "Letter to the Editorial Collective." *Broadside*, May 1983.

Valverde, Mariana, and Lorna Weir. "The Struggles of the Immoral: Preliminary Remarks on Moral Regulation." *Resources for Feminist Research* 17, no. 3 (1988): 31–34.

van Dijk, T. A. *Elite Discourse and Racism*. Newbury Park, CA: Sage, 1993.

Venegas, Mario. "Between Community and Sectarianism: Calling Out and Negotiated Discipline in Prefigurative Politics." *Social Movement Studies* 21, no. 3 (December 2020). doi:10.1080/14742837.2020.1866528.

Vickers, Jill, Pauline Rankin, and Christine Appelle. *Politics as if Women Mattered: A Political Analysis of the National Action Committee on the Status of Women*. Toronto: University of Toronto Press, 1993.

Vorauer, Jacquie, Kelley J. Main, and Gordon B. O'Connell. "How Do Individuals Expect to Be Viewed by Members of Lower Status Groups? Content and Implications of Meta–stereotypes." *Journal of Personality and Social Psychology* 75, no. 4 (1998): 917–937.

Vorauer, Jacquie, and Stacey J. Sasaki. "In Need of Liberation or Constraint? How Intergroup Attitudes Moderate the Behavioral Implications of Intergroup Ideologies." *Journal of Experimental Social Psychology* 46, no. 1 (2010): 133–138.

Walcott, R. "Theorizing Anti-racist Education: Decentering White supremacy in Education." *Western Canadian Anthropologist* 7, no. 2 (1990): 109–120.

Waldron, V. R., and K. J. Krone. "The Experience and Expression of Emotion in the Workplace: A Study of a Corrections Organization." *Management Communication Quarterly* 4 (1991): 287–309.

Walker, Margaret. "Picking Up Pieces: Lives, Stories, and Integrity." In *Feminists Rethink the Self*, edited by D. Meyers. Boulder, CO: Westview Press, 1997.

Ward, Jane. *Respectably Queer: Diversity Culture in LGBT Activist Organizations*. Nashville: Vanderbilt University Press, 2008.

———. "White Normativity: The Cultural Dimensions of Whiteness in a Racially Diverse LGBT Organization." *Sociological Perspectives* 51, no. 3 (2008): 563–586.

Ware, Vron. *Beyond the Pale: White Women, Racism and History*. London: Verso, 1992.

Weber, Max. *Economy and Society, Vol.1*, edited by Guenther Roth and Claus Wittich. Berkeley: University of California Press, 1978.

Weed, Elizabeth. "Introduction: Terms of Reference." In *Coming to Terms: Feminism, Theory and Politics*, edited by E. Weed. New York: Routledge, 1989.

Weedon, Chris. *Feminist Practice and Poststructuralist Theory*. New York: Blackwell, 1989.

Weiler, Kathleen. *Women Teaching for Change: Gender, Class and Power*. Santa Barbara, CA: Greenwood, 1987.

Weir, Lorna. "PC Then and Now: Resignifying Political Correctness." In *Beyond Political Correctness: Toward the Inclusive University*, edited by S. Richer and L. Weir, 51–87. Toronto: University of Toronto Press, 1995.

———. "Limitations of New Social Movement Analysis." *Studies in Political Economy* 40 (Spring 1993).

———. "Anti-racist Feminist Pedagogy, Self-Observed." *Resources for Feminist Research* 20, no. 3/4 (1992).

Weisman, Richard. *Showing Remorse: Law and the Social Control of Emotion*. Farnham: Ashgate Publishing, 2014.

———. "Being and Doing: The Judicial Use of Remorse to Construct Character and Community." *Social & Legal Studies* 18, no. 1 (2009): 47–69.

Wetherell, Margaret, and Jonathan Potter. *Mapping the Language of Racism: Discourse and the Legitimation of Exploitation*. Hemel Hempstead: Harvester Wheatsheaf, 1992.

Wilder, Sheila. "Racism Unresolved." *Broadside*, April 1983.

Williams, Simon J., and Gillian Bendelow. "Introduction. Emotions in Social Life: Mapping the Sociological Terrain." In *Emotions in Social Life: Critical Themes and Contemporary Issues*, edited by Gillian Bendelow and Simon J. Williams. New York: Routledge, 1998.

Wine, Jeri, and Janice Ristock, eds. *Women and Social Change: Feminist Activism in Canada*. Toronto: James Lorimer, 1991.

Wittig, M. "Local Networks for Social Change: Models for Success." Paper presented at the meeting of the Western Psychological Association, San Diego, 1979. Quoted in Bettencourt, Dillman, and Wollman, "Intragroup Dynamics."

Woo, Maylynn, and Prabha Khosla. "The Politics of Visibility: Addressing Third World Concerns." *Kinesis*, September/October 1981.

Wouters, C. "The Sociology of Emotions and Flight Attendants: Hoschchild's 'Managed Heart.'" *Theory, Culture and Society* 6, no. 1 (1989): 95–123.

Yamada, M. "Asian Pacific American Women and Feminism." In *This Bridge Called My Back*, edited by Cherríe Moraga and Gloria Anzaldúa. New York: Kitchen Table, 1981.

Young, Iris. "The Complexities of Coalition." *Dissent*, Winter 1997.

Young, Michael P. *Bearing Witness against Sin: The Evangelical Birth of the American Social Movement*. Chicago: University of Chicago Press, 2006.

Zaretsky, Eli. "Identity Theory, Identity Politics: Psychoanalysis, Marxism, Post-structuralism." In *Social Theory and the Politics of Identity*, edited by Craig Calhoun. Cambridge: Blackwell, 1994.

Zinn, Maxine Baca, and Bonnie Thornton Dill. "Theorizing Difference from Multicultural Feminism." In *Through the Prism of Difference: Readings on Sex and Gender*, edited by P. Hondagneu-Sotelo, M. A. Messner, and M. B. Zinn. Boston: Allyn & Bacon, 1997.

INDEX

Page numbers in *italics* indicate figures.

AA. *See* Alcoholics Anonymous

abolition, abolitionists and, 189–90

ACT approach to change, 234–44; asking questions component of, 245–47; collaboration component of, 247–50; taking action as component of, 250–54, 256–57

activism. *See* environmental activism

affect, racial politics influenced by, 10

affective economies, 24, 142

affective relations: definition of, 26; emotional expressions about race and, 142–44; emotion and, 22–26; race and, 12

affective sphere, 24

affect theory, 10

affinity groups, 152

African Americans: as CEOs, 13; enrollment rates in universities, 13. *See also* Black women

Aggarwal, Pramilla, 77

Agyemang, Brianna, 226

Ahmed, Sara, 16, 242; on affective economies, 24, 142; *Complaint!*, 243; *The Cultural Politics of Emotion*, 24, 142; "Declarations of Whiteness," 183; on emotion, 23; on White "pride," 123–24

Aimée & Jaguar, 162

Ain't I a Woman (hooks), 40

Alcoff, Linda, 94

Alcoholics Anonymous (AA), 223, 233, 271n155

Alibhai-Brown, Yasmin, ix

Allport, Gordon, 35, 96–97, 99. *See also* contact hypothesis

Alonso, Ana María, 50

alternatives: to moral identity, 196–97, 221–24; to workshop practices, 137–38

Amarshi, Aliya, 173

Amazing Grace, 215–16

anarchist movements, 102–4

Anderson, Benedict, 58–59, 191, 194, 289n29

anger, interpretations of, 25–26

"angry Black woman" stereotype, 115, 119, 284n133; in articles, 133; expressions of emotion and, 130–31, 180; foundations of, 128–29

Anthony, Susan B., 52, 57

anti-bias training: in community settings, 4; in corporate spaces, 4; failures of, 5–6; implicit biases and, 5; in New York City Police Department, 5; at Starbucks, 4

anti-black behaviors, at Starbucks, 4

anti-imperialism: in *Broadside,* 62; in Canadian feminist movement, 56, 60

anti-Muslim racism, 227–31

anti-political correctness, 79

antiracism, as practice: Black Lives Matter movement as influence on, 42; in *Broadside,* 65; DiAngelo as educator, 7, 240–41; emotional responses to, 18; emotional roadblocks, 235–43; failures of, 3; feminism and, 45; in feminist organizations, 79; in feminist scholarship, 40; global protests in support of, 10; historical development of, 79;

ABOUT THE AUTHOR

SARITA SRIVASTAVA is Professor of Sociology, Dean of the Faculty of Arts and Science and Director of the Global Centre for Climate Action at OCAD University in Toronto. In her prior work as an activist, she was director of a national environmental campaign for Greenpeace Canada, active in community radio and environmental education, and supported Indigenous, labor, and feminist organizing.